True West

True West

SAM SHEPARD'S LIFE, WORK, AND TIMES

—

Robert Greenfield

CROWN
NEW YORK

Published in the United States by Crown,
an imprint of Random House, a division of
Penguin Random House LLC, New York.

CROWN and the Crown colophon are registered
trademarks of Penguin Random House LLC.

Photo credits and permissions appear on page 410.

LIBRARY OF CONGRESS CATALOGING-IN-PUBLICATION DATA
NAMES: Greenfield, Robert, author.
TITLE: True west / Robert Greenfield.
DESCRIPTION: New York : Crown, [2023] |
Includes bibliographical references and index.
IDENTIFIERS: LCCN 2022041266 (print) | LCCN 2022041267 (ebook)
| ISBN 9780525575955 (hardcover ; acid-free paper) |
ISBN 9780525575979 (ebook)
SUBJECTS: LCSH: Shepard, Sam, 1943–2017. |
Dramatists, American—20th century—Biography. |
Actors—United States—Biography. | LCGFT: Biographies.
CLASSIFICATION: LCC PS3569.H394 Z69 2023 (print) |
LCC PS3569.H394 (ebook) | DDC 812/.54 [B]—dc23/eng/20220916
LC record available at https://lccn.loc.gov/2022041266
LC ebook record available at https://lccn.loc.gov/2022041267

Printed in Canada on acid-free paper

crownpublishing.com

2 4 6 8 9 7 5 3 1

FIRST EDITION

Title-page photo: Alamy Stock Photos

Book design by Barbara M. Bachman

For Donna,

who was and will always be the music

He's a walkin' contradiction / Partly truth and partly fiction . . .

—KRIS KRISTOFFERSON,
"THE PILGRIM,
CHAPTER 33"

CONTENTS

True West

—

NEW YORK, NEW YORK

I N THE OPENING SCENE OF THE MOVIE OF SAM SHEPARD'S LIFE, which he would most certainly have written, directed, and perhaps acted in as well (no doubt portraying his own father) while also possibly contributing several original songs to the soundtrack, a tall, thin nineteen-year-old man stares hungrily through the plate glass window of a White Castle in the heart of Times Square as a cook fries hamburgers in sizzling puddles of molten grease on the griddle.

Fresh off a bus after spending the past eight months touring the Midwest, the South, and New England as part of a repertory company that has been putting on plays like *Winnie-the-Pooh* and Christopher Fry's *A Sleep of Prisoners* and *The Boy with a Cart* in churches and any other venues they could find, he has left his mother, two younger sisters, and father, with whom he can no longer get along, three thousand miles away in California.

With no money and no prospects and no idea where he will sleep tonight, he is not just a stranger in a very strange land but also the kind of gangling, awkward country bumpkin who has always come to Manhattan in search of wealth and fame only to go back home again dismayed and defeated by the city.

The Times Square in which nineteen-year-old Sam Shepard stands in 1963 is dominated by a large billboard from which the painted image of a man's face blows smoke rings (actually steam) into the air above a logo reading I'D WALK A MILE FOR A CAMEL. Surrounding the billboard are smaller but equally garish neon signs for Admiral Television Appliances, Canadian Club imported whisky, Castro convertible sofas,

Planters Peanuts, Coca-Cola, and Scripto pens. Hubert's Museum and Flea Circus, where luminaries like Allen Ginsberg, Lenny Bruce, Diane Arbus, and Bob Dylan have all come to see the freaks, is still open to the public and doing business on West Forty-second Street between Seventh and Eighth avenues.

And while this stretch of Broadway has already become enshrined in American popular culture as "the Great White Way" and "the Cross-roads of the World," you can still get a prescription filled at Whelan's Drug Store or sit down for a meal at Hector's Cafeteria, Howard Johnson's, or the Horn and Hardart Automat. You can also buy yourself a snappy suit at Bond Clothiers and then spend the night at the Hotel Astor.

In 1963, the Times Square in which Sam Shepard stands is much like all of New York City and the rest of the country: still squarely rooted in the 1950s. Although Bob Dylan has already played his historic debut concert at Town Hall, and Andy Warhol is painting multiple images of Marilyn Monroe, America will not really start to change until President John F. Kennedy is assassinated in Dallas on November 22, 1963, just seventeen days after Sam Shepard (then still known as Steve Rogers, the nickname he was given by his family and the surname with which he had been born) turns twenty years old.

For what truly dies on that day in Dallas is the gleaming promise of a New Frontier as well as a particularly optimistic vision of America. Pretty much before anyone knows what hit them, the seeds of anger and discontent that have for so long lain fallow beneath the surface of everyday life in this country suddenly burst forth into full, riotous bloom. It is then that the dream really goes sour and "the sixties" begin in earnest.

And while all this will not become apparent until the decade itself is well under way, one of the first shifts in this great cultural upheaval is the utter destruction of the long-standing image of the American nuclear family as a happy, caring, and completely functional unit. Not surprisingly, in time this will become the subject of the most meaningful plays Sam Shepard ever wrote.

None of this, however, is apparent to Shepard as he stands watching a grill cook shovel mounds of fried onions above a row of sizzling hamburgers and then top them all off with a layer of white cheese slices that begin bubbling and popping like Elmer's Glue. As Shepard would later write, he has never before seen hamburgers cooked this way. Utterly clueless, he also thinks the girls in New York City must be incredibly friendly, because they all keep hitting on him as he stands there. In fact, they are working for a living and want him only to pay for their services with money he does not have.

Dead broke and hungry, Shepard remembers the advice he was given by another actor in the troupe about the easiest way to make quick money in New York. Heading down the street, he sees a big white sign in a storefront window with red letters reading GIVE A PINT OF BLOOD—GET $5 CASH. At the top of a flight of stairs that smells like garbage, with an iron handrail that sticks to his fingers, he finds a woman in a white uniform who looks like a nurse sitting behind a wooden desk in a little office. After he has filled out a form, she takes him into a back room and sits him down on a metal chair behind a green plastic curtain. Tying off a vein in his left arm with a thin rubber hose, she slowly fills her syringe with his blood. Having completed her work without ever once looking him in the eye, she hands him five dollars.

He then goes right back down the stairs and walks inside the White Castle. Sitting himself down on a chrome stool, he proudly orders a cheeseburger with fried onions. As Shepard will later write, it is one of the best things he has ever tasted.

From such humble beginnings, over the course of the next fifty-four years, Steve Rogers would go on to create an incredibly impressive body of work in theater, film, poetry, and prose while also inventing, more or less from scratch, the enduring American legend known as Sam Shepard. And while no one in New York City then even knows who he is, the beginning of his epic journey can best be described by the title of Norman Mailer's account of how John F. Kennedy came to be nominated for president at the 1960 Democratic National Convention in Los Angeles. For, insofar as the burgeoning downtown theater scene known as Off-Off-Broadway is concerned, Superman has in fact just come to the supermart. Before too long, virtually everyone involved in it will know Sam Shepard's name. As, in time, will the world.

ONE

LIFE DURING WARTIME

My dad did have a good war, I guess.
If you can call any war good.

—SANDY ROGERS

THE NOISE IN THE COCKPIT WAS SO DEAFENING THAT THE PILOT
could barely hear himself think. Although First Lieutenant Samuel
Shepard Rogers, who would come to haunt his son Sam Shepard's life
as well as much of his work, had been born and raised on a farm in
rural Illinois and had never worked in a steel mill or a foundry, he
discovered that being inside the cockpit of a B-24 Liberator was much
like finding himself inside one of them when every blast furnace was
thundering away at top volume. Unlike in those places, oppressive heat
was not one of his problems.

Because the bomber Rogers was now flying on a mission over Italy
at a cruising speed of 215 miles an hour and an altitude of two hundred
feet to avoid enemy radar was not insulated, pressurized, or heated, it
was always cold inside the cockpit, and today was no exception. Despite
this, Rogers was wearing the outfit of choice for those flying missions
designed to bring World War II to an end by destroying Nazi strong-
holds and matériel. The defining aspect of his look, which would soon
be seen in movies like *Thirty Seconds over Tokyo* and *Twelve O'Clock
High,* was a standard-issue, dark-brown U.S. Army Air Force B3 sheepskin bomber jacket with a white fleece collar, a leather helmet with
goggles perched on top, and a pair of oversize aviator headphones with
which he could communicate with his crew despite the constant din.

As the commander, Rogers was responsible for their safety at all times, even when they were on the ground. Today, that obligation had begun long before sunrise, when his men were awakened by a flashlight in the pitch-black darkness of their ice-cold barracks. After breakfast in the mess hall, Rogers and his crew attended the main briefing of the day, where they were informed of the location and importance of today's primary target, the route they would fly to reach it, the weather they would encounter on the way, and most important, the enemy defenses they would face. The briefing ended with a "time hack" so they could all synchronize their watches.

As each one of the forty B-24 Liberators of the 456th Bombardment Group in today's mission approached the end of the runway, the pilot stopped his aircraft and turned it at a forty-five-degree angle to avoid blasting the plane in line behind it. Locking the brakes, Rogers and his fellow pilots then revved their four 1,200-horsepower engines to full throttle. As the noise on the ground reached unbearable levels, the fully loaded planes, each weighing 55,000 pounds, took off at one-minute intervals.

On their way to the target, the massive bombers assembled themselves into two distinct units of twenty aircraft deployed into a pair of separate V-shaped lines. Traditionally, the least experienced crew flew the plane at the very back of the formation. This position was so vulnerable to attack by German Luftwaffe fighter planes that it was known as the coffin corner or the Purple Heart corner.

Before reaching the target zone, no B-24 pilot knew how many German fighter planes he might encounter that day. On some missions, it could be as few as nine; on others, more than a hundred. With a top speed of 652 miles an hour, the German Luftwaffe's single-seat, single-engine Focke-Wulf 190 could fly rings around the slower and far more ponderous bombers. Armed with four MG 131 machine guns, each capable of firing 475 rounds, and four MG 151 cannons loaded with explosive shells that could take down a B-24 with just three or four direct hits, German fighter planes sometimes shot down as many as six B-24s on a single mission.

As Rogers and his fellow pilots accelerated to three hundred miles an hour to begin their bombing runs, the greatest obstacle they faced was flak, as the deadly fire from large anti-aircraft artillery emplacements on the ground was called. At the time, the German 88 mm gun was widely considered the single most effective anti-aircraft weapon in the world, and flak from it could often be encountered in areas aside from the actual target.

At times, as one B-24 airman recalled, the flak "was thick enough to walk on." The concussive force alone from a shell that had exploded near a plane could pierce its Plexiglas nose, thereby causing a howling wind to suddenly course though the entire fuselage. If shells began bursting any closer, the B-24 would start to yaw and sway in the air. As the crew continued performing their assigned duties, they could only hope their pilot was skilled enough to keep them flying.

As if all this were not enough to deal with on a regular basis, there were also the kind of grievous accidents that always occurred in the fog of war. While returning from a mission in late May 1944 during which they had been unable to drop their bombs on the target, two of Rogers's fellow pilots in the 456th Bombardment Group collided their planes in midair over their home base. As live bombs began falling on the airfield, all but one of the twenty crewmen aboard both aircraft were killed.

TO A FAR GREATER degree than for many of those with whom he had served during World War II, Sam Rogers's experiences in combat would influence the rest of his adult life in ways he himself seemed never to have fully understood. Having been in complete command during a mission, Rogers would react negatively to those who later held positions of authority over him, a trait his son would also then exhibit.

After the peak experience of completing yet another mission and returning safely to base with both his crew and aircraft intact, Sam Rogers was never able to find real personal fulfillment in ordinary civilian life in post–World War II America. In time, the way he dealt with this profound sense of utter discontent became his greatest problem, wreaking havoc on not only him but all those closest to him as well.

As was true of his only son, Rogers's striking physical appearance and often stoic demeanor gave no real sense of the turbulent nature of his inner life. Accurately, Sandy Rogers, the elder of his two daughters, describes her father as "charismatic and really handsome and physically powerful. He just exuded this macho thing." All these qualities can be plainly seen in a black-and-white photograph of Sam Rogers taken shortly before he enlisted in the U.S. Army Air Force in 1941. In it, he wears a dark suit with a matching vest over a white shirt and a tie. On his head is a perfectly creased wide-brim fedora. Holding a lit cigarette in his left hand, he strides confidently across a river bridge in downtown Chicago while working as a reporter for *The Chicago Daily Tribune.* In that outfit, with a face that would not have been out of place on a movie poster, he looks like a hard-charging newspaperman right out of *The Front Page.*

Nor was it an accident that, after he enlisted, Sam Rogers was chosen to be trained as a B-24 Liberator pilot. The elite cadre of men who were selected to serve their country in this manner includes Senator George McGovern of South Dakota, the Democratic nominee for president in 1972; the actor Jimmy Stewart; Stewart Udall, the congressman from Arizona who later served as secretary of the interior under presidents John F. Kennedy and Lyndon Johnson; and director Robert Altman, who won an honorary Academy Award for a body of work that revolutionized how films were made in Hollywood.

First Lieutenant Sam Rogers flew his first combat mission on February 10, 1944. Over the course of the next six months, he successfully completed missions over Poland, Czechoslovakia, the Balkans, southern France, and Germany. By the end of 1944, he had been transferred to an airfield in Illinois, and his time of service at the controls of a B-24 bomber in war was behind him.

After he left the U.S. Army Air Force in 1948, Sam Rogers was asked to keep on flying with the Civil Air Transport group (later known as Air America), which was then defending Nationalist China in its armed struggle against Chinese Communist forces. "He said no," recalls Sandy Rogers, "and the reason he did so was because he felt his time was up. In that he had been real lucky during the war, but luck also stopped."

The rule of thumb during World War II concerning those who served on B-24 Liberator bombers was that any crew member who flew more than thirty missions had no better than a 30 percent chance of coming back alive. First Lieutenant Samuel Shepard Rogers flew forty-six. And while his service during World War II may have been the apex of his life, the consequences of it shaped who he then became and how he raised his son.

According to Spencer "Ernie" Earnshaw, who met Sam Shepard at Lincoln Elementary School in South Pasadena and became his best childhood friend, "In terms of what Sam's father did in the war, any kind of experience like that has to fuck you up in some way. There really was a lot of PTSD back then, but nobody ever talked about it. That a lot of his problems in civilian life came about because he was not in charge of the plane anymore, as he had been in combat, certainly makes sense to me. Because what we don't know about our own brains would fill the oceans."

MANY OF THOSE WHO had served their country with honor during World War II returned home only to discover that they had been unalterably changed by combat and so could not possibly pick up the threads of the life they had left behind. Sam Rogers solved this problem by simply continuing to serve in the U.S. Army Air Force long after most of those who had enlisted or been drafted to fight alongside him had resumed their civilian lives. In great part, his decision to remain in the service was motivated by the way he had been raised.

Born in Crystal Lake, Illinois, about an hour north of Chicago, on February 3, 1917, Samuel Shepard Rogers was the eldest of six sons, all of whom grew up on the family's wheat farm in nearby McHenry. Not yet the suburb it would later become, McHenry was the small-town seat of a rural county bearing the same name. The Fox River flowed through the eastern part of town, and as virtually everywhere in the Midwest, the surrounding land was flat and arable. Although heritage farms handed down from one generation to the next within a single family for decades were common in the area, the way in which the Rogers family named their sons was not.

Letting the thought flow in two long sentences with no punctuation, Sam Shepard wrote, "My name came down through seven generations of men with the same name each naming the first son the same name as the father then the mothers nicknaming the sons so as not to confuse them with the fathers when hearing their names called in the open air while working in the waist-high wheat.

"The sons came to believe their names were the nicknames they heard floating across these fields and answered to these names building ideas of who they were around the sound never dreaming their real legal name was lying in wait for them written on some paper in Chicago and that name would be the name they'd prefix with 'Mr.' and that name would be the name they'd die with."

Along with the name, a form of truly dysfunctional family trauma directly related to alcoholism had also been handed down from one generation to the next. Sam Rogers's father—whom Shepard would later portray as Dodge, the central character in *Buried Child*, the play for which he was awarded the Pulitzer Prize for Drama in 1979—was a dyed-in-the-wool drinker whose beverage of choice was muscatel, the sweet fortified wine preferred by winos everywhere for its high alcoholic content and affordable price. While he reigned as the head of the family, there was never a shortage of drama. One Sunday afternoon, one of Sam Rogers's younger brothers came down Columbine Street in Crystal Lake to see smoke pouring out of a second-story window of the family house. Rushing up the stairs, he found his father passed out in his bed with the mattress in flames all around him. He carried his father down the stairs and laid him out on the couch in the living room. After flinging the still-smoldering mattress out the window, he was hosing it down when his mother arrived home from church and angrily demanded to know why her son was ruining a perfectly good mattress. After explaining that a hole had been burned clear through it, he told her he had also just saved his father's life. As she snorted in derision and stalked off, it became clear to him that what his mother cared most about was the mattress.

While all this sounds like a scene right out of a Sam Shepard play, it pales in comparison to the description of his grandfather that Shepard wrote after making a pilgrimage by train from California to visit him in Illinois in 1962 at the age of nineteen.

> My Grandpa sits exactly as he's always sat—in a hole of his sofa wrapped in crocheted blankets facing the T.V. He's like a skeleton now. He likes the Hamm's Beer commercials. "The Land of Sky Blue Waters." The little cartoon Beaver that jumps around on the waterfall and sings the jingle. He thinks Truman was the greatest President and writes political rebuffs to the Chicago papers, signing them "Plain Dirt Farmer." He predicts "a Nigger in the White House" by 1970. He's a staunch fan of the Chicago Cubs ... He smokes and drinks continuously and spits blood into the stand-up brass ash tray like you see in the lobbies of old hotels. Sometimes he coughs so violently that his whole body doubles over and he can't catch his breath ... His world is circumscribed around the sofa. Everything he needs is within a three-foot reach.

Given Shepard's grandfather's condition, it should come as no surprise that, three decades earlier, he had managed to drink away the family farm during the Depression. As the firstborn son, Sam Rogers, then barely more than a boy, began selling Hershey bars door to door to help support his mother and five younger brothers.

As though a virulent family curse were running through all their bloodstreams, one of Sam Rogers's brothers (on whom Shepard would base the character of Ansel, the deceased son in *Buried Child*) and his wife were asphyxiated in a motel room in California on their honeymoon. Another brother (Shepard's model for Tinder in *Buried Child*) would lose a leg at the age of ten. Without ever specifying which of them had done so, Shepard noted that another brother married into what he called the "Chicago Mafia"; another cut timber in the Great North Woods of Maine, New Hampshire, Vermont, and New York; another drove a moving truck for Bekins Van Lines; and yet another raised springer spaniels, although whether he actually did this for a living is uncertain.

Little wonder, then, that Sam Rogers was in no great hurry to leave the safety and comfort of the life he had found in the post–World War II U.S. Army Air Force. By the time he finally did so, on August 31, 1948, he was thirty-one years old. By then, he had already been married for more than six years and was the father of two children, a five-year-old son whom the family called Steve and an eleven-month-old daughter named Sandy.

Unlike her brother, Sandy Rogers was born on the island of Guam, where her father was stationed in April 1946 and where the family lived for the next fourteen months. Although Emperor Hirohito of Japan had formally announced his nation's unconditional surrender a year earlier, as many as three thousand Japanese soldiers on Guam had either not heard the news or refused to believe it was true and so continued hiding in the dense jungle covering nearly half the island.

In an interview quoted by biographer Don Shewey, Shepard said because the Japanese soldiers still on Guam "had been forced back into living in the caves . . . [,] they would come down and steal clothes off the clothes-lines, and food and stuff. All the women were issued army Lugers, and I remember my mother shooting at them." According to Shepard, while she was on Guam, his mother also "drove a jeep, crashing through the jungle and brandishing her .45 just to get to the drive-in theater where she and her little boy in a cowboy hat watched *Song of the South* projected on a bedsheet."

HAD HIS FATHER NOT lost their farm during the Depression, thereby forcing his entire family to pull up stakes and move forty miles south to the village of Lombard, Illinois, Sam Rogers might never have met the girl he would marry. Born on July 16, 1917, in Lombard, a village in DuPage County, about half an hour from downtown Chicago, Jane Elaine Schook grew up in entirely different circumstances from those of her future husband. Her father, who was forty-four years old when she was born, was Frederick DeForest Schook, a well-known painter who taught for twenty-five years at the Art Institute of Chicago while also showing his work there on a regular basis. Having studied art in

England and France as a young man, Frederick Schook was cultured, civilized, and progressive. This last trait would seem to have been best evidenced by his meeting his future wife while she was posing nude for his students in his life-drawing course at the Art Institute. Four years younger than her husband, the former Amy Victoria Bynon was forty when she gave birth to their second daughter, Jane.

When she was four years old, Jane Schook began spending summers in the family's second home, a red-roofed log cabin that her father had whimsically named "the Schook Shack," with chinked walls, exposed timber beams, a stone fireplace, and a private beach on Lake Michigan.

In addition to his other qualities, Frederick Schook had a social conscience. Shortly after bringing in a team of architects to build his dream house not far from the town of Baileys Harbor, in Door County, Wisconsin, Schook persuaded a fellow professor at the Art Institute to join him in founding a program to provide summer art lessons for veterans of World War I. Funded by the federal government under the provisions of the Soldiers Rehabilitation Act of 1918, the Frogtown Art Colony is credited with making Door County a location where painters and visual artists still live and work today.

Coming from such completely disparate backgrounds, Sam Rogers and Jane Schook also lived on opposite ends of town in Lombard. And while Sam Shepard would later say his parents had known each other in elementary school, they apparently did not meet until both attended what was then known as Glenbard Township High School, a towering redbrick castle of a building replete with battlements and a rounded turret on a hill overlooking the town's man-made lake.

Although Sam Rogers and his farm boy brothers cut quite a swath through a high school whose student body had nearly all been raised in far more privileged households, Jane Schook remained curiously immune to his charms. Because his family was virtually penniless, it was not as if he would have been considered a good catch in any sense of the term. Also, unlike many of her female classmates, Jane had no intention of getting married as soon as possible and then settling down in Lombard to raise a family. In an era when just 8 percent of female high school graduates in the United States went on to attend college, she had already formulated what, for someone who had grown up in the heartland of America, was a truly daring plan.

After graduating from Glenbard High School, Jane traveled alone by train from Chicago to Los Angeles. In nearby South Pasadena, Grace Upton, her mother's younger sister, welcomed her to the two-story, red-shingled house with a porch on a quiet street in a very quiet neighborhood where she lived with her older and well-to-do husband, Charles, and their maid. As Shepard wrote, his great-aunt Grace "was Welsh and her husband was fairly wealthy ... His name was Charlie Upton, from Liverpool. And he had a penchant for whiskey and bar-room brawls. In one of these fights, he had his ear bitten off, Mike Tyson style. Bit right in half so that he only had one half of an ear on one side of his face. I forget which side it was on. But anyhow, he was wealthy enough to buy a Chrysler sedan on the black market during the War. Big heavy car. Beautiful car. Good for the open road."

Not surprisingly, Grace Upton was as outsize a character as her husband. In an era when the median age at which women married was twenty-one, she did not wed until age forty. Charles Upton was then fifty-eight. During the twenty-one years they were married, he served as a city councilman, while she spent much of her time as an unpaid volunteer for a variety of local organizations. In the words of her great-niece Sandy Rogers, "Aunt Grace was wealthy and cultured, yes, but she was also almost six feet tall. Whereas our grandmother on my mother's side, who died before I was born, had been a very short woman, almost abnormally small."

During the first year Jane Schook lived with Grace and Charlie Upton, she attended what was then known as Pasadena Junior College before transferring to Occidental College in Eagle Rock, a short drive along Colorado Boulevard from her aunt's house at 344 Pasadena Avenue. One of the oldest liberal arts colleges on the West Coast, Occidental was a private institution that had begun admitting female students as part of its first entering class in 1887 and had then opened a dormitory for women on campus in 1925.

While a student at Occidental, Jane Schook majored in English and wrote her undergraduate thesis on Thomas Hardy. She also worked on the school newspaper and belonged to the Social Club. After graduating in 1940, she returned home to Lombard, where she reconnected with, and then began dating, Sam Rogers. On December 6 of that year, Jane's mother died, leaving her to care for her sixty-eight-year-old father.

Six months later, Sam Rogers, who had attended college for a year without completing his studies and then worked as a reporter for the *Chicago Tribune*, enlisted in the U.S. Army Air Force. After completing basic training, he was assigned to radio school at Scott Air Force Base, in Rockford, Illinois. Because the base was about an hour from Lombard, he and Jane continued seeing each other for the next six months. Rogers was then transferred to Morrison Field at the Palm Beach Air Force Base in Florida for further training. On April 3, 1942, apparently with no other members of their respective families present, Sam Rogers and Jane Schook were married. The groom then spent the next nine months being trained to pilot a B-24 bomber.

Working backward from the date when Sam Shepard was born, he would have been conceived at some point during February 1943, quite possibly when his father was on leave before being assigned to join the 456th Heavy Bombardment Group of the 15th Air Force in either Utah or Idaho.

As her pregnancy approached full term in the autumn of 1943, Jane Rogers was living alone in a large house in the officers' quarters section of Fort Sheridan, the U.S. Army regional training and induction center through which half a million troops were processed during World War II. Located in Highland Park, about twenty miles north of downtown Chicago on the shores of Lake Michigan, the base was a forty-minute drive from Lombard. With her father having passed away in October 1942 and her husband now stationed two thousand miles away at the Muroc Army Air Field in California's Mojave Desert, Jane Rogers relied on her mother-in-law in Crystal Lake for support during this period.

Even heavily pregnant, Jane loved walking along the shores of Lake Michigan every day. It reminded her of the summers she had passed as a girl in Baileys Harbor. That she also spent the day before giving birth scrubbing the floors of her house says a good deal about her character as well as how she was dealing with impending motherhood.

According to Shepard biographer John J. Winters, Sam Rogers telephoned his wife long distance from California that night to report that, while preparing his B-24 bomber to fly first to North Africa and then on to Italy, he had looked up into the pitch-black desert sky and seen two shooting stars speeding by overhead. Although he had chosen to take this as some kind of a sign, Rogers was also concerned that his wife had not yet given birth, and he advised her to consult another doctor if it did not happen soon. When she woke the next morning, Jane Rogers was ready to go to the hospital. Unable to find anyone to take her there, she contacted her mother-in-law and had to wait for her to arrive, only to then take the wheel and drive them both there herself.

At 3:20 in the afternoon on November 5, 1943, Samuel Shepard Rogers was born. As soon as his mother was discharged from the hospital, she took him to Crystal Lake, where they lived for the next year with her mother-in-law. The first time Sam Rogers saw his son was in late 1944, at Chanute Field, Illinois, which was nearly a three-hour drive from Crystal Lake. Samuel Shepard Rogers, who had already been given "Steve" as his family nickname, was then about fourteen months old.

Over the course of the next four years, Jane Rogers followed her husband from one U.S. Army Air Force post to another. While being trained as a communications officer, a flight control officer, and an operations officer, Rogers was stationed in Illinois, Idaho, Georgia, and Washington State before finally being sent to Guam for thirteen months.

On August 31, 1948, by his own request, First Lieutenant Sam Rogers was discharged from the U.S. Army Air Force in Weaver, South Dakota. Thirty-one years old, with a wife and two young children, Rogers now had to decide what he wanted to do with the rest of his life.

TWO

THE ROSE PARADE

I grew up with Roy [Rogers]. He was one of the
first television cowboys I can remember watching.
I watched Roy in the flesh too, riding Trigger
down Colorado Boulevard in the
Rose Parade alongside Dale Evans.

—SAM SHEPARD,
DAY OUT OF DAYS

DESPITE THE RELATIVELY PRIVILEGED CIRCUMSTANCES IN
which he was raised, Sam Shepard was so impressed as a young boy by
those whom he watched riding past him in the Rose Parade, held on
New Year's Day in Pasadena, that they became the basis for the fully
formed persona he would inhabit for most of his adult life. Whether
Shepard would have fashioned this persona without spending his early
childhood years in what then seemed like the perfect place in America
to live, no one can say for certain. But even as a boy, he seemed to have
the uncanny knack of always being in the right place at the right time
for himself, if not also for those around him.

More than a decade after she first took in Jane Rogers, Aunt Grace
Upton welcomed her niece and her husband and their five-year-old
son and eight-month-old daughter to come live with her in that same
two-story, red-shingled house on Pasadena Avenue. Thanks to the very
generous inheritance left to her by her late husband, who had died six
years earlier at the age of seventy-nine, Aunt Grace could afford to let
the entire Rogers family live there without paying any rent. Now sixty-
seven years old, she had never had children of her own and so soon
began acting as a grandmother to Steve and Sandy Rogers, while also

exerting her power over the entire family. To her credit, Aunt Grace used some of that power to help Sam Rogers find a career.

Perhaps because he had grown up on a farm, Rogers chose to begin his civilian life as a gardener. However, his wife and Aunt Grace soon persuaded him to follow in Jane's footsteps by enrolling as a student at Occidental College. With the GI Bill providing family men like him with up to five hundred dollars a year for books and tuition and a ninety-dollar monthly stipend, nearly half the college students in America that year were veterans.

While Sam Rogers was attending college, Jane was hired to teach first grade at the Polytechnic School at 1030 East California Avenue in Pasadena. Located directly across the street from the California Institute of Technology and looking very much like an adjunct of it, "Poly" was founded in 1907 as the first nonprofit independent private school in Southern California. The long list of notable Poly alumni, many of whose parents had either taught or worked at the California Institute of Technology, included a Nobel Prize laureate, the former publisher of the *Los Angeles Times,* a current member of the U.S. House of Representatives, Julia Child, the director Howard Hawks, and the noted literary critic and former Harvard professor F. O. Matthiessen.

As Sandy Rogers says, "My mom taught little kids at this private school, and it was cool because she had all these parents who were rich and would give her the keys to their cabins and beach houses, and so we would all have wonderful vacations in these really ritzy places."

BY 1952, THE CITY of San Marino, a ten-minute drive from Pasadena, had already come to be viewed as the most exclusive enclave of old WASP money and high-born social privilege in Southern California. Because the city had grown up around the palatial mansion built in 1907 by Henry E. Huntington, the fabulously wealthy railroad magnate, businessman, and art collector, those who had chosen to live there had done so primarily to distance themselves from people of lesser means.

That Sam Rogers, who had been born dirt-poor on a farm in Illinois, would spend the next seventeen years of his life teaching at the only high school in this wealthy upper-class community seems like a story possible only in America. However, the way in which the story would end was something else again.

Far more motivated now than when he had attended college for a year before enlisting, Rogers decided to major in Latin, geography, and Spanish at Occidental. According to Shepard biographer John J. Winters, an Occidental professor recognized Rogers's ability to master foreign languages and urged him to consider a career as a high school Spanish teacher. After taking the national teacher examination that was then a prerequisite for being hired in virtually every school district, Rogers applied for a job at a high school that was still being built.

Despite their being part of the South Pasadena high school district for the past thirty years, voters in San Marino had decided they wanted a high school of their own. With administrators putting together their entire faculty from scratch as quickly as they could, Sam Rogers got in on the ground floor. Now thirty-five years old, he began teaching at San Marino High School in September 1952.

After conducting classes for a year in an administration building during construction of the new high school, Rogers moved along with the sophomore class into the large, imposing red stone structure that still towers over this section of Huntington Drive in San Marino. Behind the building, the campus included a huge parking area, a pool, two tennis courts, a baseball field, a football field, and a running track. And while San Marino High School could not have looked more different from Poly, where Jane Rogers taught, each institution accurately reflected the values of the community in which it had been built and the worldview of the parents whose children attended it.

So it was that, while Sam Shepard later chose to present a rough-hewn cowboy image to the world, his mother and father had both taught in exclusive high schools whose entire student bodies were composed of children from wealthy families.

IN AN ERA WHEN it was unusual for both a husband and a wife to set off for work each morning, the effect of having two incomes on the Rogers family was fairly immediate. By parlaying the home loan Rogers had obtained under yet another provision of the GI Bill as well as money provided to them by Aunt Grace, the family was able to buy a house of their own in South Pasadena in 1953. Ensconced in their new home on Adelaine Avenue, a quiet, leafy street lined with small houses and Craftsman cottages and bungalows, many of which had been built in the early 1900s, Sam and Jane Rogers now seemed to be living the American dream, circa 1953.

According to Spencer Earnshaw, who attended first grade at Lincoln Elementary School with Sam Shepard, "South Pasadena didn't really have a bad part of town. It was small and quiet, and most of the families who lived there were either working class or middle class. As kids, we didn't really know too much about what went on inside each family's house, but I will say there was a lot of drinking going on . . . And the fact that all those men had just come out of World War Two had to be part of it."

Sam Shepard would later say of the community in which he grew up:

> I mean, here you had all these men returning from World War II who were told to go back to work and live in the suburbs. They had no role anymore. Their role was to be a soldier. How can you compare life in the suburbs to life in a fighter jet? You can't. But the women were thinking everything was hunky-dory, and all of a sudden they turned around and the men were alcoholic schizophrenics. They'd gone off their cake, you know. And the women were all steadfast, trying to hold things together. It wasn't just the men who enjoyed battle, either, but the ones who were shell shocked by it. Where did they fit in?

As if the widespread alcoholism that afflicted many men in the community were not enough, there was also the rampant strain of racism that had long since been an integral part of the social fabric of South Pasadena. In the early 1940s, the South Pasadena city manager had decided "to bow to public demand for keeping the city an exclusive white community" by instructing "the city attorney to draw up a restrictive clause and insert it into all properties coming into the possession of the city." By doing so, he converted what had been long-standing practice in the city into official policy.

The level of legally sanctioned racism in South Pasadena, however, went far beyond allowing only whites to own property. As Spencer Earnshaw says, "South Pasadena was a sundown city. All Black people had to be outside the city limits after sundown. It was a real thing, and you could look it up, because there were other cities that were that way as well, but South Pasadena itself was one of the most conservative areas down there."

Nor was South Pasadena alone in implementing such practices. In nearby San Marino, where Sam Rogers taught at the only high school, prospective house buyers thought to be of questionable origin were required to reveal their mothers' maiden names, in order to ensure they were not Jewish. If they were, the sale would not go through. Nor was anyone of color permitted to live there.

SAM SHEPARD WAS FIVE years old and still living with his family in Aunt Grace's house on Pasadena Avenue when he began attending the stately redbrick Lincoln Elementary School on El Centro Street in South Pasadena. Although the school had been named after Abraham Lincoln, according to Charles Mingus III, the son of the legendary jazz bassist and composer, who was then living with his grandparents in nearby Duarte, "I went to school there with Sam, and by the time we were in fifth or sixth grade, I was dealing with kids who were saying, 'Let's go get that crazy nigger who thinks he can exit from the part of the school where white kids come in and go out.' They were talking about me, and this was after the *Brown v. Board of Education* decision in 1954."

In Allendale Park, a five-minute drive from where the Rogers family lived on Adelaine Avenue, Shepard and Spencer Earnshaw began playing Little League baseball for the first time that spring. "Sam and I each made different teams," Earnshaw says, "and we played like mad all the time every day during the summer. Back then, gasoline was still relatively cheap, and so the air was choked with just the most deadly smog. At the end of every day we played, our chests would hurt like hell, but we still went out and did it all the same."

By then, both boys had become accustomed to walking from Lincoln Elementary School to Aunt Grace Upton's house for lunch. "It was a really sweet deal," Earnshaw says, "because she always had soup for us and a really good sandwich, and I almost felt bad about not having eaten my bag lunch."

Because Sam and Jane Rogers were both working full time, Aunt Grace looked after their children. In *Spy of the First Person,* Shepard writes about the day in February 1953 when Aunt Grace, who had "blue hair," drove him in her black-market Chrysler sedan past the Colorado River so they could attend the Riverside County Fair and National Date Festival in Indio City, a small town east of Palm Springs, in the Coachella Valley.

After Shepard had spent two hours in the backseat of the car, surrounded by a sea of red plaid upholstery, he and Aunt Grace joined all the other festival goers at the spacious fairgrounds, where she bought them both date shakes. With the festival having instituted an "Arabian Nights" theme to attract more visitors, Shepard wrote about watching white men "from the Midwest who owned barber shops and drugstores and had thick glasses [and] had never seen the desert" dressed up "as Arabs on camels" parading "back and forth in the street wearing Shriner caps" while "pretending to be full of Arab pride."

Blessed with an extraordinary memory when it came to recalling even the most minute details of his childhood experiences, Shepard also wrote a lengthy account of the first and only time he ran away from school—by following the Arroyo Seco, a twenty-five-mile-long seasonal river that passed by the Rose Bowl on its way toward Los Angeles.

For nearly all those growing up in South Pasadena, the Arroyo was part of their everyday lives. As Spencer Earnshaw says, "Sam and I played around in the Arroyo a whole lot. It was a cement ditch with vertical walls that would then widen out into a V shape. In the middle, there was an embedded ditch to carry the little bit of runoff that would come in spring and summer. Sometimes, in a big rainstorm, the Arroyo would fill up almost to the rim, and if you went into that, you were toast. But when the Arroyo was dry, you could go a long, long way in it, all the way to Los Angeles."

Following the lead of two older boys from school, brothers who had already "been in and out of Juvenile Hall five times," Shepard, who was ten years old, let himself be persuaded to join them in what "would just be like taking a short vacation." After stealing three bicycles from someone's backyard, they headed to the Arroyo and spent the rest of the afternoon climbing around in the hills looking for snakes until one of the brothers came up with the idea of "lowering our bikes into the aqueduct and riding along the dry bed until we reached Los Angeles."

Hearing the sound of traffic on a nearby freeway, they finally left the Arroyo by climbing on one another's shoulders and hooking their belts to the top of the surrounding fence so they could clamber over it. The older brother said they were now in Sierra Madre, a small city about six and a half miles northeast of where they had started in South Pasadena. The reason he knew this was that his uncle lived nearby.

In the front room of his uncle's house, several men were sitting around drinking beer while watching *The Lone Ranger* on television. Eating spaghetti while sitting on the floor with them, Shepard eagerly watched the show. "This was the first time I'd ever seen T.V. because we didn't have one at home. (My Dad said we didn't need one.)" Shepard liked *The Lone Ranger* "a lot," he wrote. "Especially the music when he galloped on Silver and reared up waving his hat at a woman holding a baby."

As they tried to make their way back home, Shepard and the two brothers were stopped by a police car on a bridge in South Pasadena. When Shepard's mother finally appeared to drive him home, she explained that his father had not come because he was so angry at his son that "he was afraid he'd kill me."

At home, Sam Rogers whipped his son "three times with the buckle-end" of his belt. "Three times. That was it. Then he left the house. He never said a word." In an era when spanking was considered an acceptable way of disciplining a child, being whipped with the metal buckle of a belt was such an extreme form of punishment that it may have been how Sam Rogers's father had punished *him* when he was a boy.

———

WHEN SHEPARD WAS A child in South Pasadena, the Lone Ranger, Hopalong Cassidy, Roy Rogers, and the latter two's respective comic sidekicks, Gabby Hayes and Andy Devine, were always his great heroes. Visual proof of this can be found in the two photographs he provided from his own personal collection for the front and back covers of *Day out of Days*, the book of stories he published in 2010. On the front cover, Shepard, who looks to be about five years old, sits atop what he would later describe as "a dead bucking horse" (but that looks much like a statue) at the date festival in Indio. Wearing a black cowboy shirt with patterned Western yoke and black pants, he holds his black cowboy hat in his right hand with his arm stretched all the way out, much like the Lone Ranger at the end of each episode of the long-running television show. On the back cover, Shepard, now perhaps seven, sits atop a real but obviously docile white pony on a child-sized saddle with an Indian horse blanket below it. With a gaily patterned yoke and matching cuffs, his black cowboy shirt is far more elaborate than the one he wears in the other photograph. Standing beside him on the far side of the pony is his father. In a mackinaw jacket with a beat-up fedora on his head, Sam Rogers sports a heavy beard and looks much like a young John Steinbeck.

Although his parents did not have a television set in their house, Sam Shepard was a member of the first generation to grow up deeply influenced by the programs on it. Unlike most of his peers, he actually got to see the stars of those cowboy shows as they rode past him on New Year's Day in the Rose Parade on Colorado Avenue in South Pasadena.

According to Shepard biographer John J. Winters, Shepard and a friend (most likely Earnshaw) would set up a pair of stepladders on Colorado Boulevard and place boards between them so they could see the parade over the heads of those standing in front of them. Many years later, Shepard wrote about the thrilling moment when Roy Rogers and his wife, Dale Evans, rode past him on their horses looking "very straight and proper; their fringed Western outfits pressed and glittering with rhinestones. They rode ramrod straight in their matching silver concho saddles."

On New Year's Day in an era when virtually everyone in America who owned a television sat glued to the screen in their living rooms watching the seemingly endless row of elaborate floats made entirely out of flowers proceed down Colorado Boulevard in dazzling sunshine, Sam Shepard was right there watching it all happen in person.

THREE

A STRANGE KIND
OF MELTING POT

Duarte was a weird accumulation of things,
a strange kind of melting pot—Spanish, Okie,
black, Midwestern elements all jumbled together.
People on the move who couldn't move anymore,
who wound up in trailer camps.

—SAM SHEPARD, IN 1986
ROLLING STONE INTERVIEW

BURIED IN MEMORY BELOW THE EXTENDED SUBURBAN MALL Duarte has become over the last half century lie the remnants of the sleepy small town in the San Gabriel Valley where Sam Shepard spent his most formative adolescent years. Route 66, the iconic "Mother Road" of America that was storied in song as well as in a popular CBS television series of the same name, once ran right through the heart of Duarte. The empty stretches of land that separated Duarte from the equally small towns of Arcadia, Azusa, and Monrovia have now all been covered over with concrete and subsumed by faceless shopping plazas anchored by big-box stores and fast-food restaurants.

And yet, on a winter day when the sky is a perfect shade of blue, the air is crystal clear, and the towering San Gabriel Mountains framing the valley below are streaked with snow, it is still possible to get a sense of what Duarte was like when Sam and Jane Rogers moved there from South Pasadena with their fourteen-year-old son, his ten-year-old sister, and a brand-new baby girl named Roxanne.

Under the newly created California Vehicle Code, Sam Shepard was able to obtain his learner's permit at the age of fifteen and a half and begin driving on his own when he was sixteen. At the Bob's Big Boy in Duarte where everyone hung out, cheeseburgers cost forty-five cents. The "Silver Goblet" milkshake, available only in chocolate, vanilla, or strawberry, cost thirty cents. A cup of coffee or a Coca-Cola could be purchased for a dime.

In that era, Duarte embodied the "other" California, where there was no surf and where the only girls in bikinis could be found not under a palm tree on the sand but rather at the municipal pool. This was the California of hot rods and motorcycles, steel mills and foundries, A&W Root Beer stands and Bob's Big Boys, an area populated in large part by families who had migrated from the Dust Bowl during the Great Depression and then from the steel mills of the Midwest after World War II and whose teenage sons and daughters had nothing better to do on Friday nights than cruise endlessly up and down the main drag of towns where most of them would spend the rest of their lives.

Fifteen miles away, in El Monte Legion Stadium, a crumbling arena that had already seen better days, fights regularly broke out on weekend nights between kids from rival towns at rock shows hosted by deejay Art Laboe that featured Ritchie Valens and Jerry Lee Lewis. For those who drove souped-up hot rods that could go nearly 110 miles an hour on the open road, all that really mattered was shutting everyone else down at the Pomona and Irwindale speedways.

When Sam Shepard was growing up, California was still the new frontier where all things seemed possible—the true west where the outlaw spirit still prevailed. In time, this sensibility permeated his work, enabling him to present a vision of American life that had never before been seen onstage.

JANE ROGERS WAS AT a garage sale in Duarte when she fell in love with the house on Lemon Avenue. By then, she and her daughter Sandy had already been making the rounds to look at houses, one of which was on such a steep slope that Sandy Rogers would later remember thinking, "Shit, this house is going to fall right down this hill."

Concerning the home in Duarte where her family would live for the next fifteen years, Rogers says, "It was definitely kind of an oddball house but also affordable. And the reason my mother had fallen in love with it was because it reminded her of the cabin in Wisconsin where she had gone with her parents every summer and where they had always wanted to retire."

Although Duarte was less than a twenty-minute drive from South Pasadena, the two communities were, in the words of Spencer Earnshaw, who continued visiting his good friend there after the Rogers family moved in 1957, "like apples and oranges back then, really." Shepard himself would later describe the outskirts of Duarte as "dry, flat, cracked and stripped down," an empty vista where, from sunrise to sunset, an endless procession of trucks rolled to and from the rock quarries. Referring to the City of Hope, the well-known cancer research center where widespread experimentation on animals was being carried out, Shepard added, "The smoke and smell of death hangs over Duarte most of the time."

"It was an all-white town and an all-Black town," Charles Mingus III says. "The whites lived on one side of the tracks, and the Blacks lived on the other. There was a vacant lot where people dumped cars that was like a slum, because people lived in those cars. They would take extension cords and plug them into streetlights and bring their babies home from the hospital in cardboard boxes. These were Black people and Hispanics and migrant workers, some of whom were Chinese. But the one thing they had in common was that they were all poor."

Although the myth that Sam Shepard grew up on a dusty avocado ranch in the middle of nowhere would somehow manage to find its way into multiple accounts of his life, none of that was true. His family's new house was about a half mile from downtown Duarte, a small city which then had a population of thirteen thousand. Lemon Avenue, a street that was then far more rustic but still essentially suburban, rose up along a ridgeline with a commanding view of the valley below.

The street came to a dead end at Bradbury, an exclusive gated community where only those with real wealth lived.

Behind a white ramshackle fence, three gables stood atop the roof of one wing of the rambling low-slung house where Sam Shepard spent his teenage years. A brick chimney towered over the far end of the wing that adjoined it at a forty-five-degree angle. Three large umbrellas shaded the patio. In Sandy Rogers's words, "The house had its problems. When you crossed the patio, there were two bedrooms and a bathroom, and that was where my brother and I and my sister lived. So we had the best rooms. And they were completely separate from the actual house, where my parents had a big bedroom that didn't look like one during the day."

According to Shepard biographer John J. Winters, Sam and Jane Rogers slept in the living room on a foldout couch surrounded by bamboo shades. In one corner, Rogers had set up his high-fidelity record player along with two large speakers Jane Rogers then concealed with a pair of black wrought iron roosters. "It was about the worst thing she could have done for the sound," Sandy Rogers says, "but my dad just had to put up with it."

In that corner, Sam also had a card table where he studied at night and graded his students' papers. In the other corner of the room, he had placed his drum kit, replete with snare, high hat, and kick drum, so he could play along with the 78 rpm Dixieland records he loved. "So if my dad wasn't drumming," Sandy Rogers says, "he was reading or studying. And he also always worked his ass off."

Directly across the road from the house, a dense grove of towering deodar cedars, most of which were twenty to thirty feet tall and had probably been planted before the turn of the century, surrounded the house where the Banner family lived. Sam Rogers loved those trees, not just for their great natural beauty but also because they helped shield his house from the fierce Santa Ana winds that blew through the San Gabriel Valley in late fall or early winter.

The Rogers house sat on two and a half acres of land, half of which was an avocado orchard that at times had as many as sixty-five trees. "In a roundabout way," Sandy Rogers says, "both my mother and father had grown up on farms and so we had sheep and chickens, and

Sam had a champion Four-H ram. But even though my dad belonged to the California Avocado Society—and I think they had some kind of a market thing going—it was definitely not a cash crop, and we would give the avocados away."

Thirty-three years later, Shepard would write a brief but moving sketch of his father as he stood in the orchard repairing the irrigation pipes or working on the tractor only to hear a plane flying overhead. Slowly straightening up, Rogers would peel off his Mexican straw hat, squint into the sky, and then begin picking slowly at the shrapnel scar on the back of his neck that he had acquired while flying his B-24 bomber during the war on a mission over Italy. Still picking at the scar, Rogers would stand there until he could finally identify the plane. In Shepard's words, "If a formation of P-51's went over, he would almost climb an Avocado tree with ecstasy. There were planes that had let him down in the heat of combat and he would spit in their direction." Looking down at the ground again, his father would then go right back to work.

SAM SHEPARD SPENT HIS first year in Duarte completing eighth grade at Royal Oaks Grammar School. He then became part of Duarte High School's first graduating class in 1961. Because the school was still under construction, he attended classes at nearby Monrovia High School for three months before entering the brand-new home of the Duarte High School Falcons, which his classmate Charles Mingus III described as "a Frank Lloyd Wright–style building, with steel and glass and all kinds of cool stuff."

For the first three years of his high school career, Shepard was very much the all-American boy. A member of the Future Farmers of America and the local 4-H Club, he worked for two summers on a horse ranch in Chino to earn enough money (three hundred dollars) to buy his first car, a candy-apple-red 1932 Ford Deuce Coupe with black tuck-and-roll upholstery, a 1948 Mercury flathead engine, and a three-speed stick on the floor.

At Duarte High School, his athletic accomplishments included lettering for three years on the basketball team. A member of the track team as a sophomore and a junior, Shepard would later claim to have broken the school record for the 220-yard dash while under the influence of Benzedrine. Although the drug was readily available in Duarte then, his claim seems utterly at odds with his appearance at the time.

Wearing a button-down paisley shirt with his hair in a brush cut in a photograph taken for the high school yearbook during his junior year, Shepard looks the very picture of small-town innocence. Tall and rangy in another photograph taken that year, he poses with his arms outstretched while leaning backward in a line with three other fellow yell leaders. All of them wear oversize white sweaters emblazoned on the side with a megaphone jutting through a large block *D* (for "Duarte"), outrageously loud checked pants, and the kind of white buck shoes made famous by the singer Pat Boone.

Describing how he had grown up in Duarte, Shepard told *Playboy* magazine in 1984, "In that area, fighting was kind of a badge. I never enjoyed it, but I never backed down. There would be incredible slug-outs in the park. I remember some guys fought like wild men. There would even be these parties where they'd beat up people's fathers—the father of the girl who was giving the party would get wiped out on the street, with the mother screaming, calling the police." In the words of Charles Mingus III, "It wasn't that there were so many real fights in high school as [that] the strongest person would imitate a teacher in a deep voice by saying, 'Hold it!,' and if you turned around, he then had the right to punch you in the chest just as hard as he could."

And then there was the way male students were disciplined for violating school rules. "If you were lucky enough to have just lipped off in a classroom," Charles Mingus III says, "you had to go to the library and write out words from the dictionary. Which was where my vocabulary became what it still is today because I spent most of my time there. But it was the fifties, and they would also hit us in the ass with cricket paddles. They had four paddles, and one was big enough to misalign your spine with just one swat. They also had one that was the same size but with one-inch router bit holes drilled into it so it went faster and hurt more, but you would get four swats with that one. And you would get to pick which one you wanted them to use.

"Was any of this ever done to Sam? What I can say for sure is he did do some lipping off. But the point was there were three levels of punishment—isolation, laps with push-ups, and then the swats. And, of course, if you had used a curse word, then it was always swats."

SAM SHEPARD'S MOST DRAMATIC re-creation of his high school years in Duarte can be found in *The Unseen Hand*, a one-act play that opened at Café La MaMa on St. Mark's Place in Lower Manhattan on December 26, 1969. In it, a character known simply as "The Kid," who has "a blond crew-cut," appears onstage wearing "a long cheerleader's sweater with a huge A printed on it" (for Azusa High School). With his pants down around his ankles and his legs red and bleeding as though they have been whipped with a belt, he begins yelling at the unseen gang from Arcadia High School who have done this to him. Letting loose with an astonishing flood of invective, The Kid expresses the utter contempt he feels toward them for thinking they are better than him just because their fathers are rich.

"I wouldn't fuck an Arcadia girl if she bled out her asshole!" The Kid shouts. "You punk faggots shouldn't even be in the same league as us!" He then goes on and on about how, in the big game on Friday night, their football team will not score a single point but that he will be right there cheering his heart out for his team. Once the game is over, he and his schoolmates will burn the "fucking Arcadia High grandstand" right down to "the fucking ground" and then emblazon a large block *A,* for "Azusa High" on the fifty-yard line.

Sobbing, The Kid crumples to the ground and reveals that the gang grabbed him after the pep rally and took him up to Lookout Point, where they whipped him with a belt. They tried to paint his balls black, but he fought and kicked and would not let them do so. But they did manage to shove a tampon up inside him. As portrayed by Shepard here, the very worst thing anyone could have done to a young man in Duarte back then was to make him into a woman.

As the play nears its end, The Kid begins listing everything he loves about his hometown. In 235 words, Shepard describes life in Duarte back then:

This is my home! Don't make fun of my home. I was born and raised here and I'll die here, I love it! . . . I love the foothills and the drive-in movies and the bowling alleys and the football games and the drag races and the girls and the donut shop and the junior college and the outdoor track meets and the parades and the Junior Chamber of Commerce and the Key Club and the Letterman's Club and the Kiwanis and the Safeway Shopping Center and the freeway and the pool hall and the Bank of America and the post office and the Presbyterian church and the laundromat and the liquor store and the miniature golf course and Lookout Point and the Glee Club and the basketball games and the sock hop and graduation and the prom and the cafeteria and the principal's office and chemistry class and the county fair and peanut butter and jelly sandwiches and the high school band and going steady and KFWB and white bucks and pegger pants and argyle socks and madras shorts and butch wax and Hobie boards and going to the beach and getting drunk and swearing and reading dirty books and smoking in the men's room and setting off cherry bombs and fixing up my car and my mom. I love my mom most of all. And you creeps aren't going to take that away from me.

"Did anything like that ever really happen?" Sandy Rogers says. "Back then, that kind of behavior with young, stupid boys was not unusual. The thing with Sam was he remembered it all. He remembered all the stuff he did, but he also remembered all the stuff everybody else did, too. You really do get the best feel for Sam through his writing, and whether or not the things he wrote were facts didn't really matter to him, because he had a very mysterious and incredible mind even I can't describe, and so he knew you were just never going to be able to figure it all out."

WHEN IT CAME TO raising his son, Sam Rogers was a stickler for the kind of rules and regulations to which he had become accustomed in the U.S. Army Air Force. As Shepard said, "He was very strict, my father, very aware of the need for discipline, so-called, very into studying and all that kind of stuff. I couldn't stand it . . . it was really like being jailed."

Nonetheless, when Shepard was fourteen years old, his father went to a pawnshop and bought him a Ludwig drum set. After stripping the paint off the bass drum, the tom-toms, and the snares, he applied a new coat of varnish and put the set out in the avocado orchard to dry in the sun. He then began teaching his son how to play. Fortunately for both of them, Shepard took to it quickly.

Perhaps not at all surprising in light of his own family background and extensive military experience, Rogers always treated his daughters in a far different manner than his son. In Sandy Rogers's words, "The deal with my dad and my brother was that my father was every bit as charismatic and handsome and physically powerful as Sam. If you had ever been around Sam, you would know that [he] was not always very comfortable and my dad was the same way because he exuded this macho thing. But I was his daughter, and I didn't get any of that, and I saw my father in a different way. And so for the longest time, I couldn't believe what Sam was writing about him."

Shepard biographer Don Shewey quotes Shepard's younger sister Roxanne as saying, "There was always a kind of facing off between them, and it was Sam who got the bad end of that. It was always Dad who set up if it was on or off. Dad was a tricky character. Because he was a charismatic guy when he wanted to be—warm, loving, kind of a hoot to be around. And the other side was like a snapping turtle. With him and Sam, it was that male thing. You put two virile men in a room, and they're going to test each other. It's like two pit bulls."

"And he never cussed, my dad," Sandy Rogers says. "Never said a cuss word. But he might pound on the table. He might point at you, and you really felt like there was fire coming out of his eyes. He was scary. But I never saw any violence from him. He might have also been diabetic and not known it. There is nothing worse for a diabetic than to drink, but you also crave it. My dad would sit there and eat chocolate bars and drink whisky. And so while I don't think he was completely healthy, it could have been his diet, too."

In Duarte, Sam Rogers lived under a kind of constant pressure that was far more difficult to handle than what he had faced during World War II. "When we were kids," Sandy Rogers says, "my father would leave San Marino High School after teaching all day and then go to Bethlehem Steel and work until eleven o'clock at night. He was doing physical labor there, and he had another part-time job at a trucking place as well. He was a workaholic all right, but he had to pay the bills.

"Because my dad really wanted to provide for us and take good care of the family, he really wasn't around that much, and that was another gripe he had with my brother. Sam didn't work enough around the house. He didn't want to mow the lawn. He'd wake up in the morning and be gone, and that was just one of the little things they would always go back and forth about with one another."

Concerning her parents' marriage, she adds, "It's hard for me to say if my mother and father were happy with one another because I wasn't looking at it. And I really don't want to get into that because they were probably not happy with each other for quite a long time before they divorced. As were a lot of people back then. But instead of ending it quickly, they would all just let it drag on for longer than it should have."

IN AN AUTOBIOGRAPHICAL STORY entitled "A Small Circle of Friends," from *Cruising Paradise,* Shepard writes that his parents had a small circle of friends in the mid-1950s but that, by 1961, they had all disappeared. "Later, I found out this was due to my father's drinking and his ensuing temper tantrums. The kind of temper tantrums where you thought his head might explode."

In "A Small Circle of Friends," Shepard portrays his parents and their friends at a barbecue at the Rogers family home in 1957. Laughing and drinking, everyone is having a good time until a thirteen-year-old girl with whom fourteen-year-old Sam has been fooling around suddenly comes crying to her mother because of what the Rogers family's Mexican gardener has just said or done to her down by the sheep pens. After Sam's father orders the gardener to leave, the party begins breaking up. A man named Phil, whom Sam's father has always suspected of carrying on an affair with his wife, stays behind. Without any provocation, Sam's father walks up to Phil and hits him so hard the glass he is holding explodes into his face. Grabbing Phil by the hair, Sam's father smashes his face onto his raised knee again and again until his nose splits. Walking away, Sam's father then turns on the sprinklers and lets the water wash over Phil.

Although the physical violence described in the story never took place, Sandy Rogers says, "We did have an incident where our gardener was caught messing around with one of our friends' daughters at a party. She was fourteen and old enough to know what he was doing was not right. My father never beat anyone up. That is bullshit. But it was the end of the gardener. After that, he was gone."

And while Shepard's use of an act of violence to end this story may seem like a way out, he would employ this device to conclude many of his best works, *Curse of the Starving Class, True West,* and *Fool for Love* foremost among them. As a playwright, Shepard never uses violence as a form of catharsis but rather as the logical end result of long-running family dysfunction or yet another desperate and ultimately vain attempt by one of his male characters to come to terms with what it really means to be a man in America.

Concerning her parents' actual social circle in Duarte, Sandy Rogers also says, "All of my friends' fathers were alcoholics. A lot of it had to do with the war of course, but at that point in time, it was also like the American dream could only go so far and when they hit that wall, it ruined everything for them. I think what frustrated my father the most was that we had everything we needed and wanted and yet it wasn't enough. Like, 'We've got two cars, we've got the house, and so what do we do now?'"

FOUR

THE REAL
GABBY HAYES

If you are a boy, every enemy is potentially,
psychologically associated with the father image.

—JOSEPH CAMPBELL,
THE POWER OF MYTH

THINKING HE WOULD GROW UP TO BE "A VETERINARIAN WITH
a flashy station wagon & a flashy blonde wife, raising German Shep-
herds in some fancy suburb," Sam Shepard entered his senior year at
Duarte High School already knowing there was no reason for him to
apply himself to his studies now—as he had never done before—so he
could leave Duarte to go off to college. Although his plan at the time
was eventually to apply to the University of California at Davis, Shepard already knew he would be spending the next two years at Mount
San Antonio College, the local junior college known as Mt. Sac, less
than a half hour by car from his house.

Nonetheless, in what can only be described as a truly inspired bit of
fantasy, Shepard later wrote an autobiographical sketch that appeared
in the American Place Theatre newsletter in April 1971. In it, according
to biographer John J. Winters, Shepard claimed that during this period of his life in Duarte, he stole cars, drove recklessly, and was thrown
in jail for flipping off the wife of the police chief in Big Bear Lake, a
resort town in the San Bernardino Mountains.

During the course of an extensive interview twenty-six years later
in *The Paris Review*, Shepard further embellished his past by saying,
"My history with booze goes back to high school. Back then there was

a lot of Benzedrine around, and since we lived near the Mexican border I'd just run over, get a bag of bennies and drink ripple [*sic*] wine.
Speed and booze together make you quite . . . omnipotent. You don't
feel any pain. I was actually in several car wrecks that I don't understand how I survived."

In actual fact, Duarte is about 150 miles and a three-hour drive
from the Mexican border. But then, as Sandy Rogers says, "I don't
think Sam was ever a wild boy, but I remember one time he did bring
home this big sawhorse with lights on it that flashed on and off, from
a construction site, and put it in his room. He had absolutely stolen it,
and Mom said, 'You better take that back.' He put it under his bed, but
the lights just kept right on flashing on and off. And I'm really not
aware of anything else he ever did like that." Shepard's only other
known act of rebellion during his senior year at Duarte High School
was showing up late for a graduation rehearsal. "He had been late, and
so they did not let him walk," Sandy Rogers says. "We do have a picture of him in his cap and gown, but it was not taken at graduation."

During this period of Shepard's life in Duarte, his father, now
forty-four years old, was the one who began acting out in a way no one
in the family could have ignored. Precisely what triggered this behavior is impossible to say, but Sam Rogers's deep-seated dissatisfaction
with his life had already been building for years.

"My dad was an alpha male, definitely," Sandy Rogers says. "And it
was not just that people who weren't as smart and talented as him were
richer and seemed happier but the fact that he had done all the right
things—coming out west and getting himself a college degree and a
good teaching job—but those jobs didn't pay shit. Just because he was
teaching at San Marino High School in a rich neighborhood didn't
mean anything. He was making the same as anyone teaching at any
high school. And so we never had a lot of money, but we were okay.

"What also really pissed my dad off was that even though he was
the head of the language department there, he still had to do what he
was told by his boss, the principal, whose name was actually 'Mr. Din-
gus.' I remember when my dad had given this kid an F and the kid
couldn't graduate because of that, and my dad said, 'Well, he deserved
less than an F,' but the principal let him graduate anyway, and that

kind of thing happened over and over again. My dad was a tough guy and a disciplinarian, and he didn't like people stepping across his boundaries, and so all this was always very frustrating for him."

Although Rogers was displeased with his position in the chain of command at San Marino High School, the graduating class of 1960 thought so highly of his teaching abilities that they dedicated their yearbook to him. A year later, he was awarded a Fulbright Linguistic Scholarship, which enabled him to spend the summer of 1961 studying Spanish in Bogotá, Colombia.

In a letter Shepard wrote to his grandmother after spending that summer working as a veterinarian's assistant in West Covina, he brought up the possibility of not going to college at all but rather heading off to the Yukon to work in a lumberyard. Noting that Sam Rogers was due to return home from Colombia on Saturday, Shepard also wrote that his father would "probably shatter my dreams immediately."

According to Shepard biographer John J. Winters, over the course of the three months Rogers spent in Bogotá, he may have fallen in love with the daughter of his host family. In Winters's words, "There are some who say Sam Rogers left his heart in Colombia and was never the same after returning home."

KNOWN IN HINDU CULTURE as "the tree of God," the deodar cedar has survived in the Himalayas for as long as a thousand years. Those in the dense grove across the street from the Rogers house on Lemon Avenue in Duarte were far more short-lived. And so when Sam Rogers came home from work one day to see all those majestic trees gone, his immediate reaction was more than just shock and surprise. "They had all been cut down by the city, and it might have been because of some kind of tree disease," Sandy Rogers says, "but my father didn't know anything about it beforehand, and so he completely blew it. Because the neighbor across the street was on the city council, the first thing my father did was go over there and scream at those people, who of course were also friends of ours. There had been incidents before when he had been drinking, but this was different. He was devastated because there had been a forest there and now it was gone and the whole place had been completely changed. And I don't think he ever recovered from that. For him, this was the turning point. It just really sent him over the edge."

Whether or not the destruction of the deodars finally convinced Sam Rogers that he could no longer control his life as he had while piloting his B-24 bomber in World War II, and so he then decided there was no longer any reason for him even to continue trying, no one can say for sure. But from this point on, he did begin acting like an out-of-control alcoholic, thereby making everything just that much more difficult for him and his family.

In a relatively short space of time, Rogers crashed his car into a tree. He began going off on extended binges during which he would stay in a local motel, often with a woman he had met that night while drinking in a bar. He would then return home just long enough to dump his dirty laundry on the kitchen table along with a note instructing his wife not to starch his shirts. How he was still able to show up to teach at San Marino High School five days a week can only be explained as the kind of behavior high-functioning alcoholics can sometimes maintain for long periods of time.

As Shepard described it, the final confrontation between him and his father in Duarte took on the air of Greek tragedy. During an interview with Terry Gross on National Public Radio's *Fresh Air* in 1998, Shepard called the incident "a holocaust" in which "the old man" literally "destroyed the house . . . Broke windows, tore the doors off, stuff like that." According to biographer John J. Winters, Shepard wrote another account of the incident in a notebook entry dated May 20, 2008. In it, he stated that his father had smashed windows in the house, torn the front door off its hinges, and then set the backyard on fire. In his *Paris Review* interview in 1997, Shepard referred to his father as "a maniac, but in a very quiet way. I had a falling-out with him at a relatively young age by the standards of that era. We were always butting up against each other, never seeing eye-to-eye on anything, and as I got older it escalated into a really bad, violent situation. Eventually I just decided to get out."

By far the single most personal statement Shepard ever made about how deeply his father's drunken behavior affected him can be found in a story titled "Orange Grove in My Past," from *Day out of Days*. In it, he writes:

> I thought I had done my level best, done everything I possibly could, not to become my father. Gone out of my way in every department: changed my name, first and last, falsified my birth certificate, deliberately walked and swung my arms in exact counterpoint to the way he had; picked out clothing the opposite of what he would have worn, right down to the underwear; spoke without any trace of a Midwestern twang, never kicked a dog in the ribs; never lost my temper over inanimate objects, never again listened to Bing Crosby after Christmas of 1959, and never ever hit a woman in the face. I thought I had come a long way in reshaping my total person. I had absolutely no idea who I was but I knew for sure I wasn't him.

"As far as I know," Sandy Rogers says, "my dad never laid a hand on my mom. As far as I know. I swear. I never saw him touch her. In my life, he never touched her. But just like there were so many things I did not tell my brother, there was stuff that happened to Sam he never told me about or that I didn't see. I mean, I can guess, but I don't know. Because I cannot know.

"Now, I was there the night when my mother locked my dad out of the house, but there was no physical violence. Well, yes, there was physical violence, because my dad took a crowbar to the door. And then Sam came out of his room and said, '*Dad!*' And then my dad turned around, and my mom began screaming, but nothing came of it except for the broken door. And my dad never set the yard on fire. Sam's writing makes it all sound better than it really was from my point of view, but I was there when it happened."

In the same letter to his grandmother in Illinois expressing his fears about what would happen when his father came back home from Colombia, Shepard also wrote that he intended to major in education at Mount San Antonio College. Having already signed up for the golf team, he was also thinking about trying out for track as a high jumper.

As he began the first of his three semesters at a school best known for its agricultural program, Shepard abandoned these plans and joined the drama club instead. He then appeared in four plays. By far, his most notable performance was as Elwood P. Dowd, the central character in *Harvey*, a genial fantasy written by Mary Chase that had already been made into a popular movie starring James Stewart, who was nominated for the Academy Award for Best Actor for his performance.

A perpetually pixilated eccentric who liked to hang out in bars but who did not resemble Sam Rogers in any way whatsoever when he was drinking, Dowd is accompanied throughout the play by his best friend, a six-foot, three-inch rabbit named Harvey whom only Dowd can see. "I saw Sam in *Harvey* at Mt. Sac, and he was amazing," Sandy Rogers says. "He was just great and I think he also did some writing while he was there. Then he linked up with the Bishop's [Company Repertory] Players at the Pasadena Playhouse and worked with them there for a little while."

During his freshman year at Mt. Sac, Shepard also wrote his first play. Discovered in the college archives by biographer John J. Winters with the help of a current faculty member, *The Mildew*, a one-act comedy, occupied ten pages in the school's 1961 student literary journal. Although the play was never performed, Winters wrote that "for a community college freshman it shows a remarkable eagerness to experiment and a transgressive sense of humor." But, as he also noted, "Shepard's first play lacks a traditional ending." Whatever *The Mildew*'s merits and faults may have been, Shepard still thought of himself as an actor rather than a writer and it was this self-characterization that enabled him to finally leave Duarte for good.

After dropping out of Mt. Sac in the spring of 1963, Shepard worked on a horse farm in Chino, California. He then delivered newspapers from his red-and-white Chevrolet in Pasadena. It was while doing so that he saw a classified ad in the newspaper for the Bishop's Company Repertory Players, which was looking for actors, and decided to audition for a place in the troupe.

In what has become yet another integral part of his legend, Shepard was handed a book of Shakespeare's plays at the audition but was so nervous—and so completely untrained as an actor—that he read not only his assigned dialogue but also the stage directions accompanying it. Young, eager, and good-looking, he was nonetheless hired for the princely sum of ten dollars a week to join the Bishop's Company on its cross-country tour, which eventually brought him to New York City.

By then, Sam Rogers was no longer even living in the house on Lemon Avenue. "He kind of left and came back a couple times," Sandy Rogers says. "And then my dad was around the area, but we didn't know where. I remember driving with my mother one day, and there he was, walking down the street, and I went, 'Mom, *stop*! I want to see Dad.' So, my mother stopped and he was all pissed off, because he thought she had been out looking for him."

After being married for twenty-five years, Sam and Jane Rogers divorced in 1968. By then, Rogers had already begun spending time with a woman who played piano in one of the local cocktail bars where he was a regular. Eventually, the two got married and moved to Altadena, but the marriage lasted for only a few years.

Despite having worked at San Marino High School for seventeen years, Sam Rogers was fired from his position as a teacher and the head of the language department in 1969. "I really don't know why or even when he got fired from his teaching job," Sandy Rogers says, "but I do know he dropped his thermos in the teacher's lounge one day, and there was whisky in the coffee. And he had been showing up drunk and teaching drunk. And then he took off. There were times when I would be with Sam, and he would say, 'It's the old man.' Meaning that what he [Sam] was doing was because of [our father]. I will tell you this: Sam was haunted by my dad. He was definitely haunted by him."

IN A FIVE-PAGE STORY entitled "The Real Gabby Hayes," from *Cruising Paradise,* Shepard created a chilling portrait of his father as a man who had already lost his way in mid-1950s America. George "Gabby" Hayes was a movie and television actor who played the perpetual sidekick to cowboy luminaries like Hopalong Cassidy, Roy Rogers, and Gene Autry and to movie stars like Randolph Scott and

John Wayne. Hayes was also often cast as the laughing, babbling, half-mad old coot who had spent far too many years on the range rounding up strays or out in the desert panning for gold he never found.

Written in the first-person voice of a seven-year-old boy, "The Real Gabby Hayes" has a simple plot. Acting solely on the promise of the glossy brochures a door-to-door real estate salesman has shown him, the boy's father buys a piece of land in a remote location in the Mojave Desert. Father and son journey out there together, but instead of the "glistening swimming pools, emerald-green golf courses, and a club-house" featured in the brochures, they see nothing but "virgin desert."

In the first of a series of odd and inappropriate remarks, the father says he wants to bring a rattlesnake home so the boy's mother will not think he has been "tomcatting around." When the boy asks if this is the real reason he brought him here today, his father gets angry and starts tossing one can after another up into the air and firing at them until his .22 pistol is empty without ever once hitting his target.

Continuing to "take long sips from a fifth in a paper bag that he had stuffed in his hip pocket," the father explains that what he really has in mind for this place is "a little desert hideaway," because he can't "always be the family man." Living out here together, he and his son would keep burros, take hikes, and go looking for buried treasure.

After driving back across the desert sand to the blacktop highway, the boy's father stops at a date shake shack and asks the Mexican owner for directions to "a place called the Shadow Mountain Inn—some kind of country club he'd remembered from his air force days." Parking right outside it, the father carefully wraps his .22 in an old racing form and stuffs it beneath the front seat.

As the two of them walk across the parking lot, the boy's father says that because this is "a very exclusive club," they should act like they belong here. After sitting down together at the mahogany bar, he orders a martini with white pearl onions floating around in it. Just then, the boy sees Gabby Hayes. Or, as he says in the story, "the real Gabby Hayes."

Although it is 109 degrees outside, and the blacktop is melting, Gabby Hayes sits in a corner booth wearing a shiny tuxedo and a black string bolo tie. "Hypnotized by his big white beard," the boy cannot stop staring. With Hayes are two young blondes "decked out in slinky cocktail outfits, dripping with jewelry and sex. Even at seven, I could recognize sex when I saw it."

While dangling shrimp dipped in red sauce in front of Hayes's nose, both women continue "giggling and nibbling on his fuzzy ears." Beneath a white linen napkin, one of them also has her hand in his lap. Excitedly, the boy directs his father's attention to Hayes. Turning around to gaze at him, his father says, "That's what fame and fortune'll get you. Couple a blond chippies and a shrimp cocktail. How 'bout that?"

As Sandy Rogers says, "My dad had bought real estate in the desert, and so we did have a piece of property out there." Concerning the dismissive remarks the father in his story makes about Gabby Hayes, Shepard told *New York Times* drama critic Mel Gussow in 2002, "That is my old man talking."

FIVE

THE VILLAGE GATE

Sam said he needed an apartment, and I said,
"I got this apartment. The rent is a little steep.
Sixty bucks. Let's split it. At least it will save
you from being on the street."

—CHARLES MINGUS III,
IN "THE WRITE STUFF,"
THE GUARDIAN

BEFORE SETTING OUT ON THE TOUR THAT BROUGHT HIM TO New York City in the fall of 1963, Shepard was cast in a Bishop's Company performance of Thornton Wilder's *The Skin of Our Teeth* at the San Gabriel Mission Playhouse, a large, ornate theater built in the 1920s that seated nearly fourteen hundred people.

An allegory in three acts that shattered a host of the theatrical conventions of the time, *The Skin of Our Teeth* won the Pulitzer Prize for Best Drama in 1943. Employing the kind of stereotypical racial language still common in that era, Wilder's original stage directions in Act 2 specify "three roller chairs, pushed by melancholy Negroes, file by empty. Throughout the act they traverse the stage in both directions." And while no one in Hollywood would ever have bought this as a plot point in the movie of Sam Shepard's life, those stage directions began the improbable friendship that helped him launch his career as a playwright in New York City.

In 1947, after Camille Jeanne Gross left the legendary jazz bassist and composer Charles Mingus for the final time, thereby ending a marriage that had always been tumultuous, she brought their four-year-old son, Charles Mingus III, and his one-year-old brother, Eu-

gene, to Duarte so they could be raised by her parents. As Charles
Mingus III says, "My grandfather was an Austrian Jew and my grandmother was Native American. He davened and so I was Jewish and I
then became bar mitzvahed in the second-oldest synagogue in the
United States. My grandfather was a real estate guy and in Duarte, we
were not living on the wrong side of the tracks. We were living *on* the
tracks. At one point in time, the family owned four city blocks. They
lost most of it to taxes, but my grandfather had built a house on the
property and that was where I grew up."

According to Shepard biographer Ellen Oumano, the only contact
Sam Shepard and Charles Mingus III had at Duarte High School was
a fistfight over a remark that neither of them could later remember.
"When I saw him the second time," Mingus III told Oumano, "I didn't
think about the fight, but he'd made an impression. I was eating in a
diner on Route 66, like in the movie *Diner,* only everyone was black.
Sam was looking around, vaguely nervous . . . He saw me first, came
over, said, 'Hi,' something like 'We went to school together' and asked
me to be in a Bishop's Company production, *Skin of Our Teeth,* at the
[San Gabriel] Mission [Playhouse] theater. What he was really looking for was someone who looked like Sammy Davis, Jr., because the
guy who was supposed to do this part in the play never showed up.
Sam didn't know I would be [at that diner]. It was totally by accident
that he bumped into me."

Because he had never rehearsed with the cast and had apparently
not read the play before being pressed into service, Mingus III thought
he was just doing Shepard a favor until he learned—apparently during
his performance—that his role was as one of the "melancholy Negroes"
who push rolling chairs across the stage during the second act. "I didn't
flip out," Mingus III says. "I just said, 'No way, folks. Fuck this! You
want someone to push a chair, push it yourself.' And then I threw the
chair off the stage. Fortunately, the front row was about thirteen feet
away, because I could have killed some people. But Sam thought that
what I'd done was fucking hilarious."

Unfortunately for Mingus III, no one in the audience for that performance shared Shepard's opinion. "They turned on the lights," Mingus III says, "and a guy stood up, pointed at me, and said, '*Kill . . .*

that . . . nigger!' There was no logic in it. It was just absolute rage, like in a lynching. My mom, my stepdad, and my baby brother were sitting in the front row and they all just disappeared."

Running out the back door of the theater, Mingus III climbed a telephone pole because he thought no one would ever think of looking up there for him. "Panicked, freaked out," and "turned inside out," Mingus III was clinging to "the pole in the back parking lot and then Sam came swaggering out of the place and whistling and he said, 'I know you're out here, Mingus.'" Quickly, Shepard led Mingus III to his old red pickup truck. "If he hadn't had that," Mingus III says, "I think I'd be dead, because the entire town was still looking for me the next morning. I scooched down and got in the truck beside him, and he took me home."

Despite what Mingus III had done onstage at the San Gabriel Mission Playhouse, Shepard remained a member in good standing of the Bishop's Company, then set off with them on a cross-country tour. Like so many other places he would pass through during his life, Duarte was now in his rearview mirror forever.

AFTER GETTING ON A bus that took him to Pennsylvania, Sam Shepard joined one of the small troupes of actors the Bishop's Company kept out on the road. In what then became his apprenticeship in the world of professional theater, as well as a forerunner to his habit of driving obsessively across America for the next fifty years, Shepard spent the next eight months moving constantly from one place to another in New England, the South, and the Midwest as part of a troupe that rarely stayed anywhere for more than a single night.

Performing in churches and college auditoriums while sleeping in Best Western motels or private homes, the actors traveled together in a pair of Ford station wagons, each vehicle pulling a small trailer loaded with costumes and sets that could be used for a variety of productions, a version of *Winnie-the-Pooh* among them. As Shepard later said in *The Paris Review,* "It was actually a great little fold-up theater. We were totally self-sufficient: we put up the lights, made the costumes, performed the play and shut down."

While on the road, Shepard began to understand how what he later called "the vitality of theater" always sprang from what had been written on the page. Falling in love with the sheer power of words he seemed able to string together in long, frenetic bursts, he began envisioning the characters who would speak those words onstage.

Putting an end to his career as an actor in theater, Shepard decided to focus his energy and attention on writing plays rather than performing in them. Or, as he said many years later in *The Paris Review*, "Anyway, one day we got to New York to do a production at a church in Brooklyn, and I said, 'I'm getting off the bus.'"

After selling a pint of his blood in Times Square so he could buy himself a cheeseburger at White Castle, Shepard put to good use another "hot tip" he had picked up from a fellow actor in the Bishop's Company troupe by applying for a job with the Burns Detective Agency, for which he was immediately hired. Dressed in a khaki uniform with a bright silver badge and the "Marine looking" hat he had been given by the agency, along with a night stick and a time card clock in a black leather holster, Sam Shepard took on his first job in New York City, guarding a fleet of coal barges tied up to the docks on the East River.

For performing this existential task five nights a week from ten P.M. until four A.M., he was paid what was then the legal minimum wage of $1.25 an hour, which resulted in a weekly salary of $52.50 (a sum now worth about eight times that much). Stationed in a small, four-by-fourteen-foot wooden hut "set on the edge of the docks overlooking the Con Ed smokestack and the shimmering oily river," he made regular rounds of the docks every fifteen minutes while "stopping at designated steel posts with little boxes on them containing keys." He would fit each key into a slot in his punch-out clock, making a notch on a paper disk he would then drop into a box at the end of his shift in order to prove he had carried out his appointed rounds. As he later wrote, "It was probably the most peaceful job in New York City, and I never could fathom why anyone would want to vandalize a coal barge."

In "Fear of the Fiddle," a story in *Cruising Paradise*, Shepard writes about an Appalachian fiddle player named Ansel Cartwright he met on the Lower East Side who introduced him to crystal Methedrine by "mixing the bitter powder with Coca Cola" so they could both "then belt the whole thing down. Our personal record for no sleep was five consecutive days." After a few hits on their bottle of doctored Coke, they would both feel "impervious to cold and time." As Cartwright played his "lacquered candy-apple green" fiddle "with a pin-striped spider web painted in black on the back" that "was electrified but could be unplugged and played acoustic" in that tiny hut at the edge of the East River, Shepard would beat out the rhythm against his hands and knees with "a pair of nickel-plated soup spoons."

Every fifteen minutes, Shepard would go outside to make his rounds, sometimes with Cartwright following him while keeping right on playing. Back inside the guardhouse again, they would "discuss the ancient fear of the fiddle, a belief the early American colonists had inherited from European religious fanatics of the Middle Ages, that the fiddle was an instrument of the Devil himself."

A week after he began playing with Cartwright, Shepard writes, he became so absorbed in "an extended version of Soldier's Joy," a popular fiddle tune dating back to the eighteenth century, that he forgot to make his rounds and so was summarily fired by the agency the following day. Because they wanted their uniform, cap, nightstick, clock, and badge back, Shepard returned "everything but the clock, which I threw in the East River."

While the character of Ansel Cartwright is based upon Shepard's longtime friend Peter Stampfel of the Holy Modal Rounders, the two men had not yet met during this period and so, in many ways, the story exemplifies how Shepard would integrate real details about his own life into an otherwise fictional framework.

Now unemployed, Shepard considered returning to his career as an actor and may actually have begun making the rounds with his head shot and résumé before deciding he did not want to spend the rest of his life auditioning for others. He then read an item in Hedda Hopper's nationally syndicated gossip column in which she expressed her dismay that Charles Mingus's son had been reduced to working as a busboy at the Village Gate, a popular nightclub in Greenwich Village.

With Mingus III as his connection, Shepard was hired at the Village Gate at 158 Bleecker Street in the heart of Greenwich Village.

Bussing tables three nights a week for as much as fifty dollars a night, he was now able to afford his share of the rent for the apartment where Mingus lived on the corner of Tenth Street and Avenue C, a two-minute walk from Tompkins Square Park, and so promptly moved in with him.

In their apartment, Shepard slept on a mattress on the floor with, as Charles Mingus III says, "the bumper of a 1957 Chevy, not as a headboard but at the far end of the mattress in my studio space, which was the front room of the apartment and had a nice view out of the window." Their other roommate was Dannie Richmond, the renowned jazz drummer, who came and went while backing up Charles Mingus, with whom he worked for twenty-one years.

Despite Richmond's drug issues, Shepard idolized him as a musician. "The only rule I had," Mingus III says, "was 'No shooting up in my apartment.' If anything, what we were doing back then was booze and, occasionally, a really expensive joint. You know what a joint cost in those days? Or a bottle of whisky?"

Confirming this, Shepard said, "I never shot up, but I mean I used everything on the street." While doing so, he and Mingus III became best friends. Running wild together, they played different roles on the street with each other, switching characters while mimicking the voices of everyone from gangsters to old ladies. They also nearly got themselves arrested for holding an impromptu concert on the roof of their apartment building. At one point, Shepard and Mingus III, both of whom loved Laurel and Hardy, even considered becoming a professional comedy team, a concept they then quickly abandoned.

"Sam was safe on the Lower East Side because of me," Mingus III says. "He could have been seen in the wrong light, because sometimes he could be very rude to people and didn't have any real street smarts at all. He'd see a blond girl and go right up to her and say something fresh and find out she was a Puerto Rican girl with bleached blond hair and curse her out."

Shepard described his sex life during this period on the Lower East Side in a 1985 *Newsweek* cover story about him by saying, "I rode everything with hair. Charles had this knack of picking up these amazingly straight women—stewardesses and secretaries. Charlie was always spattered with paint and I didn't take too many baths back then. And there were cockroaches all over the place. But these women would show up in their secretarial gear. It was wild. I couldn't believe it."

Although he may well have availed himself of his fair share of the women who found themselves in that apartment on the Lower East Side, Shepard was by then already involved in a relationship that had begun soon after he arrived in New York City. "I met Charles before I met Sam," says Lee Mason, who had just dropped out of New York University and was working for a temporary agency while sharing a fifth-floor walk-up apartment on Suffolk Street with four other women. "But I always knew him as Steve Rogers. He had only just arrived from California, and while I was aware there had been some kind of scratchiness between him and his father, he was not yet ready to unburden himself about it. He was still trying to breathe and let his shoulders drop down below his earlobes.

"At that point, I didn't know many Californians and he was rather tall and slender and lanky and laconic. We were friends and we hung out together and we became good friends, and then we became better friends. We kept company for about the better part of a year and I never had the sense he was seeing other women. Not that there would have been anything wrong in that, but he was so kind in his attentions to me that I don't think he had anyone else in his life.

"We parted because I needed some private time away from him. He didn't do anything bad. In retrospect, it was just my own misconception of things."

THE FRIENDSHIP BETWEEN SAM SHEPARD and Charles Mingus III was always far too intense not to cool down. In the words of Marianne de Pury, a musical composer and theater artist who was then seeing Mingus III, "Sam and Charles eventually separated. They were still friends but didn't see each other that often anymore. Charles had come east because he wanted to connect with his father. Sam had come because he wanted to become a famous playwright. And while Sam always knew exactly what he was going to do and then did it and was brilliant, Charles was more the artist. The two of them had different lives, and they also had really different lifestyles."

Despite all this, the bond between the two men was so powerful that Shepard would later say he was greatly influenced by Mingus III throughout this period because, as an artist, Mingus III was "very not into selling out, and keeping himself within his own sphere of reference."

Together one night, Shepard and Mingus III went to a roadside church in New Jersey with a Wollensak tape recorder to capture ambient sound for Shepard's first play, *Cowboys*, only to be rousted by the state police, who then escorted them back onto the New Jersey Turnpike.

And after Shepard's play *La Turista* was performed at the American Place Theatre in March 1967, Mingus III created the pop art image of a roll of toilet paper that appeared on the cover of the Bobbs-Merrill edition of the play. "That was the last project I ever did for Sam," Mingus III says. "I introduced him to Chris Cerf, who was then an editor at Random House. He gave Sam a book contract for *La Turista*, which Sam then used as leverage for a deal with Bobbs-Merrill he had actually wanted all along without telling me. So I ended up ripping off Chris Cerf's time as well as a contract while Sam had his usual fishing expeditions going."

But the incident that finally led to the end of their friendship occurred when Shepard and Mingus III were having breakfast together one day in a Lower East Side restaurant. Amused by the behavior of three Mafia-type thugs at the next table, Shepard began laughing out loud at them. He then made the situation even worse by, in the words of Mingus III, "getting hysterical and hyperventilating" because the man who took their money at the cash register "looked exactly like Elmer Fudd." Already pissed off at Shepard "for mocking them," the thugs grabbed Mingus III from behind and dragged him out into the street. As two of them held his arms and lifted him into the air, "this little runty guy with a pinky ring started cursing and calling me names and hitting me like I was a punching bag," Mingus III says. "All through this, Sam was nowhere to be seen." When the thugs finally released Mingus III, he stood there stunned until Shepard walked up, handed him his glasses, and said, " 'You didn't think I was going to help you, did you?' He was a fucking coward."

In Lee Mason's words, "Charles told me the story and that Sam had done nothing and did not lift a hand to help him. I was dumbstruck and asked Charles how he could stay in contact with [Sam] after this happened, and he said, 'Well, that was one of several things that caused Sam and I not to be in touch anymore.'"

Asked by director Michael Almereyda during a 2011 interview who in New York City had been "a particular accomplice or guide or friend" to him, someone who helped shape his work, Shepard said, "Well, Charles Mingus Jr. was a great friend of mine. I went to high school with him and he was always close to me, but then our friendship got distorted and warped because of his . . . Hell, I hate to say *paranoia*, but I started to feel as if the influence I was getting from him was more and more negative. I didn't quite know how to handle it, so I broke off the friendship.

"But he definitely had an influence on me, and so did his father and all of the jazz musicians around that scene because I felt like jazz was really the art form of that decade. I don't know what it was about that music, but when you saw it live, there was something deeply glowing about it. The way those musicians presented themselves on stage . . . They were the heroes of that era."

UNLIKE THE HALF NOTE and the Five Spot, the Village Gate was not a club where only jazz artists performed. Comedians like Woody Allen, Flip Wilson, and Bill Cosby, whom Charles Mingus III would later describe as "a B- or C-list guy at the Village Gate back then," regularly worked there. Blues artists like Memphis Slim and Willie Dixon, soul singers like Aretha Franklin, and folk artists like Pete Seeger also appeared at a venue most people simply called "the Gate."

Founded in 1958 by Art D'Lugoff, who with his neatly trimmed goatee and black wool fisherman's cap was the very picture of a hip downtown entrepreneur, the Village Gate was located in what had been the basement laundry of the Mills Hotel. Built in 1897 as Mills House No. 1, a residential hotel for impoverished men, the Mills had more than fifteen hundred tiny rooms, each of which originally rented for twenty cents a night, with meals costing fifteen cents.

When Sam Shepard began working at the Village Gate in 1964, Edward Herbert Beresford "Chip" Monck, who was twenty-five years old, had already served as the club's lighting director for five years. In time, Monck would become best known as the Voice of Woodstock for warning the crowd at the festival that "the brown acid that is circulating around us is specifically not too good."

Far too busy working the lights during shows, Monck never even noticed Shepard in the Village Gate. However, as Monck made his way back to the club one afternoon while carrying a twenty-foot-long section of inch-and-a-quarter pipe he had lifted from a nearby construction site, he found himself trapped in the middle of Bleecker Street. As traffic rushed by him in both directions, a young man whom Monck did not know came up to him and said, "You look like you need a hand. I'll take an end." Together, they headed toward the stairs leading down into the Village Gate.

Inside the club, both men carefully laid the pipe down on the stage. Because Monck wanted to hang the pipe as a light bridge but needed to get ropes and a chain to do so, he asked the young man if he had time to stick around to help him. The young man said he did. After they finally finished the job two hours later, the young man said he had to go work. When Monck asked where he worked, the man said, "Here." When Monck asked for his name, he said, "Sam." When Monck offered to pay him for his time, he said, "No." As Monck says, "And that was about it. Years later, I realized it was Sam Shepard, because he never did give me his last name."

When Shepard's nights at the Village Gate finally ended at one or two in the morning, he would head for his apartment near Tompkins Square Park. On the way, he would sometimes stop off for a bowl of hot borscht and an order of pierogi at Veselka, the Ukrainian restaurant on Second Avenue that was open twenty-four hours a day. As for Monck, when his night at the Gate ended, he would head out the back door of the club, turn left, and walk into the kitchen of his apartment. In a small nook just beyond it, he had an office with a green carpet on the floor, a bed, and a desk with an IBM Selectric typewriter on it.

At about six thirty each night, as customers began filing into the Village Gate before the first show, a singer-songwriter with whom Monck had made an arrangement would arrive in his office. Sitting himself down at Monck's typewriter (which then cost $450, an astronomical sum equal to ten times that much today), he would begin writing lyrics to his songs. "He was extremely private and very seldom spoke," Monck says. "And so we did not have a gabby relationship. But he did once say to me, 'Listen, you can read what I've written. But if you're thinking about making suggestions, I don't need a fucking co-writer, because I ain't about to pay one.'"

Although Bob Dylan, by then already viewed by many in Greenwich Village as the second coming of Woody Guthrie, and Sam Shepard, who was earning $150 a week hauling dirty dishes, glasses, and cutlery off tables at the Village Gate, were in very close physical proximity on a nightly basis, they would not meet until years later when both were about to go out on the road on one of the most iconic rock-'n'-roll tours in history.

AS HILTON ALS, the Pulitzer Prize–winning drama critic, wrote in a moving obituary entitled "Sam Shepard's Soul," for *The New Yorker* in August 2017:

> After Amiri Baraka, Sam Shepard, who died last week, at the age of seventy-three, was this nation's first hip-hop playwright. In astonishing early works like "The Tooth of Crime" (1972) and "Angel City" (1976), he merged his love of jazz and jazz culture with stories about impossible love affairs and male competitiveness ...
>
>   Like hip-hop—or rap set to an electronic beat—Shepard's first scripts were hopped up on their own language about race and women and guys doing guy stuff that they didn't understand and didn't question ... And while he was associated in

films and onstage with the West—or an Old West that his looks made one nostalgic for—his real terrain was black music.

At the Half Note, the Five Spot, and the Village Gate, Sam Shepard saw many of the greatest jazz artists of an era that was about to end. He saw Eric Dolphy, the great alto sax, bass clarinet, and flute player whose sudden death at the age of thirty-six on June 29, 1964, would reduce Charles Mingus to tears for the rest of his life. Years later, Shepard wrote about "Dolphy's Egyptian pharaoh goatee, long with a knob at the end, hieroglyphic" as the musician sat with "eyes pinned to the bandstand floor, seeing right through it as Mingus mashed away with his meaty fingers, cruel smile" while doing "Fables of Faubus." Bearing the name of Governor Orval Faubus of Arkansas, who in 1957 had summoned the National Guard to prevent nine Black students from integrating Little Rock Central High School, this was the most overtly political composition Mingus had ever written. Shepard would remember Mingus "unleashing torrential angry riffs through 'Fables of Faubus,' chanting 'FAUB-ASS' into the face of a mostly white audience."

At the Gate, Shepard saw "Thelonius Monk mauling the piano with his huge hands, doing his little shuffle-step hat dance around the stage then returning to the stool to begin the hauntingly simple melody line of 'Round About Midnight.'" He saw Cannonball Adderley and his brother Nat "shaking the whole place down with saxophone frenzy. Dizzy Gillespie busting his round face into that weird-looking horn with the gold bell pointing straight up to the rafters." He saw Ella Fitzgerald, Gerry Mulligan, Sonny Rollins, Mongo Santamaría, Coleman Hawkins, and Roland Kirk.

Shepard also saw the groundbreaking singer, songwriter, pianist, and civil rights activist Nina Simone. Each night after Simone had finished performing, Shepard would bring her "a whole big gray plastic bus tray filled with ice to cool her Scotch," and she "was always nice to me." According to Mingus III, "Sam did not bring Nina Simone ice. I did. She would come off sweating and I would get her fresh terrycloth towels and ice water and napkins."

Peeling off her blond wig, Simone would throw it on the floor.

"Underneath," Shepard wrote, "her real hair was short like a sheared black lamb." Removing her fake eyelashes, she would paste them to the mirror. "Her eyelids were thick and painted blue. They always reminded me of one of those Egyptian Queens like I'd seen in *National Geographic*." Still soaked with sweat from her performance, Simone would lean forward with both elbows on her knees as the perspiration "rolled off her face and splashed on the red concrete floor between her feet."

Nina Simone always ended her set with "Pirate Jenny," the song Kurt Weill wrote for Bertolt Brecht's *The Threepenny Opera*. "She always sang that song like she'd written it herself," Shepard later wrote. "Her performance was aimed directly at the throat of a white audience . . . She was like a warrior—and a tyrant. When she sang the 'Pirate Jenny' song, the hair on your neck stood up."

Right from the start, Shepard "recognized that this was the real thing. This was music unschooled, totally inspired, and coming directly" from the souls of the gifted artists who were playing it "like a story by a campfire in the middle of nowhere." Stumbling out of the Half Note, the Five Spot, or the Village Gate at daybreak, he would head home thinking, "The only thing to be in this life is an artist. That's the only thing that makes any sense."

SIX

THEATRE GENESIS

Sam knew he was different, and he thought
differently, and he always remained completely
himself, separate from those around him.

—MARIANNE DE PURY

ALTHOUGH HIS FATHER HAD ENLISTED IN THE U.S. ARMY
Air Force to serve in World War II, Sam Shepard had no desire whatsoever to be drafted so he could go off to fight in a war in Vietnam that
only those in power seemed to understand or even think was actually
worth winning. However, as required by law, he had registered for the
draft in the fall of his senior year at Duarte High School. After he
dropped out of Mount San Antonio College in the spring of 1963,
thereby forfeiting his student deferment, the Selective Service notice
ordering him to report for his physical examination would have been
sent to the house on Lemon Avenue. Once that notice was forwarded
to Shepard in New York, he would have reported for the pre-induction
physical at the cavernous army induction center on Whitehall Street
in Lower Manhattan. If he passed his physical examination with flying colors—and he was in excellent health—he would receive an induction notice in the mail and then be sent off to Fort Dix in New
Jersey for six months of basic training.

With the number of U.S. troops serving in Vietnam having grown
from around 23,000 in 1964 to more than 184,000 in 1965, Shepard
might then have seen combat in Southeast Asia. However, because the
massive escalation in recruitment for the war did not begin until
July 1965, when it more than doubled from 17,000 to 35,000 men each

month, those who wanted to avoid the draft in the fall of 1964 could still do so even in New York City by pretending to be homosexuals, drug addicts, or just plain crazy.

According to Shepard biographer John J. Winters, Shepard's 1964 play *Up to Thursday* "is supposedly based on [his] flunking his draft board physical by pretending to be strung out on heroin." According to Joyce Aaron, who first met Shepard while auditioning for the show, "By then, Sam had already gotten himself out of the draft by acting like he was schizophrenic or crazy, which was something he was very good at. At the time, I was training people on how to do this by acting crazy at their physical. Because you *had* to get out."

Confirming that Shepard had played this role before in real life, Charles Mingus III says that one reason those Mafia thugs got so upset at breakfast in that restaurant was because "Sam just kept looking at them and getting more and more hysterical. This was before we were both dosed with LSD, but Sam was already nuts. By that I mean he could be indifferent nuts and hostile to everybody like he was crazy. This was also how he got out of the army and so it was also a kind of celebratory insanity."

As he so often did while writing about his real-life experiences, Shepard came up with yet another version of how he had managed to avoid being drafted during the Vietnam War. A year after he had cracked two vertebrae in his back by falling off one of his polo ponies in 1987, he was asked by a reporter from *The Washington Post* how the war in Vietnam had affected him. "I was 4F," Shepard told him. "I had a busted back. Two broken vertebrae."

DESPITE BEING WILLING TO do whatever he could to avoid being drafted, Shepard remained curiously removed from all the social and political protest movements then swirling around him in the East Village. Explaining why he had felt this way, he told Matthew Roudané in 2000:

The sixties, to me, felt extremely chaotic. It did *not* feel like some heroic effort toward a new world, like many people make it out to be ... Vietnam of course shaped everything ... And I suppose you could say that it was morally correct to be against the war. But people got swept up in idealisms ... and it was very confusing.

And then when the Civil Rights Movement kicked in, everything just doubled and doubled, until all the barrels were wide open and everybody was shooting and it felt very awesomely confusing to me. Still, even after the Kennedy and King assassinations and all the killing in the war, it was the idealism that continued to astound, and it just seemed so naive. The reality of it was chaos, and the idealism didn't mean anything.

I was up against the war myself and was very much against it. But I wasn't about to become a Marxist; I didn't think Marx was the answer to Vietnam any more than "flower power" ... and the Berkeley thing turned me off completely. I never went to college. You know that great Creedence Clearwater song, "I Ain't No Fortunate Son"? I always identified with that tune: I mean this was my anthem. "It ain't me!" And that's exactly how I felt throughout the sixties.

While Shepard was certainly entitled to his opinion about the era, the civil rights movement in the United States actually began years before the first massive anti–Vietnam War demonstrations. Assuming that he was referring to Robert Kennedy, who was assassinated two months after Martin Luther King, Jr., in 1968, the "idealism" Shepard cited had by then also long since been supplanted by anger. Also, having attended classes at Mt. Sac for a year and half, Shepard did in fact go to college. And despite being a musical scholar of the first order, he seems not to have understood that John Fogerty wrote "Fortunate Son" as a protest song about those born to wealth and power in America who were only too happy to support the flag, the president, and the war in Vietnam.

In the same interview, Shepard went on to say, "And that's the way I kind of felt throughout the sixties. I was on the tail of this tiger that was wagging itself all over the place and spitting blood in all directions. It was weird, very weird. And then to make it even more weird was acid. When acid hit the streets, then it became a circus. Then it became totally unfathomable because nobody has a *clue*."

Concerning LSD, Shepard did have firsthand knowledge, albeit of the worst possible kind. "Sam and I were dosed," Charles Mingus III says. "We were in the kitchen of a brownstone owned by some very wealthy people on the West Side of Manhattan, and we found this pint of orange sherbet in the freezer. Sam took one scrape of his spoon across the top of the stuff and said, 'I don't like it.' And then I ate the whole pint.

"What we found out later was that someone had taken this pint of sherbet, thawed it out into a liquid, and then combined it with fifty thousand dollars' worth of LSD so they could drag sugar cubes across it, wrap them in aluminum foil, and then sell each one for five dollars a dose. Sam had never taken acid before. I'd already had mescaline, psilocybin, and peyote by then, but this really changed both of us.

"Sam lost his filter because of LSD. After it happened, he went to Joyce Aaron's place for shelter and she told me he was bouncing up and down on her bed like it was a trampoline and writing stuff on her bedroom wall. Joyce also thought I was the one who had dosed Sam and gotten him so fucked up. That was why she came up to me afterward and threatened to have me killed if I ever had anything to do with Sam again."

Fantastic as all this may seem, Marianne de Pury seems to confirm this: "I think Charles and Sam were dosed with LSD. This was one of those things I didn't believe at the time but was true." And while many writers and critics have commented on the influence of LSD on the dialogue in Shepard's early plays, he told an interviewer for *Playboy* magazine in 1984, "I was on a different drug—crystal Methedrine, which has much more of an edge; when you walk down the street, your heels sparked."

ABOUT A YEAR AFTER arriving in New York, Steve Rogers changed his name to Sam Shepard. He was publicly identified this way for the first time as the author of two plays, *Cowboys* and *The Rock Garden*, that opened on October 16, 1964, at Theatre Genesis, a brand-new black-box performance space in St. Mark's Church in-the-Bowery on East Tenth Street and Second Avenue.

While, in part, this was the name Shepard had been born with, anyone who had not seen it spelled out could easily have confused him with Dr. Sam Sheppard, the prominent neurosurgeon in Cleveland, Ohio, who was accused of bludgeoning his wife to death in July 1954. After a lengthy trial covered in a sensational manner on the front pages of newspapers all over the country, Sheppard was found guilty of second-degree murder and sentenced to life in prison. Ten years later, in the summer of 1964, the doctor's name was still in the news when Lee Mason met Sam Shepard. In response to a writ of habeas corpus filed by his defense attorney, F. Lee Bailey, Dr. Sam Sheppard had been released from prison that year. (Two years later, the U.S. Supreme Court would strike down his conviction because of the carnival atmosphere in which the original trial was conducted.) "I must also say I was always amazed that someone named Sam Shepard had then become the idol of millions," Mason says.

As Charles Mingus III says, "People were confused when Sam changed his name from 'Steve Rogers' because Dr. Sam Sheppard's case was in court. I guess Sam did this to paper the house"—i.e., increase audience size—"which I found to be an interesting technique." Amplifying this statement in an interview with Shepard biographer Ellen Oumano, Mingus III added, "Sam Shepard never called himself Sam Shepard. All of a sudden, he changed his name. It was too coincidental in a way, and in a way, it was a good trigger because it was excellent publicity. The guy I knew would exploit that . . . because people would actually go to the play . . . thinking, 'I wonder what this guy who killed his wife and got away with it wrote?' There were people like that and that was fascinating to Sam and to me . . . And Sam was freaking out and laughing, and at the same time, there was a profit motive involved. He was aware of box office."

Over the years, Shepard supplied a wide variety of reasons for changing his name. Asked by Robert Coe why he went from calling himself Steve Rogers to Sam Shepard for a profile that appeared in *The New York Times Magazine* in November 1980, he replied, "Because it's shorter." When Pete Hamill posed the same question three years later for *New York* magazine, Shepard said he had done so before coming to New York while still on tour with the Bishop's Company. Although this was not true, he added, "I always thought Rogers was a corny name because of Roy Rogers and all the associations with it. But Samuel Shepard Rogers was kind of a long handle. So I just dropped the Rogers part of it." Laughing, Shepard went on: "Years later I found out Steve Rogers was the original name of Captain America in the comics."

FROM THE MOMENT THE host of an off-campus "beatnik party" at Mt. Sac handed him a copy of *Waiting for Godot*, Sam Shepard recognized Samuel Beckett as "the only guy. He could be the only playwright on earth . . . all we need is Beckett. I idolize Beckett from every aspect. He represented the epitome of the modern playwright. Nobody was doing that stuff . . . nobody was doing what he started. He totally reinvented it. He absolutely stood it on its head. There had never been anybody like him."

Eugene O'Neill's *Long Day's Journey into Night*, which Shepard first experienced via the 1962 black-and-white film that was nearly three hours long, became the other great influence on his work. After he read the play, Shepard felt an odd connection with the subject matter because "There was something wrong with the family . . . a demonic thing going on that nobody could put their finger on, but everybody knew the ship was sinking . . . So I thought there was something about that that felt similar to my own background, and I felt I could maybe write some version of that."

That it would be fifteen years before Shepard wrote *Curse of the Starving Class*, the first of his great family dramas, speaks to how long and hard he had to work to master the craft of playwriting. For, as he would later admit, "When I first started, I didn't really know how to structure a play. I could write dialogue, but I just sort of failed beyond that, and kind of went wherever I wanted to go, which is how I ended up with these shorter pieces . . . These things I was writing were all experiments of just tiptoeing into the waters of what it's like to write a play."

In yet another act of serendipity, Shepard could not have chosen a better place to begin his career as a playwright than the Village Gate. Unlike at the Five Spot and the Half Note, many of those who worked at the Gate were also involved with theater on the Lower East Side and so provided him with a relatively easy entrance into a world about which he knew almost nothing.

HAVING JUST BEEN DISCHARGED from the U.S. Air Force after serving for two years as a low-level intelligence analyst in Germany, Lee Kissman arrived in New York City in the spring of 1963. To support himself while attending acting classes, Kissman began working as a host at the Village Gate. He then became part of a group of waiters who were permitted to use the stage when the club was empty so they could audition for agents and casting directors.

When Kissman went off to work elsewhere, he stayed in contact with Ralph Cook, the headwaiter at the Gate. A tall man with shaggy hair and a thick black moustache and goatee, Cook was in his mid-thirties. Despite being an atheist, he had enrolled his three children, whose custody he shared with their mother, in Sunday school at St. Mark's Church so he could go to a nearby coffee shop and read the newspaper.

On Easter Sunday in 1964, Cook found himself in St. Mark's listening as the Reverend Michael Allen, the bearded thirty-seven-year-old Episcopalian rector who had graduated from Harvard, studied at the Sorbonne, and then worked as a journalist at *Look* magazine before deciding to enter the priesthood, delivered what Allen would later characterize as one of his "more depressing sermons." Recognizing Allen as a kindred spirit, Cook approached him after the service and the two men spent the afternoon together in conversation. A dedicated social activist who would march with Dr. Martin Luther King, Jr., and visit Hanoi with Joan Baez, Allen was fully committed to developing "a parish-based arts program" and so decided to enlist Ralph Cook to help him make this a reality.

What began as a children's drama group in the basement of the church soon gave way to Cook's desire to present plays for adults. To do so, he converted a space on the second floor of the parish hall into a seventy-seat black-box theater with sixteen lights, nine dimmers, skeletal sets, and a minimal number of props. The first production at what Cook had decided to call Theatre Genesis—he viewed it as "the beginning, the Genesis, of a cultural revolution"—was *Study in Color,* a play written by Allen's fellow activist Episcopalian priest Malcolm Boyd. The second production was a double bill of plays written by a busboy at the Village Gate who had just renamed himself Sam Shepard.

Even before Ralph Cook began looking for original material to present in his brand-new performance space, he had heard that Shepard was writing plays. Cook went to visit him in his apartment, and it was there he read *The Rock Garden* for the first time. Because the play was fewer than twelve and a half pages, it could not have taken him long. To his credit, Cook immediately recognized Shepard's gift and decided on the spot to present the play at Theatre Genesis. Because *The Rock Garden* was too brief to sustain an evening of theater, Cook asked Shepard if he had another play that could be added to form a double bill.

After telling Cook he did not, Shepard went off and quickly wrote *Cowboys.* Asked many years later how long it took him to discover his voice as a writer, Shepard explained how he had worked back then by saying, "For me, that wasn't a problem. There were so many voices that I didn't know where to start. It was splendid, really. I felt kind of like a weird stenographer. I don't mean to make it sound like hallucination, but there were definitely things there, and I was just putting them down."

Within a week, both plays had been cast and rehearsals had begun. Lee Kissman was chosen to play the character named Boy in *The Rock Garden.* Kevin O'Connor, a waiter at the Village Gate who had helped Kissman find a job there, was cast as the character named Man. Robbie Lyons, yet another waiter at the Gate, joined O'Connor onstage as one of the two characters in *Cowboys.*

Although none of the actors was being paid, they spent an entire month rehearsing. During this period, Shepard was at the theater fairly constantly and although he would later characterize himself as somewhat of "a pain in the ass," he seems to have been of great help to

Lyons and O'Connor, both of whom came to the first rehearsal and, as Lee Kissman wrote, "admitted they didn't know what *Cowboys* was about."

Because the play took place in the apartment Shepard and Mingus III shared, the original script called for a set with three black walls and a sawhorse with a yellow blinking light on it, much like the one Shepard had hidden under his bed in his family's house on Lemon Avenue. Throwing themselves into all aspects of the production, Shepard and Mingus III did their best to create a complete theatrical environment by bringing in sand and gravel to cover the stage. Following Chip Monck's lead, they appropriated from a neighborhood construction site a sawhorse with a blinking light that could not be turned off. During the play itself, the sound of passing traffic they had recorded during their visit to New Jersey was blasted from a stereo.

Very much inspired by Beckett, *Cowboys* has no plot and consists entirely of random incidents with no real connection. The second show of the evening, *The Rock Garden*, was far better written than *Cowboys*, with characters who spoke in paragraphs rather than rapid bursts of sheer verbiage and so created their own reality onstage. Many years later, in *The New York Times Magazine*, Shepard described *The Rock Garden* as being "about leaving my mom and dad."

In terms of pure stagecraft, Shepard's intuitive sense of how to use blackouts, short scenes, and entrances and exits to move the play along remains impressive. After meandering along for twelve pages, *The Rock Garden* ends with an explosive, sexually explicit monologue that seems shocking even now. The speech begins with the phrase "When I come, it's like a river," and then becomes even more graphic in its description of various sexual techniques and positions. According to Shepard biographer Don Shewey, the theater critic for the *New York Herald Tribune* was so offended by the language in this scene that Michael Allen felt compelled to defend *The Rock Garden* in print by saying, "I believe this whole generation of young people is saying to us in effect, 'Look, you use beautiful words and do ugly things; we'll take ugly words and make beauty out of them.'"

Because *Cowboys* was longer than *The Rock Garden*, Ralph Cook had chosen to begin the evening with it. In terms of the initial critical reaction to Sam Shepard's debut as a playwright, this would prove to be a truly consequential decision. Jerry Tallmer, who had served as the theater critic for *The Village Voice* since its inception in 1955 and who created the awards for independent downtown theater that became known as the Obies, had left the *Voice* in 1962 and was now working for the *New York Post*. Having helped foster the downtown theater scene, Tallmer was a revered figure whose approval of any production was always crucially important.

And so, when Tallmer's thoroughly negative review of what he had seen at Theatre Genesis ran in the *Post* on October 12, 1964, beneath a headline reading, "Tell Me about the Morons, George," it seemed the kiss of death not just for the double bill but also for the career of its fledgling playwright. But while Tallmer had opened fire with both barrels on *Cowboys*, he made no mention at all of *The Rock Garden* in his review. The reason for this was that he had left the theater before the second half of the double bill was performed.

After reading the review, Shepard was, in Lee Kissman's words, "more than a little distressed" and "had decided to give up writing and move back to California." Whether he really meant to do so, no one can know for certain. However, his reaction to this attack on his work did influence the way he would then respond to all forms of criticism during the rest of his career.

In an article about the history of Theatre Genesis in *The New York Times* fifty years later, Shepard said, "It was shocking to be produced; I was writing more or less as a private experience. I don't know if you want to call it a meditation. Probably not. It was just amazing suddenly to have actors, an audience. And kind of embarrassing, like listening to your own voice on a tape."

Ten days after Tallmer's negative review in the *Post*, when the next issue of *The Village Voice* hit the streets of the Lower East Side, Sam Shepard's world suddenly turned itself upside down. In his review of the double bill, the weekly newspaper's drama critic Michael Smith wrote that, at Theatre Genesis:

They have actually found a new playwright. The playwright's name is Sam Shepard, and I know nothing about him except that he has written a pair of provocative and genuinely original plays . . . The plays are difficult to categorize, and I'm not sure it would be valuable to try. Shepard is still feeling his way, working with an intuitive approach to language and dramatic structure and moving into an area between ritual and naturalism, where character transcends psychology, fantasy breaks down literalism, and the patterns of ordinariness have their own lives . . . His voice is distinctly American and his own.

This sudden reversal of fortune, which paved the way for Shepard's career, was put into motion by Lee Kissman, who had invited Bill Hart, a talented director who would become close to Shepard both professionally and personally, to attend the Sunday evening performance of the double bill during the second weekend of its monthlong run. Hart brought Michael Smith with him that night.

After the double bill ended, Kissman and Hart went to Smith's apartment in the West Village, where "neither of them could stop talking about" what they had both just seen. As Kissman walked back home that night, he felt fairly certain that Smith would review the double bill favorably in the *Voice*. In fact, the review was an unqualified rave.

Up to that point, people had been trickling into Theatre Genesis. But during the final two weekends of the run, in Lee Kissman's words, "We packed them in, and they weren't just the hip downtown audience, either." As Kissman launched into his final monologue in *The Rock Garden* one night, he looked "out toward the audience and three nuns were sitting in the front row immediately in front of me. They seemed to be enjoying themselves; they didn't flinch."

According to Michael Smith, who would go on to a long career as a director, playwright, lighting director, and critic, "Everybody else in theater was writing this kind of artificial realism which was then the dominant style, but Sam seemed completely free. He could do anything and have people say anything, which was the way reality actually was. His plays were alive, and they kept on surprising you as they went along, as opposed to playing out some plan.

"It was a quantum leap even from Edward Albee, who was still working with conventional characters and situations, whereas Sam had caught the actual rhythm of the way people who were smoking pot back then were thinking. He wrote monologues that made it possible for them to spin off into their heads in the middle of a play and nobody else was doing that."

Five years after *Cowboys* and *The Rock Garden* closed at Theatre Genesis, Jacques Levy, who had already directed two of Shepard's plays, chose to incorporate the shocking monologue that ends *The Rock Garden* into his Off-Broadway production of *Oh! Calcutta!*, the erotic revue of songs, sketches, and dances in which all eleven performers in the show appeared completely naked onstage at one point or another. After transferring to Broadway in 1971, the show ran for more than thirteen hundred performances. Revived in 1976, it ran for another thirteen years and nearly six thousand performances, thereby becoming the longest-running revue in Broadway history.

During its initial Broadway run, Shepard was paid $68 a week in royalties (about $475 a week today) for the use of his *Rock Garden* monologue. If he learned anything from this experience, it was that there was real money to be made by defying social convention onstage with language that had never before been heard in a Broadway theater.

SEVEN

LA TURISTA

At that point, Sam was extremely handsome.
Oh, he was beautiful. The lost artist look, definitely.
I really had to take care of him because he was still
a kid and just beginning to get famous, and
The New York Times would be calling for interviews.

—JOYCE AARON

FIVE YEARS ON, THE GRINNING, AWKWARD-LOOKING TEENAGER in Sam Shepard's high school yearbook photograph had somehow managed to transform himself into a soulful, sensitive artist who would not have looked out of place at a table in the Café de Flore on Boulevard Saint-Germain in Paris during the early 1950s.

In a photograph taken outside Caffe Cino on Cornelia Street in Greenwich Village, in the winter of 1965, Shepard, dressed all in black with his hair parted on the left and brushed up and back on the right, stares directly into the camera. With the left side of his head in shadows, the brightly lit planes of his face are so sharp and smooth and his gaze so intense that he looks like a cross between Montgomery Clift and James Dean.

"Back then," Joyce Aaron says, "Sam was really still a kid. Don't forget, he took a suitcase of his plays to Edward Albee and knocked on his front door. Now, who would have ever done something like that? But that was what Sam did, and for him, it worked." By then, Albee had already achieved critical success in Lower Manhattan with *Zoo Story* and then both great critical and commercial success on Broadway with his Tony Award–winning play *Who's Afraid of Virginia Woolf?*

Along with his producing partners in the Playwrights Unit, Albee then presented *Up to Thursday,* Shepard's one-act play about avoiding the draft, at the Village South Theatre on November 23, 1964.

Shepard himself happened to be sitting at the back of the theater while Joyce Aaron auditioned for the play. After reading her lines, she was instructed to laugh. "I was laughing as part of the audition," Aaron says, "and Sam started laughing. I was laughing and he came up to me and we had a drink. We came back to my apartment on Second Avenue across from the Gem Spa and he never left."

Eight years older than Shepard, Joyce Aaron had grown up in privileged surroundings in Scarsdale, New York. After graduating from Sarah Lawrence, she studied at the Neighborhood Playhouse with Sanford Meisner and Martha Graham. A year before meeting Shepard, Aaron had joined the Open Theatre, founded by Joe Chaikin, who in time would become Shepard's close friend, artistic mentor, and collaborator. Half Sicilian, half Jewish, Aaron was a powerhouse in her own right. Deeply in love with Shepard, she quickly became his protector, most notably warning Charles Mingus III as she dug her fingernails into his arm that if he ever let Shepard get dosed with LSD again, she would arrange to have him killed.

"I didn't really know what Sam was doing back then," Aaron says, "but he was always high and very paranoid about all these people who wanted to meet him and talk to him and write about him, and I helped him by guiding those people away from him. Later on, he was into giving interviews, but I'm talking about this twenty-two-year-old guy who had suddenly become the biggest thing Off-Off-Broadway and was in the Sunday *New York Times* arts section, and he just really wasn't up to any of that then."

During this period, Aaron brought Shepard to the Open Theatre, which was then located in a warehouse on Spring Street. "That was where Sam met Joe Chaikin. They did not hit it off right away. I think Sam was kind of intimidated by Joe and I think Joe was attracted to who Sam seemed to be. Joe was very close to me and then eventually it all worked out and everybody got close to whom they were going to get close to."

Now writing so constantly that eighteen of his one-act plays would be produced over the next three years, Shepard left the apartment he had shared with Charles Mingus III to live with Aaron. He was now not nearly as happy as he had once been about working at the Village Gate. He did not like having to line up for inspection before each shift or being told he needed to be alert and available to patrons while bussing their tables. Despite being admonished for his attitude, Shepard continued working at the club until the night he deliberately dumped his entire bus box into the lap of a man whom Charles Mingus III described as dressed in a tweed suit with a vest and a cap while also carrying a cane.

"Sam should have gotten fired for what he had done," Mingus III says. "Because that guy was totally innocent. Sam just hated the guy for his British persona and for wearing that Sherlock Holmes hat and so he did it on purpose, and everybody saw it happen." As Mingus III also told Shepard biographer Ellen Oumano, "Sam didn't care about the outcome. I apologized—Sam was reckless."

According to Shepard biographer John J. Winters, even though Joyce Aaron had "a little family money that helped them squeak by," she and Shepard partially supported themselves during this period by waiting tables at Café La MaMa. Thirty years later, Shepard would write about working as a busboy at the Hickory House, a legendary jazz joint at 144 West Fifty-second Street, where, as he remembered, a table was always reserved for Duke Ellington and his family.

In 2011, Shepard told director Michael Almereyda that, after leaving the Village Gate, he worked as a busboy in the Oak Room of the Plaza Hotel, where Mary Lou Williams, "one of the great piano players," performed at the horseshoe bar. "It was Duke Ellington's favorite place for dinner," Shepard said. "He'd come in every night with his entourage and his family and sit down in this huge booth. I remember bussing his table many nights. Sir Duke. It was kind of awesome."

Although Mary Lou Williams performed regularly at the Hickory House in 1965, she never appeared in the Oak Room of the Plaza Hotel. Also, given what happened to end his previous stint as a busboy at the Village Gate, nor does it seem likely that Shepard could have gotten hired to work in what was then perhaps the top-of-the-line establishment bar in New York City. But then, in the world according to Sam Shepard, reality was not just fungible but also always subject to his own form of artistic embellishment.

KNOWING THAT JOYCE AARON was about to go off to Chicago to perform in *The Knack,* a play by Ann Jellicoe that then became a film directed by Richard Lester, Shepard wrote *Chicago* in a single day. Although the play cannot have taken more than twenty minutes to perform onstage, the opening monologue—which the lead character delivers while sitting in a bathtub much like the one in Shepard's former apartment on Tenth Street and Avenue C—is an exercise in the kind of rhyming that can now be found in rap.

As Lee Kissman, who performed in *Chicago,* says, "Mostly, those early plays were like happenings. They were filled with energy and that was the good part because they were funny and entertaining and then at the end enigmatic. People were saying stuff onstage that had never been said there before and it was the birth of a new sensibility."

Not long after he wrote the play, Shepard traveled by train to Chicago to join Aaron. From there, they went to Philadelphia, where she had been cast as the female lead in *Slow Dance on the Killing Ground,* a play by William Hanley that had closed on Broadway a year earlier after eighty-eight performances. While they were in Philadelphia, Shepard wrote *Red Cross,* a one-act play that was performed for the first time on January 20, 1966, at the Judson Poets' Theater at Judson Memorial Church in Washington Square, in a production directed by Jacques Levy.

Continuing their cross-country journey, Shepard and Aaron were in Milwaukee on the Fourth of July. After watching the holiday fireworks, Shepard wrote *Icarus's Mother,* a one-act play directed by Michael Smith that was first presented at Caffe Cino on November 16, 1965. What may have been most noteworthy about *Icarus's Mother* was the scathing review of the play Edward Albee wrote for *The Village Voice.* Beginning his critique by describing Shepard as "one of the youngest and most gifted of the new playwrights," who gives the impression that he is "inventing drama as a form each time he writes a play," Albee then noted, "His new theatre piece, 'Icarus' Mother [*sic*],' is presently on view at the Caffe Cino. Sad to say, it gives the impression of being a mess."

By now, however, Shepard's theatrical career had already taken flight. Ten days after Albee's utterly negative review appeared, *The New York Times Magazine* ran that photograph of Shepard looking like a cross between Montgomery Clift and James Dean as he stood outside Caffe Cino. Above it, the caption read, "OOB TALENT—Sam Shepard, 22, the author of several plays, is generally acknowledged as the 'genius' of the Off Off Broadway circuit." At the end of the year, he won his first Obie Award for Distinguished Play for *Chicago, Red Cross*, and *Icarus's Mother.*

WHILE JOYCE AARON WAS performing in Milwaukee, she and Shepard stayed with friends of hers. On a night when she did not have to perform, Aaron took LSD for the first time. "I would never have taken it if I had to do a show," she says, "but Sam was not tripping. Instead, he was watching over me. I went into a fit of depression on the acid and then got catatonic, and he kind of saved my life by figuring out what I was going through, because it was all very, very tricky."

In an untitled story in his 1982 book *Motel Chronicles*, Shepard fictionalized this episode by writing about how he had returned to the apartment where he lived with Aaron on Second Avenue only to find her sitting silently on her bed with the curtains drawn and her head down between her knees. When he asks her a question, she is not able to answer him. Instead, strange and meaningless noises begin coming out of her mouth. He hands her a pencil, but she is unable to write about what she is now going through. Instead, she draws a duck and then somehow manages to say the word.

Falling backward, she suddenly begins moaning "in a voice I'd only heard in animals giving birth . . . At the peak of it, I thought for sure she was dying." Just as quickly as it all began, she is back to normal again. She then walks to the phone and calls her mother in New Jersey to say she was about to visit her. In response to her mother's questions, she says her former boyfriend (i.e., Shepard) was now gone and even though she did not know where he was, he definitely did not live there with her anymore.

"The friends we were staying with in Milwaukee," Aaron says, "had young children. And so the way Sam got me out of my catatonic state was to give me a baby's bottle of milk he had found in the house. The story he wrote about it was really interesting, because he used what had happened without ever bringing up that the acid had caused my breakdown. Me calling my mother at the end of the story to tell her I was no longer with him was Sam reflecting on his own pain about our breakup. I mean, he had even gone with me to my father's funeral and so he was really in my life quite a lot at the time."

After Aaron completed her run in the play in Milwaukee Shepard rented a car and they set off on a road trip to visit his grandparents in Illinois and his family in Duarte. As though their summer had not already been strange enough, things then began to get really weird.

AFTER GOING WITH HIS mother and father to visit his grandparents in Illinois when he was nine years old, Shepard had returned on his own to visit them in 1962. For a nineteen-year-old who had never traveled any farther than from Pasadena to Palm Springs, it was a dramatic gesture. By then, however, he had already begun searching for clues to his identity by trying to find out what life had been like for his father but not his mother before the two met, married, and brought him into the world.

"Sam was really into finding out about his ancestors," Sandy Rogers says. "He was intrigued by the subject and did so much research into it. Part of his fascination with it was trying to get my dad to tell him stories, but that was really hard for both of them. Because they were so much alike. Both of them were so strong and had that shield, that impenetrable thing you just could not get through."

In 1980, Shepard wrote about this second visit in *Motel Chronicles*. The story begins with him picking up a "Tuesday Weld–type–of blonde girl, maybe fifteen, in bare feet" in the train's dining car. He and the girl end up in her compartment, where they have sex "all the way from Winnemucca through the Great Salt Lake Desert." In Salt Lake City, the girl gets off the train. As he travels on, Shepard imagines that after the blonde's father learns about everything that happened, he suddenly appears on the train with a twelve-gauge shotgun. Now too paranoid to remain on the train all the way to Chicago, Shepard gets off in Missouri, calls his grandmother, and lets her know he plans to come see her and his grandfather the next day.

Once they have welcomed him and gone to sleep, Shepard heads upstairs so he can stare for as long as he likes at the framed photographs of his uncles, all of whom "carry the bones of my Grandpa's face." As Sandy Rogers says, "In terms of Sam looking at those photographs in that story, I think this is what a lot of men do. They look for what it means to be a man and what they have to do to become one. You have to drum yourself up to be a man. And I think Sam did that."

When Shepard visited his grandparents with Joyce Aaron in 1965, the scene remained very much the same. "Sam's grandfather was bundled up in that chair with the television on," Aaron says. "He was a full-on alcoholic and he wanted liquor and I went and got it and brought it back to him just like Vince does in *Buried Child*."

For the first time since he left home two years earlier, Shepard then returned to Duarte. He and Aaron stayed with his family in the house on Lemon Avenue. Sandy Rogers, who was then in high school, says, "What I remember most about that visit was my mom making this big pact with Sam and Joyce that I thought was completely unnecessary and then telling my father they were married, because he would not have wanted them in the house otherwise—which, to me, was ridiculous, because my father wouldn't have cared one way or the other. I also remember Joyce very, very vividly, because I thought she was so cool and I remember Sam calling her 'Baby,' which I thought was just so weird."

"They had avocado trees and a horse and sheep, but they were not farmers," Aaron says. "They just liked the country life. They also had some kind of an RV or a trailer, which coming from New York was totally foreign to me. I also got to know Sam's father very well, because we were there quite a while. He would disappear and go out and get drunk and then show up two days later and that was wild. I could also feel the anger. It was underneath everything, and his father was very seductive with me and Sam observed that and so I was very careful with his father. And although I didn't think Sam's mother was exactly a saint, she did hold that family together. Without his father, I do think Sam would still have been a writer, but not the one he became."

CONTINUING THEIR JOURNEY, SHEPARD and Aaron boarded an airliner at Los Angeles International Airport to fly to Mexico City, a 1,550-mile journey that took a little less than four hours. Everything went well until the plane hit a patch of bad air. Sitting beside Aaron, Shepard suddenly began freaking out. "I don't think Sam had ever been on a plane before," Aaron says. "Because if he had, he would never have gotten on that flight with me. Just as he then never flew again for years and years. Sam was not stoned on that plane. He just couldn't believe we were up there in the sky. Sam knew he couldn't get out by jumping and so he just went crazy."

Although Sam Rogers had been a decorated B-24 bomber pilot in World War II, his son was so terrified of flying anywhere that he would happily drive across the country by himself again and again rather than ever set foot in a plane again. When he could drive no more, he would pull off the road to spend the night in some roadside motel. The next morning, he would get back behind the wheel and begin driving all day long once more.

From Mexico City, Shepard and Aaron traveled by bus to Oaxaca, a journey of three hundred miles that, back then, could take as long as eight hours. After checking into the Hotel Nacional, they both got sick with the virulent form of gastroenteritis known to visitors to Mexico as Montezuma's Revenge or *la turista*. To their credit, Shepard and Aaron found their situation so awful yet also absurd that much of what they were going through seemed hysterically funny to them.

After they recovered, the two embarked on an even longer and more difficult journey by bus to Chiapas, in the southeastern corner of Mexico near the border with Guatemala. With just sixty-five dollars left to their names, they then made their way back to Mexico City and returned to New York by riding on another bus for four days and nights, a journey Shepard thought "was just cool."

Shepard began writing *La Turista,* his first two-act play, while he and Aaron were still suffering in their hotel room in Oaxaca. He dedicated the play to her because, as she says, "I was the one who had taken him to Mexico." Back in New York City, Aaron connected Shepard with Wynn Handman, her former acting teacher.

Then forty-five years old, Handman was the artistic director of the American Place Theatre, located inside St. Clement's Episcopal Church on West Forty-sixth Street. A legendary figure who had co-founded the theater and would spend the next four decades of his life working there, Handman was a revered acting teacher and director whose constant search for new talent enabled a host of actors and playwrights to begin their careers.

Although Shepard's theatrical output to this point had consisted entirely of relatively brief one-act plays, his first draft of *La Turista* comprised three acts. Although Handman was baffled by the play, he thought the writing was "superb." More than twenty years older than Shepard, he also thought the play was about the alienation from society many young people were then feeling.

Set in a hotel room in Oaxaca inspired by the one where Shepard and Aaron were sick together, *La Turista* opens with Salem and Kent lying side by side in single beds. From then on, the action grows progressively more surreal. During one sequence, a Mexican witch doctor with two live chickens hanging from his wrists enters with his son. To banish the evil spirit inhabiting Kent's body, the witch doctor's son cuts the heads off both chickens so his father can drizzle their blood over Kent's back.

Unlike the tiny downtown venues in which all his plays had been presented to this point, the American Place Theatre seated 165 people, nearly all of whom were regular subscribers. For the first time in Shepard's career, he now had a budget for sets, costumes, and all the special effects he had created. As Jeremy Gerard noted in his book about Handman and the American Place Theatre, this was also the first time a Shepard play had been presented "north of Fourteenth Street."

With Jacques Levy directing and Joyce Aaron and Sam Waterston cast as Salem and Kent, the two leading characters, the play went into rehearsals. As Shepard told Gerard, "We struggled and struggled with it. It was so long winded, it just went on and on. And at the last minute, at the end of rehearsals, I pulled the rug out from under Wynn. I said, 'Listen, man, it's too long, let's make it a two-act play.' He didn't even blink an eye. He just said, 'Fine, whatever works.'"

La Turista opened at the American Place Theatre on March 4, 1967. Although no critics were invited, a review of the play appeared in *The New York Review of Books* on April 6, 1967, by which time the play had already closed after a monthlong run. Written by Elizabeth Hardwick, the critic and novelist who co-founded *The New York Review of Books*, the review was an unqualified rave: "*La Turista* by Sam Shepard, in a dazzling production at the American Place Theater [*sic*], is a work of superlative interest." Hardwick then took her fellow theatergoers to task by writing, "The night I saw *La Turista* the American Place audience was, for the most part, utterly depressing; middle-aged, middle class, and rather aggressively indifferent: a dead weight of alligators, dozing and grunting before muddily sliding away." She also disparaged those who did not "get" the brilliance of Shepard's baffling new play.

Although Handman and his staff found a way to fake the death of the chickens at every performance, the play came as a rude shock to many of those who regularly attended shows at the American Place. As Handman said, "We lost a lot of subscribers with *La Turista*." In Shepard's words, "So that was an eye opener, that suddenly you were held prisoner by this audience of people who were putting their dollar down and most of them were geriatric. I thought it was very strange, it seemed intrinsically wrong for a writer. You weren't getting the experience of an audience just coming in raw."

Nonetheless, *La Turista* won the Obie Award for Distinguished Play in 1967. As Shepard noted forty years later, "It's still kind of an odd play, a pretty weird play. I wouldn't write a play like that now. I was totally arrogant then. I didn't read anybody else's plays. I didn't go to anybody else's plays. I hated theater . . . I was a belligerent asshole back then. Really. I mean I was really not a pleasant person to be around. I was rude and belligerent."

———

BY THE TIME *La Turista* closed in the spring of 1967, Sam Shepard and Joyce Aaron had been living together two and a half years. "When Sam was with me," Aaron says, "I don't think he was ever with any other women. But because he was so attractive, women were after him all the time. Sam and I were going to get married, but after I had taken the blood test you needed back then to apply for a marriage license, I looked at myself in the mirror and said, 'Joyce, he's a druggie, he's a womanizer, he has a father who is an alcoholic . . . Stay with him, do whatever you want, but don't get married.' And so I broke it off. I know I made the right decision. There was no question about it."

Despite ending their relationship, Aaron remained close to Shepard. In July 1967, she was on her way to London with Joe Chaikin to perform in Jean-Claude van Itallie's play *America Hurrah* at the Royal Court Theatre. As she says, "Sam wrote me he really wanted to come along and wanted us to get back together again, but I said no."

In 1967, Bobbs-Merrill published the first collection of Shepard's work. Entitled *Five Plays*, the volume included *Chicago, Red Cross,* and *Icarus's Mother.* After dedicating the book to Joyce Aaron, Shepard wrote, "Whose loving companionship for more than three years molded the shape and content of these five plays. Love, Sam."

—

EIGHT

FORENSIC AND THE NAVIGATORS

Well, here we are again, along with
Sam Shepard, our drummer who also
writes plays and is a Scorpio.

—PETER STAMPFEL,
LINER NOTES, 1967 ALBUM,
INDIAN WAR WHOOP

SAM SHEPARD WAS SITTING IN A FUNKY JOINT ON SECOND
Avenue on the Lower East Side of Manhattan one day in September
1966 when a young guy with black, Beatles-length hair and a thick
pirate's moustache walked in the door with a fiddle case under his arm.
Without knowing that the guy had only just gotten the fiddle out of
hock to play a gig—or that he had pawned it in the first place to buy
speed—Shepard asked him if he could play electric bass.

Twenty-eight years old, Peter Stampfel was already a well-known
musician on the Lower East Side. He had co-founded the Holy Modal
Rounders with Steve Weber before they both joined the Fugs, the
groundbreaking band formed by the poets Ed Sanders and Tuli Kup-
ferberg. In what for Shepard was yet another fortuitous coincidence,
Stampfel was now forming a brand-new band to be known as the
Swamp Lilies and so had just begun teaching himself how to play
bass. Shepard himself had been accompanying a guitar player on bongos in a duo he had named the Heavy Metal Kid after a character in
William Burroughs's novel *The Soft Machine.*

When Shepard offered Stampfel the nonpaying gig of joining him and his guitar player on bass, he accepted and they soon began rehearsing together on a regular basis. "Sam didn't even have his own drum kit back then," Stampfel said, "and he was playing hand drums, not bongos. When I first met him, I had no idea who he was. And he didn't know who I was. I'm sure he knew who the Rounders and the Fugs were, but he didn't know that was me."

A talented multi-instrumentalist who played guitar and banjo as well as fiddle, Stampfel had attended the University of Wisconsin for two years before getting kicked out for refusing to join ROTC and for flunking too many courses while playing music with fellow students. By the time he began performing alongside Steve Weber in the Holy Modal Rounders, Frazier Mohawk, the record producer who discovered and briefly managed Buffalo Springfield, called Stampfel (according to Stampfel) "the most stoned person I'd ever met in my life." With their eponymously titled 1964 debut album, the Holy Modal Rounders became the first band to use the word *psychedelic* (which they spelled "psycho-delic" in their lyrics) in popular music. And then there was the Holy Modal Rounders motto: "If it doesn't make you feel horny, it's not art."

Inspired by being in a band whose real goal, it often seemed, was to be as flat-out loony as possible, Shepard integrated rock music into his work for the first time in *Melodrama Play*, which opened at Café La MaMa on May 18, 1967. Directed by Tom O'Horgan—who, one year later, would win a Tony Award for directing *Hair*—*Melodrama Play* charts the travails of a long-haired singer-songwriter named Duke Durgens as he struggles to create a follow-up hit to "Prisoners, Get Out of Your Homemade Beds," his "one original, million-dollar, gold-label, award-winning song."

A consummate musician, O'Horgan also wrote the score that accompanied Shepard's lyrics, some of which were more than two pages long. In *Melodrama Play*, Shepard also created a role for a four-piece rock band that would play live during the show, and in which he performed on opening night. He also specified that the stage be set with "a huge black-and-white photograph of Bob Dylan without eyes" and "an equally large photograph" of Robert Goulet, the cabaret singer best known for playing Sir Lancelot in the Broadway production of *Camelot*, also to be pictured without eyes.

At one point in the play, as Duke tries to explain his continuing inability to write a new hit song, he points to each image in turn. As Bob Dylan and Robert Goulet were then the alpha and the omega of the music business, Duke's unspoken message was that he had somehow gotten himself trapped between the two. As the Holy Modal Rounders were hell-bent on defying every music business convention in the book, this was not a situation in which they had ever found themselves.

On June 16, 1967, less than a month after *Melodrama Play* opened at Café La MaMa, the Monterey Pop Festival kicked off what, due in no small part to unrelenting coverage by the mainstream media, became known as the Summer of Love. One hundred thousand young people then flocked to the Haight-Ashbury District in San Francisco in search of peace, love, and flowers, but the scene on the Lower East Side of Manhattan bore little or no resemblance to what was happening in California.

As Peter Stampfel wrote, "Being 1967, it was the 'Summer of Love,' which annoyed the hell out of all of us. One July day, I walked into the . . . practice space on East Fourth Street, and there was this nearly bald, scary-looking guy pounding away at the drums, his back to me. I thought some local hood had stormed in—and was Sam gonna be mad! But then he turned around, and it was Sam. He had gotten a real short crew cut to protest the Summer of Love."

Still hoping to persuade Joyce Aaron to reconsider her decision to break up with him before she left for London, Shepard seems to have experienced his own very brief and entirely theatrical version of the Summer of Love by spending time with a group of actors and directors, and the playwright Murray Mednick—all of whom had come together at Theatre Genesis. To help fully develop a two-page scenario for *The Hawk*, Mednick's play about a heroin dealer who purposely overdoses female junkies while being followed by his double, Shepard and director Tony Barsha had traveled with nine actors to the Keystone dairy farm in the Pocono Mountains, a recreation area about a hundred miles from New York City in northeastern Pennsylvania.

Blurring the lines between theater and the counterculture, Mednick wanted the actors to create the text and structure of the play through improvisation while living together in a communal situation. During their two-month stay on the farm, they also availed themselves of marijuana, LSD, and speed.

The youngest actor in the troupe was O-Lan Johnson. Small in stature with large, round eyes and a sensual mouth, she was born on May 23, 1950, in Los Angeles and would celebrate her seventeenth birthday on the farm. She had been accompanied there by her mother, Scarlett, who had been born in England and named her daughter after the indomitable female protagonist of Pearl S. Buck's novel *The Good Earth*. Mother and daughter would co-star in *The Hawk* when it opened at Theatre Genesis in October 1967.

Describing a childhood during which the qualities exhibited by her namesake might have served her well, O-Lan Johnson (who would later change her last name to "Jones") wrote (in the third person) on her website that she was "raised by a free-spirited Philosopher Queen in various ghettos across America (Los Angeles, Chicago, Austin, New York) with stops in London and the jungles of Yucatan where they lived in a hut in a village of 80 Mayan Indians, Jones began her acting career at 16 in the hotbed of New York's off-off Broadway scene in the late 60's."

Jones's childhood odyssey began after her father walked out on the family in Los Angeles, leaving them with little to no money. Scarlett, O-Lan, and O-Lan's younger sister, Kristy, then began making their way across the country, supporting themselves by scrubbing floors and taking in laundry. According to Shepard biographer Don Shewey, they were so broke while living in Chicago that O-Lan had to come home early from school one day so her mother could put on her daughter's boots to go to work.

Having quit school at fourteen, Jones began working in theater while living in a walk-up apartment on Second Avenue and Eleventh Street in the East Village with her mother, younger sister, grandmother, and a cat named Bartley. Due in no small part to the way she had been raised, Jones seemed much older and far more sophisticated than her age and so was accepted into Theatre Genesis as its youngest member.

Nearly twenty-four years old when he came to visit Keystone Farm that summer, Sam Shepard seems to have immediately noticed Jones. But director Tony Barsha, who was then twenty-nine, had done so as well and would soon begin living with her on the Lower East Side. Right from the start, there was no love lost between the two men. "He was a quiet guy; he didn't have a lot to say," Barsha said of Shepard to biographer John J. Winters. "He was almost like a nerd-y guy, kind of a gawky kid type. He seemed more childlike than anything. Then I found out he belonged to the Future Farmers of America. I said, 'That figures.'"

Six months after their first meeting, Jones was cast to play the female role in Shepard's new play, *Forensic and the Navigators,* which opened at Theatre Genesis on December 29, 1967. The name of her character was "Oolan." Even in the no-holds-barred world of theater in Lower Manhattan, it was a novel way of letting someone know you were interested in them.

Much as Murray Mednick had done at Keystone Farm, Shepard began rehearsals for *Forensic and the Navigators* with a five-page scenario to which the cast—which included Lee Kissman and Walter Hadler, both of whom had also helped develop *The Hawk*—began adding text on a daily basis. In a reaction that would not have been out of place in a Hollywood romantic comedy, O-Lan Jones was, as Shepard biographer Don Shewey wrote, "quite mystified to audition for a play and discover a character in it bearing her name and saying things she herself had said. It finally dawned on her that the author was this 'crazy, skinny guy' she'd seen hanging around Theatre Genesis."

Difficult to characterize, *Forensic and the Navigators* is a weird, futuristic science-fiction take on the nature of revolutionary politics in the counterculture. It was also, by far, the funniest play Shepard had ever written up to this point in his career. In it, he also began exploring the bifurcated nature of personality, which would become a major theme in works like *The Tooth of Crime, True West,* and *Simpatico.* As

Stephen J. Bottoms points out in *The Cambridge Companion to Sam Shepard*, Forensic and Emmett, the central characters, "appear on one level to be two sides of the same divided consciousness" and so represent "Shepard's first, sketchy attempt at exploring the doppelganger theme," a concept Bottoms also notes as having been "common currency at Theatre Genesis during the later 1960s."

Although it is often given relatively short shrift in critical appraisals of Shepard's work, *Forensic and the Navigators*—which, along with *Melodrama Play*, won the Obie Award for Distinguished Play in 1968—represented yet another major step forward in Shepard's ability to create a unique and completely convincing alternate reality onstage.

At the end of the play, the band, with Shepard playing drums, would come out onstage and begin making what Ralph Cook, who directed the show at Theatre Genesis, described as "this noise that was so bad that all you wanted was to get out. There was a woman singing with them, she was just screeching into the microphone as loud as she could, everybody playing in dissonance against her. People were outraged. But Sam wanted it that way."

Entirely punk in nature decades before that movement began, the utterly bizarre finale was yet another example of how Shepard had begun bringing hard-core rock music into the world of straight dramatic theater as no one before him had ever done. "A big difference about Sam," says Marianne de Pury, who managed the Open Theatre, "was that he was involved with rock 'n' roll. Jean-Claude van Itallie wasn't. Megan Terry wasn't. Joe Chaikin wasn't. So it was a completely different world. And we admired Sam because he would hit the road with the Holy Modal Rounders. We were a little more old-fashioned. And then, later, rock 'n' roll *became* theater."

ON THE WEEKEND THAT *Forensic and the Navigators* opened at Theatre Genesis, Sam Shepard was in a drugstore on the Lower East Side when a man with dark hair who "had a red plaid shirt on" and "looked like Kerouac" walked over to him and said, "I saw your play last night and I wondered what drug you were on?"

Twenty-seven years old, Johnny Dark had been, in his own words, "bought (adopted) in 1942 at about a year old for $6000 the way you buy a puppy." Because his stepfather ran a successful plastics business, Dark had grown up in a house in Jersey City with living room furniture "from another century," a fireplace with "phony logs and a red light behind them," and a swinging door between the kitchen and the dining room, so his mother had to ring "a silver dinner bell to call the maid."

Shepard's first thought about Dark was "I like this guy because he's not a hippy & he just talks like a guy with no agenda & no ambitions of any kind," and so the two men left the drugstore together. Still talking, they walked to the front stoop of the house where Dark lived so they could sit down and begin a conversation, one that would continue for the next four decades. Almost immediately, Shepard and Dark both began talking about their upbringing and how neither man had ever been able to live up to his father's demands.

Not surprisingly, Dark's stepfather had wanted Dark to take over his business. By then, however, Dark had already read Jack Kerouac's *On the Road.* Unable to wait any longer "to see America from the front seat of a car at four in the morning and descend into a valley of lights," Dark left home in 1958 at the age of eighteen to go off on his own. Even after he had driven across the United States several times, his idealistic vision of the open road never became real until he finally found himself traveling with "fifty joints, a bottle of Vodka between my knees and a blonde in boots riding shotgun."

A fervid devotee of Kerouac who spent his life emulating the free-wheeling ethos embodied by Neal Cassady, Dark first got a job as a lifeguard in Asbury Park, New Jersey. He then worked as a massage therapist, a bookstore clerk, a dogcatcher, a veterinarian's assistant, and a delicatessen counter clerk in a supermarket.

Even though the man sitting beside him on the stoop was a complete stranger, Shepard bared his soul to Dark in what for him was a completely uncharacteristic manner. In Dark's words, "Sam said his father was an alcoholic and always had him doing all these chores and was completely crazy. Suddenly, we were talking as sons. I had just started living with this woman who had two daughters. So I said, 'Why don't you come up tonight? I'm going to make spaghetti.' And I ended up marrying the mother, and he ended up marrying one of the daughters. So we were related."

Dark had met Scarlett Johnson, who was thirty-four years old in 1967, in someone's apartment about a year earlier. Accompanied by one of his many girlfriends, Dark met Scarlett for the second time in her apartment. He then traveled to Tangier—while Scarlett and her daughters went to live in Yucatán—before returning to New York via Mexico City and Los Angeles. The third time Dark met Scarlett was when she dropped by a friend's apartment at three in the morning. He then walked her home and they became a couple.

On September 18, 1972, Johnny Dark and Scarlett Johnson were married at the Marin Civic Center in San Rafael, California, at which point Dark became stepfather-in-law to Shepard (who had married Jones in 1969) and what Chad Hammett, who edited *Two Prospectors: The Letters of Sam Shepard and Johnny Dark,* described as "the playwright's confidant and sounding board for both his writing and his personal life. Dark is the closest thing Shepard has to a brother."

A FEW DAYS AFTER Dark and Shepard's 1967 spaghetti dinner, Michael Smith's wildly enthusiastic review of *Forensic and the Navigators* appeared in *The Village Voice.* In it, Smith wrote that while the entire play may well have been "a smoke-dream . . . the smoke that fills the theater at the end is real. So are the people, for all their elusiveness as dramatic characters, and so is the paranoia of our times, which Shepard expresses better than anyone else now writing."

By then, Sam Shepard was on an ocean liner headed across the Atlantic to begin his screenwriting career by working with a man who had already earned worldwide recognition as one of the great film directors of his time.

NINE

ZABRISKIE POINT

I didn't know how to continue with what Antonioni
wanted. He wanted political repartee and I just
didn't know how. Plus, I was twenty-four and just
wasted by the experience. It was like a nightmare.

—SAM SHEPARD, IN 1975
VILLAGE VOICE PROFILE

DURING THE SECOND WEEK IN DECEMBER 1966, MICHELANGELO
Antonioni, who was then fifty-four years old, journeyed from Rome to
New York for the opening of *Blow-Up*, his first English-language film.
At some point during his visit, Antonioni read a newspaper article
about a young man who had stolen an aircraft and then been killed
while trying to return it. After seizing on this incident as the basis for
his next film, Antonioni was able to launch, primarily because of the
great critical and commercial success *Blow-Up* had enjoyed in America, what soon became the extremely ambitious and very expensive
project known as *Zabriskie Point*.

Plotted like a mystery thriller and set in swinging London at the
height of its fashionable but vacuous decadence, *Blow-Up* was a visually stunning work that accurately portrayed a world few had ever seen
before onscreen while reflecting the sense of utter dislocation felt by a
younger generation the world over. Widely praised as the best movie
of the year, *Blow-Up* cost less than two million dollars to produce but
earned more than three times that much in its first year of release.

After Antonioni returned to Rome, he began working on *Zabriskie
Point* with his longtime collaborator Tonino Guerra, with whom he
had co-written the script for *Blow-Up*. According to Shepard biogra-

pher Don Shewey, the two men came up with a scenario "about a semi-committed student activist and his apolitical girlfriend, who undergoes some sort of political enlightenment when he is killed by policemen."

Unlike the work they had done together on *Blow-Up*, Antonioni felt the English dialogue he and Guerra had written did not sound convincing when spoken by American characters. While Shepard was visiting Murray Mednick and his troupe of Theatre Genesis actors in the Poconos, Antonioni flew to New York to find a writer who could solve this problem, before then embarking on a cross-country journey to scout locations for a movie that did not yet have a shooting script. Although this may not have been the most efficient way to put a movie together, Antonioni was an artist and he did have a vision. When he discovered *Five Plays*, the collection of Shepard's work that had been published two weeks after *Blow-Up* opened in New York, the director was immediately certain that this was the writer he had come to America to find.

In the fall of 1967, the two men met for the first time. "He got in touch with me," Shepard said. "He came to New York looking for writers for this scenario and he read my plays. I had a play called 'Icarus's Mother' which had an airplane in it; he figured that since he had an airplane in his movie we had something in common."

Far more than the airplane, it was the way the play's characters seemed estranged from society as well as from one another that made Antonioni believe Shepard could deliver the first draft of the script he wanted. The way Shepard looked, the way in which he carried himself, and the bohemian neighborhood where he lived all served to reinforce the impression Antonioni had already formed of him.

Much like Shepard when he first came to New York City in 1963, Michelangelo Antonioni, thirty years older than his newfound collaborator, was also very much a stranger in a very strange land. In the end, this flaw in Antonioni's artistic vision would doom his film to failure.

NOTHING HE HAD EVER done before could have prepared Sam Shepard for the day-to-day reality of working in the Italian film business. In Rome, script meetings were rarely held in offices. Rather, they were conducted over long, leisurely lunches and wine-soaked dinners in the very fashionable trattorias and *ristoranti* favored by Antonioni and his fellow Italian film luminaries like Federico Fellini, Luchino Visconti, and Vittorio De Sica.

To be sure, Shepard was now traveling in very heady and rarefied circles indeed. Carlo Ponti, who was providing the initial funding for his good friend Antonioni's new movie, had discovered and married Sophia Loren before she won the Academy Award for Best Actress in 1961 for her role in *Two Women,* a film Ponti produced. By 1967, Ponti had been in the film business for twenty-seven years and produced more than fifty movies, *Dr. Zhivago* and *Blow-Up* among them. As Shepard said, "I like Michelangelo a lot—he is incredible—but to submerge yourself in that world of limousines and hotels and rehashing and pleasing Carlo Ponti is just . . . forget it. I spent almost two years, off and on, around the whole business."

During the two months he spent working with Antonioni in Rome, Shepard came up with a first draft. Later that spring, the two men boarded an ocean liner to New York before continuing on separately to Los Angeles, where preproduction for the film that was now titled *Zabriskie Point* had already begun. Tellingly—especially in terms of the final screenwriting credits, which Shepard would end up sharing with five others, Antonioni among them—the director would not permit Shepard to return to the United States with his own copy of the script. Still unwilling to board an airplane, Shepard drove across the country in a van with an astrologer named Nancy whom he had begun seeing the previous summer.

In Los Angeles, he reunited with Peter Stampfel and Steve Weber to record an album called *The Moray Eels Eat the Holy Modal Rounders.* On his debut effort in the studio with Stampfel and Weber for *Indian War Whoop,* an album that had been recorded in just four sessions before being released in 1967, Shepard could be heard laying down an insistent tom-tom drumbeat on the title track while also keeping a rapid and steady rhythm going on "Soldier's Joy," a traditional Appalachian fiddle song.

Although he was credited only for having played the tambourine on *The Moray Eels Eat the Holy Modal Rounders*, Shepard did recite the Pledge of Allegiance on the final track, which was entitled "The Pledge." As an out-of-tune chorus sings "America the Beautiful" in the background, Shepard begins the pledge using a funny voice. Freaking out in the middle, he says "I forgot the words. I forgot the words! I'm going to get an F! *Mom! Pop!*"

In Stampfel's words, "Weber and I were on speed for the whole album except for a few sleep breaks. Not Sam, though. I've heard a lot about all the drugs he took back then, but I hardly ever saw him take any. Maybe he did all that before we met." Not surprisingly, Elektra Records did not send the Holy Modal Rounders out on tour to support their new album.

Nonetheless, Stampfel and Weber somehow managed to get the band booked as the second act on a bill headlined by Pink Floyd on August 2, 3, and 4, 1968, at the Avalon Ballroom on Sutter Street in San Francisco. Owned and operated by Chet Helms and fellow members of his Family Dog collective, the Avalon, which could accommodate five hundred people on a good night, was the groovy hippie alternative venue to Bill Graham's Fillmore Auditorium. Having already made plain what he thought of the Summer of Love, Stampfel was nonetheless shocked by the hippie scene in San Francisco one year later. "We were on our way to the gig," he says, "and these kids, who were like twelve or thirteen years old, were hitchhiking and so we gave them a ride. They started going on and on about the prices of marijuana and I thought, 'Hey, I don't think it's a good idea for them to be smoking that stuff at their age.' I was also thinking, 'Oh, fuck this. Let's just go buy some fucking bourbon, man.' We did, and the crowd at the show was outraged we were drinking onstage. Like, 'Bad karma, man.'"

While in San Francisco, the Holy Modal Rounders did not stay in a hotel. Rather, according to Sandy Rogers, who was then living not far from Golden Gate Park, "I saw them open for Pink Floyd, and then they all came and slept on the floor of my apartment. That was fun. Because they were all just so crazy."

Although no one in the Holy Modal Rounders would have agreed with this assessment, the highlight of their career may have occurred on October 14, 1968, when the band performed as the only musical act on *Laugh-In,* the hour-long comedy show on NBC watched each week by 18.5 million people, which made it the highest-rated network television show in America that year. Doing what can only be described as an awful punk version of "You Got the Right String but the Wrong Yo Yo," a song written by Piano Red or his brother Speckled Red that had been covered by many artists, Carl Perkins foremost among them, Peter Stampfel can be seen howling the lyrics like a hippie version of Johnny Rotten.

Looking long, lean, and impossibly young with flowing hair, Shepard goes right on playing the drums with great enthusiasm as Ruth Buzzi, wearing a hairnet while portraying her old lady character, Gladys Ormphby, wanders onstage. A beat later, she is followed by Arte Johnson, who plays the dirty old man who pursues her everywhere in one of the show's long-running bits. Doing shtick with every step, they weave their way in and around the band, making it seem as though the Holy Modal Rounders had been invited to appear on the show only so they could be viewed by those watching at home as freaks. True to their ethos, Stampfel, Weber, and Shepard all seemed to be taking great delight in playing that role.

Putting his career with the Holy Modal Rounders into perspective, Shepard spoke on camera for *Bound to Lose,* the documentary about the band released in 2006: "We were on *Laugh-In?*" he says. "No, I don't remember any of this. What kind of drugs were we on then?" After Stampfel points out that the band was not even allowed to complete their song on the show, Shepard wryly says, "And right on the verge of success."

ALONG WITH HIS GIRLFRIEND Nancy the astrologer, Shepard attended the wedding of his sister Sandy in Duarte. As *Zabriskie Point* went into preproduction and then began filming in various Southern California locations, he split his time between his family's home on Lemon Avenue in Duarte, crashing with the Holy Modal Rounders in their Los Angeles house, and staying at the Chateau Marmont on the

Sunset Strip, courtesy of Metro-Goldwyn-Mayer, the major Hollywood studio that was now bankrolling Antonioni's new film.

Not long after the director began filming in July, Michael Smith, the *Village Voice* drama critic who had helped start Shepard's career and directed the initial production of *Icarus's Mother*, visited him on the set Antonioni had constructed on the roof of a building in downtown Los Angeles. As the crew spent the entire day waiting for the weather to clear so they could get a shot of yet another building, Smith remembered seeing Shepard, who seemed far more involved with the Holy Modal Rounders, hanging around so he could watch the business of moviemaking at close range "out of curiosity, rather than working on it."

That Shepard was even on the set was extraordinary. By then, he had already been relieved of his duties as the screenwriter for the movie. "I wrote the very first version of *Zabriskie Point*," he said, "and as Antonioni got into it, he got more and more politically oriented. I didn't want anything to do with that, so I dropped out of that. However, he used quite a bit of my original stuff, up to the point where it begins to speak for radical politics. Antonioni wanted to make a political statement about contemporary youth, write in a lot of Marxist jargon and Black Panther speeches. I couldn't do it. I just wasn't interested."

The illogic of the script's still being created while the movie was being shot paled in comparison to the way *Zabriskie Point* had been cast. After a widely publicized six-month nationwide campaign, the male and female leads, twenty and seventeen years old respectively, were selected primarily for their looks. Neither had ever acted before, and it showed. Still carrying a torch for the woman who had been his great teenage crush, Shepard suggested that Tuesday Weld would be perfect for the female lead, only to be told by Antonioni that Weld was now too "emaciated and worn down" to play the role.

Although nearly every decision Antonioni made only added to the chaos, Shepard remained involved in the project throughout the summer. At one point, the playwright even asked for a camera so he could go out into the desert to film some of the action on his own. However, neither Antonioni nor MGM, which now found itself bankrolling a film with a budget of $7 million (the equivalent of $55 million today), was willing to let him do so.

Indirectly, Shepard was also involved in the scene for which *Zabriskie Point* is still remembered, but which also put the entire project into legal jeopardy. During his time in New York City earlier in the year, Antonioni had been inspired by seeing the Open Theatre perform *The Serpent,* a spoken-word piece about the fall of Adam and Eve from the Garden of Eden co-written by Jean-Claude van Itallie and the Open Theatre troupe. In what came to be recognized as one of the classic examples of experimental theater in that era, male and female actors, all of whom were completely clothed, writhed about onstage, often on top of one another.

To ensure that what was called the "Love Scene" in *Zabriskie Point* would look and feel like what he had seen onstage in Lower Manhattan, Antonioni brought Joe Chaikin and fifteen Open Theatre actors, Joyce Aaron among them, to Las Vegas. They then began rehearsing with two hundred extras who had been hired to perform in the massive hippie orgy Antonioni planned to shoot in Death Valley.

To accelerate the process of breaking down their inhibitions so they would be able to embody Antonioni's vision of unbridled sexual freedom, someone dosed the extras with LSD. One very straight young woman who had never before smoked a joint or even had a drink began freaking out and screaming in distress. When her boyfriend, a staunch Republican who was running for Congress, learned what had happened to her, he filed a criminal complaint against the movie and its producers with the U.S. Department of Justice.

As Shepard looked on in Death Valley as the "Love Scene" was shot, the Open Theatre actors, most of them fully clothed, rolled around in twos and threes on the desert sand. In the film, the scene lasts for seven minutes as Jerry Garcia plays a psychedelic lead guitar solo from "Dark Star" with the Grateful Dead.

Shortly after filming was completed, eleven people were summoned before a grand jury in Sacramento, California, "to testify about the movie's alleged anti-Americanism, as well as possible violations of the Mann Act, which forbids the transporting of women across state lines for immoral purposes." Although Shepard said, "I think people got screwed on the desert, for real, you know," no charges were ever filed.

Finally released in February 1970, *Zabriskie Point* was greeted by a universal chorus of truly awful reviews. One critic called Antonioni "an ignoramus." Roger Ebert labeled the film "a silly and stupid movie." In *The New York Times*, Vincent Canby characterized the orgy scene in the desert as "unintentionally funny." Despite becoming the greatest critical and commercial failure of Michelangelo Antonioni's career, *Zabriskie Point* thrust Sam Shepard headlong into the movie business, where he would spend the next five decades earning large sums of money not just by writing screenplays, some of which he also directed, but as an actor who then became an authentic movie star.

TEN

MAXAGASM

Well, it's the old syndrome: if you get one, you get a
hundred. So as soon as you start writing a movie
you get these scripts showing up in the mail.
Can you do this one? Can you do that one? Twenty
thousand for this one and 30 thousand for that one.
It's like an open auction—suddenly you're in
the screenwriters market. I find it exhausting:
not only exhausting—debilitating.

—SAM SHEPARD, IN 1975
VILLAGE VOICE PROFILE

BEFORE HE BECAME THE TOAST OF THE TOWN IN HOLLYWOOD
based on his association with Antonioni on a film that had not yet
been released—and so could afford to turn down a plum screenwriting
assignment like the script for a movie based on *Alice's Restaurant,* Arlo
Guthrie's epic eighteen-and-a-half-minute song—Sam Shepard was
already working on his second screenplay. And while there might have
been nothing remarkable about this, the same could not be said about
where he was writing it.

Surrounded by a deep moat, the two-story thatched-roof country
house in which Shepard was now an honored guest had been built
during the Elizabethan era. Roughly four hundred years old, the black-
and-white half-timbered exterior closely resembled structures from
the Middle Ages. Located about two miles from the tiny seaside town
of West Withering on the southern coast of England, Redlands was

where Mick Jagger and Keith Richards of the Rolling Stones, Jagger's girlfriend Marianne Faithfull, and the art dealer Robert Fraser, all of whom were tripping on LSD, had been busted for possession of drugs on February 12, 1967. The most sensational arrest of any rock star up to that point, the bust became headline news all over the world.

How Shepard, who was then still completely unknown in England as a screenwriter or a playwright, came to live in Keith Richards's country manor in the spring of 1968 while writing a screenplay for the Rolling Stones, was in and of itself a story worthy of cinematic treatment. In June 1967, *Barbarella*, a film directed by Roger Vadim based on a popular French science-fiction comic book, began shooting in Rome with Jane Fonda, who was then married to Vadim, in the title role. Anita Pallenberg had been cast as the Black Queen.

Having recently parted company with Rolling Stones co-founder Brian Jones, Pallenberg had begun a relationship with Keith Richards. On the set one day, she met Tony Foutz. Physically imposing and handsome, with thick black hair, Foutz, the son of a Walt Disney executive, was hanging out in film business circles in Rome. Six months later, he appeared briefly in *Candy*, a movie based on the bestselling 1958 novel by Terry Southern and Mason Hoffenberg, in which Pallenberg played a supporting role.

When Shepard arrived in Rome in January 1968 to work with Michelangelo Antonioni on the script for *Zabriskie Point*, he met Foutz, who then introduced him to Richards. By then, Foutz had already pitched Richards on a science-fiction scenario for a film starring the Rolling Stones that would "feature the group as a band of unemployed mercenaries wandering through [the] Moroccan desert in a plot that involved UFOs and Mayan-style human ritual sacrifice."

Unlike Mick Jagger, who would go on to enjoy a long career as both an actor and a producer in the film business, Keith Richards's primary concern was always the Rolling Stones' music. Nonetheless, he was sufficiently impressed with Foutz's scenario, and with Shepard, to invite the playwright to stay at Redlands for as long as he needed to write the screenplay so the band could make their onscreen debut. In an interview a year later, Shepard conveyed the impression that he and Richards had hunkered down together at Redlands for six weeks to work nonstop on a screenplay entitled "Maxagasm: A Distorted WESTERN for Soul & Psyche."

Based on information Shepard supplied in that interview, biographer John J. Winters wrote, "With a couple of elderly locals bringing them milk and steaks and stoking the fire, Shepard and Richards worked most days in a hash-fueled haze from morning to about 3 A.M. When things got too 'heavy,' Shepard hitchhiked into town to escape for a bit. Overall, the situation was 'groovy,' he recalled."

With the Rolling Stones then under great pressure from Decca Records to come up with a hit single, the idea that Keith Richards would have spent six weeks collaborating with anyone but Mick Jagger on anything but new songs for the next Rolling Stones album seems implausible at best. From the end of February until mid-March when Shepard was at Redlands, Richards, Jagger, and the Rolling Stones were rehearsing and recording at R.G. Jones Studios in Morden, Surrey, and at Olympic Studio in London. Given that the Stones often spent all night recording and that Morden was eighty miles from Redlands but just six miles from Richards's London townhouse, with Olympic Studio even closer, Richards may occasionally have come and gone while Shepard was at Redlands, but they could not possibly have spent all that much time there together.

Asked if he had any recollection at all of Shepard at Redlands, Richards replied in classic fashion through his manager that while he did recall hanging out with "Sam," he quite honestly "did not remember where it was," as they had both been a bit "out of it" at the time.

Although Shepard would later claim "Maxagasm" was "a really great movie," he devoted the first 7 pages of the undated second draft, which runs to 136 single-spaced pages, describing all twenty-two characters in great detail. With each shot and scene numbered, the script would have required 361 separate setups (i.e., camera position, lighting, and blocking), many of them very elaborate.

Describing Cowboy, the film's lead character, Shepard wrote, "A cascading wealth of shoulder length blond hair crowns his magnificent carriage . . . a demon lurks behind his beautiful facade: Vanity." The female lead is called Child. Feelgood is "the dynamic leader of a band of unemployed mercenaries." Honkie is a "Negro member" of the mercenaries. Taco is a Mexican member. There is also a loner named Panama Red and an albino named Nightmare.

Although the opening scene is well written and cinematic, the characters then begin speaking in an entirely wooden, fake cowboy jargon. In scene after scene, the conversations drag on and on, making the story painfully slow. The title refers to a ritual sacrifice in which a man and a woman are killed to achieve a form of transcendence known as Maxagasm. And while the final scene bears some relationship to the desert orgy in *Zabriskie Point*, it is also virtually impossible to comprehend.

At no point in the script is it possible to imagine the Rolling Stones, either as individuals or a group, portraying any of the characters in "Maxagasm." Because Shepard had been hired to write a movie for the band, this would seem to have been the point of the entire exercise.

IN JULY 1968, MICK JAGGER arrived in Los Angeles to do overdubs and begin mixing *Beggars Banquet*, the album the Stones had been busy recording during Shepard's time at Redlands. In Peter Stampfel's words, "One day, Sam, who had just got together with the Stones, who were in town, brought an unreleased copy of 'Jumping Jack Flash.' 'Look what I've got!' he said, running up to the house we were all renting (except Sam). He held the forty-five over his head with the sun directly behind him, which gave the record a brilliant halo. We played it about five times. A little later, Sam introduced me to Mick Jagger at the Chateau Marmont, where the Stones were staying. I reached out to shake hands with him, but Jagger pulled his hand behind his back as if I had cooties or something. He seemed to be a lot shorter than I thought."

And while "Jumpin' Jack Flash," which would then go to number one on the *Cash Box* chart, had actually been released in the United States five weeks before Jagger arrived in Los Angeles, Sam Shepard was now most definitely on a first-name basis with both Jagger and Richards. As with so many others who crossed their path in that era, their effect on him would prove to be more than just casual.

In February 1971, Shepard went to the Chelsea Theater Center at the Brooklyn Academy of Music in New York City to see *AC/DC*, a mad futuristic fantasy written by the English playwright Heathcote Williams that would greatly influence Shepard's own play *The Tooth of Crime*. Forty-six pages into the text of *AC/DC*, a female character rips a necklace bearing a plastic picture of Mick Jagger off the neck of another female character. She then says, "The cat that gets him, he's really gonna get it off . . . This cat's had sixteen million teenybopper orgasms laid on him, so the cat that gets him, and it won't be long after Altamont, he's really gonna get it off. He's really gonna pick up a heavy-duty flash . . . He's really gonna get loaded behind THAT charge when he rips it off." Mortally offended that anyone would even dare suggest killing Mick Jagger to appropriate his powers for themselves, Shepard suddenly leaped angrily to his feet and stormed out of the theater, shouting, "You can't talk that way about Mick Jagger!"

At a time when rock stars were not yet appearing in works of serious fiction, Shepard wove both Mick Jagger and Keith Richards into a short story entitled "The Curse of the Raven's Black Feather," which appeared in *Hawk Moon: A Book of Short Stories, Poems, and Monologues,* his first collection of prose, which was published in 1973. In the story, the unnamed narrator, who seems to be Shepard, is driving at high speed through the night while thinking about "Keith Richard" (as the rocker was then known, per Rolling Stones manager Andrew Loog Oldham).

"The thing about Keith is his shark tooth ear ring," Shepard wrote, "his hawk face, and his name. Not Richards but Richard. Keith Richard, two first names . . . And he kicked some Scotch guy in the teeth from the stage in the early days when they played in Scotland before jeering crowds." Although this incident actually occurred in Blackpool, England, during the annual drunken gathering known as Scots Week, Shepard could only have learned of it from reading an article about the band's farewell tour of Great Britain in *Rolling Stone* magazine in April 1971, and so the playwright does seem to have been somewhat obsessed with the band during this period.

Continuing the Rolling Stones thread in his short story, Shepard references a line from "Moonlight Mile," the final song on *Sticky*

Fingers, an album released a week after the *Rolling Stone* article was published. Shepard then envisions Richards standing alone outside in the California night "in his Python boots staring at a kidney shaped pool. The kind Brian died in. Staring at the water. The air blowing his crow feather hair."

ALTHOUGH HE HAD BEEN warned not to do so by someone much closer to the Rolling Stones than he was, Tony Foutz nonetheless continued to pursue his film project with the band by journeying to Brazil in December 1968, where Mick Jagger, Marianne Faithfull, Keith Richards, and Anita Pallenberg were on an extended holiday together. As Jagger, Richards, and Pallenberg sat outside their house in the jungle besieged by flies, Foutz, who now wanted to direct "Maxagasm" as well, suddenly drove up to join them. Joining their traveling party, he continued on with them through Brazil to Peru.

In the end, Foutz's efforts proved of no avail. At some point after Brian Jones had drowned in his own swimming pool in July 1969, Mick Jagger finally decided to pull the plug on "Maxagasm." Although Shepard would later say Jagger did so because he felt the script was "dated," it was also utterly incoherent.

ELEVEN

O-LAN

He was always looking for a fight and looking
for a joke and looking for who loved him,
who was going to ignite the longing and
keep him warm for a while.

—O-LAN JONES,
"RUNNING OFF WITH SAM"

AFTER HIS FIRST REAL TASTE OF THE HIGH LIFE DURING HIS
time in Rome with Antonioni, at Redlands with and without Keith
Richards, and in Los Angeles at the Chateau Marmont, Shepard returned to New York City in the fall of 1968. Despite having written a
new play during his time in California, he was now convinced his real
future was as a screenwriter.

Shepard then began a curiously unfocused and relatively unpro-
ductive period in his life by being awarded the first of his two Guggenheim fellowships. Twice a week, he also commuted by train to New
Haven, Connecticut, where, along with fellow downtown playwrights
like Megan Terry, he attended filmmaking courses at Yale taught by,
among others, the well-known film critic, editor, and author Stanley
Kauffmann. Shepard also involved himself in the New York City underground film scene. Greatly influenced by *Faces,* the Academy
Award–nominated *cinéma vérité* film written and directed by John
Cassavetes, he began working on *Blood.*

Directed by his good friend Bill Hart, with whom Shepard was now
sharing an apartment next to a police warehouse in Lower Manhattan,
the film featured Joyce Aaron and Charles Mingus III. Although the
footage has been lost, the film, much of which was improvised, was

about white people imitating Black styles as well as Black power, a subject that would later embroil Shepard in controversy.

"We shot the movie in Columbia Presbyterian hospital in Harlem and in a lot of taxis, and Joyce Aaron and half the Open Theatre were in it," says Mingus III. "In this one improvised scene between Bill Hart, Sam, and myself, Bill was pretending to be a guy who had picked us up to try and hustle us and so we gaffer-taped him. Every time we heard him say something stupid, we taped him more.

"We taped his mouth and he was still trying to communicate. Then we started throwing beer cans at him. There was now a pyramid of beer cans in Bill's apartment and then the cameraman said, 'Cut!' Which was fortunate, because we could have really hurt Bill. In came a couple of makeup guys, who put chocolate syrup on the floor where Bill was supposed to fall so it looked like blood. Because in a black-and-white movie, chocolate looked like blood. Bill was still rocking back and forth and he said, 'I almost made the front page of the *New York Post* today. And the headline would have been "Two Actors Kill Director."'"

A year later, Shepard performed in *Brand X*, an absurdist comedy written, directed, and filmed by Win Chamberlain, a realist painter who had become part of Andy Warhol's circle. Replete with full-frontal nudity, the film starred Taylor Mead along with other downtown luminaries like Sally Kirkland, Candy Darling, Ultra Violet, and Abbie Hoffman. Shepard's entire contribution to this project consisted of appearing in one scene in which he and a blonde, both naked from the waist up, scream "U.S.A.!" over and over again.

Shepard did work on one film during this period that would have a lasting impact on cinema. At the end of 1967, Robert Frank, the photographer whose critically acclaimed book of black-and-white images, *The Americans*, featured an introduction by Jack Kerouac, was shooting and directing *Me and My Brother*, a film he had also written. Intending to make a movie based on *Kaddish*, Allen Ginsberg's epic poem about his mentally ill mother, Frank had started working on the project in 1965 only to abandon it for lack of funding. A year later, he began following Ginsberg and his lover, Peter Orlovsky, as they toured the country reading their poems. While doing so, Frank chose as the subject of his film Orlovsky's schizophrenic brother, Julius, a catatonic who had just spent fifteen years in a mental hospital.

When the real Julius Orlovsky wandered off and disappeared in San Francisco—he returns in the final scene, the only shot in color—Frank cast Joe Chaikin, Shepard's friend and mentor from the Open Theatre, to portray Julius in what had become a film within a film. By combining both documentary and staged footage to examine the nature of mental illness, Frank broke new ground, and so, in time, *Me and My Brother* would come to be recognized as an iconic work of cinematic art.

Shepard, who was listed with Frank as one of the writers on the film—both Ginsberg and Peter Orlovsky were also credited, but only for their poems—would later characterize his involvement in the project as a really nice experience. Frank himself did not share this feeling. "Well," he said, "Sam Shepard wrote just one little scene, and then Antonioni asked him to do *Zabriskie Point*. Sam Shepard left for the glory of the glory."

According to novelist and screenwriter Rudy Wurlitzer, who by then "had already known Robert Frank forever" and had brought Shepard to the project, "Sam always had a running confrontational dialogue with authority and so what was sort of amazing to me was that he could exist as he did in the film world." Aside from being close friends who worked together on several films, one of which they co-directed, Wurlitzer and Frank also shared an abiding love for Cape Breton, in Nova Scotia. After going there for the first time with his friend the composer Philip Glass, who was then also driving a cab in New York City, Wurlitzer had bought an old lodge on eighty acres of land where he and Glass built separate houses where they still spend their summers.

"I took Sam up there as well for the first time back then and he loved it right away, because it was wilderness and off the grid," Wurlitzer says. "He had enough money to buy some land and a house, which was a couple hours from where I lived, and so we didn't get to hang out together all that much up there. But Robert Frank had a place a lot nearer to me, and so we would always see one another in the summers." Over the course of the next fifteen years, Shepard would return with his family to spend the summer in the two-story clapboard house he had bought not far from the Bay of Fundy, where the world's highest tides rolled up against the six-hundred-foot cliffs towering over the black-sand beaches.

Six years older than Shepard, Rudy Wurlitzer had been named after his great-grandfather, a German immigrant who in 1853 had founded the company bearing his name, a manufacturer of pianos and the massive pipe organs that became standard operating equipment in movie theaters all over America. After dropping out of Columbia University, Wurlitzer was drafted and then spent a year stationed in the Arctic testing cold-weather equipment.

Returning to New York City, Wurlitzer took up residence in a "pretty funky" rent-controlled apartment on Twenty-third Street in Manhattan where he was working on *Nog*, the first of his four experimental novels, when he met Shepard. As Wurlitzer says, "In those days, neither one of us was really making any money from our writing. And that was why I got into films and that was why he got into films. Because they paid you whether or not they made your script and we were grateful for that."

In many ways the older brother Shepard had never had, Wurlitzer understood him as few others did. "Sam was very complex and very smart and interested in all aspects of artistic culture," Wurlitzer says, "and so he was fun to talk to because we had quite a large frame of reference together. Sam was also not easy to understand, because he could barely understand himself. And that was what his journey was all about. He came from a different sensibility, and he was an explorer who was always outside of his own being but not conscious about it. And so I don't know if he even ever thought of himself that way."

ALTHOUGH IT HAD BEEN less than a year since *Forensic and the Navigators* opened at Theatre Genesis, O-Lan Jones knew that Sam Shepard had been "off writing a movie with Antonioni in Italy, and then in L.A.," and so was no longer "really part of our little Off-Off-Broadway world anymore; rather he was on the magic carpet to success."

For all these reasons, she found it strange that Shepard had chosen to join her and a group of other actors as they worked with director Tony Barsha to develop *The Vision Piece* (also known as *The Body Piece*) for Theatre Genesis. Although Shepard had done very little acting, Jones soon discovered that he was "full of life." That he might have also joined the group because she was in it never seems to have occurred to her. But when everyone stood in a circle to do their sound and movement exercises, Shepard would always come over to her while "doing some wild shapes and sounds for me to copy. I got the feeling he did crazy stuff just to see me go crazy." One day, as Shepard was doing repetitive movements that consisted of bending all the way over with his hands on the floor only to suddenly straighten back up as though he were now "pulling up gallons of thick taffy . . . and then throwing it over his head with a growl," she "mirrored him." Timing it "just right so that during the little bit of time when we were standing up straight facing each other," Jones whispered, " 'We can't go on meeting like this!' . . . I knew he'd get it. I knew it only confirmed all the looks and accidental bumps and jokes we made for each other." What until then had been a fairly innocent flirtation suddenly became something far more serious and exciting.

Although Jones was still living with Tony Barsha in his sixth-floor walk-up on First Avenue, she and Shepard began to "steal away and drive around in his car at night." As he drove her through the city with no specific destination in mind, she would watch his hands as he changed gears "in the rolling light from the streets." To her, his car, a beige Volvo station wagon, "didn't seem like him; it was something you'd find in a suburban driveway. It was placid and boxy, but he was jagged, vibrant; the air rippled around him. He'd walk into any dark place, and not because he wasn't scared—it was okay to be scared, it would all be gone someday anyway."

After a rehearsal one night, Jones and Shepard walked into Max's Kansas City only to see Murray Mednick, with whom Jones had worked on *The Hawk*, sitting by himself. After they squeezed themselves into his booth, Mednick asked Shepard what was going on. Shouting so he could make himself heard over the music, Shepard said, "O-Lan and I are moving in together." As Jones later wrote, "I froze—nobody knew about us sneaking around, and now he had crossed us over into the real world. No consultation, just said it. I was numb, feeling my life being changed again without my consent; barely even questioning that he had the right or that I could say no." Although it had been "a thrill sneaking around with Sam, [and] he was way more fun than Tony," she was still "looking for my own solo life to get going."

And so, when Tony Barsha showed up at Max's Kansas City along with others who had been at the rehearsal, Jones was still "off balance and getting my bearings" as well as frightened that Mednick "might blurt out something about the plans Sam had just made for us." Thinking it would be better for all concerned if she told Barsha about this in private, Jones asked him to take her home. In a cab on the way there, she informed him that when the show they were doing was over at the end of the month, she was going to move in with Shepard. Even though she had just said this out loud, it still did not seem real to her. This feeling was compounded by Barsha's silence during the rest of the cab ride and by the hour he then spent alone in the bedroom without speaking to her.

When Barsha finally re-emerged into the living room, he said, "You're not moving out at the end of the month; you're moving out tonight. Call him up right now if that's what you're going to do." Because she did not have Shepard's number, Barsha had to find it for her in his director's notes. Jones then called Shepard, who said he would be there as soon as possible. Barsha returned to the bedroom while she "kept quiet in the living room. The mood was too dangerous: The wrong move, too sudden, too loud, could crack the atmosphere and cause an explosion."

About half an hour later, there was a quiet knock at the door. When Jones opened it, Shepard was standing there "bundled up in his brown suede Afghan jacket with the sheep fur around the collar and down the front, red and blue embroidery following its lines. His eyes were slanting up up up and all the bones and angles of his face were sharp. He was nervy and excited and he pulled me out of the apartment and held both my hands. We looked at each other in the stark overhead light of the hallway, jolted by the sudden change in our lives—the laughter bubbled up, and we went running down the stairs to his station wagon double-parked in front."

About to begin a relationship that would continue for the next fifteen years, the couple drove off in Shepard's beige Volvo station wagon. As Barsha said of Shepard to biographer John J. Winters, "He was a tricky guy. He couldn't be entirely trusted. I couldn't trust him with my girlfriend, and he ran off with her."

IN THE LATE SUMMER or early fall of 1969, after Shepard and Jones had been living together for some months, she became pregnant. On Sunday, November 9, 1969, they were married in a dual ceremony along with actors Walter Hadler and Georgia Lee Phillips in the main chapel of St. Mark's Church, the home of Theatre Genesis where, nearly two years earlier, Jones had performed in a play written by her groom.

Clad in white vestments with shaggy hair and a thick beard as he stood before the huge wooden cross on the altar, the Reverend Michael Allen began the ceremony by saying, "In a broken world and a polluted land, nothing could be more beautiful than a marriage."

Unlike Jones, who "was wearing a long Empire-waisted yellow dress with flowers in kind of a wreath in her hair," Shepard had chosen to get married in an outfit that made him look as though he had just come from lip-synching his brand-new single on *American Bandstand*. Rock-'n'-roll sharp, he wore an untucked, outsized, gaily patterned shirt with a large, floppy collar over a pair of black corduroy bell-bottom trousers rolled up into wide cuffs over his boots. At the altar, flanked on one side by Bill Hart, the best man, and on the other by Jones's younger sister, Kristy, the maid of honor, Shepard towered over his diminutive bride.

Confirming that the hippie vibe at the wedding came from the bride's side of the aisle, one of Jones's fellow actresses said, "I remember I was shocked at O-Lan's mother, Scarlett—she seemed to be so young. She was in jeans and had a suede vest with fringe, and I thought to myself, 'Boy! My mother is not like that.' She was really kind of cool."

Making the event yet more festive, purple tabs of acid had been passed out as everyone filed into the church. According to Albert Poland, who would produce Shepard's next play at Café La MaMa, the Holy Modal Rounders, who performed in the parish hall after the ceremony, with Shepard on drums, were the ones who had distributed the LSD. "The Rounders played at the wedding," Peter Stampfel wrote, "and I read years later that we also passed 'purple acid' around to everybody. I don't remember that, but maybe we did. I don't remember much about the wedding, except meeting Richard Brautigan. Like I said, maybe we did."

Whether it was the acid, the anti-establishment attitude of most of the guests, or a combination of the two, the ceremony itself did not proceed as it was meant to. Nor is it possible even now to reconcile accounts of the event from those who were there. Although two female guests say Jones was visibly pregnant that day, she shows no sign of being so in a photograph of her standing beside Shepard at the altar.

Watching it all from the balcony of the church, Gretchen Amussen had both a clear and a completely sober view of the proceedings. A sixteen-year-old student at the Bronx High School of Science, she had first been brought to the church by her father, the editor in chief of Bobbs-Merrill who would publish Shepard's first collection of plays. Although she had studied only piano, Amussen had sat in for the church's regular organist when she went on vacation. "And then, when this wedding came up," she says, "I don't know why, but they thought it would be cool to have this sixteen-year-old play. I think they wanted me there because these were not regular church people and so somebody played the guitar, and then somebody read a poem and it was all kind of really folk-y or hippie."

It was also theatrical. At one point in the ceremony, the Reverend Michael Allen asked, "Who gives these people to be married to one another?" As one, the entire congregation supplied the answer by shouting, "We do!" As Amussen says, "I was in the balcony playing the organ and I had not a clue about people having taken LSD. What I do remember is that in the middle of the service, the best man suddenly said, 'We've had enough of this. This has gone on long enough.' And that was the end of the ceremony, because everyone left."

The Reverend Michael Allen's daughter would later tell biographer John J. Winters her father's favorite story about the wedding was "that before he could proclaim them husband and wife, Sam picked O-Lan up and ran down the aisle, with my dad yelling the proclamation after them." Without further ado or a honeymoon of any kind, the newly married couple repaired to an apartment of their own, conveniently located below the one Shepard had shared with Bill Hart, to await the birth of their child. And while he may not have realized this at the time, Sam Shepard had not just married O-Lan Jones but also her entire family.

AS THERE WAS THEN no way to know the sex of a child before birth, the name Shepard and Jones chose for a girl was "Kachina," a spiritual being in the religious culture of the Pueblo people, the Hopi and Zuni tribes among them. Their name for a boy was "Jesse," after the outlaw Jesse James, with the middle name "Mojo," as in the voodoo charm referenced in song by Black blues musicians, Muddy Waters foremost among them.

In May 1970, Jesse Mojo Shepard was born. In a black-and-white photograph taken when he was about three months old, Jones leans against a tree holding him tenderly in her arms. The look on her face is one of utter bliss. Bearing absolutely no resemblance to how he looked at their wedding, Shepard stands over them with one arm against the tree. Bare-chested and skinny with a patch of black hair right above his sternum and a battered old fedora on his head, he looks like he has just walked out of some remote hollow in Appalachia. Responding to Jones's joyful expression, he gazes down at her with a tender smile on his face.

If in fact every picture tells a story, no two people who had just welcomed the arrival of their newborn child had ever been this happy, or so much in love.

—

TWELVE

OPERATION SIDEWINDER

I am truly an American. I was made in America.
Born, bred and raised. I have American blood.
I dream American dreams. I fuck American girls.

—SAM SHEPARD,

OPERATION SIDEWINDER

A MONTH AFTER THEY WERE MARRIED, IN DECEMBER 1969, Sam and O-Lan Jones Shepard were both working on different plays on separate floors at Café La MaMa. As befitting his return to theater in Lower Manhattan after a two-year absence, Shepard was in the larger first-floor space, making his debut as a director with his new play, *The Unseen Hand*. One floor above him, in the slightly smaller cabaret space, Jones was rehearsing her role in *Sprint Orgasmics*, an experimental drama by the Austrian playwright Wilhelm Pevny. Originally written in German, the play evoked ancient Greek theater through an onstage choir.

While another playwright directing his own work for the first time might have driven everyone crazy with demands, Shepard was far more casual. During rehearsals, he spent a good deal of time playing poker with his actors onstage rather than working with them on character, blocking, or performance.

While all this was taking place at Café La MaMa, producer Albert Poland and director Jeff Bleckner, who had graduated from Yale with an MFA a year earlier, were trying to mount an Off-Broadway revival of *Forensic and the Navigators* as part of a double bill with another new Shepard play entitled *Back Bog Beast Bait*. After hearing the actors auditioning for the play read his text, Shepard decided that *Back Bog Beast Bait* was not yet ready for production.

For a variety of reasons, he then invited Poland and Bleckner to attend a rehearsal for *The Unseen Hand*. Blown away by what they saw, they expressed their eagerness to pair *The Unseen Hand* with *Forensic and the Navigators* for their Off-Broadway double bill. Shepard suggested that Bleckner replace him as director of *The Unseen Hand*. Once he had done so, Poland used the play's run at Café La MaMa, which began on December 26, 1969, to raise money for the Off-Broadway production.

According to Lee Kissman, who had been cast in *The Unseen Hand* as Willie the Space Freak, an alien who has come to earth only to find himself stranded in the desert outside Azusa, California, with an aging derelict named Blue Morphan, "Sam started directing *The Unseen Hand* at Café La MaMa but then stopped a couple of weeks into it and found Jeff Bleckner. It wasn't difficult being directed by Sam, because he got us all on the same wavelength, but I think he just got bored. It became something he didn't want to do because it was an investment of too much time for him."

In truth, Shepard's decision enabled him to redirect his attention to the play he had been trying to get produced ever since his return to New York City more than a year before. He had begun writing *Operation Sidewinder* during the summer of 1968 while performing with the Holy Modal Rounders in Los Angeles and hanging out on the set of *Zabriskie Point*. As Peter Stampfel told Shepard biographer Ellen Oumano, "A lot of the songs we were practicing at the time seemed to segue neatly into the plot of *Sidewinder* so he wrote the songs into the play."

After Shepard returned to New York in the fall of 1968, the Yale Repertory Theatre, which had been founded two years earlier by Robert Brustein, the drama critic and playwright who had become dean of the Yale School of Drama, optioned *Operation Sidewinder* for $500 (the equivalent of $3,500 today). Scheduled to open on January 23, 1969, the play, which was to be directed by Jeff Bleckner, had already been cast when six of the seven Black students at the Yale School of Drama (out of an enrollment of nearly two hundred) made their objections to it known to Dr. John Clark, a fellow in psychiatry at Yale Medical School, who then became the spokesman for the group.

A play in two acts with twelve scenes, eleven songs, and thirty-seven characters, *Operation Sidewinder* is a mad farrago of themes, thoughts, and ideas that never become more than the sum of their parts. The title character, a very large sidewinder rattlesnake, is in fact an advanced computer designed by a mad scientist for the U.S. Air Force. After somehow escaping from the laboratory, the sidewinder must be retrieved before it falls into the hands of Black militants who are working with a young white political radical and a half-Irish, half-Native American named Mickey Free to dump a large quantity of LSD into the water supply of the air force base. Throughout the play, the action advances in fits and starts only to then suddenly veer off in yet another direction.

On December 26, 1968, Clark told Sam Zolotow, the veteran *New York Times* theater reporter, that the Yale students were objecting to the way in which the three Black militants in the play were portrayed "as stereotypes reminiscent of Stepin Fetchit and 'Amos 'n' Andy'" and as characters unable to formulate or carry out their own plans without relying on white people for help.

The group's other objections were aimed at the university. In their view, the Yale School of Drama had not met the needs of its Black students because there were no Black teachers on staff. There were also no Black representatives on the committee that selected the plays to be put on at the Yale Repertory Theater. To date, no work by a Black playwright had been performed there; nor had any play been brought to its stage by a Black director.

During its first two seasons, the Yale Repertory Theater had presented works like *Volpone* by Ben Jonson and Aeschylus's *Prometheus Bound*. The only plays even faintly resembling *Operation Sidewinder* had been Samuel Beckett's *Endgame* and *Viet Rock* by Megan Terry, both of which had been put on by visiting companies. Whatever the reasoning behind the decision to produce Shepard's new play might have been, it soon proved to have been a serious error in judgment.

As Robert Brustein was about to leave campus to spend his post-Christmas holidays in Barbados, he released a statement reading:

Mr. Shepard withdrew the play against the will and advice of the school administration. It had been approved by the school's play committee, consisting of a dozen students and faculty members, without the slightest anticipation that it would offend anyone's sensibilities. We remain convinced that the play is completely harmless on the black question by any objective standard; and indeed the three black actors in the cast were vigorously opposed to any cancellation of the play. The playwright, however, disturbed by the atmosphere in which his work was about to be produced, decided to withdraw it. We regret the implications of this situation for the future of free theater in a university setting.

While Brustein's account of why Shepard decided to withdraw his play was accurate, how he had been persuaded to do so was far more interesting. Arnold Weinstein, a poet and playwright who was teaching at Yale and who fully supported the Black students' demands, had taken it upon himself to provide them with Shepard's telephone number. The students then appeared on Shepard's doorstep and asked him to withdraw the play. According to biographer Don Shewey, Shepard conceded to their demands "not because he agreed with their assessment but because he declined to have his play become the scapegoat for grievances between the black students and the university faculty."

Nonetheless, Shepard allowed *Esquire* to publish the play in May 1969. In the magazine, the text above the play's title read, "The New Theatre presents the work of its greatest living playwright." Directly below the title, the magazine identified him as "Sam Shepard, age 25." Below that, a line of italics enclosed in a set of parentheses stated, "Read it as a play, but think of it as a warm, wet kiss." Making it all that much worse, *Esquire*'s editors had also chosen to run a large, lurid illustration of a busty young woman on the facing page. In a tight sleeveless blouse and skintight pants, and with her mouth agape, she reacts in horror to the massive sidewinder rattlesnake that has wrapped itself around her waist and thigh and has its mouth wide open to reveal its fangs.

Unwisely, Shepard also permitted the magazine to publish a scene that did not appear in the play when it was finally produced. After a musical interlude, the audio of a speech made on August 24, 1968, in Los Angeles by Stokely Carmichael, the former chairman of the Student Nonviolent Coordinating Committee, who had become the "honorary prime minister" of the Black Panther Party, can be heard. As the stage lights come up, the three Black militants listening to the speech are revealed to be sitting in "an orange '59 Cadillac convertible, chopped and channeled in the style of the Fifties, with a TV in the back seat. Blood, a Black Nationalist dressed in a black beret and black leather jacket and wearing dark glasses, sits behind the wheel. In the back seat are two more Black Nationalists dressed like Blood."

That they are listening to Stokely Carmichael speak from a television set in the backseat of a car, a classic bit of Shepard surrealism, is not the problem. The problem is the car. To have placed three Black militants in a vehicle that many white people assumed only a Black pimp could afford to drive was a racist stereotype of the first order. And so, in the produced version of the play, Blood begins the second act sitting behind the wheel of a 1957 Chevrolet convertible he has just parked at a drive-in restaurant.

Similarly, Stokely Carmichael's speech, which goes for so long in the printed version of the play that Shepard may actually have recorded and transcribed it himself, is gone from the staged version. Instead, a young white female carhop at the drive-in repeats several lines from the speech while Blood seems far more interested in ordering his dessert than what she is saying.

In the printed text, the opening stage directions for Act 2 refer repeatedly to the two militants who accompany Blood as "Negroes." In the produced version, they have become "Blacks." Shepard had also given them both names. And when the cute-as-a-button, very sassy young white female carhop asks the three Black militants if they are with the Panthers, the one named Dude replies, "No, we're with the Rams."

In the end, yet another of Shepard's attempts to portray a counterculture he seems never to have understood as well as the radical political movements it spawned, whose strident rhetoric he had been unable to portray in *Zabriskie Point*, had led him into the kind of very public controversy he did not anticipate. Far more significantly, *Operation Sidewinder* marked the start of what soon became such a calamitous turn in Sam Shepard's career that it sent him into exile.

WHILE THE UNIVERSALLY NEGATIVE critical reaction that greeted *Zabriskie Point* after it was released on February 9, 1970, and its dismal performance at the box office had to have been incredibly disappointing for Shepard, his theatrical career was now moving forward at a rapid pace. In great part, this was due to the work being done on his behalf by his agent, Toby Cole. A former actress and political activist who was born Marion Cholodenko in Newark, New Jersey, Cole had resurrected the careers of actors like Zero Mostel, who had been blacklisted during the McCarthy era, while also championing the work of playwrights like Peter Handke, Bertolt Brecht, and Luigi Pirandello in America.

Thanks to Cole, a fledgling Off-Broadway producer had optioned *Operation Sidewinder* and then leased the rights to the Repertory Theatre of Lincoln Center. Formed in 1965, the theater had been run ever since its inception by Jules Irving (along with his partner Herbert Blau, who resigned after the first season), both of whom had been brought in from the San Francisco Actor's Workshop to present works in the newly constructed Vivian Beaumont Theater.

The only Broadway-class theater in New York City not located in or around Times Square, the Eero Saarinen–designed Vivian Beaumont featured a thrust stage and stadium seating that could accommodate eleven hundred people. With virtually unlimited technical capabilities, it was the perfect venue for a play that could never have been presented in the tiny downtown theaters where Shepard had made his name. "It's impossible to stage in a poverty situation," Shepard said of *Operation Sidewinder* in a *New York Times* article that appeared three days after he and Jones were married. "Forty actors! My idea was to write a movie for the stage."

Only someone like Jules Irving, whose own theatrical background had predisposed him to this kind of radical material, would have dared bring a play described by Shepard biographer Don Shewey as "an apocalyptic comic strip" to an institution that embodied the artistic values of the cultural elite. Well aware of this conflict, Shepard also told *The New York Times* that he rarely attended shows on Broadway and had never seen a play at Lincoln Center. "I couldn't bring myself to go up there," he said. "It's a total bourgeois scene." When he was asked why he had allowed Lincoln Center to put on *Operation Sidewinder*, he said, "The main reason is because no one can really afford to do it anywhere else."

Many years later, John Lahr, the author and theater critic who was then the literary manager at Lincoln Center's Repertory Theatre (and who also reviewed *Operation Sidewinder* in *The Village Voice*), would write, "In the fractious early seventies, it was a shocking thing for the darling of downtown theatre to cross the Maginot Line of Fourteenth Street, and it proved traumatic for all concerned." Accurately, Lahr also labeled Shepard's decision as "a move that in Off-Off-Broadway circles was the equivalent of Dylan going electric."

And so when Shepard and Jones, whose pregnancy was then very advanced, came to see the initial preview of the play at the Vivian Beaumont Theater on February 26, 1970, in Lahr's words, "the bartender tried to shoo us out of the lobby because we looked too scruffy . . . Communication between cultures soon turned into a collision." Concerning Shepard's feelings about the production, which featured the Holy Modal Rounders onstage performing eleven songs, Peter Stampfel told biographer Don Shewey, "The first time he came to rehearsal, he hated it so much he left. When he came back a few days later, he hated it even more, so he never came back."

After watching ticket holders take their seats before the first preview of *Operation Sidewinder*, Shepard conclusively proved he had no real idea what he had gotten himself into at Lincoln Center by telling Lahr, "Gee, it's not like Theatre Genesis. I don't know anybody in the audience." Once the preview was over, Jules Irving called Lahr into the stage manager's office and handed him the audience's written comments. "Except for two," Lahr wrote, "the comments are horrific: 'Terrible, terrible, terrible.' 'Infantile.' 'The artistic director and anyone connected should be fired.'" Concerning the effect *Operation Sidewinder* had on the theater program at Lincoln Center, Lahr later said, "We lost about 10,000 subscribers."

After thirteen previews, *Operation Sidewinder* opened at the Vivian Beaumont Theater on March 12, 1970, and ran for fifty-two performances before closing on April 25, 1970. In his review in *The New York Times,* Clive Barnes wrote, "The difficulty of the play is in the writing . . . It seems as though Mr. Shepard has been so busy making his points that he has almost forgotten to write his play . . . Probably the best performance came from the mechanical snake devised by Jean Delasser."

In the Sunday *New York Times,* Walter Kerr, the Pulitzer Prize– winning theater critic after whom a Broadway theater was later named, noted, "There is only one thing wrong with Sam Shepard's deliberately non-rational, surreal, fancifully pictorial, carefully mythic, conventionally angry, heavily overproduced and rock-group-interrupted *Operation Sidewinder* now at the Vivian Beaumont. It isn't interesting."

ON APRIL 1, 1970, *The Unseen Hand* and *Forensic and the Navigators* opened at the Astor Place Theatre at 434 Lafayette Street in Lower Manhattan. Much as she had done with the Lincoln Center production, Toby Cole had orchestrated Shepard's Off-Broadway debut by urging Albert Poland to present the double bill in the stylish three-hundred-seat theater that had opened two years earlier. Describing the first time he met Shepard, Poland told biographer Don Shewey, "He told me he'd had awards and Café La MaMa and all these things, and now what he really honestly wanted was a commercial hit."

After attending the double bill with his wife, Robert Redford, who had become a major Hollywood star seven months earlier with the release of *Butch Cassidy and the Sundance Kid,* optioned the film rights to *The Unseen Hand* for $5,000 (the equivalent of $33,000 now), with the proviso that Shepard write the screenplay. Although he never fulfilled that part of the deal, Shepard did use the money to buy the house on Cape Breton where he would spend his summers.

Perhaps the most astonishing aspect of *Forensic and the Navigators,* the second show of the evening, was that despite being eight months pregnant, O-Lan Johnson-Shepard, as she was then being billed, was somehow able to re-create the role she had played in the original production at Café La MaMa more than three years earlier. Her "funny and charming" performance as Oolan required her to move constantly across the stage while also taking refuge with another character beneath a small table for an extended period of time. Five weeks after opening night, she gave birth to a son.

In his *New York Times* review, Clive Barnes wrote, "Despite my worst instincts, I cannot prevent myself from mildly loving the plays of Sam Shepard. He is so sweetly unserious about his plays, and so desperately serious, about what he is saying. Mr. Shepard is perhaps the first person to write good disposable plays. He may well go down in history as the man who became to drama what Kleenex was to the handkerchief. And just like Kleenex, he may well overcome."

Although Barnes then urged his readers to see the production, business at the box office was not good. The double bill closed two and a half weeks later and was judged yet another failure for Shepard. As Albert Poland told Shepard biographer Don Shewey, "I felt terrible for causing the playwright I thought was the best in America to have a flop."

In a diary entry he wrote on the night the double bill opened, John Lahr described an entirely different reality. "Seeing Sam in the lobby—cigarette dangling from his mouth as he smacks away at the drums, squalling into the microphone—loose, easy[,] confident. The atmosphere is intimate. People are happy—how different from the Lincoln Center production. I couldn't help feeling we failed him. This, at least, felt right: that he was having fun—and fuck it!—that's what theatre is about."

AS SOMETIMES HAPPENS WHEN people come together to put on a play, the drama surrounding the opening night of *The Unseen Hand* and *Forensic and the Navigators* was just as intense as the action onstage. As elaborately planned as it was absurd, a failed attempt to kidnap Sam Shepard was engineered by Joey Skaggs, a self-described "fine arts painter and performance artist" whom Shepard and Albert Poland both knew from having hung out with him at St. Adrian's, a basement bar on Broadway between Bleecker and Third streets.

Although his "imaginary abstract" landscape paintings had been hung on the walls of the Astor Place Theatre lobby, Skaggs, along with five of his friends, Jones's former boyfriend Tony Barsha among them, decided that the publicity Shepard had been receiving lately was, as Skaggs wrote, "inflating his ego. We believed he was buying into the accolades of the status quo (i.e., he was becoming marketable and successful), and we wanted to 'rescue' him." To do so, Skaggs and his friends decided to storm into the Astor Place Theatre on opening night and abduct Shepard. After they had done so, "The idea was to take him up to the Port Authority and let him go with a one-way ticket to Azusa."

As the second play of the evening ended, Albert Poland, Jeff Bleckner, and Shepard were standing at the back of the theater watching everyone in the house vanish as a wall of smoke came off the stage where *Forensic and the Navigators* had just ended. Suddenly, a black 1937 four-door Pontiac sedan with running boards, large fenders, and torpedo headlights pulled up outside the theater. Wearing double-breasted pinstripe suits, the six would-be kidnappers leaped out of the car and headed into the lobby. Led by Skaggs, who was carrying a violin case as though he had a Tommy gun inside it while the others brandished fake guns, they all made a beeline for Shepard.

It was then that O-Lan Johnson-Shepard began to scream. As Skaggs wrote, "Tony Barsha thought the plan was backfiring because Sam was paranoid, believing Tony was really out to cause him harm." Or, as Barsha noted, "They recognized me and maybe they thought I was out for revenge." Despite how reasonable this assumption seemed, Skaggs and his crew then began laying their hands on Shepard, who "started throwing fists, swinging wildly, and yelling," as Johnson-Shepard, who was eight months pregnant, "was freaking out." Realizing their plan was not working, Skaggs and his crew "made a hasty retreat, jumped into the waiting car, and took off, laughing our asses off. Sam and everyone else did not think it was funny. In retrospect, can you blame them?"

As if all this were not enough excitement for the evening, the gun-toting boss of the Union Square club where the opening night party was being held decided at 12:30 A.M. to put a sudden end to the celebration, which had been scheduled to go on until 2. Two and a half hours later, according to Albert Poland, there was an explosion. As Poland later wrote, "The next morning the *Daily News* carried a front-page photo of the building. It was a pile of rubble. It had been occupied by the headquarters of the Black Panthers, and shortly after 3:00 A.M., it was blown off the face of this earth." And while there seem to be no independent sources confirming this actually happened, it would have been the perfect finishing touch to an opening night that in many ways was far more surreal than the onstage material Sam Shepard had created for it.

On July 20, 1970, *Shaved Splits*, a one-act play that took little more than an hour to perform, opened at Café La MaMa. Directed by Bill Hart, the play ran for only four midnight performances. When Albert Poland contacted Toby Cole about moving it to another theater, she referred to the fairly damning critique Clive Barnes had written of *Forensic and the Navigators* by telling him, "Sam doesn't want anything moved anymore—he doesn't want his plays called tissue paper."

As Poland said in Winters's biography of Shepard, "He had a triple whammy at the time, because *Sidewinder* had opened to a not-good response at Lincoln Center, *Zabriskie Point* opened to bad reviews, and he was devastated."

THIRTEEN

COWBOY MOUTH

Some people are one-woman men.
And some people never figure out which
one woman to be with.

—CHARLES MINGUS III,
IN *THE NEW YORK TIMES*,
2017

THE FIRST TIME PATTI SMITH EVER SAW SAM SHEPARD, HE WAS playing the drums onstage at the Village Gate in 1970 with the Holy Modal Rounders. Toward the end of the set, Shepard performed a song of his own entitled "Blind Rage" with lyrics like "I'm gonna get my gun / Shoot 'em and run." Having already noticed Shepard because he "seemed as if he was on the lam and had slipped behind the drums while the cops looked elsewhere," Smith suddenly realized that he truly embodied "the heart and soul of rock and roll."

"Patti Smith did not know who Sam was," Peter Stampfel said. "She had come that night to review the Rounders, and Sam did 'Blind Rage.' It was one of the most incredible performances I had ever seen in my life, because he'd lost the pages with the song on it and forgotten the lyrics. So what he did was basically proto-punk. And it blew her mind."

Along with Todd Rundgren, who had brought her to the show, Smith then went backstage, where she was introduced to Shepard, who told her his name was "Slim Shadow." Despite not yet having been published, Smith told Shepard she wanted to write an article about him for *Crawdaddy*, the hip rock journal founded in 1966 by Swarthmore College student Paul Williams.

In her memoir *Just Kids*, Smith writes that Shepard agreed to let her interview him and they both went back to the loft on Twenty-third Street where she lived with her former lover and friend, the photographer Robert Mapplethorpe. Making up stories as though he knew this was what she wanted to hear from him, Shepard began the interview by saying he had been born in a trailer. He then went right on telling tales Smith described as "even taller than mine . . . In my mind, he was the fellow with the cowboy mouth."

To those who had witnessed their initial meeting, the immediate effect Shepard and Smith had on each other was obvious. "After the set, instead of talking to me as she had asked to do," Stampfel said, "Patti made a beeline for Sam. I didn't listen to their conversation, but it was obviously intense. Years later, an English music writer interviewed me about Patti and Sam's first meeting. I said, regarding Sam, he 'copped her entire mind.' . . . He sure did. And so did she. Cop his entire mind."

One day after Smith had shoplifted two steaks from a nearby market, she ran into Shepard in the street. As they began walking together, Smith told him what she had in her pocket. Pulling a slab of meat out in the middle of Seventh Avenue, Shepard said, "Okay, sugar, let's eat." Once in her loft, Smith used her grandmother's cast iron pan to fry up the steaks for them on Smith's hotplate.

Concerned that Smith was not getting enough to eat, Shepard came by a few nights later to ask if she liked the lobster at Max's Kansas City. When she told him she had never eaten there because it was too expensive, Shepard said, "Get your coat. We're getting some grub." At the restaurant, he ordered for her by telling the waiter, "Bring her the biggest lobster you have."

According to Smith, it was only then that Jackie Curtis, the drag queen who was an Andy Warhol superstar, let her know that the "really good-looking guy" with whom she was having dinner was Sam Shepard, the playwright who had already won multiple Obie Awards. Shepard, Curtis told her, could take Smith "straight to Broadway."

Unlike Robert Mapplethorpe, who had teased Smith about her childhood desire to shatter windows, Shepard told her, "Kick it in, Patti Lee. I'll bail you out." With him, Smith felt she could be herself. "He understood more than anyone how it felt to be trapped in one's skin."

Soon after, Shepard and Smith moved into the Chelsea Hotel together. In that setting, their relationship became the stuff of myth, much of it self-created.

NOBODY EVER STAYED AT the Chelsea Hotel for its creature comforts. As soon as anyone stepped through the front door, the funk of ancient carpeting that had never been cleaned, spilled wine, stale cigarette smoke, body odor, and God only knew what else would hit them right in the face. As though this was their living room, long-term residents of the hotel, some of whom had lived at the Chelsea longer than they could remember and apparently had nothing better to do with their time, filled the lobby at all hours of the day and night.

The Chelsea Hotel was where Dylan Thomas died after boasting he had just drunk eighteen straight whiskies at the White Horse Tavern. It was where William Burroughs wrote *Naked Lunch* and where Edie Sedgwick, the Andy Warhol superstar who was one of Patti Smith's heroines, set fire to her room. The Chelsea Hotel was where Bob Dylan wrote "Sad Eyed Lady of the Lowlands," the eleven-minute, twenty-two-second paean to his wife Sara Lownds. It was where Janis Joplin stumbled into the elevator at three in the morning and told Leonard Cohen she was looking for Kris Kristofferson, only to have Cohen respond, "Little lady, you're in luck. I *am* Kris Kristofferson."

When Patti Smith had moved with Robert Mapplethorpe into the Chelsea Hotel two years earlier, they paid fifty-five dollars a month to live in its smallest room. Because Shepard was now paying their rent, Smith found herself in a room with a balcony that passed for luxury accommodation at the Chelsea. On that balcony in the spring of 1971, the rock photographer David Gahr took a photograph of Shepard and Smith that still says everything about who they both were back then.

Dressed in a long-sleeved polo shirt and faded jeans, arms crossed over his chest and strands of hair falling into his eyes, Shepard stares at the camera with a look of either puzzlement or faint bemusement on his face. By his side, Smith stands with her right hand looped casually over his shoulder. Posing like the model she had once wanted to be, she wears a dark tie-dyed top with one shoulder torn off in a classic punk manner. Over the snakeskin belt holding up her black jeans, a wide swath of bare stomach can be seen. With bracelets on both wrists, chains around her neck, and a moody expression on her face, she stares off into the distance at something only she can see. Around Smith's face, an astonishing mane of thick, shaggy black hair falls in mad profusion. Her overall look can only be described as Slum Goddess of the Lower East Side meets Cher singing "Gypsies, Tramps and Thieves."

Aside from the intense sexual heat the two of them generate simply by standing next to each other, Shepard and Smith make it plain in this photograph that the rules of conventional behavior simply do not apply to them. A pair of artists who are also young and beautiful, they seem completely free. Along with this freedom came what Smith later called a blatant disregard for how their actions might affect others. By then, Smith had already met O-Lan Jones, whom she recognized as "a young and gifted actress." As Smith said in an interview, "Me and his wife still even liked each other. I mean, it wasn't like committing adultery in the suburbs or something."

On a daily basis, Smith and Shepard's relationship was incredibly frenetic. An acquaintance remembered walking with them to see a play at Caffe Cino as they began having an argument that soon became "the weirdest fight I ever saw," each of them walking for half a block in utter silence before saying "something totally inconsequential but hostile to the other." Now very much at home at Max's Kansas City, Smith and Shepard would often also drink too much there and start fights. In Smith's words, "Everything you heard about us in those days is true. We'd have a lot of rum and get in trouble. We were hell raisers."

Although Smith loved their room at the Chelsea Hotel, she also missed Shepard badly when he was not there and remembered how she would throw her leg around him in bed as they stayed up all night together to watch the sunrise. As she wrote about Shepard in her diary, "Like any snake, you've rattled your way into my heart."

At the Chelsea Hotel one night, Smith and Shepard both got tattoos from Vali Myers, the "beatnik-witch" artist from Australia who had been one of fourteen-year-old Patti Smith's great heroes. Because

Smith had been reading about Crazy Horse, who had tattooed the ears of his horses with lightning bolts, she elected to have one put on her right knee. Shepard had a small crescent moon inked between the thumb and index finger of his right hand, because, as he wrote, "Hawk Moon month November month my birthday month month of cold . . . snake mouth painted hand and lightning bolt month of washing long black hair my month of birth month—the Hawk Moon month." Smith and Shepard also had the tattooing filmed by the same woman who had shot Robert Mapplethorpe having his left nipple pierced while Smith talked about it in a voiceover.

After Shepard learned that Smith had given her guitar to her sister, he offered to buy her another. Together, they went to a pawnshop where Smith looked at several Martins, some with mother-of-pearl inlays, only to fall in love with "a battered black Gibson, a 1931 Depression model. The back had been cracked and repaired and the gears of the tuning pegs were rusted. But something about it captured my heart." Once Shepard had made certain this was the guitar she wanted, he paid the pawnshop owner two hundred dollars for it. His "beautiful gesture" reminded Smith of the film title *Beau Geste*, the classic 1939 film starring Gary Cooper, and so she decided to call the guitar Bo.

Over the next five decades, Patti Smith would write most of her songs on that guitar. At the time that Shepard bought it for her, she was able to play only five chords, and the first song she ever wrote on it was for him.

ON FEBRUARY 10, 1971, PATTI Smith was offered the opportunity to read her poetry at one of the events regularly sponsored by the Poetry Project at St. Mark's Church. Over the years, those who had appeared there included Allen Ginsberg, Amiri Baraka, William Burroughs, John Ashbery, Ted Berrigan, Diane di Prima, Lawrence Ferlinghetti, Laurie Anderson, and Ishmael Reed. Smith had already attended one of these events with the Beat poet Gregory Corso, who had relentlessly heckled those reading onstage by shouting out, "Shit! Shit! No blood! Get a transfusion!" Determined not to bore anyone in the audience while she was at the lectern, Smith began thinking about how to make her reading more dynamic.

During her time at the Chelsea Hotel with Robert Mapplethorpe, Smith had met Kris Kristofferson, Roger McGuinn, Todd Rundgren, Janis Joplin—who referred to Smith as "the Poet"—and Bobby Neuwirth, Bob Dylan's close friend and touring companion. As a teenager growing up in New Jersey, Smith had immersed herself in rock 'n' roll and spent nights at home dancing with her younger brother and sister to James Brown, the Shirelles, and Hank Ballard and the Midnighters. While working as an usher at the Fillmore East, Robert Mapplethorpe had made it possible for her to see a performance by the Doors, a rock band with a poet for a lead singer.

Nonetheless, Shepard was the one who suggested that Smith integrate music into her reading, thereby making it into a performance. "Her writing blew me away," Shepard said. "She's a really great poet and she wasn't even singing back then, she was just doing poetry readings. I said: 'Y'know, you can get up there and do this poetry reading and make like you're a rock star—or you can actually be a rock star.'" To accompany her onstage, Smith enlisted Lenny Kaye, a rock writer and guitar player whom she had met while he was working behind the counter at Village Oldies, the well-known record store on Bleecker Street.

On a full-moon night when the evening's feature attraction was Gerard Malanga, a poet, photographer, filmmaker, actor, and the creative force behind much of Andy Warhol's best work, most of those who crowded into St. Mark's Church had come to see him. The audience included Andy Warhol, Lou Reed, Todd Rundgren, Robert Mapplethorpe, Brice Marden, record producer Sandy Pearlman, the rock writers Richard and Lisa Robinson and Lillian Roxon, and, of course, Shepard.

After Anne Waldman, one of the co-founders of the Poetry Project, introduced her as a "terrific poet and great songwriter and a really great friend," Smith took to the stage with Lenny Kaye. In a little-girl voice with a street accent then still far more pronounced than it would eventually become, Smith announced that because this was Bertolt

Brecht's birthday, she was going to honor him by singing "Mack the Knife" (i.e., "Die Moritat von Mackie Messer," by Kurt Weill, from *The Threepenny Opera*) in German, a language she did not speak. She followed this with a brief spoken-word piece that ended with "Christ died for somebody's sins, baby, but not mine." This then became the opening line of her classic version of "Gloria."

During the first set of her career, Smith dedicated one of her songs to Bobby Neuwirth and a poem to François Villon, "who was, like, really neat because he was a poet, but he was a murderer, too." While each of her pieces was greeted by rapturous applause, Sam Shepard could be seen hanging over the balcony railing, enthusiastically urging her on throughout the entire performance.

Smith's final song of the night was "Ballad of a Bad Boy," the poem she had written for Shepard in the Chelsea Hotel. In Smith's words, "I didn't capitalize on that performance because I didn't have a design except to make the night a little more exciting. It was a bit controversial because we had sort of desecrated the home of poetry with an electric guitar but on the other hand it got quite a good reception."

EVEN THOUGH SHEPARD HAD taken up residence with Smith in the Chelsea Hotel, he continued to regularly visit Jones and their son, Jesse, in Brooklyn, where the two were now living. His monosyllabic responses to her questions about his current situation soon led Jones to believe that he had no real idea what he was doing. Although this only heightened her concern for him, trying to pull information out of him was such a frustrating process that she finally decided to allow him to tell her whatever he wanted and just let it go at that. She was now also seeing someone else.

Complicating matters even further, Shepard (using the alias "Slim Shadow" in the program) was playing electric guitar and tambourine in the three-man band he had assembled to provide musical accompaniment for *Mad Dog Blues,* his new "Two Act Adventure Show," which opened at Theatre Genesis on March 4, 1971. With Jones (billed simply as "O-Lan" in the program) in a feature role as Mae West in a beaded evening gown (her wedding ring clearly visible on her left hand) and with other actors portraying Marlene Dietrich, Captain Kidd, Paul Bunyan, and Jesse James, *Mad Dog Blues* was Shepard's most self-conscious recycling of pop culture mythology. As always when Jones appeared in one of his plays, reviewers singled her out for her charming onstage presence.

Reflecting Shepard's state of mind during this period, when an actor with whom he had often worked before showed up drunk to a rehearsal, Shepard warned the man that if he said another word, he would punch him in the jaw. The actor said another word and Shepard broke the actor's jaw, thereby forcing director Robert Glaudini to perform that part on opening night.

That Sam Shepard was in what can only be described as a fevered state of mind throughout this period of his life would become clearly evident in the only play he ever wrote with someone else. That his collaborator was the woman for whom he had abandoned his wife and child only served to further raise the stakes of his ongoing real-life drama. For reasons even he seems never to have understood, Shepard then compounded it all by deciding to appear onstage along with Patti Smith so they could both portray their current real-life situation for one and all to see.

JUMPING OUT OF THE bed he shared with Smith in the Chelsea Hotel one night, Shepard returned with his typewriter in his hands and said, "Let's write a play." When Smith told him she did not know anything about writing plays, Shepard assured her it was easy.

To demonstrate what he meant, he began the play by writing a detailed description of the utterly chaotic state of Smith's loft, a collection of wildly diverse objects that included several hubcaps, an old tire, raggedy costumes, a boxful of ribbons, lots of letters, a pink telephone, stuffed dolls, crucifixes, license plates from southern states nailed to the wall, photographs of Hank Williams and Jimmie Rodgers, and a dead crow named Raymond.

Shepard then introduced his character, Slim, "a cat who looks like a coyote." Shoving the typewriter toward Smith, he said, "You're on, Patti Lee." Smith decided to call her character Cavale, "a chick who looks like a crow," after the title of a novel written by Albertine Sarrazin while she was in prison for armed robbery. About Slim and Cavale, Shepard wrote, "They are both beat to shit."

Although *Cowboy Mouth,* the play Shepard and Smith wrote together in two nights, is just twenty-seven pages long, it is also incredibly dense and far more literate than any of Shepard's earlier works. The text begins with Shepard explaining the play's setup by writing, "Cavale has kidnapped Slim off the streets with an old .45. SHE wants to make him into a rock-and-roll star but THEY fall in love. We find them after one too many mornings. THEY'RE both mean as snakes."

Because Shepard and Smith were both already steeped in Bob Dylan's work, the reference to "One Too Many Mornings," a song from Dylan's 1964 album, *The Times They Are a-Changin',* is intentional. Dylan himself is later referenced by name when Cavale says, "People want a street angel. They want a saint with a cowboy mouth . . . what Bob Dylan seemed to be for a while." Addressing Slim a few moments later, she tells him, "You gotta be like a rock-and-roll Jesus with a cowboy mouth." Completing their homage to Dylan, Smith chose *Cowboy Mouth,* a line from "Sad Eyed Lady of the Lowlands," written in the Chelsea Hotel, as the title for the play.

In terms of sheer psychodrama, the volume of personal information Shepard integrated into the play seems shocking even now. Erupting in anger after Cavale demands to know what he has done with her dead crow, Slim brings up the wife and kid from whom she has kidnapped him. After Cavale spins out a fantasy of getting a cradle and booties for her dead crow, Slim retorts, "I ain't gettin' no cradle for no dead crow. I have a baby! My own baby! With its own cradle! You've stolen me away from my baby's cradle! You've put a curse on me! I have a wife and a life of my own!" Slim also says, "I don't know who I am anymore. My wife's left me. She's gone to Brooklyn with the kid and left me. And here I am stuck with you." When Cavale tells Slim to go back to them, his agonized response is "I don't want! I do want! I don't want! I want you!" When Cavale tells him to stay, he says of his wife, "I want her too."

In Smith's words, "The characters were ourselves, and we encoded our love, imagination, and indiscretions in *Cowboy Mouth.* Perhaps it

wasn't so much a play as a ritual. We ritualized the end of our adventure and created a portal of escape for Sam."

AS HE HAD NEVER done with any of his plays before, Shepard approached Wynn Handman at the American Place Theatre with an
offer. Along with *Back Bog Beast Bait*, which Shepard had rewritten
but which had still never been performed, the playwright wanted
Handman to present the brand-new play he had written with Patti
Smith. Having never heard of Smith, Handman was understandably
reluctant to put on a play in which she had written all the dialogue for
a character she was now also going to play onstage. Doing what he
could to allay Handman's fears, Shepard said, "She's great—she's going
to be a big star." Then he added, "It's the most important thing in my
life and I want to act in it." In Handman's words, "When he said that,
I said, 'Fine.'"

And so Sam Shepard was now acting in a play he had written with
the woman for whom he had left his wife and child. On a nightly basis
in the same theater, his wife was also in another play he had written,
directed by Tony Barsha, the boyfriend she had left for him. Adding to
all this Sturm und Drang, Jones had to sit backstage while *Cowboy
Mouth* was being performed so she could then take the stage in *Back
Bog Beast Bait*. "On the surface, it was amicable," Tony Barsha told
Handman's biographer, "but she was having a hard time . . . That it was
all under the surface made it worse. No one was yelling or screaming
or doing anything like that."

Despite all the offstage complications, Shepard was, in Smith's
words, really excited about *Cowboy Mouth*, "because the play was good,
but the reality of exposing himself on stage was stressful." After they
had rehearsed together in their room at the Chelsea Hotel and onstage
at the American Place Theatre, "the first preview was for local school-
children, and it was liberating as the kids laughed and cheered and
egged us on." Shepard's friend and best man, Bill Hart, told biographer
Ellen Oumano that the schoolkids at the preview were "out of control,
talking to the actors." At one point in the play, when he was about to
perform a song, Shepard stepped up to the microphone, "yelled 'Fuck

you,' hit the guitar, and the amplification overwhelmed them . . . from then on it went on smoothly. His was a great performance."

Peter Stampfel found the play "riveting, one of my all-time favorites. The play started with Sam on a tricycle making believe it was a scooter and going 'Rhhhm! Rhhhym! Rhhhym!' while Patti was having a conversation with her dead crow. It was psychodrama in that they were acting out their love affair onstage, and it was fucking amazing to see."

After two previews, *Cowboy Mouth* and *Back Bog Beast Bait* opened at the American Place Theatre on April 29, 1971. Because critics had not been invited, there were no reviews—which was just as well, because on the night of April 30, Shepard was nowhere to be found, and so only *Back Bog Beast Bait* was performed. "It didn't work out because the whole thing was too emotionally packed," Shepard told biographer Don Shewey. "I suddenly realized I didn't want to exhibit myself like that, playing my life on stage. It was like being in an aquarium."

Smith wrote that Shepard, before heading off to New Hampshire to hang out with the Holy Modal Rounders as they performed in Franconia, left $1,000 (about $6,200 today) in an envelope for her on the bureau in their room at the Chelsea Hotel. In Smith's words, he also told her, "You know, the dreams you had for me weren't my dreams. Maybe those dreams are meant for you."

Offering another version of their parting, Wynn Handman told Shewey, "O-Lan didn't know where Sam was and Patti kept coming to the theater every night hoping he would show up. It was very sad." Shepard biographer John J. Winters wrote that an unnamed friend of Patti Smith's "would recall an inebriated Smith being carried out of Max's Kansas City, at one point screaming Shepard's name."

In a 2019 interview with Maureen Dowd of *The New York Times*, Smith made a point of addressing "stories about me being carried out of Max's Kansas City drunk and sobbing and screaming Sam's name. I mean, first all, it just never happened. I could laugh at it because it's so stupid but they keep repeating it."

Describing the experience of writing and performing *Cowboy Mouth* for her and Shepard, Smith said, "We were only trying to talk about two people that were destined—two big dreamers who came together but were destined to come to a sad end. It was the true story of Sam and I. We knew we couldn't stay together. He was going to go back to his wife and children [*sic*], and I was gonna go on my way."

AFTER RETURNING TO New York City from his brief sojourn with the Holy Modal Rounders in New Hampshire, Shepard, in Peter Stampfel's words, "informed O-Lan that they were getting back together (it was Sam's way to dictate to women and they tended to go along with it)." As Jones told Johnny Dark many years later, Shepard called her up one day and informed her that he was now through with Smith. If Jones refused to let him move back in with her, Shepard said he was going to "do something drastic like move to South America." When Jones told Dark that she had then agreed to reconcile with Shepard, Dark said, "Well, I guess you hadn't written him off after all." To which Jones replied, "No, I guess I hadn't."

"I think Patti was very seductive to Sam at first, and he went mad for her for a little while," Joyce Aaron says, "but he didn't stay all that long with her at the Chelsea Hotel, and then he went back to O-Lan. I don't think she was blithe about any of it, but I do think she forgave him . . . not forgave him . . . because that's too ordinary. But, then, you were not going to be with Sam if you expected a guy with a tie in a business suit to come home after having worked an eight-to-five day."

FOURTEEN

THE TOOTH
OF CRIME

I'd exhausted whatever I was doing in New York.
I'd really exhausted it and I'd been living on the
streets too much. A lot of stuff was just frayed.
I needed to get into another environment.
It was kind of an escape.

—SAM SHEPARD,
IN 1976 *INDEPENDENT
PROFILE*

OVER THE PAST EIGHT MONTHS, SAM SHEPARD HAD BEEN
forced to withdraw a play about to go into production because Black
students had objected to the stereotypical nature of its Black characters. The first film for which he had written a script had turned out to
be an unalloyed critical and commercial disaster. In an unsuccessful
attempt to extend his theatrical career beyond the Lower East Side of
Manhattan, he had allowed Lincoln Center to present a play he could
not even bear to watch. Envious of his newfound success, a group of
"friends" had tried to kidnap him. Nearly wrecking his marriage, Shepard had abandoned his wife and young son to live with Patti Smith,
only to then leave the play in which they were both appearing without
giving notice that he had no intention of ever coming back.

"When I first got to New York," Shepard told British director Kenneth Chubb in an interview in *Theatre Quarterly*, "it was wide open,
you were like a kid in a fun park, but then ... things got more and

more insane ... And also I was into a lot of drugs then—it became very difficult, you know, everything seemed to be sort of shattering."

Deciding that the only way he could possibly save his life, his career, and his family was to leave New York City, Shepard, along with Jones and three-year-old Jesse, boarded the *Queen Elizabeth 2* during the summer of 1971 for what was then a five-day transatlantic voyage. Among its many features, the massive ocean liner, which could sail backward faster than most ships could go forward, offered its nineteen hundred passengers their choice of five restaurants, three cafés, three swimming pools, a five-hundred-seat movie theater, a library consisting of six thousand books, and the only known synagogue at sea.

Although bargain basement airfares from New York to London were then available, Shepard still could not bring himself to travel by air and so paid nearly $2,500 (the equivalent of nearly $17,000 today) to book passage in a basic cabin on the ship. Arriving in Southampton, where they would have been granted the standard six-month tourist visa that specifically denied visitors the right to work legally in the United Kingdom, Shepard and his family traveled on the boat train to Waterloo Station in central London. They then began looking for a flat to rent.

In the same interview with Chubb, Shepard also claimed he had come to London "really to get into music, you know. I was in a band in New York and I'd heard that this was the rock 'n' roll center of the world—so I came here with that kind of idea ... My favorite bands are The Who, groups like that, so I had this fantasy that I'd come over here and somehow fall into a rock 'n' roll band." A brilliant put-on, the statement was nearly on a par with the claim he would make many years later when he told a writer from *Playboy* magazine that he had "sat in for Charlie Watts and jammed with the Rolling Stones."

Although the back pages of music business trade papers like *Melody Maker, Disc,* and *The New Musical Express* were then filled on a weekly basis with notices taken out by bands seeking guitarists, bass players, and drummers, Shepard never once played onstage anywhere during his time in London. And while the Who had performed for the first time as a band in Shepherd's Bush, it was not for this reason that Shepard and his family chose to begin their stay in England in what was then still a gritty, unfashionable working-class district in West London.

As Shepard explained in a 1998 PBS documentary about himself, although the English loved dogs and did not mind if a tenant owned one, it was then very hard for a family with a small child to find a flat in London. With the rent in Shepherd's Bush even cheaper than rents on the Lower East Side of Manhattan, Shepard's decision to live there made practical sense on many levels. Immediately settling down to work, he then spent three months writing a three-act play about rock 'n' roll set inside a prison. "At the end," he said, "it was a complete piece of shit, so I put it in the sink and burnt it, and then an hour later, I started to write this one."

In what Charles Marowitz of the Open Space Theatre described to Shepard biographer Shewey as "a series of lined notebooks," Shepard set his new version of the play in "an unrecognizable space and time" while also "using an invented language derived from several American idioms which included pop, underworld slang, sports jargon, and that ever-changing vernacular that musicians continually keep alive among themselves."

Although as a playwright, Shepard seemed never to run out of ideas, he had borrowed this one from someone else. Twenty-four years after *The Tooth of Crime* opened in London, he acknowledged this in the preface to a revised version of the play, writing, "Back in the sixties I was playing with the idea of a war of language—a duel where words were the actual weapons, the bullets. When I arrived in London in the early seventies, a largely unheralded play, *AC/DC* by Heathcote Williams, struck me as being an opening in that direction. Not only was the language uncanny but it also had the aura of assault about it."

The first play ever to move from the Royal Court's Theatre Upstairs to its main stage, *AC/DC* had ended its run there more than a year before Shepard arrived in London. However, he had seen and reacted to it in a very dramatic fashion at the Brooklyn Academy of Music in February 1971. Shepard's characterization of *AC/DC* as "a largely unheralded play" is also incorrect. As Roger Croucher, one of its co-directors at the Theatre Upstairs, says, "*AC/DC* was a hell of a production to do and caused a sensation." In his front-page review in *The Times Literary Supplement*, Charles Marowitz, who would then produce *The Tooth of Crime* at the Open Space Theatre, called *AC/DC* "the first play of the twenty-first century."

Without question, Heathcote Williams was then the leading playwright of London's underground theater scene. A celebrated playwright, poet, political activist, and well-known man about town, he was also, as his close friend the graphic designer Richard Adams says, "mad as a snake." Williams spent four years writing *AC/DC*.

Originally entitled *Skizotopia*, it is a play about madness, the deleterious effect of mass media on the brain's ability to process information, and the utterly overwhelming and essentially vapid nature of modern celebrity. In a play where celebrities' names flow like water and no bodily function is ignored for long, even Elizabeth Taylor's clitoris becomes a topic of discussion. According to Nicholas Wright, who managed the Theatre Upstairs, "*AC/DC* may well seem more insane now than it did back then, but that is because no one really took it up. Nobody could have, because Heathcote was like Congreve. You had to be a genius of English to be able to write that."

In the end, Heathcote Williams may have had no greater admirer than Charles Marowitz. On the basis of *The Local Stigmatic* and *AC/DC*, Marowitz placed Williams in the pantheon of great British playwrights that included Harold Pinter, John Osborne, and John Arden. He also considered Shepard's *The Tooth of Crime* "the finest American play" he had read since *Moonchildren*, by Michael Weller.

GUIDED BY CHARLES MAROWITZ, Shepard and his family moved into a small basement flat at 62 Pilgrims Lane in Hampstead that was a far cry from both Shepherd's Bush and Manhattan's Lower East Side. Just four stops from Central London on the Northern Line, Hampstead was a quiet, leafy, and discreetly bohemian village that was also almost entirely self-contained.

Composed of nearly eight hundred acres of dense and unspoiled woodland dotted with winding trails and bathing ponds, Hampstead Heath was just a five-minute walk from the flat where the Shepards now lived. According to Michael March, a poet who had been the New York editor of *Fusion* magazine before moving to London in 1970, "I lived in the attic at 62 Pilgrims Lane, and Sam and his family lived in the basement. Their flat was very small, but it did have central heating, which was more than I could say for mine, where the need to keep the paraffin heater always going in the winter nearly killed me."

Along with central heating, a luxury in London then, the basement flat had a private bathroom and a small private garden in back. At a time when many people in the city did not own a car, Shepard drove a small, used green Ford Anglia van around London and also sometimes took it on solitary trips into Wales. "Sam had money," March says. "He had more money than anybody I knew at the time, and I was making seventeen pounds [about forty-one dollars] a week working in a book-store. Sam bought a greyhound and he had a van. But he was not a cheap guy. He was a generous man and people liked him very much."

In a city where the center of all social life was "the local," the neigh-borhood pub where those who lived nearby gathered together on a nightly basis, March says, "I don't ever remember Sam drinking when I knew him in London. He had talked to me about his father being an alcoholic and I think Sam wouldn't drink because of the Freudian na-ture of their relationship. I also never knew Sam to smoke hash back then, as I think he was in a recovery period from whatever he had been doing in New York."

Although Shepard and March had "many conversations about Mayakovsky and Brecht," Shepard "never introduced me to any of his theater friends in London," March says. "We would meet and talk, but our worlds were absolutely really separate." Nonetheless, March did introduce Shepard to another American writer who was then in Lon-don.

Fifty-seven years old, William Burroughs already looked as though he had long since died and been mummified. On Duke Street, in a dimly lit flat as devoid of color as Burroughs himself, March brought Shepard and Murray Mednick, who had come to spend a month with Shepard in London, to meet the legendary author of *Naked Lunch*. "It was like East meets West," March says. "Burroughs was this tremen-dous Easterner and so he did not like Sam's rawhide effects. In that meeting, William was also very anti-Semitic. He saw Murray was a Jew and made him into Dr. Benway, a character in *Naked Lunch* who would perform surgeries and drop his cigarette ashes into the wounds of his patients. William was tremendously nasty to Murray, and of course Sam was taken aback by it all and was quite defensive. Burroughs was a genius and a workaholic and if he wasn't taking heroin, he was drinking a bottle of Jameson's a day. By the time we got there, it was late afternoon and so William was already fairly drunk."

At another time on a different day, the two men could have conversed about Jack Kerouac, whom Shepard revered and Burroughs had known and influenced. They could have discussed Allen Ginsberg, whom Burroughs had known since 1943 and whom Sam had met while working on *Me and My Brother*. They could have spoken about Charles Marowitz, whose production of Shepard's *The Tooth of Crime* was opening at the same venue where Burroughs had portrayed Judge Julius Hoffman in *Chicago/Conspiracy*. They might also have discussed Rimbaud, a poet whose work they both loved.

However, because William Burroughs was drunk, what might have been a real and substantive dialogue between two iconic American writers from different generations instead became just another rather odd and wasted afternoon in London.

CHARLES MAROWITZ DID NOT DRINK. He also would not eat anything red, neither vegetables nor meat, because the color reminded him of blood. Marowitz was born on the lower East Side of Manhattan on January 26, 1932, to Orthodox Jewish parents who had emigrated from Poland and spoke only Yiddish at home. "They were very poor," says his wife, Jane Windsor Marowitz, "and lived in a tenement with a toilet down the hallway. Charles was always basically self-taught. He taught himself to read and play the piano, and if he had not been a writer and a director, I think he would have become a composer."

After graduating from Seward Park High School, Marowitz was drafted into the U.S. Army during the Korean War. "He didn't really serve, darling," says actress Thelma Holt, one of the grande dames of

English theater, who was Marowitz's founding partner at the Open Space Theatre. "If he had, America would no longer be there. You would have lost everything."

Stationed in France, where he lived in a chateau and served as editor of the base newspaper, Marowitz later used the GI Bill to attend LAMDA (the London Academy of Music and Dramatic Art) and the University of London. He then began running workshops in which he introduced the improvisational techniques of Elia Kazan's Actors Studio as well as the Group Theatre to Great Britain.

Six feet tall, "with a Mephistophelian beard and an abrasive manner that could burn off pretension and patronage like paint stripper," Marowitz was never easy to get along with. "The best way to describe Charles," Jane Windsor Marowitz says, "is that he had a fierce intelligence. He took no prisoners. It was either his way or the highway. And if he didn't like you or something you were doing in theater, he wasn't afraid to write about it, which made him a lot of enemies."

In 1968, Marowitz found an unused basement at 32 Tottenham Court Road in Central London. With the help of Thelma Holt, who persuaded her father-in-law to pay for the construction costs, Marowitz converted the basement into the 128-seat performance space that became the Open Space Theatre. Although Shepard would later be unable to remember why he contacted Charles Marowitz about *The Tooth of Crime* in the first place, the two men had actually already met during one of Marowitz's visits to New York City. As for Thelma Holt, she had seen Shepard perform onstage with the Holy Modal Rounders.

Eleven years after *The Tooth of Crime* opened at the Open Space Theatre on July 17, 1972, Shepard said, "I guess Marowitz's theater was the theater in London at the time that was doing new stuff. So I thought he'd be open to something new. And he was. But when we got into production, we had a big falling-out. He mounted the first production of *Tooth of Crime* but he wanted to twist it in his direction and we had a big falling-out."

Explaining the two men's initial affinity for each other, Thelma Holt says, "I can imagine why Sam and Charlie became friendly when they first met, because Sam was a very attractive man. He was also fun and a bit shy, which made him even more attractive. Because I was the one who ran the Open Space, what I remember best is I never had any trouble with him. In terms of what occurred between them during rehearsals, I witnessed strife between everybody I ever worked with in England all the time. But it was far more apparent if you were working with an American. Because Americans respond. And so Sam quarreled more than the Brits. All of our daggers always went right in the back. We are really good at that." In Jane Windsor Marowitz's words, "It all came to grief between Charles and Sam during rehearsals and they almost came to blows because they didn't see eye to eye on a lot of things. I think that sometimes happens when two writers are working together."

The real issue that led to their blowup was about who controlled the rights to have the play produced in the United States. Shepard wanted the Public Theater to present *The Tooth of Crime* "on a proscenium stage with amplified rock music like a concert." He also wanted Rip Torn, who had been the inspiration for Hoss, the former reigning rock star now in perilous decline who is the play's lead character, to portray him.

Unbeknownst to Shepard, Marowitz had already agreed to allow Richard Schechner, the founder of the Performance Group in Lower Manhattan, to present the play in a manner intended to break down the traditional barriers between the audience and the performers. That Marowitz might have done this without bothering to consult or even inform Shepard would not have surprised those who knew him. "If Charles had sold the American rights to *The Tooth of Crime* to Richard Schechner," Thelma Holt says, "that was not the way it was supposed to work. Did Charles need money? Charlie always badly needed money and so would probably have done it for that reason without discussing it with me, because he knew it would have troubled me. Had it been Alan Ayckbourn or Harold Pinter, Charlie would not have been able to do that, because I would have been the one who had signed the contract."

Unaccustomed to being treated in this way by anyone in theater, Shepard contacted Clive Goodwin. A well-known writer, actor, and iconic figure from the London pop scene during the early 1960s,

Goodwin had become the literary agent who represented Toby Cole's clients in England. From London, Goodwin managed to put a halt to Schechner's U.S. production, which was then already in rehearsals.

Three months after the play opened at the Open Space Theatre, *The Tooth of Crime* had its American premiere at Princeton University's McCarter Theatre, with Frank Langella in the leading role. In his review in *The New York Times,* Clive Barnes noted that although some people took advantage of the intermission to walk out on the show, "apparently in anger at what they felt was the obscenity of the language, some in pure bafflement . . . Mr. Shepard has gathered his forces and produced a splendidly provocative play."

After exchanging several letters with Richard Schechner, Shepard, who might also have needed the money, finally agreed to let the Performance Group present *The Tooth of Crime* in their space on Wooster Street in SoHo in March 1973. At Princeton's McCarter Theatre, the play, as Barnes wrote, was presented "in a conventional theater and was seen as a ritual between throne room and pop arena. It seemed perfect and was very boldly acted." Schechner's production ran along decidedly different lines. With Spalding Gray as Hoss, the Performance Group's version of *The Tooth of Crime* was, as Barnes also wrote, put on "in an open space filled in part with stairs, ramps, and various climbing structures . . . The audience clambers around these structures, and the performance takes place in the interstices between wood and bodies." Adding insult to injury insofar as Shepard was concerned, the actors re-created the songs he had written for the play without using instruments. Although the playwright won yet another Obie Award for *The Tooth of Crime,* he "actively hated" what the Performance Group had done to his work.

Twenty-two years later, a revised version of what Shepard called *Tooth of Crime (Second Dance),* with Vincent D'Onofrio as Hoss and a brand-new set of songs by the musician, songwriter, and record producer T Bone Burnett, was presented at the Lucille Lortel Theatre, on Christopher Street in Greenwich Village. As Ben Brantley noted in his *New York Times* review of the play, "And in the enlightened year of 1996, audience members are still fleeing in disgust at intermission . . .

Are those leaving like the concertgoers who booed the first performance of Stravinsky's 'Rite of Spring'? Satisfying as it would be to answer yes, the bolters are just showing good sense."

A decade later, the La MaMa Experimental Theatre Club presented *The Tooth of Crime* in its original form at the Ellen Stewart Theatre on Fourth Street in Lower Manhattan. Because Shepard had officially "disowned" his original version of the play, Ellen Stewart, the founder of Café La MaMa, had to get special permission from him so the production could be mounted during the theater's forty-fifth-anniversary season.

In his *New York Times* review of the production, Brantley wrote, "It is both gratifying and a little frightening when a play you had consigned to the crypt returns as a living prophecy for our times . . . In bringing clarity to a work often dismissed as a smoky head trip, this interpretation makes a compelling case for 'The Tooth of Crime' as one of Mr. Shepard's best plays . . . and perhaps the best American drama on the cancerous nature of fame."

SHORTLY BEFORE *The Tooth of Crime* opened at the Open Space Theatre, Shepard discussed his new play with a writer from *Time Out*, the ultimate weekly guide to everything hip and cool in London back then, by saying, "The idea was like a gang-warfare situation, where the gangs had been split up into individual mobile warriors that fought from Maseratis and Lamborghinis with all kinds of fancy aluminum weapons. And using those people in a rock 'n' roll context. They're all killers, but they treat their situation like a rock musician." Shepard also noted he was "real interested" in "this whole 'macho' thing, y'know, this masculinity trip," because there was now "a lot of that going on in every aspect of American life, from pimps up to Nixon. People competing in life and death situations with their images of who they are."

Providing an insight into why he had left the United States a year earlier, Shepard added, "And the other thing I was thinking of was what happens when people get so carried away with death, to really craving that. Because death has become really hip in New York. The more self-destructive you become, the hipper it is. The more against yourself, like junkies. It's like a code, a badge . . . And that's what I was interested in in the play."

Shepard adapted the title of *The Tooth of Crime* from "Anguish" (also sometimes translated into English as "Distress"), a poem by the nineteenth-century French symbolist poet Stéphane Mallarmé—"But while there exists in your breast of stone / A heart which the tooth of no crime can wound, / I flee, wan, undone, / In terror of dying while sleeping alone."

Throughout *The Tooth of Crime*, Shepard plays with language in a manner that far outshines his earlier attempts to create idiosyncratic forms of diction for his characters. Galactic Jack, a disc jockey who is "white and dressed like a 42nd Street pimp," talks "like Wolfman Jack" in a Black-inflected hipster rhyming jive infused with 1950s slang. Crow, the young up-and-coming challenger to Hoss's reign, speaks in an argot so incomprehensible that it sometimes seems to have come straight out of Anthony Burgess's *A Clockwork Orange*.

Insofar as Shepard was concerned, the songs he had written for *The Tooth of Crime* were an integral part of the text. Cast in the play as the astrologer Star-Man, Michael Weller, whose own play *Moonchildren* had been on Broadway six months earlier, says, "Sam had figured out all these songs on guitar, which he could play in a really rudimentary way. When he would come to my place, he would sort of improvise a little on guitar and then bring his drumsticks out, and we would just fuck around and get stoned and play music. He was a casual musician, but he loved it. And he really did know rock music."

When it came to discussing the issues that Shepard was having with Marowitz during rehearsals, Weller says, "He never communicated his feelings to me. That was not how he related to other people. He would say, 'Let's go to the dog races.' And then he would start talking about, 'Hey, you heard of this guy Brecht? Fucking crazy play he wrote, huh?' It was like he was just learning this stuff. All of a sudden, people were taking him seriously, and it was like he was going, 'Wow, I better bone up on this shit.'"

Inspired in part by *In the Jungle of Cities*, a play written by Bertolt Brecht in the early 1920s, *The Tooth of Crime (A Play with Music in Two*

Acts) opens with an evil-looking black chair that resembles an Egyptian pharaoh's throne on an otherwise empty stage. A live band begins to play what Shepard describes in his stage directions as "dark, heavy, lurking Rock and Roll" that "should be like 'Heroin' by the Velvet Underground." The central thread of *The Tooth of Crime* is the battle for supremacy between Hoss, who, in his black rocker gear with silver studs and a pair of black kid gloves, "should look like a mean Rip Torn but a little younger," and Crow, who, in his "high-heeled green rock and roll boots, tight greasy blue jeans, a tight yellow T-shirt, a green velvet coat, a shark tooth earring, a silver swastika hanging from his neck, and a black eye-patch covering his left eye . . . looks just like Keith Richards."

Entirely American in context, the references in *The Tooth of Crime* to El Monte Legion Stadium, Ripple wine, and the Coasters, as well as a scene in which a basketball referee keeps score as costumed cheerleaders urge Hoss and Crow to battle on, would have gone right over the heads of an English audience. Nonetheless, as Thelma Holt says, "At that time, there was very much a fascination with American culture in London. The Yanks were in favor, and so the audience welcomed the play." As *The Tooth of Crime* nears its end, Hoss and Crow pick up microphones and engage in the kind of verbal combat that closely resembles "the Dozens" as well as what would later come to be known as a rap battle. Conceding that Crow has defeated him, Hoss puts a gun into his mouth, pulls the trigger, and falls dead on the stage.

Reviewing the play in *The Times* of London, Irving Wardle wrote, "Its central battle to the death between an aging superstar and a young pretender to his throne is as timeless as a myth . . . If any classic has emerged from the last twenty years of the American experimental theatre, this is it."

Intent on his getting his own back while also having the last word on Sam Shepard, Marowitz wrote an article for *The Village Voice* describing how he had felt when Shepard asked him to read *The Tooth of Crime*. "My first reaction was to beg off as I was no true champion of his earlier work . . . but if you've ever met Shepard, you will realize that he is the personification of that conquering charm that is sometimes bred in the southern and western sections of America. Despite his 28 years, his febrile hassles with Antonioni and the jet set, and his Lincoln Center tribulations, he remains Huckleberry Finn minus the fishing rod. (In time I was to learn he was also something of a Peter Lorre and a Bela Lugosi, but at the time the Huck Finn facade obliterated all other persona [*sic*].)"

FIFTEEN

THE ROYAL COURT

Meanwhile, here in boring London we're
freezing our asses off . . . It's only dog racing and
consciousness (the promise of) that keeps me here.

—SAM SHEPARD,
1972 LETTER

AFTER VISITING SHEPARD AND HIS FAMILY ON PILGRIMS LANE
in the summer of 1972, Naseem Khan, who reported on and reviewed
fringe theater productions in London for *Time Out*, wrote that they
were living "in one of those transit basement furnished flats dotted
with personal paraphernalia—nappies, kid's toys, a guitar."

Posted on the wall was a notice listing the names of the six greyhounds that had been entered into the eighth race of the day, most
likely at White City Stadium in Shepherd's Bush. "On the divan,"
Khan wrote, "Keywall Spectre dozes sloppily. He's a very large black
greyhound that forms part of the Shepard stable of 2½ dogs . . . and
was bought for 200 pounds." The equivalent of $3,000 now, and then a
fair price to pay for a greyhound Shepard described as "a real champ,"
this was an astonishing amount of money in London at the time. In
real terms, it would have taken the Shepards' upstairs neighbor Michael March three months to earn that much.

By then, Shepard had already become utterly fixated on the sport
of greyhound racing. In the words of Nicholas Wright, who, as the
manager of the Theatre Upstairs at the Royal Court, had commissioned Shepard to write a play on the subject, "The greyhound races
were kind of a working-class pursuit. Nobody in the theater would
ever go see them because they were for old geezers in cloth caps who

read *The Sun* newspaper. I don't know where Sam got it from, but he absolutely loved the greyhound races."

Recalling the summers he had spent mucking out stalls at Santa Anita when horse racing was so popular that the stretch call there was broadcast live on radio, Shepard said, "I really used to like the horse-track, we lived right near one. But it's very expensive, as far as actually getting involved in it. Then, when I came here, I found dog-racing is the second biggest spectator sport in England . . . and suddenly, it was like all your romantic childhood dreams come true—only with dogs . . . Being around the track, punters and all, that kind of stuff—I like that world."

Shepard also liked betting on the dogs. "I had never been to the greyhound races before," Michael March says, "and Sam took me for the first time. I knew nothing about any of it and put ten pence on a dog. Because Sam knew it was the first time I had ever done this, he asked me for the number of the dog and bet quite heavily on it, and we both won. His instinct was tremendous, because every other race I bet, I lost money."

Shepard became so thoroughly hooked on greyhound racing that he wrote an article about the sport entitled "Less than Half a Minute" (the amount of time it took to run each race), for *Time Out*. "So those few seconds are what it's all about," he wrote. "Less than half a minute and all that money, all that feeling, all that pounding energy has been pushed out into the night. And at the heart of it is this strange event of six dogs doing something that comes natural to them. Chasing something small, something moving, something that isn't even what they think it is."

During his time in London, Shepard's other central obsession was his involvement in "the Work," the consciousness-raising system based on the teachings of G. I. Gurdjieff, the Armenian-born spiritual teacher, mystic, author, and composer who died in Paris in 1949. Both Shepard and Jones had been introduced to the Gurdjieff movement during the summer of 1970 by Johnny Dark and Scarlett, who were living in the Haight-Ashbury, a section of San Francisco then still oc-cupied primarily by hippies.

During the late sixties and early seventies, Gurdjieff's *Meetings with Remarkable Men,* the second volume of a trilogy he wrote in Russian in 1927 but that was not published in English until 1963, was one of the essential books for those who had embarked on the spiritual path. The man who encouraged Shepard to join a Gurdjieff study group in London was Peter Brook, who eight years later would direct the film version of *Meetings with Remarkable Men* with Terence Stamp in the leading role.

Although Brook and Shepard had "only a few brief meetings" in London, and Shepard did not "know him that well," the director exerted an extraordinary influence on Shepard's career. In his words, "Character has become much more important to me. I learned that from Peter Brook." Just as important for Shepard's development as a playwright, Brook also "once said that everything is, in a certain way, storytelling."

Incorporating a variety of practices from other spiritual disciplines, the Gurdjieff method (also known as the Fourth Way) had at its core the concept of "self-remembering." Simply defined, this was being aware of one's own awareness. Similar in many ways to the Zen Buddhist notion of mindfulness, it was also what the American spiritual teacher Ram Dass meant by the phrase "Be here now." What differentiated all these disciplines from one another were primarily the techniques employed to evoke this state of mind.

Unlike other spiritual practices embraced by members of Shepard's generation, the Fourth Way did not rely on ecstatic experiences induced by psychedelics. It did not encourage its followers to worship their teachers as perfect masters who could do no wrong. Nor did it demand that devotees surrender all their worldly goods in return for spiritual salvation. Because it was a discipline centered on the mind, the Gurdjieff movement allowed Shepard, who had never been willing to join any group or submit himself to someone else's power, to retain his independence while also becoming part of something greater than himself.

This did not also mean the playwright was now in a state of constant bliss. In a letter to Johnny Dark on October 19, 1972, written on stationery from the *QE 2,* Shepard began by noting that he and Jones had just come back from their "first re-introduction to 'the work,'" and he was feeling "mean as a snake." Virtually every aspect of the meeting had pissed him off. For starters, he did not like "the movements," the sacred dances created by Gurdjieff as a form of physical meditation. To perform them, Shepard and Jones had had to journey into Central London to "buy some dumb ballet shoes at some fruity ballet store."

At the meeting, they had to move "like little wooden soldiers all in lines to some morbid piano music all in the same rhythm being dictated by some fat little tank of a woman in a long black dress." As if this were not bad enough, they were also "snubbed by all these stoney faced English twerps who're all taking themselves so seriously it's hard to imagine how they got out of bed in the morning."

For Shepard, the final straw was learning that he and Jones would have to attend a meeting in Bray, a picturesque village on the Thames about forty minutes from London by car "on the very day that they're running the Anglo-Irish challenge cup at White City—the four fastest greyhounds on the planet and I gotta miss it!" Despite all the problems the Work was causing him, Shepard added, "Still there's something that keeps me hanging on to all this like a drowning man. I know that without it I got no chance for anything in life."

Nearly two months later, Shepard wrote Dark another letter in which he described the Christmas reception he and Jones had attended at the house in Bray where his teacher, Basil Tilley, lived with his wife. Arranging all those in attendance in a half circle around him, Tilley talked about what it had been like for him to spend Christmas with Gurdjieff himself. "I felt like a little kid through all this," Shepard wrote. "At last I'd found a father. I felt protected and sheltered from the world outside, as though nothing mattered but this experience— this huge family with Mr. Tilley at its head. And behind him, in the shadows, I could almost feel Mr. Gurdjieff smiling on us from above." After Shepard and Jones left the house, she began to cry. As it now seemed almost miraculous that they had found themselves "under this kind of influence," Shepard wrote, "There's no way of thanking you for putting us in touch with this man but somehow I feel we're all very lucky to be in the world together at same time. Merry Christmas!"

A month later, Shepard and Jones were back in Bray for another gathering, at which Tilley played music Gurdjieff had composed,

much of it based on traditional chants and folk melodies he had collected during his extensive travels throughout the Middle East and
North Africa. "It was like a tidal wave taking me over," Shepard wrote.
"My heart started beating like a chicken being led to the slaughter. I
felt just like I used to when approaching a girl's door for a date in High
School. There was nothing I could do but sit there and take it as it
came. A flood of terror and ecstasy all at once. I didn't know whether
to run or come inside myself." Once it was over, he and Jones drove
back to their flat on Pilgrims Lane "with something quite different
than we brought with us."

ASIDE FROM THE PEOPLE he encountered while doing the Work,
Shepard's social circle in London consisted of those whom he had met
in, around, or through the Theatre Upstairs at the Royal Court. Most
of them were already avid admirers of his work. "I had read about
Sam's plays because the New York avant-garde was quite important in
the kind of theater circle I was in," Nicholas Wright says. "Back then,
one used to get these little published editions of plays by people like
Lanford Wilson and others, and Sam was the one I thought was obviously the most interesting."

When Wright opened the Theatre Upstairs at the Royal Court in
1969—a performance space he had helped create by removing the "low
and oppressive" ceiling to reveal an attic adorned with decorative iron-
work that gave the room real character—the third play he presented
there was Shepard's *La Turista*. Four years later, Wright asked Jim
Sharman, "a very, very, very brilliant" Australian director, to choose a
play to put on at the Theatre Upstairs. Having seen *The Tooth of Crime*
at the Open Space Theatre, Sharman met with Shepard to talk about
a film project they never got around to discussing. Instead, Shepard
suggested Sharman direct the London premiere of *The Unseen Hand*.

"I was very excited by the prospect of putting on *The Unseen Hand*,"
Wright says, "because the play called for this huge vintage American
automobile on the stage." Precisely how to get it there was a problem.
A relatively small space that could seat just sixty-five people, the Theatre Upstairs could be reached only by means of a winding staircase. "I

knew," Wright says, "it would be very theatrical if the audience came into this not-very-large room and found a huge car in it and then wondered, 'How the fuck did that get there?' I solved the problem by having the automobile cut up in the alley outside and then pulling it up with ropes through the window so we could weld it all together again."

When *The Unseen Hand* closed after the usual three-week run at the Theatre Upstairs, Wright paid Shepard about a hundred pounds (the equivalent of about fifteen hundred dollars today) to write a new play he also asked him to direct. "At the time," Wright says, "I had this theory that it was always interesting to see a play done the way the playwright thought it should be. I don't know if I particularly thought Sam would be a wonderful director, but I did know we would get a fantastically good cast because he was such an incredibly chic and at-tractive figure that actors would really want to be in a play directed by him."

Eight years earlier, Heathcote Williams's one-act play *The Local Stigmatic,* which is centered on the world of greyhound racing, had been performed during the Sunday night series at the Royal Court. In the play, Williams describes greyhound racing as "half an hour of boredom and agony for a few seconds' pleasure" and quotes Winston Churchill as calling the sport "animated roulette."

Despite their shared subject matter, Shepard's *Geography of a Horse Dreamer* differs radically in tone from *The Local Stigmatic.* Subtitled *A Mystery in Two Acts,* Shepard's play begins with "The Slump," in which Cody, who has been kidnapped from Wyoming because he can pick winning horses in his dreams, lies spread-eagle on a bed in a hotel room with his arms and legs handcuffed to the bedposts. Two gang-sters named Beaujo and Santee, who look and talk as though they are from the 1930s, keep a close watch on him.

Once able to generate "a quarter million bucks in a day," Cody's powers are now fading, and so Santee announces that their boss has ordered Cody to begin picking the winners of greyhound races. Going in and out of sleep, Cody ends the first act by speaking the name of the winning greyhound in the seventh race at Wimbledon.

Entitled "The Hump," the second act opens in a fancier hotel room, with all the characters wearing different clothes. Cody is now free to move about the room. Fingers, the Englishman who is Beaujo and Santee's boss, enters with the Doctor. Because picking greyhounds instead of horses has completely unhinged Cody, the Doctor is going to cut the "dreamer bone" out of his neck. As the Doctor is about to perform the surgery, Cody's two brothers, their cowboy clothes covered in dust because they have just come from Wyoming, burst into the room carrying twelve-gauge shotguns. After killing the Doctor and Santee, they lead Cody out of the room. The play ends with Fingers moaning on the floor to the sound of Clifton Chenier's "Zydeco sont pas salé."

And while even the most ardent admirer of Shepard's work might have been hard-pressed to realize this while watching the play, Ross Wetzsteon, the longtime theater critic for *The Village Voice,* who also chaired the Obie Award committee for many years, characterized *Geography of a Horse Dreamer* as a "work of art that ostensibly deals with another subject but which is actually an extended metaphor for the personal dilemma of the artist himself." And so the way Cody's dreams have been turned into money by those who so ruthlessly exploit him is meant to mirror Shepard's own experiences in both the film business and theater.

The cast for the production featured Stephen Rea, Bob Hoskins, and Kenneth Cranham, all of whom were, in Nicholas Wright's words, "already established actors and, in art theater terms, also really big and exciting names." Having already met Rea, Shepard had written the role of Cody for him. He then cast Hoskins as Beaujo. Kenneth Cranham, who had studied at RADA, the Royal Academy of Dramatic Art, and who had portrayed one of the bank robbers in the West End production of Joe Orton's *Loot,* played Santee. In Shepard's words, "They were so superb that it was bearing witness. I just sat there and watched these guys."

Cranham—who said that the reason Shepard had come to London was because "he was sort of resting up after being Patti Smith's boyfriend in New York and doing all that stuff"—described rehearsals for *Geography of a Horse Dreamer* by saying, "Sam came to work on the first day with a record player under his arm and played the three of us ... me, Bob Hoskins, and Stephen Rea, a track of the records he had brought. He played me 'Careless Love,' by Sidney Bechet, and I couldn't work it out. I thought, 'What does he mean by this?' But, of course, my character was a romantic, and he was longing for a life he did not have. It was the most brilliant way to direct me, because I will always remember someone's favorite song ... It's much more informative to me than the books they read or their favorite author."

The song Shepard played for Stephen Rea was by Hank Williams. "There was no messing about," Rea said. "Sam just let you do it. There was no directorial ego going." Once the work was done, Shepard, Rea, Hoskins, and Cranham would often spend their afternoons playing poker, a practice Cranham describes in a Royal Court Theatre history as "a way of sort of getting into the world of the characters and getting to know one another in a suitably villainous context." In Nicholas Wright's words, "And Sam absolutely also took all three actors to White City to see the greyhound races. I think what he was doing was just letting the charisma of his personality and his devil-may-care masculinity rub off on them. Not that they needed much rubbing off. I think for them it was just a very exciting thing to do."

Although Wright says he did "not know how much directing Sam actually did," because whenever he looked in on rehearsals, Shepard and the three actors were playing poker onstage, the actor whom Shepard cast as the Doctor, "because he looked like Sydney Greenstreet," turned out to be utterly unable to learn his lines. In Wright's words, "It made enormous demands on Sam to coach this elderly guy through a speech he showed no signs of ever getting to know. But Sam was incredibly patient with him. At that point, I thought, 'You really are taking this very seriously.'"

"What was extraordinary about Sam," Cranham said, "was the beauty he possessed. It was like working with a film star. And then he actually became a film star. And all the wives and girlfriends would come along, and they would all completely fall for him, he was so gorgeous. He looked great in a polo neck with his hair falling around his collar."

As Nicholas Wright puts it, "You had to experience him. He really was like the best-looking man you had ever seen in your life. People just fucking died because he was so fucking handsome. It was like Henry Fonda and Gary Cooper rolled into one walking into the room."

UNDER THE RULES AND regulations governing employment for those who had not been born in England or become citizens, Sam Shepard was able to earn a living in London only because Thelma Holt had gotten him a work permit. O-Lan Jones could not work at all. "I got a call from the casting director at the Royal Court Theatre because Sam was working there," says Nancy Meckler, "saying O-Lan was looking for workshops. I was doing a workshop one night a week at the Freehold, the experimental fringe theater company I was running, and she came to those workshops and I would give her a ride home. She kept talking about her husband being a writer and finally I said, 'Well, what's his name?' And she said, 'Sam Shepard.' And I couldn't believe it. Then she invited me in for tea, and that was when I finally really met him."

Born in New York and raised on Long Island, Meckler had attended Antioch College and New York University, where she studied with Richard Schechner. After coming to England in 1968 to study acting at LAMDA, she met and married David Aukin, a solicitor with a law degree from Oxford who went on to become a film and theatrical producer.

Eager to present a Shepard play at the Freehold, Meckler asked Jones if Shepard would grant her permission to do a workshop of *Icarus's Mother*. "O-Lan wanted to be in it," Meckler says, "but we had just done a very arduous physical workshop for three weeks with a Japanese mime artist and she felt exhausted. So I did it without her and Sam came to a couple of rehearsals and the performance and really loved it, and as a result, he gave me several premieres of his plays after that, which was fantastic."

It was through Nancy Meckler that Shepard had first met Stephen Rea, a member of the troupe who would later describe the Freehold as the most "vigorous of all companies" when it came to training actors and putting on performances. "Sam and O-Lan got to know all my Freehold people very well," Meckler says, "and actually got closer to some of my actors than I was." One of these was Dinah Stabb, who was then nearly seven months pregnant.

What all these associations led to was *Little Ocean*, the most distinctive play of Shepard's career. "He wrote it about three women," Stabb told a journalist for *The Independent*. "His wife, O-Lan, who'd had a baby; me, who was about to have a baby; and Caroline Hutchinson, who hadn't had a baby. Because I was seven months pregnant, I couldn't really do anything, and O-Lan couldn't really work in this country. One day, [Shepard] said, 'I'll write something for you.' So we all held our breath, crossed our fingers, and waited. It was extraordinary: It was written by a man, but it didn't feel like that."

Directed by Stephen Rea, who was Hutchinson's boyfriend at the time, *Little Ocean* was presented just once, on March 25, 1974, as a late-night show at the Hampstead Theatre, which was then being run by David Aukin, Nancy Meckler's husband. According to Shepard biographer Don Shewey, the play began with Jones tuning her guitar as Caroline Hutchinson blew smoke rings into the air while asking where the habit of handing out cigars when a baby was born had come from. This was followed, as recounted in Shewey's biography of Shepard, by "O-Lan's hymn to the masculinity of General Motors, Caroline's dream of a tadpole swimming through the little ocean of the womb, and Dinah's fantasy of the Garden of Eden (she wonders if Adam was a sissy and Eve had to get it on with a very sexy snake to start the human race). At the end, threatened in the park by stone-throwing hoodlums, the three women chase off their attackers with a soft-shoe and a song."

In an obituary for Sam Shepard that appeared in *The Guardian* after his friend's death, Stephen Rea wrote, "The play was about being pregnant and he wrote it for a need those women had: firstly a need to work and also to talk about something so essentially feminine. It was never published and when I asked him about it recently he said he didn't even have a copy; he wrote it for that moment and for those women, no one else, and in a way that's what he was all about."

ON JANUARY 25, 1974, SHEPARD wrote a letter to Johnny Dark in which he outlined the direction he wanted his life to take over the next decade. He began by expressing his frustration at having to "write these fucking letters all the time. I want some real live flesh and blood stuff. You know, us in the white Chevy cruising around, looking like detectives and talkin philosophical. Suddenly having a moment of thinking we're REALLY HERE IN THE FROZEN FOOD DEPARTMENT and then some creamy chick floats by making sure not to look like she's on the make."

Conceding that all this was just "food for fantasy," Shepard explained "the depths" of his dreaming by writing, after he and Dark had gone through the pros and cons of buying a house together in earlier letters, "We finally settle on this nifty little ranch somewhere on the outskirts of one of those suburbs. Not too far from all the newsstands and supermarkets yet just far enough so that we have a couple of acres or so."

Blessed with a visual imagination second to none, Shepard wrote, "Out in back through huge plate glass windows with the golden sunshine glaring in we get a view of a neat little corral. An Appaloosa mare with [a] foal is peacefully nibbling on some fresh alfalfa and whisking away a blue bottle [*sic*] fly with her tail. Off to the left is a long green paddock full of about six varieties of purebred hounds with puppies nipping at their heels."

Having painted a vivid picture of domestic tranquility in which Jones, her mother, and her sister are working on a jigsaw puzzle at the kitchen table while Shepard and Jones's son, Jesse, tries to learn how to play the guitar and Dark takes pictures of himself as he types and smokes a cigar, Shepard closed his letter by writing, "Yessir, we're on our way boy!"

SIXTEEN

MAGIC THEATRE

Sam Shepard is a lean and handsome man with
a lot of luck. He plays a fast, good, loud set of drums
and he writes plays that interest me very much.
A part of luck is energy and a part is genius
and part is quickness.

—MICHAEL MCCLURE,
INTRODUCTION, "*MAD DOG
BLUES*" *AND OTHER PLAYS*

IN THE FALL OF 1974, NINE MONTHS AFTER WRITING THAT
letter to Johnny Dark while living in a basement flat on Pilgrims Lane,
Shepard and his family arrived in Marin County, California. Asked
by a reporter why he had come to live there, Shepard said, "I came
out here because of my family and the weather, and because there's
very little theater being produced out here. New York and London are
polluted with theater, and everyone goes to the theater with ready-
made assumptions. Out here, there's a possibility of getting something
going."

In 1974, Marin County was still very much a world unto itself.
About a half-hour drive across the Golden Gate Bridge from San
Francisco, the small, sleepy towns of Mill Valley, San Anselmo, Corte
Madera, Larkspur, and Fairfax were where rock stars like Janis Joplin
and Van Morrison had lived and where various members of the Grateful Dead, Jerry Garcia and Bob Weir foremost among them, were still
in residence.

Shepard and his family began their time in Marin County by
moving into the tract house near Corte Madera where Johnny Dark,

Scarlett, and O-Lan's younger sister, Kristy, were then living. Shepard biographer Ellen Oumano quotes a friend who described the house as "the kind of place with paisley felt wallpaper in the bathroom." Shepard himself called the neighborhood "an area that looks like the outcome of a recent battle between opposing bands of landscape architects, having nothing to do with the original lay of the land." Although Shepard was now where he wanted to be, the house itself bore no resemblance whatsoever to the bucolic ranch he had envisioned. Because the problem was money, he went looking for a theater to present his work.

His first choice was the American Conservatory Theater, the acclaimed repertory company that had come to San Francisco in 1967. Faced by the challenge of having to fill two large downtown theaters on a regular basis, ACT was by 1974 presenting plays by Shakespeare, Ibsen, Edmond Rostand, Elmer Rice, and Tom Stoppard. Apparently unaware of the company's preference for mainstream drama, Shepard was not pleased by its response to plays he had written before leaving London. In his words, "They told me I could maybe do them in the ACT basement or whatever—you know, with no public audience invited. They were totally unenthusiastic. It's like they're asleep, lobotomized over there."

In his introduction to a collection of Shepard's early work, Michael McClure, the Beat poet and playwright who had been part of the historic Six Gallery reading in San Francisco in 1955, had written, "The plays are virile and crack like a whip and glitter like light in a snake's eye—they are also feral and viable, with part of themselves mysterious and still clinging to blackness while the actors move and sing in the light."

Dubbed "the prince of the San Francisco scene," McClure had read from the stage during the Human Be-In at Golden Gate Park in 1967. An actor and a musician, he co-wrote the song "Mercedes Benz" with Janis Joplin and served as a role model to Jim Morrison of the Doors. In 1966, *The Beard,* McClure's play about the sexually charged relationship between Hollywood bombshell Jean Harlow and Billy the Kid, the iconic American outlaw, was declared obscene in both Berkeley and San Francisco. Directed by Rip Torn, it went on to win two Obie Awards in New York City.

Not long after Shepard arrived in Marin County, McClure invited the playwright to his house in San Francisco so he could introduce him to John Lion. During the past five years, Lion had presented ten of McClure's plays, many of which Lion also directed, at the Magic Theatre, which he had founded. Thirty years old, Lion had graduated from the University of Chicago and then done his graduate work at UC Berkeley. In 1967, he staged his master of fine arts thesis production of *The Lesson* by Eugène Ionesco at the Steppenwolf Bar on San Pablo Avenue in Berkeley. An unexpected hit, the show ran for months and Lion decided to form his own theater company.

Painted on one of the outside walls of the bar—which was owned by the publisher of the *Berkeley Barb*, Max Scherr, to whom Lion was related—was a quote from the novel by Herman Hesse after which the bar had been named: MAGIC THEATRE—FOR MADMEN ONLY—PRICE OF ADMISSION—YOUR MIND. Lion then chose to make "Magic Theatre" the name of his new company.

Having presented *La Turista* for the first time on the West Coast in 1970 while also playing Kent, the leading male role, Lion knew when he first met Shepard at Michael McClure's house that it was more than a casual social engagement. As Shepard seemed to like "Lion's easygoing attitude," the three of them agreed to begin a collaborative relationship in which each man would bring his own projects to the theater. Over the course of the next ten years, McClure and Shepard would both serve as playwrights-in-residence at the Magic Theatre.

Because *The Tooth of Crime* had not yet been seen on the West Coast, Lion wanted it to be the first Shepard play he presented at the Magic. Establishing what became the pattern of their relationship, Shepard instead persuaded Lion to put on a double bill of *Action* and *Killer's Head,* a short one-act play he had written a few months earlier. He also insisted that he be allowed to direct the plays. Unwilling to get off on the wrong foot with the playwright, Lion acceded to both demands.

Action, a one-act drama with four characters, had first been produced at the Theatre Upstairs at the Royal Court in October 1974, with Nancy Meckler directing. Along with *Killer's Head,* it was then presented at the American Place Theatre in New York City in April 1975. What made the Magic Theatre production different was that when the double bill opened a month later in San Francisco, Shepard was actually there to see both plays performed onstage for the first time.

HEAVILY INFLUENCED BY SAMUEL BECKETT and Harold Pinter, *Action* is unlike any play Shepard had written before or would ever write again. Ironically entitled *Action* because of the conspicuous lack of it in the play, the work reads like a weird, post-apocalyptic episode of *Friends* in which two male and two female characters in their mid-thirties who are completely estranged from one another as well as the outside world sit around a table talking and drinking coffee before "celebrating" Christmas with a turkey dinner. While Shepard never specifies the nature of the cataclysmic event that has brought them together, he does strew copious hints throughout the play about the current dismal state of the world.

As one character notes, *Action* occurs in a place of "no sound, no time, just a cold space." When one of the female characters asks if anyone remembers "the days of mass entertainment," the answer given by the male character named Jeep is a brief and blunt "No." Jeep ends the play with a speech in which he describes how everything changed for him after he got arrested. "Everything disappeared. I had no idea what the world was. I had no idea how I got there or why or who did it. I had no references for this."

Asked what *Action* means, Nancy Meckler wrote in an email in 2019, "I remember Sam offering one thought as to what the play was about. 'Fear of time passing.' And I guessed that had to do with his struggle to find meaning in life when we are constantly aware of mortality. Once I took on the idea of the characters living in heightened terror and fear of time passing, everything fell into place. Any activity was an attempt to find focus or meaning or to feel anchored and safe. Hence, cooking a turkey, having a Christmas tree, hanging out the washing, filleting a fish."

As Clive Barnes, the *New York Times* drama critic, wrote, "The play is about time and action—or rather no time and inaction. Time has almost run out, has, in Aldous Huxley's phrase, almost had a stop. And the people are imprisoned in the cell of their own inability to act—they are modern Oblomovs, unable to muster the moral force needed for decision."

By the time Meckler's production of *Action* opened at the Theatre Upstairs at the Royal Court in October 1974, Shepard and his family had already left London for New York on one of the final voyages of the transatlantic ocean liner the SS *France*. Before continuing on to join Johnny Dark and Scarlett in Marin County, Shepard spent time at his summer house in Nova Scotia and began working on a three-act family play entitled *The Last American Gas Station*, which he would resurrect four years later as *Buried Child*.

Although Shepard never saw the London production of *Action*, Meckler did send him photographs of the show. Forty years later, a picture of Stephen Rea onstage beneath an overturned chair during that production was still hanging on a wall in Shepard's home in Santa Fe, New Mexico. Having forged both a close personal and professional relationship in London, Shepard and Meckler continued corresponding throughout this period. And so when Shepard wrote to tell her the Chelsea Theater Center in Brooklyn had passed on *Action* and that he was now giving the play to Wynn Handman to produce at the American Place Theatre, she wrote Handman a letter putting herself forward to direct it.

Although he readily accepted Meckler's offer, Handman's real concern was that he "couldn't imagine doing a play without the author being there." According to Handman, Shepard said, " 'Look, New York is a nightmare for me.' Plus, he didn't fly, and he's so creative—once he writes a play, it's out there. He doesn't sit on it like a hen on an egg." Because *Action* was "really short" and ran for only fifty-five minutes, Handman asked Shepard to write "something to go with it." As Meckler says, "Hence, *Killer's Head*, which is barely eight minutes long but very demanding."

On a slightly raised platform in the center of a bare stage, Mazon, a rodeo cowboy who in many ways is the initial incarnation of the character Eddie from *Fool for Love*, sits in an electric chair facing the audience. His hands, arms, legs, feet, and neck are bound to the chair with steel bands. In a T-shirt and jeans, he is barefoot and blindfolded. As the lights slowly rise on him, he begins speaking in "a clipped, southwestern rodeo accent."

Mazon says this is the day he will buy himself that blue pickup truck with the 350 horsepower V8 engine and an eight-foot bed so he can drive back and forth from Santa Rosa to get his mare bred by an Appaloosa stud. On and on Mazon goes about halter shows up north, yearling fillies, quarter mares, martingale tack, and the equine triathlon known as the Snaffle Bit Futurity.

Suddenly stopping, he sits in silence for a full minute. Then he starts talking about how he expects to get almost four hundred dollars off the list price of the truck. Once he puts some big magnesium wheels on it, he'll be able to pull a two-horse trailer all the way to Los Angeles. "Highway Five all the way. Right down through the center. Over the Grapevine. Bakersfield. Should pull that okay." Stopping again, he sits in silence. Taking a full minute, the lights on stage dim to black. Once they do, "the chair ignites with an electric charge that lights up Mazon's entire body. The electric charge is very short, just long enough to take in the illuminated body, then back to black."

Dismissed by Clive Barnes as "a sketch" and "a one-joke tragedy," *Killer's Head* remains of interest if only for what Shepard decided to leave out of it. Mazon never mentions what he has done to bring himself to this moment. Nor does he express any regret for it. Rather, he engages in a pure stream-of-consciousness monologue about pickup trucks and horses. *Killer's Head* is also now best remembered for the breakthrough performance given by the relatively unknown acting student whom Wynn Handman chose to play the role of Mazon.

"Wynn was also an acting teacher," Meckler says, "and so he brought in some of his students to read for the male roles in both plays. Because Wynn thought Richard Gere was special and was also sure he was going to be very big, I think he was the only student who read for *Killer's Head*." Twenty-five years old, Richard Tiffany Gere, whose mother and father were both Mayflower descendants, had previously appeared in a rock opera that closed after three performances on

Broadway, as an understudy in the original Broadway cast of *Grease*, and as Danny Zuko in the West End production of that musical.

Meckler cast Gere for the part because "he was reminiscent of Sam. Slim and good-looking but with no small talk and a bit distant. But mostly he was a good actor. Although he was very quiet and laid back, he was open to the exercises we did and worked very hard. He was also very grateful for the part." Shepard was not about to drive from California to New York City to participate in the production, Meckler says, so "one day we rang Sam so he and Richard could talk on the phone. I wanted Richard to hear Sam's voice and feel connected to him."

In his review of *Killer's Head*, Clive Barnes took note of Gere's "great virtuosity." As Gere later wrote about playing Mazon, "I had nothing to use. My body was strapped. It was all in my voice and my emotions. It certainly took me to another place as an actor. And it was very well-received, so it was a stepping-stone, and put me in a different place as an actor in New York."

ON MAY 2, 1975, ABOUT three weeks after the *Killer's Head/Action* double bill opened in New York at the American Place, Shepard's version made its West Coast debut at the Magic Theatre, then located at 1618 California Street in the Polk Gulch section of San Francisco. As she explained in her review, Berna Rauch, the drama critic for the *Berkeley Barb*, was not able to offer an opinion on *Killer's Head* because she had been outside the theater looking for a parking spot while it was being performed. However, she did follow up on her assignment by calling Shepard so they could discuss the deeper meaning of his plays over the phone.

Noting that Shepard sounded a lot like his work, Rauch wrote that the playwright was not particularly interested in being interviewed because "the communication is in the writing and directing of the play. I want to say it through that means." Insofar as *Action* was concerned, Shepard said, "The play was an experiment with space and language. I was hoping that something would be seen that never had been seen before."

Asked to be specific about the kind of theater that had inspired him to write, Shepard said, "Most of my inspiration comes from the race track. I learn more at the race track than from Shakespeare. It's a real situation where the audience has something at stake—namely their own money." He also made it clear that he now wanted to direct his own plays, because other directors tended to use his work to say what they wanted, and "after a while I get tired of that."

After *Killer's Head* and *Action* ended their five-week run of weekend performances on June 8, 1975, Shepard applied for his third Rockefeller grant. The first time he had done so was in 1966. Describing the playwright's personal and professional situation, one sentence in that earlier, official-looking, single-spaced grant document read, "At present, he is 'making ends meet' by serving as a waiter at the Cafe La Mama [*sic*], supplemented by the occasional earnings of his actress wife." Although Shepard and Joyce Aaron did occasionally earn money by serving patrons at Café La MaMa, they were not married in 1966. Still, having never been all that concerned with the line between reality and what he imagined, Shepard may have felt that having an actress wife who was also working to support him would increase his chances of being awarded a grant.

Based on the work Shepard had already done, the Rockefeller Foundation decided to "make available the sum of $5,500 to be used by Mr. Shepard approximately as follows: $4,800 toward basic living expenses over a twelve month period; up to $500 toward costs of local or international travel; and up to $250 toward purchase of tickets for productions." (In today's terms, these funds were equivalent to $39,000 for living expenses, $3,500 for travel, and $1,750 toward the purchase of tickets.) Still unwilling to fly, Shepard would not have had extensive travel expenses in 1966. Adamantly, he also refused to attend any plays but his own. And while he did accept these funds as part of his grant, he apparently used them for another purpose. Concerning the titles of Shepard's plays, biographer Don Shewey wrote that they were "a pleasure to recite. They also provide the key to Shepard's rock 'n' roll heart— the part that inspired him, when he got his first major Rockefeller grant . . . to spend the money on a Dodge Charger and a Stratocaster guitar."

In need of money again two years later, Shepard received a second grant from the Rockefeller Foundation, this one for $6,800 (the equivalent of nearly $44,000 today). The stated purpose of this grant was to enable him to keep writing while allowing him to visit drama centers in Europe, something he had never done.

Seven years after that, Shepard's priorities had changed significantly. In the letter requesting a third grant, which he submitted to the Rockefeller Foundation in 1975, he wrote that during the past twelve years:

> I feel like I've gone more than full circle in my search for the right environment and more importantly, the right director for my work. Sometimes in my search I have even gone so far as to allow a play to be totally dismantled and re-structured by a director and even to have sections of a play taken out of context and placed in a revue . . .
>
> Last year in London, I took the opportunity to direct my own work for the first time . . . By stepping into the role of director I was actually stepping into the experience of the play . . . That one experience was so strong for me that when I came to San Francisco and got in touch with John Lion I insisted I try it again with Action and Killer's Head . . . I'm convinced now that the only way to grow as a playwright is to become directly involved in the production of a play in this way.

In truth, Shepard had never worked with a director who had totally or even partially dismantled or restructured any of his work. In theater then as now, the playwright was the final authority on the text and no director would ever have dared alter significant portions of Shepard's work without first consulting him. The only section of one of his plays that had ever been "taken out of context and placed in a revue" was the scene from *The Rock Garden* that Jacques Levy had included in *Oh! Calcutta!*, thereby providing Shepard with a steady income for years.

By exaggerating how he had been treated during his theatrical career, Shepard was doing all he could in his grant application to be awarded monies that would allow him to write and direct his own plays. He concluded his essay by noting that his intention now was "to form a small company in conjunction with the Magic Theatre to explore ways and means to produce my own work."

Although he never followed through with this plan, the Rockefeller Foundation awarded Shepard a $15,000 grant (the equivalent of $72,000 now). The money enabled him to move his extended family from the tract house where they had all been living to the kind of idyllic ranch in Marin County he had envisioned while still living in London. It also enabled him to mount any production he liked at the Magic Theatre, thereby giving him complete control over the work he presented there. And while this arrangement curtailed John Lion's power at a company he had founded, the agreement proved in the end to be beneficial for both men.

Over the next decade, the Magic Theatre presented twelve new plays by Sam Shepard, three of which were collaborations with Joe Chaikin. Four of those plays, *Curse of the Starving Class; Buried Child*, which won the Pulitzer Prize for Drama in 1979; *True West;* and *Fool for Love*, served to establish Shepard's reputation.

In 1985, Shepard ended his association with John Lion and the Magic Theatre. As a result, *A Lie of the Mind*, which he directed, was presented at the Promenade Theatre, a large Off-Broadway venue in New York City. As *San Francisco Chronicle* drama critic Steven Winn wrote, "The break with Shepard was painful for Lion. And the Magic was never quite the same glamour address without its famous house playwright offering his new works there."

After spending twenty-three years at the Magic Theatre, Lion himself was forced out of the company by the board of directors in 1990. Returning to graduate school, he received a Ph.D. in drama from Stanford University and then became the director of the American College Drama Festival at the Kennedy Center in Washington, D.C. In 1999, at the age of fifty-five, he was about to assume his new position as chairman of the theater arts and dance department at California State University in Los Angeles when he died of a heart attack, leaving behind a wife and four children under the age of twelve.

In a letter to Johnny Dark dated March 28, 2000, Shepard wrote, "Oh, while we're reminiscing, I don't know if I told you that John Lion died very suddenly of a heart attack. He was about our age, I guess. I remember him as being someone like the Mr. Jones in the Dylan song. Nice enough guy but I always felt uneasy around him, like he wanted to get 'in' on something that in reality didn't even exist."

—

SEVENTEEN

ROLLING THUNDER

First thing he says to me, "We don't have to make
any connections." At first, I'm not sure if he's talking
about us personally or the movie. "None of this has
to connect. In fact, it's better if it doesn't connect."

—SAM SHEPARD,
*THE ROLLING THUNDER
LOGBOOK*

A S JOHNNY DARK DROVE SAM SHEPARD'S WHITE CHEVY NOVA
through downtown San Anselmo carrying a heavy load of roofing
paper and galvanized nails in late October 1975, he kept talking about
how Bob Dylan could never again be what he was back in the sixties.
Having landed a three-year lease on a twenty-acre property on Bay-
view Drive called the Flying Y Ranch, not far from the Panoramic
Highway and Muir Woods, Shepard was far more concerned about all
the work he and Dark still had to do before their families could move
into their new home next week.

To prepare the old and fairly stodgy-looking two-story house for
the winter rains, Shepard and Dark had already repaired the roof and
windows, painted the exterior, and installed wood-burning stoves.
They had also put up fencing for corrals where the Appaloosa mares
Shepard intended to buy could give birth to their foals.

Despite his concerns as he listened to Dark, Shepard's mind wandered back to when he had danced naked in an older woman's bedroom
to Dylan's "Like a Rolling Stone" in 1965. Doing his best to keep up his
end of the conversation, Shepard told Dark how it had blown his mind
when he first heard Dylan singing "Everybody Must Get Stoned," from

the jukebox in a restaurant on Christopher Street in Greenwich Village, because "I couldn't believe you could play that kinda stuff in public while you were eatin' your cheeseburger." Shifting gears while "talking to the windshield" as they headed down Paradise Drive toward their rented house in Corte Madera, Dark kept right on following his train of thought about how relatively brief the life expectancy of a star even of Bob Dylan's magnitude was until both men were back home again.

Inside the house, surrounded by cardboard boxes from Safeway packed with books and toys for the move, Shepard saw a note written on green paper lying on the kitchen table. Picking it up, he read it and stood there staring at it for a beat. Then he said, "Dylan called? . . . Dylan called here? Why would Dylan call? I don't even know him."

Making his way through the kitchen while repeating the message as though this would help him make sense of it, he finally noticed the Los Angeles area code at the bottom of the note. After returning the call, Shepard slowly began making his way through a web of Dylan functionaries whose job it was always to protect the artist from those he did not know. Finally, Shepard was allowed to speak to someone who began explaining what this was all about.

In short, "Bob," as the disembodied voice called Dylan, was about to go on a secret tour of the Northeast called the Rolling Thunder Revue. That "this chump" had the temerity to refer to Dylan by his first name immediately pissed Shepard off. Angrily, he demanded to know what any of this had to do with him. After being told that "Bob" was going to make a movie of the tour and that he had been looking for someone to write it, Shepard's attitude abruptly shifted. Now definitely interested, he asked about the exact nature of the project only to be informed that he would be "somehow providing dialogue on the spot for all the heavies." After the man at the other end of the line informed Shepard that this was "going to be a high-pressure situation," he added insult to injury by saying, "You're used to working under the pressure, right?"

After assuring the man that he did not scare easily, Shepard was asked when he could leave. Stalling for time so he could think about it, he said that he had not flown since 1963 and so would have to travel to New York City by train. Because the journey would take a week, which was when the tour was scheduled to begin, the man told Shepard that if he wanted the gig, he would have to leave the next day.

And while this was the version Shepard chose to tell in the opening pages of his *Rolling Thunder Logbook,* the way he actually came to find himself out on the road in America with Bob Dylan, Joan Baez, Allen Ginsberg, Ramblin' Jack Elliott, and Joni Mitchell, as well as a constantly changing cast of supporting characters, was not nearly so dramatic. However, it was far more complicated.

JACQUES LEVY AND SAM Shepard's personal and professional relationship dated back nearly a decade to when Levy had directed the debut of *Red Cross* at the Judson Poets' Theater in January 1966. A year later, he directed Joyce Aaron and Sam Waterston in the debut of *La Turista* at the American Place Theatre. Two years after that, he helped subsidize Shepard's playwriting career by including the closing monologue from *The Rock Garden* in *Oh! Calcutta!*

According to Claudia Carr Levy, an artist and art gallery owner who met Jacques Levy in 1975 and married him five years later, "Sam and Jacques were fast friends. They had hit it off together right from the start and were always pretty much on the same wavelength. Like Sam, Jacques had been traumatized by his father, and so they were also very simpatico."

Eight years older than Shepard, Jacques Levy grew up in the Yorktown section of Manhattan as the only child of an Alsatian Jewish family without much money. Levy attended Stuyvesant High School in Lower Manhattan and then graduated from the City College of New York. After receiving his master's degree and a doctorate in psychology from Michigan State University, he became a clinical psychologist at the Menninger Foundation in Topeka, Kansas.

Returning to New York City, Levy began working with Joe Chaikin and the Open Theatre. He directed plays by Shepard, Terrence McNally, Jack Gelber, Jean-Claude van Itallie, and Bruce Jay Friedman. A stocky man with a black beard and thick, shaggy black hair, Levy had always loved music but could not read musical notation or play an instrument. Nonetheless, he managed to inveigle his way into rock 'n' roll in 1969 by sending his girlfriend to the Fillmore East to tell Roger McGuinn of the Byrds that her boyfriend was writing a Broadway musical and wanted McGuinn to compose the score. Although the musical was never staged, Levy and McGuinn then co-wrote the Byrds' FM classic hits "Chestnut Mare" and "Lover of the Bayou."

Having already met Bob Dylan in California, Levy stepped out of his house on LaGuardia Place in Greenwich Village one night in July 1975 only to literally bump into him as the singer-songwriter made his way to the Other End, a nightclub where Levy also sometimes hung out. After having a drink together, they went back to Levy's apartment and co-wrote "Isis." Over the course of the next month in Dylan's house in the Hamptons, Levy collaborated with him on seven of the nine songs on the *Desire* album, among them "Hurricane," "Oh, Sister," "Sara," "Romance in Durango," and "Mozambique." Although Dylan regularly performed these songs on the Rolling Thunder Revue, the album itself was not released until after the tour was over.

As Levy told Shepard biographer Ellen Oumano, "Dylan and I wanted to do this tour and do all the new songs we'd written and have a traveling circus. Bob also wanted to shoot a film while that was going on, and find some way to make it work as a kind of *Children of Paradise*," Levy said, referring to the classic romantic film directed by Marcel Carné in France during the last years of World War II. "He didn't know anything about Sam, so I gave him a collection of his plays. He read them, and he didn't have a great response. He said to me, 'Do you think this guy is really the right guy?' And I said, 'I really do. I think the two of you would really have a good connection,' and we let it drop there."

On his own, Dylan then hired a film crew. In a conversation about who should write the movie, somebody on the crew brought up Shepard's name again. Dylan then called Levy and asked if they should contact Shepard. "I said, 'Yeah, we should,'" Levy said. "I knew Sam would come."

Although he was not part of the film crew, the odds-on favorite for who had put in yet another good word for Shepard was Rudy Wurlitzer, who had first introduced him to Robert Frank and then to the beauty of Nova Scotia. Obsessed with the legend of Billy the Kid, Dylan had shown up unannounced two years earlier at Wurlitzer's apartment on the Lower East Side to discuss playing a part in *Pat Garrett and Billy the Kid,* the film for which Wurlitzer had written the script Sam Peckinpah was about to direct. After Wurlitzer wrote Dylan into the movie as a minor character named Alias, the two flew to Durango, Mexico, where Dylan began writing the score. Wurlitzer was sitting next to Dylan on a flight to Mexico City when he decided to write a song for the death of the character played by Slim Pickens, which was to be filmed the next day. By the time the plane landed less than two hours later, Dylan had completed "Knockin' on Heaven's Door."

When asked why Shepard had dedicated *The Rolling Thunder Logbook* to "Rudy Wurlitzer—who helped me get over the first hump of this thing," Wurlitzer says, "I don't know. They never asked me to write that script, because I was too busy with other things, and so I probably got him the gig. But we all helped each other back then, and Sam was easy to help because he was so expansive in his way."

Confirming that Shepard's account of how he had been summoned to join the Rolling Thunder Revue was mostly fiction, Claudia Carr Levy says, "I was there when Jacques called Sam about coming on the tour. And I think Jacques really thought, 'What a fabulous opportunity for Sam.' And I know Sam thought he was going to be writing a big movie, because he told me that himself."

JUST AS HE HAD first done as a nineteen-year-old in 1962, when he went to visit his grandparents in Illinois, Sam Shepard was again crossing America on a train. Now, however, he was, in his words, "On the road to see the 'Wizard.'" After making his connection in Chicago, he journeyed on until his train finally reached Grand Central Station. Paralyzed by the realization that he was now actually back in New York City, Shepard stayed in his compartment until almost everyone else had left the train.

After being taken to meet Louie Kemp, the close friend whom Dylan had put in charge of the tour, Shepard found himself being escorted past multiple levels of security into the Studio Instrument

Rentals facility on Thirty-sixth Street off Tenth Avenue. There, he first came in contact with many of those who would also be on the tour, including Allen Ginsberg, who did not remember having met Shepard when he was working with Robert Frank on *Me and My Brother*, as well as Bobby Neuwirth, another of Dylan's longtime friends, who brought back for Shepard shared memories of nights during the sixties when they had both been part of the scene at Max's Kansas City.

All this was just a preamble to the evening's main event, the first meeting between Sam Shepard and Bob Dylan. Like a pair of large and powerful planets revolving in entirely separate solar systems, the two men had slowly been gravitating toward each other since they had first been in such close proximity at the Village Gate without ever knowing it.

After being led down a long, dark hallway, Shepard discovered Dylan lying across a metal folding chair in a dark back room with his ragged cowboy boots propped up on a metal desk. Insofar as Shepard could see, Dylan was "blue." He was "all blue from the eyes clear down through his clothes." For "about six minutes straight," as he stared at Dylan, Shepard saw only how he had looked on all the album covers that had been part of the decor in every funky apartment on the Lower East Side of Manhattan and in hippie crash pads all over America for more than a decade.

Right behind Dylan, Jacques Levy, whom Shepard identified in *The Rolling Thunder Logbook* simply as the co-author of "Hurricane," was on the phone with a record company lawyer. So that they would not all be sued for libel, the two were busily rewriting the lyrics for the Dylan song about Rubin Carter, the imprisoned former middleweight boxer, that would be released as a single in less than a week. Although this sudden development had everyone else on edge, Dylan seemed oblivious to it all.

After having made that gnomic comment about their not having to connect personally that made Shepard wonder if he meant in real life or in the scenes for the movie they were about to shoot, Dylan asked Shepard if he had ever seen *Children of Paradise* or *Shoot the Piano Player*. Having seen them both, Shepard asked Dylan if that was the kind of movie he wanted to make. "Something like that," Dylan said, before lapsing into a silence so deep and profound that Shepard could hear those words playing back to him over and over again in his head.

Doing his best to fill the void, Shepard mentioned a scene he and the film crew had already begun thinking about shooting with Ramblin' Jack Elliott in the bathroom of the Gramercy Hotel, where everyone on the tour was staying. His face lighting up, Dylan said that what he needed most now was to get out of the city. Once everyone was on the road, they would be able to really get into this film together.

THAT THE MERE MENTION of Ramblin' Jack Elliott's name would have caused Bob Dylan's mood to brighten should have come as no surprise to anyone on the Rolling Thunder tour, because in the world according to Bob Dylan, Jack Elliott was true royalty. He was the living, breathing connection to Dylan's great idol Woody Guthrie, who had inspired the former Robert Allen Zimmerman of Hibbing, Minnesota, to begin the journey that would lead to his being awarded the Nobel Prize for Literature in 2016.

As luck would have it, Shepard had run into Elliott in the lobby of the Gramercy Hotel just before his initial meeting with Dylan. Born Elliot Charles Adnopoz in Brooklyn, Ramblin' Jack Elliott—then forty-four years old with a headful of black curls peeking out from under his ever-present cowboy hat—still looked much as he had back in 1950 when he shared an apartment in Coney Island with Woody and Nora Guthrie and their four children.

Describing his initial meeting with Shepard, Ramblin' Jack—whose nickname refers not just to his incessant travels but also to his ability to spin fantastic and seemingly endless yarns at the drop of a hat—says, "I was walking into the hotel on my first day on the Rolling Thunder tour in my cowboy hat and cowboy boots when this guy I didn't know and who didn't know me came up and said, 'Wow! That hat and those boots make me homesick, man. Because that's all I wear when I'm home. See, I raise quarter horses, but here I am wearing my Ivy League clothes.'

"'Hang on, stranger,' I said. 'I'll be right back.' I then went up to my room and grabbed a beautiful, brand-new, slate-gray Dobbs cowboy hat I had brought with me along with one that was snow white. I went back downstairs and gave it to the guy and said, 'You can wear this one for the duration of the tour.' Which he then did.

"It was a little too small for him and so he gave it back to me and then I gave it to Joan Baez for her little boy, Gabriel. Three years later, I ran into them both at a Rolling Stones concert and he didn't know me from Adam. But when I said to him, 'So, do you still have that cowboy hat?' his eyes opened wide as the sky and he looked at me like maybe I was someone special."

Captivated by Elliott after watching him being filmed in his room at the Gramercy Park Hotel, Shepard headed for the elevator "wondering about cowboys. About the state of cowboys. About 'real life' and 'fantasy.' About making yourself up from everything that's ever touched you. From Pecos Bill to the Rolling Thunder Revue."

CHRIS O'DELL, TWENTY-EIGHT YEARS old, blond, thin, and attractive, was having breakfast with Dylan and Bobby Neuwirth in the coffee shop of the Gramercy Hotel when a "good-looking fresh-faced guy in a plaid checked jacket" who "looked like he was still in college" and "like a farm boy" walked over and sat down next to Dylan. Shutting everyone else out of their conversation, the two men began talking intently about a film. Although O'Dell had no idea who this guy was, what struck her right away was how Dylan treated him like an equal while also deferring to him about how things should be done on this film she still knew nothing about.

It was not until O'Dell was back out on the street that a member of Dylan's retinue told her the guy was Sam Shepard, a playwright who had been hired to write the film about the tour. Since she had never seen or even heard of his plays, his name meant nothing to O'Dell. What did matter was that he "was so damn cute."

By 1975, Chris O'Dell had already established herself as a member in good standing of the elite rock-'n'-roll touring support staff hierarchy. After beginning her career seven years earlier at Apple Records in London by working for Derek Taylor, the press officer for the Beatles (not to mention the Byrds, the Beach Boys, and the Mamas and the

Papas), O'Dell had become good friends with George Harrison and his wife, the former Pattie Boyd of "Layla" fame, who then married Eric Clapton.

In 1970, Leon Russell wrote the song "Pisces Apple Lady" for O'Dell and the two began an affair. Three years after that, George Harrison wrote "Miss O'Dell," the B-side of the single "Give Me Love (Give Me Peace on Earth)." In the summer of 1972, O'Dell had worked on the Rolling Stones' extensive and very profitable cocaine-fueled tour of America while carrying on an affair with Mick Jagger no one knew about until she chose to write about it in her memoir thirty-seven years later. During the lesser-known second half of the Rolling Thunder Revue in the spring of 1976, she was also romantically involved with Bob Dylan.

A seasoned veteran of life on the road, O'Dell had just come off an exhausting Santana tour of Europe on which the band played thirty shows in thirty-nine days. Officially listed as a tour manager on the Rolling Thunder Revue, she was tasked with solving the unforeseen problems that always occurred on the road while maintaining the positive attitude for which she was known.

On October 30 and 31—with the second gig falling on a Friday night that was also Halloween—the Rolling Thunder Revue began in the fifteen-hundred-seat Memorial Hall in Plymouth, Massachusetts. As Shepard wrote, Plymouth was "a donut of a town. The kind of place you aspire to get out of the second you discover you've had the misfortune to have been raised there." As O'Dell says, "It was actually in Plymouth that Sam started making himself known to me. He came up to me in the concert hall and he reminded me of a guy I would have gone to high school with. Clean cut, and his hair was kind of sloppy, and he was wearing a plaid shirt but was really naive looking. He seemed like the boy next door, very American, and with something straight about him, too."

One night after the show was over, everyone went to the replica of a seventeenth-century Pilgrim village that was just outside town to shoot a scene for the movie, only to discover it could not be lit because there was no electricity. "We were all walking through the village," O'Dell says, "and Sam was following me, and I thought, 'I think this guy is coming on to me.' But that happens on tours, and so it wasn't all that unusual. He kept coming on to me, but I was sort of staying away from that a little."

When they did finally spend the night together, "It was pretty surprising because once we started talking, he told me a lot about his childhood and how he had grown up on a ranch. He presented himself like a cowboy. He also told me he was married and had a son. He wasn't hiding that part of it. But, then, a guy who sleeps with you when he already has somebody else never tells you the truth. There are always problems."

Five days into the tour, Shepard's biggest problem had nothing to do with his marital status. Having once believed that "the only place to write was on a train," he had already put the time he had spent traveling cross-country to good use by starting work on the movie he thought Bob Dylan had hired him to write. By the time he arrived in New York City, he had written what Jacques Levy said were "two scenes for some movie that he had in his head, which he thought Bob would want to do. It was a total misperception. They tried a little bit of work on the two scenes he'd brought—I wasn't involved . . . and none of it worked out."

On November 5, 1975, his thirty-second birthday, Shepard found himself sitting in front of three cakes, a giant pen, a studded sex frog, and other assorted goodies in the Red Lion Inn in Stockbridge, Massachusetts. In Springfield, Massachusetts, the next night, he told O'Dell he had no idea what he was doing on the tour. Although Dylan had brought him on to write the script, everything about the film project was so disorganized and chaotic that Shepard confessed he had no idea how to relate to "this rock-and-roll lifestyle."

Opening himself up to O'Dell, he explained that because nobody ever showed up to film scenes when they were supposed to, they now wanted him to "write the dialogue after it happens."

Remembering a conversation they had shared a few days earlier, she told him, "But, Sam, you told me you wanted to be a rock-and-roll star."

"Yeah," he replied, "but I just wanted to play music. I didn't want to do *this*."

In *The Rolling Thunder Logbook*, Shepard describes this moment on the tour as "where the film experiment" began "to get interesting. We've abandoned the idea of developing a polished screenplay or even a scenario-type shooting script," as it had become obvious that the musicians, T Bone Burnett, Roger McGuinn, and David Bowie's lead guitarist Mick Ronson among them, were not about "to be knocking themselves out memorizing lines in their spare time." Because they were all either "rehearsing all night playing a concert, or jamming, and then crashing out at six or seven in the morning," it was almost impossible to "even get two or more of them together at the same time in front of the camera." And so Shepard and the film crew had now "veered into the idea of improvised scenes around loose situations."

Despite Shepard's travails insofar as the film was concerned, he and O'Dell were getting on well. As she says, "He was just sweet and gentle and romantic in his own weird way. The way it felt to me was that he was looking for a girlfriend." O'Dell also saw "another side of him that was pretty weird. When we first started seeing one another, we were pretty quiet about it, but people began finding out all the same. We went to a gig one night and when we came back to the hotel, they had put all my stuff in his room and all his stuff in my room. That really pissed him off, and I had never seen him so angry.

"They always did these kinds of things on tour as a joke, but it also meant people knew what was going on between us and Sam did not like people fucking with him. That really pissed him off. Why, I don't know, but it was like his space and his stuff and nobody else should have been there."

Having repeatedly stated that his real goal in life had always been to become a rock-'n'-roll star, Shepard simply could not tolerate the day-to-day madness of life on the road. "Sam hated it," O'Dell says. "He hated everything about it. He hated the moving from place to place. He hated that he had to be at a certain place at a certain time, all of that. He was upset and he wanted to leave the tour, because the whole film thing was just kind of a mess."

On a tour where the pretension had reached brand-new levels after just a few days of working on the film, Louie Kemp called Shepard into "a secret meeting" about what was now needed "to get this film off the ground." Kemp's idea was to bring in either Francis Ford Coppola or Orson Welles to take over the project. As Kemp told Shepard, "We're after heavyweights, you understand."

As always, copious amounts of alcohol helped to sustain the madness. As Ramblin' Jack Elliott later said, everyone on the Rolling Thunder Revue was pretty much drunk all the time for thirty-one straight days. There was also so much cocaine available on the tour that Joni Mitchell, who had never done the drug before joining the Rolling Thunder Revue, asked to be paid in the substance rather than money.

Acknowledging the ubiquitous presence of the drug, Allen Ginsberg wrote a four-line poem in which he noted that nobody was going to save America by snorting cocaine, but "when it snows in your nose, you catch cold in your brain."

ON NOVEMBER 13, 1975, JONI Mitchell had flown in from Los Angeles to join the Rolling Thunder Revue in New Haven, Connecticut. After recording six critically acclaimed albums over the past seven years, she was at the height of her career. A groundbreaking artist whose music would only grow in stature over the next five decades, Mitchell was also, much like Bob Dylan, a once-in-a-generation talent.

Despite his relationship with Chris O'Dell, none of Joni Mitchell's charm was lost on Shepard. In Niagara Falls just two days after Mitchell joined the tour, O'Dell looked everywhere for Shepard after the show but could not find him. At breakfast the next morning, she heard someone say that Shepard had been seen hanging out with Mitchell the night before. When O'Dell saw him later that morning, she ignored him while also noting that he looked guilty. When he did not appear in the hospitality room where he would usually meet her after the show, she decided to take matters into her own hands by knocking on his hotel room door.

After identifying herself, O'Dell waited until Shepard finally came to open the door. In a scene that would not have been out of place on a sitcom, Shepard returned to his bed, laced his hands behind his head, and looked at O'Dell with "a sweet little smile." When she asked him why he had not come down to the hospitality room, he said he was tired and so had "just been lying around here."

It was then that O'Dell, who by then had entered his room and was sitting with her back to the door, heard the door open and close. The very picture of innocence, Shepard said, "Oh, what was that?"

Knowing that Joni Mitchell had been hiding in the bathroom all the while and had just sneaked out of the room, O'Dell said, "Sam, who was that?"

"No one," he answered.

"You know what?" O'Dell told him. "You're a shit." And then she went out the door as well.

The next day, as O'Dell was sitting on the bus waiting for it to depart for Worcester, Massachusetts, Bobby Neuwirth came up the steps and stopped right in front of her. In what he most likely intended as a note of caution, he told her, "You know Sam's having it on with Joni. You need to take care of yourself." Unfortunately, he said this in a voice loud enough for everyone to hear. Not knowing how she might react, various members of Dylan's backup band stared at her before moving on to their seats.

Wondering what could be worse than a guy who had cheated on his wife with her and then turned around and cheated on her, O'Dell decided the tour did not need this kind of drama and neither did she. Not about to screw up her job for some guy and knowing she could never compete with Mitchell, O'Dell decided to "withdraw from the competition" and let the singer-songwriter have him. However, despite her decision to carry on as though nothing had happened, "It hurt like hell."

UNLIKE ALMOST EVERYONE ON the Rolling Thunder Revue, Larry Sloman knew Sam Shepard was an Obie Award–winning playwright. Sloman, who had a master's degree in deviance and criminology from the University of Wisconsin, had begun his time on the tour reporting for *Rolling Stone*. Dropping that assignment because "all they wanted to know was how much money Dylan was making from this tour— which, to me, was a great cultural event," he began an epic struggle to be allowed to remain on the Rolling Thunder Revue so he could write a book about it.

Nicknamed "Ratso" by Joan Baez because she thought he looked like Ratso Rizzo, the character portrayed by Dustin Hoffman in *Midnight Cowboy,* Sloman first met Shepard in the lobby of the Red Lion Inn in Stockbridge immediately after two burly security guards charged with keeping Sloman away from the principals on the tour had unceremoniously dumped him onto a couch. In Sloman's words, "Sam was standing by the front desk and I started complaining and he started complaining to me." On the occasion of his thirty-second birthday, Shepard told Sloman, "I'm pissed off. I've been lied to . . . I'm ready to quit, go home. They made some assurances to me in terms of money that they didn't follow through on."

As Sloman says, "Sam was a malcontent for the entire tour. He had all those Obies and a name and an ego and then he came on this tour and got slapped around by Dylan, who basically threw out everything Sam had written and said, 'Let's just make it all up.' There was no script for that movie. They were just flying by the seat of their pants and had no idea what they were doing."

The yawning gap in sensibility between Sloman, who later described himself as being "clinically manic, out of my mind, and totally rock-and-roll" on the tour, and Shepard was best illustrated by their wildly varying accounts of the night of November 21, 1975, when they set off together between shows in Boston on an expedition to the Combat Zone. In *On the Road with Bob Dylan,* his behind-the-scenes account of the Rolling Thunder tour, Sloman devotes a single sentence to his taking Shepard, "the Western greenhorn," through the notorious and incredibly seedy section of Boston that, on any given night, could make Times Square seem tame by comparison.

In *The Rolling Thunder Logbook,* Shepard devotes an entire chapter to a jaunt that began with him feeling stoned on Lomotil, "an opium derivative designed to counteract the 'trots'" whose many "unforeseen side benefits" included "elongated color perception, high pain tolerance, a certain sense of predetermination in all muscular activity, and a wonderful warm glow in the frontal lobe."

As Sloman says, "I don't know how much of what Sam wrote about the tour was exaggerated, but I've been to Mexico a lot and taken Lo-motil and it doesn't give you hallucinations. All it does is make you constipated." He also wonders, "Was this Sam's version of gonzo jour-nalism? Because the whole notion of Lomotil being a psychedelic is very much like something Hunter Thompson would have written."

Leading Shepard into a brightly lit sex shop, Sloman gleefully set about trying to find the perfectly inappropriate present for Dylan. In *The Rolling Thunder Logbook*, Shepard writes that the entire place then began "doing cartwheels off" his brain cells as his body headed toward the door while his head was "on the ceiling somewhere." All the while, Sloman was still trying to select a gift for Dylan from a variety of sex toys, boxes of dildos, "motorized cocks, and religious figures with erect members." At long last, he decided to buy a "toy monk whose joint springs out between his habit when you squeeze him."

As Sloman told Shepard biographer Ellen Oumano, "I couldn't get past Sam. On one hand he's got that macho cowboy exterior, on the other he's got that suburban bourgeois mentality. It's a weird contra-diction. Here's this shitkicker walking through the Combat Zone holding his nose and saying, 'Look at these prostitutes, look at these sex shops, look at these weird people.' I felt like I was with William Buckley."

Despite how odd everything had already been, the evening became yet even weirder when Shepard and Sloman went backstage to see the Tubes perform in support of their debut album, *White Punks on Dope*. As Shepard wrote, his reason for attending the show was to see Jane, "a friend from San Francisco." In a vain attempt to talk his way past security, he told the guard at the door that the friend's name was also "Lila the Snake [*sic*]." A well-known figure in the San Francisco rock scene, Jane Dornacker had been the lead singer and songwriter for Leila and the Snakes. After joining the Tubes as a backup singer and dancer, she co-wrote the song "Don't Touch Me There." Also an ac-tress, Dornacker would appear in Shepard's *Inacoma* at the Magic The-atre and then with him in *The Right Stuff*.

Seeing Dornacker coming offstage "completely naked save for a couple of buttons and some panty hose," Shepard called out to her. Followed by "four other equally naked girls," she led him and Sloman up to a dressing room, where "long lines of snow" were "being inhaled across a record jacket."

Having already slagged off Prairie Prince, the drummer of the Tubes, for "slashing away at his kit as though he was caught in his own mosquito netting," Shepard could only wonder, "What are all these kids doing watching this shit when they could be hearing good music?" Expanding on this theme, he thought it was because they wanted "to see some action" and "brains dripping from the ceiling. Is that the generation stuff that you hear about all the time? . . . Am I part of the old folks now? Is Dylan? Could it be that like Frank Sinatra and Bing Crosby, Dylan himself was now actually not known in certain circles?"

The thirty-two-year-old playwright's concern about how the music of his generation was being perceived by those a decade younger was matched by his sense of dislocation on the Rolling Thunder Revue. Although bassist Rick Danko of the Band and guitarist Sandy Bull joined the tour three days later in Hartford, Connecticut, Shepard could now no longer even make himself go out front to watch the show. He was so utterly frustrated by the lack of progress on the movie that he felt like he had become "a backstage parasite."

And while Sloman would remember the Rolling Thunder tour as "the greatest thing in the world" and "still the highlight of my life," Shepard felt as though he was "cracking up behind" it while also being transported back to "the mid-sixties when crystal meth was a three-square diet with 'yellow jackets' and 'black beauties' for chasers."

Completely losing it in print, Shepard wrote, "I DON'T WANT TO GET BACK TO THE SIXTIES! THE SIXTIES SUCKED DOGS! THE SIXTIES NEVER HAPPENED!" Three days later, in Bangor, Maine, he got into a rental car and left the Rolling Thunder tour by driving to New York City.

WITH THE TOUR SCHEDULED to cross the border into Canada the next morning for shows in Quebec City, Toronto, and Montreal, Chris O'Dell visited Joni Mitchell in her dressing room so she could give her an itinerary and describe the tour's upcoming travel plans.

Asking O'Dell to sit down, Mitchell said, "You know, I really admire the way you're handling this thing. You just seem so confident and able to deal with this. I really respect that. I wish I could do the same." Bowled over by this, O'Dell responded by saying how much she appreciated what Mitchell had just said. As O'Dell later wrote, both of them also knew that because Shepard had a wife waiting for him at home, it was only a matter of time before he cheated on Mitchell as well.

When the Rolling Thunder Revue took the stage in a ten-thousand-seat hockey arena in Quebec City two nights later, Mitchell had already set her feelings about Shepard to music. Having written only the first two verses of a song to which she continued adding lyrics during the final week of the tour, Mitchell performed "Coyote" in public for the first time.

The brilliance of the song begins with the opening line, in which Mitchell directly addresses Shepard as a "coyote," the animal he used to describe his character in *Cowboy Mouth* and with which he also identified in *Back Bog Beast Bait.* In her lyrical account of what seems to have been a great rock-'n'-roll romance, Mitchell identifies herself as a hitchhiker who realizes she is just a prisoner of the white lines on the freeway (as well as the fine white lines of cocaine) that have now become the metaphor for her life.

The real nature of their relationship was something else again. As Chris O'Dell says, "Sam made it plain to me that after they had been together for a night or two, Joni wanted him to go back to where she lived and move in with her, because she was in love with him, but he said no. Sam pretty much told me, 'Look, she was driving me crazy.'" More than forty years after the Rolling Thunder tour ended, Mitchell dismissed the time she and Shepard spent together as "a flirtation" that ended when "he got scared of me," while adding that, "on coke, I found him very attractive."

Nonetheless, in a handwritten note she sent Shepard in February 1983, Mitchell wrote that she had just read about his new play, *Fool for Love,* but could not find it anywhere and so wondered if it had yet been published. Having started painting again, she also sent him a sample of her work. Closing her note, she wrote that she was about to go off on a world tour. Urging Shepard to keep up the good work, she ended the message with love and her first name.

AFTER THE TOUR ENDED and Chris O'Dell returned to Los Angeles, Shepard continued calling her and trying "to have conversations with me. He even hung up on me once because his wife had walked into the room." He then came to visit her in Los Angeles with Johnny Dark, who, he told her, was "his best friend." After learning that O'Dell and her boyfriend were staying at the Chateau Marmont, Shepard checked in there with Dark.

Eight months later, on August 5, 1976, O'Dell was at a Roger McGuinn concert at the Roxy Theatre on the Sunset Strip in Los Angeles when Shepard and Johnny Dark suddenly appeared. In O'Dell's words, "Sam started coming on to me and wanted me to leave with him. And I said, 'No, I'm not going with you. I'm with someone now, and I'm going to stay with him.'" Despite her efforts to elude Shepard, he and Dark followed O'Dell up to McGuinn's dressing room after the show. "Sam was hurt and angry at me and so there was a big scene there because I wouldn't go with him."

Although this was the last time O'Dell ever saw Shepard, she did receive a letter some weeks later from Dark in which he "asked how I was doing and said Sam was wondering how I was. Of course, Sam had Johnny write me that letter. I never for a minute thought it was just Johnny's idea."

ON DECEMBER 8, 1975, THE Rolling Thunder tour ended with a sold-out benefit concert for Rubin "Hurricane" Carter before fourteen thousand people in Madison Square Garden. Joining the pantheon of stars who had performed thirty shows over the past forty days were Muhammad Ali, Coretta Scott King, Robbie Robertson, and Roberta Flack. The dramatic nature of the final concert notwithstanding, Shepard himself had other things on his mind. In four days, *Geography of a Horse Dreamer,* a play no one in New York City had seen, was set to open at the Manhattan Theatre Club, a ninety-seat venue then located on East Seventy-third Street between First and Second avenues.

Adding to the pressure of having every major newspaper critic in the city review Shepard's play, Bob Dylan and his wife, Sara, had told Shepard they wanted to see the show. He then invited them to the first performance only to learn that it would also be a preview for the press. As he writes in *The Rolling Thunder Logbook,* "Great, an audience full of critics and Bob Dylan. Couldn't be worse."

Despite his multiple responsibilities on the tour, Jacques Levy had chosen to leave it so he could spend two weeks directing rehearsals for *Geography of a Horse Dreamer,* which Shepard also attended. On the play's opening night, Levy was also willing to hold the curtain until Dylan, whom Shepard later described as being "plastered," finally arrived with Sara, Bobby Neuwirth, Louie Kemp, and another of his people in tow.

From his place at the back of the theater, Shepard knew his play was dying on its feet by the deafening sound of silence in the house. As he stood there "cringing in the dark," he could only ask himself why, of all his plays, Dylan had chosen to come to this one rather than those with music or dialogue that would have made the audience laugh.

Unable to take any more, Shepard headed out a back door and was about to leave the theater when Levy came toward him. Offering him the joint in his hand, the director said, "Here's something for the pain, Sam." Availing himself of the offer, Shepard took a heavy hit and then realized that he had no choice but to steel himself for the agony of watching what he had written in private be transformed into a public event in the most painful way imaginable.

Stoned out of his mind, he made a beeline for the bar during the act break only to quickly turn around and head back up the stairs when he saw the size of the crowd there. As bad as it had all been for him until now, Shepard took comfort in thinking Dylan had walked out on the show and so would not be around for the second act.

Without warning, Dylan then suddenly emerged from the men's room. Stuffing a bottle of brandy into his pocket, he began fumbling with the notes he had scribbled during the first act. Spying Shepard, Dylan asked him how the play ended. He also wondered why one of the greyhounds in the play was named "Sara D.," having taken this as a reference to his wife.

Less than halfway into the second act, Shepard saw that two of the most important newspaper critics in the city were now fast asleep. At the point in the play when Cody was about to be injected with a syringe so his "dreamer bone" could be removed, Dylan suddenly jumped to his feet and shouted, "Wait a minute! . . . Wait a second! Why's he get the shot? He shouldn't get the shot! The other guy should get it! Give it to the other guy!"

As Louie Kemp began hauling Dylan back into his seat and Neuwirth told him over and over to shut up, the critics down front suddenly came back to life. When Cody's two cowboy brothers entered the scene, Dylan leaped to his feet again and shouted, "I DON'T HAVE TO WATCH THIS! I DIDN'T COME HERE TO WATCH THIS!" Fighting to escape Kemp's "hammer-lock grip" as Neuwirth and others tried pulling him back down again, Bob Dylan simply would not be denied. All the while, he kept insisting, "HE'S NOT SUPPOSED TO GET THE SHOT! THE OTHER GUY'S SUPPOSED TO GET IT!" As soon as the play ended, Dylan was out the door and gone.

Loyal to both Dylan and Shepard, Jacques Levy explained to Shepard biographer Ellen Oumano that Dylan had not been at all "rowdy" that night. He also described Shepard as "amused" by Dylan's reaction, because "he was really in the play." Levy added that he "wished more people in the audience were doing that."

TWO YEARS AFTER THE Rolling Thunder Revue ended, Shepard and Jacques Levy were working together again on a project entitled *Jackson's Dance,* based on the life of the abstract expressionist painter Jackson Pollock. Shepard had written the play in London in 1972, intending to have Murray Mednick direct it at Theatre Genesis. When that production failed to materialize, he gave the material to Levy, who then wrote most of the lyrics for songs composed by a husband-and-wife team of folksingers.

In a space at the Public Theater provided by Joe Papp, Levy began staging the play. Although Papp and Levy did not get along, Papp presented a workshop performance of *Jackson's Dance* that Shepard did not attend. Only then did Lee Krasner, Pollock's widow and a well-known abstract expressionist painter in her own right, finally read the play. As Claudia Carr Levy says, "Lee Krasner had given her okay as well as the rights to do the play. She adored Jacques, but after reading the play, she said, 'You'll do this over my dead body. I don't want anything more to contribute to the myth of Jackson Pollock.' She killed it, and that seemed to be the end between Sam and Jacques."

And while the two men may never have seen each other again after the Rolling Thunder tour ended, Levy—who served as assistant director of *Renaldo and Clara,* the three-hour-and-fifty-minute impenetrable farrago of a film that incorporated footage shot on the tour with a story not worth following—told biographer Ellen Oumano that he may have been "responsible for Sam's film career as an actor" because of scenes in which Shepard "looked so wonderful and had this mysterious, cool character going and that boyish smile."

Whether Shepard was ever aware of this, no one can say for certain. Nonetheless, as Claudia Carr Levy says, "Jacques had been so important to Sam in his career and as a friend as well, and then, it was like Sam just disappeared. And Jacques said, 'Well, that happens. Sometimes when you're on your way up and you finally get to the top, you don't want to remember how you got there.' And, excuse my French, but I used to say, 'That fucking Sam is around the corner, and he doesn't connect with you? I can't believe it.' And he would say, 'That's just Sam.' And he didn't let it be a thing for him."

DESPITE CUTTING OFF ALL ties with the man who had brought them together, Shepard continued his relationship with Bob Dylan. In October 1984, he met with Dylan in his Malibu home to work on a song entitled "New Danville Girl" that Dylan had already recorded but did not choose to include on his *Empire Burlesque* album. In the spring of 1985, Shepard and Dylan spent two more days together transforming "New Danville Girl," which had been inspired in part by Woody Guthrie's "Danville Girl," into the eleven-minute song "Brownsville

Girl," the standout track on Dylan's critically panned 1986 album, *Knocked Out Loaded.*

Impressed by how Dylan kept coming up with new verses even as he was recording the song, Shepard wrote an eight-page treatment for a film based upon it. When that did not materialize, he suggested turning the song into a ninety-minute opera. Although neither project was ever realized, the noted rock critic Robert Christgau praised the song as "one of the greatest and most ridiculous of Dylan's great ridiculous epics."

In Shepard's words, Dylan was "a lot of fun to work with, because he's so off the wall sometimes. We'd come up with a line, and I'd think that we were heading down one trail over here, and then suddenly he'd just throw in this other line, and we'd wind up following it off in some different direction. Sometimes it's frustrating to do that when you're trying to make a wholeness out of something, but it turned out OK."

In the summer of 1986, Shepard flew to Los Angeles to conduct an interview with Bob Dylan in his Malibu home. In July 1987, *Esquire* magazine published "True Dylan" (a nod to Shepard's *True West*) with the subtitle "A one-act play, as it really happened one afternoon in California." Shepard biographer John J. Winters, who listened to the interview tapes, wrote that throughout the session, "a petulant Dylan" continued "noodling ceaselessly on an acoustic guitar" as Shepard tried "time and again to break through and engage him." Noting Shepard's "nervous laughter and jittery prompts," Winters characterized their encounter as "a little brother trying to get the attention of an older brother."

Beginning with Shepard's stage directions, "True Dylan" does read like a play. Dylan begins what becomes an extended meditation on fame and death in American popular culture by noting he had just passed through the spot on the highway outside Paso Robles, California, where James Dean died in his Porsche in September 1955. As they continue talking about Dean, Elvis Presley, Ricky Nelson, and Hank Williams, Shepard breaks up the interview with a series of phone calls Dylan never made.

Near the end of their conversation, Shepard gets Dylan talking about his legendary 1966 motorcycle accident in Woodstock, New

York. As he was recovering from his injuries after spending a week in the hospital, the singer-songwriter had "started thinkin' about the short life of trouble. How short life is. I'd just lay there listenin' to birds chirping. Kids playing in the neighbor's yard or rain falling by the window. I realized how much I'd missed. Then I'd hear the fire engine roar, and I could feel the steady thrust of death that had been constantly looking over its shoulder at me. (pause) Then I'd just go back to sleep."

EIGHTEEN

DAYS OF HEAVEN

I remember thinking—"The movies! I can make
lots of money and I won't have to ever again apply
for a Guggenheim grant or a Rockefeller grant or a
National Endowment grant or write a play for Joe
Papp to get a crumby five thousand so I can pay the
fucking rent to some whacked out landlord."

—SAM SHEPARD,
TWO PROSPECTORS

HAVING JUST SPENT TWO PHYSICALLY AND EMOTIONALLY
exhausting months on the road on a rock-'n'-roll tour, Shepard returned for the first time to the ranch he had only been able to dream
about while in London. Once there, he settled quickly into his new life
as the center of an extended family, all of whose members depended
on him for both financial and emotional support. He also began
spending much of his free time with Johnny Dark. A de facto brother
to the playwright, Dark was now constantly by Shepard's side, serving
happily as his faithful companion and comrade-in-arms. As he had
not done during his time in London, Shepard was now drinking again
and also smoking pot on a regular basis.

Under the influence, Shepard and Dark, both fervent admirers of
Jack Kerouac's *On the Road,* transformed themselves into their own
version of Sal Paradise and Dean Moriarty. Because neither man was
working, they were both able, as Dark said in a documentary entitled
Shepard & Dark, "to get stoned and talk and make stuff up all day
long."

Thirty-five years later, Dark would write Shepard a letter in which he recalled the good old days when, as the only members of "the Garcia y Vega club," they would lock Shepard's seven-year-old son, Jesse, out of the basement room where the two of them got high together, smoked cigars, and talked about women. When the boy would begin banging loudly on the door asking if he could join them as well as what they were doing in there, Shepard would tell him it was none of his business and that he should go away. Dark, who in time would become Jesse Shepard's caretaker and surrogate parent, would explain that they were wrapping presents. Shepard would then end the conversation by informing his son that if he wanted to get one of them, he would stop banging on the door.

Then there was the day when a friend who had just returned from Mexico brought Shepard and Dark a bottle of mescal. Because the powerful alcoholic beverage distilled from the agave plant was not yet widely distributed in America, the bottle contained the traditional red worm (*gusano rojo*, in Spanish) that some consumers, after partaking of the liquor, would eat in the mistaken belief that it had hallucinogenic properties. After spending the better part of the day getting high while also polishing off the mescal, Shepard and Dark became fixated on their need to obtain a copy of *The Dog of the South*, the novel Charles Portis wrote after achieving both literary acclaim and great commercial success with *True Grit*.

As acquiring the book became what Dark described as "a matter of life & death," both men hopped into Shepard's white Chevy Nova and drove at top speed to the library in San Rafael only to discover that it was about to close for the day. In Dark's words, they both began "begging & pleading with the librarian how desperate our situation was—how far we'd traveled to get there—how we needed to have that book as though it was our last drink of water."

Although they had driven only twelve miles to get there, the librarian was swayed by their pleading and let them go inside to find the book they could not live without. Afterward, Dark wrote, "As I remember, neither one of us managed to read more than five pages of the damn thing, & we were on to the next mad caper—stealing bathrobes or something like that. Those were indeed rare & cherished days full of a wild sense of being alive but not having a clue why or what or how."

In a 2000 letter to Dark, Shepard was just as rapturous about this period in his life, writing, "We were in our thirties and we'd get bombed on weed, jump on our bikes and cruise down through the back streets in the middle of the night having long convoluted conversations then convulsing into laughter so hard, I thought my insides were turning to knots . . . Those were truly high times and I remember thinking at the time that this was something completely unique and amazing—two 'grown' men able to essentially have a relationship like two kids, like two boys out of time with the rest of the world."

ON THE DAY DIRECTOR Terrence Malick came to Marin County to offer Shepard a starring role in *Days of Heaven,* the film he intended to begin shooting in Alberta, Canada, Shepard and Johnny Dark were "running around in the mud" feeding "forty some head of boarding horses" on the Flying Y Ranch.

Despite knowing why Malick was coming to see him that day, Shepard—who had liked *Badlands,* the director's first feature film, which Malick had written, directed, partially financed, and produced— did nothing at all to facilitate their interaction. Nor had he been bothered to do so when Jacob Brackman, the executive producer of *Days of Heaven,* made his own earlier visit to Marin County to ask Shepard to join the cast.

Then thirty-two years old, Brackman had collaborated with director Bob Rafelson on the script for *The King of Marvin Gardens,* a 1972 movie starring Jack Nicholson. Brackman then wrote the lyrics for many of Carly Simon's songs, among them "That's the Way I Always Heard It Should Be" and "Haven't Got Time for the Pain." Nonetheless, Shepard had chosen to view him as "a suit," a derogatory term for a movie company executive who was not an actual filmmaker, and so their meeting had not gone well at all.

Returning to Hollywood, Brackman told Malick he had not been able to persuade Shepard to accept a role in *Days of Heaven.* Rudy Wurlitzer, who had originally urged Brackman to consider Shepard for the film—an idea Malick had approved after seeing Shepard in

Renaldo and Clara, the movie shot on the Rolling Thunder tour, which was still being edited in Los Angeles—then intervened on his friend's behalf. "I had not read the script," Wurlitzer said, "but I knew what it was about from talking to Terry and so I told him, 'Stay in the hunt with Sam, because he will be great in this kind of story.'"

Still "totally devoted to writing," Shepard was fearful about how he might fare in front of the camera. The hard lesson he had learned from committing so quickly to collaborating with Bob Dylan on the Rolling Thunder movie was also still fresh in his mind. Despite Shepard's reservations, Malick eventually persuaded him to play the role of the Farmer in *Days of Heaven.* And while Shepard would later concede that earning enough money to continue living with his extended family on the Flying Y Ranch was "definitely a motive" in his decision, he also recognized Malick as a fellow artist. As the playwright noted thirty years later, "Terry has always been an enigma to me but you got to love him."

SET IN 1916, *Days of Heaven* is the story of Bill, a Chicago steelworker who accidentally kills his supervisor and then flees the city with his girlfriend, Abby, and his little sister, Linda. In the Texas Panhandle, they begin working in wheat fields owned by "the Farmer," who is suffering from a fatal disease. In the best line of dialogue in the film, Bill describes the Farmer as having "one foot on a banana peel and the other on a roller skate." Nonetheless, Abby falls in love with the Farmer and marries him.

In *Days of Heaven,* the plot and characters finish a far distant second to the astonishing look of a film still widely regarded as one of the most visually stunning accomplishments in modern American cinema. Richard Gere, whose star had continued to rise since his performance in Shepard's *The Killer's Head,* was cast as Bill.

Although Shepard never read the script before accepting the role of the Farmer, he had reacted positively to something Malick said to him during one of their initial conversations. "Terry told me very early on that he wanted to make a silent movie. He didn't want dialogue and

I knew what he meant—dialogue in some ways engaged the audience too much. He wanted almost a voyeuristic thing from the audiences, to witness the image."

Despite his willingness to work with Malick, Shepard immediately got off on the wrong foot with the film's producers by deciding to drive a rented Ford Mustang the fifteen hundred miles from Mill Valley to the remote location in Alberta where *Days of Heaven* was to begin shooting in August 1976. As Jacob Brackman says, "Unlike everyone else, Sam would not come up to the location in Canada in the normal way. He wanted to drive up and so needed a gas allowance and a per diem, because it was going to take him three or four days to get there. Then there was some kind of hassle at the border and someone from the crew had to go down there just to get him into Canada."

While virtually no one on the Rolling Thunder Revue had known Shepard or his work, he did have a direct connection with Bob Dylan and Jacques Levy. On the set of *Days of Heaven*, Shepard was far more isolated than when he had been out on the road on the rock-'n'-roll tour. And as if the pressure of having to perform before the camera as an actor for the first time were not enough, he now also found himself involved in yet another chaotic attempt to shoot a movie from a script that was still being written.

Although Shepard and Brackman, in Brackman's words, "seriously disrespected one another" and had "an extremely testy relationship" on *Days of Heaven*, they were constantly thrown together, because Malick "saw the script as just a blueprint for something better the actors would come up with, but of course, it didn't work that way." Rather than let Brackman travel to the set with him in his car in the morning, Malick instructed him to ride out to the location on the bus with Shepard so the two could write new dialogue for the scene being shot that day. Not a fan of writers like Jack Kerouac, "who didn't revise," Brackman would sit there as Shepard scribbled away madly in his notebook for "like three minutes, and then he was done ... The last thing in the world he wanted to do was collaborate with me."

While shooting *Badlands*, Malick had been able to rely on Sissy Spacek and Martin Sheen to improvise their own dialogue, which allowed him to concentrate on framing his shots in purely visual terms.

On *Days of Heaven,* he was working with actors who could not do this, and so, in Brackman's words, "it was the opposite of the kind of rapport he'd had on *Badlands,* and in a way, it was amazing Sam went on as an actor after the experience he had with Terry."

Whenever Malick asked Shepard to do several takes of a scene to make what he was doing in front of the camera seem bigger, Shepard would go off by himself "in a state of high anxiety" and do all he could to work himself up to the emotional pitch the director wanted. After this process did not prove successful, Malick came up with another solution. "Terry was constantly saying, 'Just squint your eyes. Think you're a gunslinger,'" Brackman says. "And then Terry would have them shoot him from below, so you would get Sam's jaw structure and the sky above him as opposed to putting him into the kind of close-up you would have used with an actor like Robert DeNiro."

Soon enough, those who assembled in the editing room each day to view the rushes began asking one another, "Is today's work worthy of a Sammy?" Not so much what Brackman called an "award for being a terrible actor," the question referred to "someone in the tradition of Robert Redford—as opposed to Richard Gere, who would chew up the furniture."

With the film on location in the wheat fields outside Alberta for weeks on end, the drama behind the camera was often more intense than in front of it. Brooke Adams, who was then twenty-seven years old, had appeared only in uncredited parts in four movies before being cast as Abby. The romantic arc of her character in the film became her own during filming. "She started out having a romance with Richard Gere until they broke up on film," Brackman says, "and then she started having a romance with Sam during the second half of the filming. They also broke up, because she started going with my brother-in-law who had come to visit me and when the picture wrapped, he and Brooke went off to Europe together."

On top of all these other complications, O-Lan Jones made the long journey from Mill Valley to spend a week with her husband on the set. Biographer Don Shewey wrote that she was "apparently unruffled by Sam's affair." The same could not be said for how Richard Gere and Shepard dealt with the situation. "The thing about Sam was that he really had a mean streak," Brackman says. "Especially when he drank. He could really be a mean drunk. Both Sam and Richard Gere had episodes of trashing stuff in their rooms. Like getting drunk and throwing something through a picture window or a TV. They did this separately because of their respective romances with Brooke but never fought with one another. Because Sam and Richard Gere didn't have the slightest bit of a real relationship, they completely avoided one another offscreen."

Eleven weeks into shooting *Days of Heaven,* Shepard wrote a letter in which he noted that even though it was the third week in October, there was already "a thick blanket of snow covering everything outside" and that it was also "getting very cold up here." Having never before experienced life on a movie set in a remote location, he also could not believe he was "still doing this thing." Because Malick himself had just gotten sick from "inhaling too much smoke from the fire sequences," work on the film would now be "delayed even more." Shepard hoped to be home for his birthday in twelve days, but as it turned out, filming continued until long after then.

For Shepard, the "roughest part of this whole experience is having so much spare time." Unlike being at home, he was "really in limbo." Stuck in his trailer "on the high plains of Canada day after day starts to do things to you. I go through orgies of reading then writing then back to reading then I think 'maybe I'll take a walk'—but you walk out and there's nothing there. Just plains as far as you can see & a few crazy humans huddled around a camera yelling things at each other."

DUE IN NO SMALL part to Malick's predilection for shooting as much of *Days of Heaven* as he could during "magic hour," the brief period before sunset each day, when the light is particularly soft and golden, principal photography dragged for thirteen weeks. Nor did Malick's obsessive quest to obtain cinematic perfection end once he was done filming. One year into the editing process, the director summoned Shepard and Gere to Los Angeles so he could shoot some inserts (i.e., shots from different angles) with them. Malick also had Jacob Brackman work with Linda Manz, who played Linda, in New York City, to create the voiceover the director then used to tie the film together.

Days of Heaven was released in September 1978. In his otherwise thoroughly negative review of the film in *The New York Times,* Harold Schonberg noted, "The dramatist Sam Shepard demonstrates that he knows how to act." In the *Chicago Sun-Times,* Roger Ebert began his review by stating, "'Days of Heaven' is above all one of the most beautiful films ever made."

Twenty-two years after the release of the film, Shepard wrote Johnny Dark a letter in which he recalled his fear that by acting in a movie, "I was about to enter a whole new world and that world was somewhat scary in its connectedness to the public and the fear of becoming maybe 'famous' and how I might lose something of myself as a writer." Shepard had by now also realized that his decision to accept Malick's offer was one of those "monumental turning points in a life that cannot be denied" and "one of those moments where the consequences (good and bad) keep ringing out until you die."

However, this was not how he felt about the experience at the time. Despite still having pickup shots (i.e., shots filmed to augment existing footage) to do, he packed his truck in the middle of the night and set off before dawn to drive home without saying goodbye to anyone or letting the producers know he was leaving. "During the entire shoot," Brackman says, "Sam was pissed off at everything and everybody. The truth was he didn't have a friend on the picture. But, of course, everybody would have thrown him a going-away party with hugs and all that, but that was not what Sam wanted. Instead, he just left like a wolf going off in the night."

NINETEEN

CURSE OF THE STARVING CLASS

The break-up of the family isn't particularly
American; it's all over the world. Because I was born
in America, it comes out as the American family.
But I'm not interested in writing a treatise on
the American family. That's ridiculous.

—SAM SHEPARD, IN 1984
AMERICAN THEATRE
INTERVIEW

AT SOME POINT WHILE HE WAS IN NEW YORK CITY WORKING
with Jacques Levy on *Geography of a Horse Dreamer* as the Rolling
Thunder tour was coming to an end in late 1975, Shepard was summoned to meet with Joe Papp, the well-known theatrical producer,
director, and impresario who had founded the Public Theater as the
Shakespeare Workshop in 1954 and now ran the institution from the
iconic redbrick building on Lafayette Street in Lower Manhattan that
had once housed the Astor Library.

Fifty-four years old when he first met Shepard, Papp was already
legendary in New York City for having brought free performances of
Shakespeare to Central Park in the summer as well as to public schools
in all five boroughs. At the Public Theater, which opened at its present
location in 1967, Papp had presented *Hair* and *A Chorus Line*. Both
plays had gone on to win multiple Tony Awards while enjoying profitable runs on Broadway.

Born to Yiddish-speaking parents in the Williamsburg section of

Brooklyn, Josef Yosl Papirofsky grew up in crushing poverty. As a boy, he shined shoes, plucked chickens, and sold peanuts from a pushcart to help his family survive. After serving in the U.S. Navy during World War II, he became the managing director of the politically active left-wing Actors Laboratory in Hollywood before returning to New York to pursue a career in theater.

Always contentious, Papp fought with New York City bureaucrats. He fought with foundations, unions, critics, and playwrights. When Robert Moses, the power broker who transformed the geography of the greater New York City metropolitan area, decided for purely political reasons that a fee would have to be charged for performances of Shakespeare in Central Park, Papp fought him as well, and won.

Insofar as Sam Shepard was concerned, central casting could not have found a more perfect male authority figure than Papp for him to defy. Not surprisingly, the tension between the two men began when they sat down together for the first time ever in the fall of 1975 to discuss the possibility of Shepard's writing a new play for the Public to produce. Describing his one and only face-to-face encounter with Shepard, Papp told Kenneth Turan, the co-author of *Free for All*, the oral history of Papp and the Public, "I was as warm to him as I could be to a young writer. He was kind of broke, and he said he'd heard that I was interested in plays about fathers and sons. Well, I had that reputation. It's not entirely untrue, but it's not entirely true, either." According to Papp, Shepard said he had already written "a family play." Because he needed money, he offered to let the Public Theater option and produce all the plays he would write during a specified period in return for an up-front payment on which he could live.

Based solely on *Curse of the Starving Class*, a title Papp thought "sounded very socialistic, and also dramatic," the producer said he agreed to pay Shepard $5,000 (the equivalent of nearly $25,000 today) for the right to have a first look at all his new plays over the next five years. In the words of Gail Merrifield Papp, who was then director of plays and musical development at the Public Theater and who would marry Joe Papp a year later, "It was a lump-sum payment to cover whatever Sam wanted to give Joe over a period of five years, with the understanding [that] he didn't actually have to give him anything.

Back then, that was a lot of money to give a playwright without a definitive commitment as to how many plays he might write."

From the start, neither Papp nor Shepard seems to have been able or willing to recall the actual sequence of events leading to the production of *Curse of the Starving Class*. Contradicting Papp's account of their meeting, Shepard said he had not yet written *Curse* when they met in New York City. That he already had the idea for the play and supplied Papp with the title seems far more likely. Nor did Papp and the Public Theater graciously endow the playwright with an up-front payment of five thousand dollars.

Instead, as Shepard biographer John J. Winters wrote, Papp sent Shepard a check for five hundred dollars on December 18, 1975. Shepard then spent the next four months writing the first three-act play of his career that was presented onstage. When he mailed the script to Papp on April 5, 1976, he included a handwritten note asking the Public Theater to make a copy of the play and send it back to him, as he could not afford to have the manuscript copied on his own.

It was then the conflict between Papp and Shepard began in earnest. In March 1975, Papp had agreed to manage both the Vivian Beaumont and Mitzi E. Newhouse theaters at Lincoln Center. By doing so, he hoped to be able to raise more money for the Public Theater, which was in dire financial straits. Despite a disastrous first season at Lincoln Center, Papp wanted to present *Curse of the Starving Class* in the Vivian Beaumont during his second season there. Whether he knew that this was where *Operation Sidewinder*, the greatest failure of Shepard's theatrical career, had been staged in March 1970, no one can say for certain.

From opposite coasts, the two men then began a protracted negotiation over the contract. For Shepard, the money he was being offered was a problem. For Papp, scheduling the play at Lincoln Center became an issue. They also could not agree on who would direct it. As they continued to haggle with each other, months went by. With the five hundred dollars Papp had paid him now long gone, Shepard took matters into his own hands by sending *Curse of the Starving Class* to Nancy Meckler in London. By doing so, he hoped to persuade her to come to New York City to direct the play. When Meckler explained that it would be too disruptive for her two young sons for her to spend that much time away from home, he authorized her to put the play on in London.

As Meckler began preparing to go into rehearsals on *Curse* in London in early 1977, Shepard was spending six weeks and a significant portion of his Rockefeller grant working with Joe Chaikin at the Magic Theatre on an experimental piece that could just as easily have been presented a decade earlier at the Open Theatre in Lower Manhattan.

Based loosely on the story of twenty-one-year-old Karen Ann Quinlan, who spent ten years in a coma as her parents fought a series of well-publicized court battles for her right to die, *Inacoma* was created by Shepard and Chaikin in collaboration with a troupe of eight actors, O-Lan Jones, Peter Coyote, and Fred Ward among them, as well as eight musicians who called themselves the San Francisco Theatre Jazz Ensemble. Three hours long, *Inacoma* received decidedly mixed reviews when it opened on March 18, 1977, at the Magic. In keeping with the way the piece had been created, Shepard himself greeted the audience on the second night of its run by telling them they were all in for a special treat, as the company was not going to do the second act as he had written it. Rather, as a group, they were going to improvise it.

In London, Shepard's reputation was already so well established that when Nancy Meckler's production of *Curse of the Starving Class* opened at the Royal Court in London on April 21, 1977, the play was not staged in the small performance space upstairs but rather in the 465-seat main theater. In an interview meant to stimulate interest in the production, Shepard spoke to Roger Downey for an article entitled "Inside the Words" that appeared in *Time Out*. In a fairly fanciful account of his initial meeting with Joe Papp that then appeared in two biographies of the playwright, Shepard described a phone call with Papp that began when Shepard breezily demanded to know why in all the time he had been working in theater in New York City, the producer had never before offered to put on one of his plays. After Papp responded by saying he wanted to do one now, Shepard asked, "How much money will you give me? And he said $200. $200: sheeee! I got him up to $500. So I asked Joe, what kind of play do you like? And he said, oh, a family, two sons, one stays home, one goes off to Vietnam or anyway to war and gets fucked up. So I said, OK." In fairly accurate detail, Shepard had just described the plot of *Sticks and Bones* by David Rabe, a play Papp had presented at the Public Theater in 1971 before moving it to Broadway, where it won the 1972 Tony Award for Best Play and Best Performance by a Featured Actress.

As Gail Merrifield Papp says, "Sam's account of Joe calling and saying he wanted him to write a play about a family in which one brother goes off to war and the other stays home is what you would call a legend. It's a legendary account because I was there in the room with them when they met and Joe never talked that way. Sam might have known Joe was a great fan of David Rabe, but he was also a very eclectic producer who put on all kinds of stuff."

IN THE SAME INTERVIEW in which Shepard gave his version of how Papp had commissioned him to write *Curse of the Starving Class,* the playwright said, "'Curse' is the first time I've ever tried to deal with my family. Not really *my* family, just the, what do you call it, nuclear family. I've always been kind of scared of that . . . I mean, it doesn't stop at one family or generation, the reactions keep spreading out and repeating themselves."

As a play, *Curse of the Starving Class* also represents Shepard's first venture into social realism, albeit in a manner very much his own. Clearly modeled on his teenage years in Duarte, the supremely dysfunctional Tate family lives on a farm in California. The play begins with Wesley, the teenage son, picking up the pieces of the front door his father, Weston, shattered during a drunken rage the night before. In a long monologue delivered by Wesley consisting primarily of two- and three-word sentences, Shepard graphically re-creates the terror he himself felt as a teenager lying in bed at night as his drunken father tried to break into the house while cursing and screaming threats at his mother like a man who had gone insane.

Much as Shepard's father had done after he began spending most of his time outside the family house in Duarte, Weston, who is "un-

shaven and slightly drunk" when he first enters, has brought home a
duffel bag filled with his dirty laundry. Noticing that his daughter is
gone, he carefully instructs Wesley to tell her to do his laundry with no
"bleach in anything but the socks and no starch in the collars." Having
also just returned from checking on his piece of land in the desert
much like the one Sam Rogers owned, Weston describes it as "a real
piece of shit. Just a bunch of strings on sticks, with the lizards blowing
across it."

With the possible exception of Wesley, none of the characters in
Curse of the Starving Class is likeable or even really comprehensible,
except as archetypal figures who have lost their way in an American
dream that has long since gone seriously wrong. After a succession of
melodramatic events, the very convoluted plot finally resolves itself
with the family completely self-destructing. Despite how much of
Shepard's own personal trauma is on display here, the play is somehow
funny, yet heartbreaking as well.

Despite having not yet opened in New York City, *Curse of the
Starving Class* won the 1977 Obie Award for Best New American Play.
Along with the award came a check for $1,000. With the Rockefeller
grant and the money from *Days of Heaven* gone, Shepard was now
once again struggling to earn a living. After Applause/Urizen Books
made an offer of a paltry $500 advance for the publication of *Angel
City, Curse of the Starving Class, and Other Plays,* Shepard's new agent,
Lois Berman, managed to persuade them to go up to $1,500 (the
equivalent of $6,500 today).

Three months after *Curse of the Starving Class* was published, the
play was produced by Joe Papp at the Public Theater, opening on
March 2, 1978. With a cast that included Olympia Dukakis, Pamela
Reed, James Gammon, and Michael J. Pollard, it was directed by Robert Woodruff, who had co-founded the Eureka Theatre in San Francisco in 1972.

Woodruff had met Shepard for the first time in 1977, at the Bay
Area Playwrights Festival, which he had also founded. Woodruff asked
Shepard if he had any plays that had not yet been produced and the
playwright gave him a thirty-minute musical entitled *The Sad Lament
of Pecos Bill on the Eve of Killing His Wife,* which he had written for a

bicentennial project but that had never been used and so was "sitting in his drawer." Woodruff staged the piece, which, in his words, was "just a little shorter than the title." Although Shepard never saw the production, "he heard good things about it." At some point during the lengthy process of producing *Curse of the Starving Class* at the Public, in Woodruff's words, Shepard "told Joe Papp, 'Well, why don't you get this guy?' . . . So Joe called me up. I was . . . doing theater in a church basement in San Francisco and, well, Joe Papp calls you up. So you go to New York."

As Woodruff told Kenneth Turan, "I loved the material. I had a great ensemble of actors, and the audiences were agog. Joe was very supportive to the company, and working at the Public at the time was really the most exciting thing you could do in American theater." Although Woodruff had spent only half an hour discussing the play with Shepard over the phone before directing it, the playwright gave him "total license, total freedom . . . to just go and do it. That's what he said, 'Just do it.' He'd never seen it performed, so he said, 'If you don't want something, cut it.'"

Citing his unwillingness to fly as the reason, Shepard did not attend the opening of *Curse of the Starving Class* in New York City. The show ran for sixty-two performances but was not extended beyond its scheduled five-week run. In Woodruff's words, Shepard had "a lot of friends in New York, and the reports that he had were wonderful . . . he was not concerned about the work."

In his *New York Times* review of *Curse of the Starving Class*, Richard Eder identified "the central notion" of the play as hunger for a kind of "phony food that doesn't bring satisfaction, only a new voracity," while "American life is controlled by crooks and swindlers, who delude the people and end up stripping them . . . Unfortunately, much of the force hangs in the air. It plays like a play that reads well, as if Mr. Shepard had failed to consider what would happen when his parable took physical form on the stage, and his images were played out by real actors performing in real time."

Despite describing the characters as "grotesque archetypes" whom Shepard had "deliberately dehumanized" so that "they become messages," Eder praised the cast. He ended his review by writing, "The director, Robert Woodruff, has allowed the action to drag excessively, accentuating the play's tendency to self-indulgence."

In Gail Merrifield Papp's words, "There were no problems when we put on *Curse of the Starving Class*. It worked, and we liked that play. The problems came with *True West*."

TWENTY

BURIED CHILD

I've been in a few rodeos, and the first team
roping that I won gave me more of a feeling of
accomplishment and pride of achievement than
I ever got winning the Pulitzer Prize.

—SAM SHEPARD, IN 1984
AMERICAN THEATRE
INTERVIEW

ALTHOUGH HE HAD NOW FOUND THE SUBJECT OF AND THE
style in which he would write four major plays over the course of
the next seven years, Shepard also found himself confronted by what
seems to have been a major case of writer's block after completing
Curse of the Starving Class. During the summer of 1977, "one of his
lowest points," in the words of biographer Don Shewey, the playwright
"felt stymied, unsatisfied. He complained in his journal that he felt like
writing but had nothing to say, and then he berated himself for complaining."

Day after day, Shepard "brooded around the house, causing O-Lan
to protest that she had to read his writing to know what he was thinking." After immersing himself in the works of Jack London, William
Faulkner, James Joyce, and Flann O'Brien, he went through what
Shewey called the playwright's "Irish phase . . . referring to himself as
a mick" as "he and Johnny Dark went through a spell of compulsively
talking in phony brogues."

This period of malaise ended when Shepard returned to *The Last
Gas Station,* the play he had begun writing in Nova Scotia after leaving
London in the summer of 1974. Now entitled *Buried Child,* the three-

act play begins with Dodge, the character based on Shepard's grandfather, watching television from the couch in the living room of his farmhouse.

As he had never done before in any of his works, Shepard employs rapid-fire bursts of dialogue and short poetic monologues to convey an immense amount of information about yet another supremely dysfunctional family. Unlike the Tates in *Curse of the Starving Class*, these characters are firmly grounded in their own history and in the rural area where they have lived for generations. The core element of the play is the curse Dodge has brought upon his family and their now-failing farm by what he did after his wife became pregnant even though they had not slept in the same bed for six years. Unable to "allow that thing to grow up right in the middle of our lives" because it "made everything we'd accomplished look like it was nothin'," Dodge drowned the child "like the runt of a litter."

In many ways, *Buried Child* is Shepard at his best. Only someone haunted by the ghosts of the men who had come before him—all of whom had wreaked havoc on not just themselves but also those closest to them—could have written the play. Shepard's deep engagement with the characters makes them all more real, believable, and ultimately terrifying than those in *Curse of the Starving Class*, thereby elevating *Buried Child* to another level of theater entirely.

AFTER DIRECTOR ROBERT WOODRUFF had auditioned hundreds of actors for a play with seven roles, *Buried Child* opened at the Magic Theatre on June 27, 1978, where it ran for six weeks. Two and a half months after it closed in San Francisco on October 19, 1978, the play opened in Lower Manhattan at the former Tabernacle Baptist Church on Second Avenue and East Tenth Street, which had been converted into three performance spaces. Although Shepard chose not to attend the premiere, one of his plays was again being performed within walking distance of the apartment on East Tenth Street and Avenue C where he had first lived in New York City fifteen years earlier.

Although Shepard had accepted a thousand-dollar yearly stipend from the Public Theater for the right of refusal on every new play he wrote during this period, Joe Papp was not producing *Buried Child*. According to biographer Don Shewey, this was because Shepard "had already promised" it to Crystal Field and George Bartenieff, who had co-founded the company Theater for a New City in 1971 and whom Shepard knew "from his New York days." That they were able to give Shepard "a small commission for the play" and were "happy to have Woodruff direct the play" also figured in his decision. However, "the disadvantage was that they could only guarantee a three-week run in a tiny theater."

In Gail Merrifield Papp's words, "When Sam gave *Buried Child* to another theater, Joe was not happy about it. He was totally blindsided by that and felt it plainly came within the parameter of what they had talked about in his office, and so he was very surprised the play went elsewhere all of a sudden. That he only heard about it really late in the process was also puzzling to him."

In his *New York Times* review of the Theater for a New City's production of *Buried Child*, Richard Eder called the work less interesting as "a piece of writing" than *Curse of the Starving Class* but a play that "seems to work far better on the stage." He also wrote, "In the very gifted production directed by Robert Woodruff," the play "manages to be vividly alive even as it is putting together a surreal presentation of American intimacy withered by rootlessness." Thanks to the interest in the play generated in part by this review, *Buried Child* moved to the 299-seat Theater de Lys (now the Lucille Lortel Theatre) at 121 Christopher Street in Greenwich Village on December 5, 1978. After 152 performances, far more than any Shepard play had had before in New York, the show closed on April 15, 1979.

In a letter dated April 3, 1979, Brendan Gill, the drama critic for *The New Yorker*—writing on behalf of his fellow jurors Richard Eder and Edwin Wilson, the drama critic for *The Wall Street Journal*—notified Professor Richard Baker of the Graduate School of Journalism at Columbia University that they had "voted unanimously to recommend for the Pulitzer Prize in Drama the play called 'Buried Child' by Sam Shepard." Citing "the remarkable body of work" Shepard had produced over the past years, Gill wrote, "He is widely held to be one of the most talented of his comparatively youthful generation, as well as unquestionably the most industrious. As a playwright, he has devoted himself to American themes—perhaps more self-consciously than any of his colleagues, he has taken for his subject the nature of contemporary American life."

By writing the first Off-Off-Broadway play ever to win the Pulitzer Prize for Drama, Shepard helped move what in London had been known as fringe theatre into the mainstream of commercial American drama. In the process, he won yet another Obie Award for Best Dramatic Writing. He also set the stage for his final confrontation with Joe Papp.

As Gail Merrifield Papp says, "And then, of course, *Buried Child* won the Pulitzer. I wouldn't say Joe was furious about it, but he was irritated. The people from Theater for a New City were in residence at the Public Theater in 1966 and 1967, and so they were all friends of ours. I don't want to call what Sam did underhanded, but he and Joe did have an understanding."

IN JANUARY 1979, DON SHIRLEY, who wrote about theater for *The Washington Post*, came looking for Sam Shepard in Mill Valley so he could speak to "the visionary playwright and fledgling movie star" as *Curse of the Starving Class* was about to open in the nation's capital. Although Shepard had not yet won the Pulitzer, he still proved maddeningly hard to find. After a "crunching drive down the muddy country path" leading to the Flying Y Ranch, Shirley was told by a woman grooming a horse that Shepard had moved away from there two years ago.

In truth, Shepard had left the ranch just a couple of months earlier. Unable to come up with enough cash to buy the property when the lease expired in October 1978, he and his extended family had moved into Mill Valley. For a more affordable price, Shepard and Jones purchased a four-bedroom, three-bathroom, white-paneled house with two garages on the corner at 33 Evergreen Avenue, just a short walk from the downtown area.

Proceeding to that address, Shirley found Shepard's white Chevy Nova parked in the driveway. After a neighbor confirmed that the playwright did live in that house, Shirley looked through the window and spotted a framed cover of Shepard's *Rolling Thunder Logbook* hanging on a wall. The younger of the two women who answered the door (either O-Lan or Kristy along with Scarlett) told Shirley she did not know Shepard, had never met him, and had the book cover on the wall only because she was a fan.

Nothing if not persistent, Shirley returned to the house several hours later to be greeted by Johnny Dark. To prove this was his real name, Dark showed the writer his driver's license. He then told Shirley that although Sam Shepard did not live there, perhaps the owner of the downtown bookstore where Dark had bought *The Rolling Thunder Logbook* could help the writer find him.

In his article for *The Washington Post,* aptly entitled "Searching for Sam Shepard," Shirley wrote, "Sam Shepard, theatrical navigator of American myths, is becoming something of a mythic figure in the American theatrical world. As his fame and influence increase, he is becoming more introspective and private. He is a man of mystery, and this probably pleases him no end."

And while the elaborate runaround Shirley had been given in Mill Valley by various members of the Shepard clan may now seem amusing, Shepard himself had entered into what might be called his Greta Garbo phase, during which time the playwright repeatedly made it plain that all he really wanted was, as Garbo had said, "to be alone."

Although Shepard turned down *The New York Times Magazine*'s offer to publish an extended feature about him after he won the Pulitzer Prize, the playwright changed his mind fifteen months later. With *True West* about to open at the Public Theater, he allowed Robert Coe to write a lengthy profile, entitled "Saga of Sam Shepard," for that publication. In a conversation with Amy Lippman originally published in 1983 in *The Harvard Advocate,* Shepard said, "Dealing with the media makes you believe that you have an importance beyond your actual importance. It leads to a lot of false assumptions about who you are."

A year later, the interview was republished in the debut issue of *American Theatre* magazine along with an article about Shepard by John Lion, in which Lion described Shepard's long association with the Magic Theatre and offered a detailed critical assessment of the playwright's role in American culture. In a cover photograph designed to attract readers to the brand-new magazine, Shepard posed in full cowboy mode with a straw Resistol hat, a plaid flannel shirt, and a white T-shirt. Staring out of frame with a long filter-tip cigarette dangling from his lips, he looked like James Dean in *Giant*.

SHORTLY AFTER DON SHIRLEY left Mill Valley without managing to corner his very elusive quarry, Shepard got into his pickup truck to begin the nearly eighteen-hour drive to San Antonio, Texas, where principal photography on *Resurrection* was scheduled to begin on January 29, 1979.

Based on a script by the Academy Award–nominated screenwriter Lewis John Carlino and directed by Daniel Petrie, the film starred Ellen Burstyn as Edna Mae McCauley, who after dying in a car crash that also killed her husband comes back to life with the power to heal people through her touch. Shepard was cast as Cal Carpenter, a working-class tough who gets stabbed in a bar fight. After Burstyn's character saves his life, the two become lovers.

Affecting a southern accent as Cal, the name of the character James Dean had played in *Giant,* Shepard looks every inch the part. Young and thin with long hair, Cal rides a motorcycle. When he is not bare-chested in bed alongside Burstyn, he wears a John Deere cap, a jean jacket, blue jeans, and a black T-shirt.

Unlike the way he spent his free time on the set of *Days of Heaven,* Shepard approached *Resurrection* as an opportunity to begin learning how to act onscreen. He did this not just by watching Burstyn, whom he considered "a genius," but also by marking up his script with the kind of detailed notes a theater director would have given an actor to use onstage. To help himself understand his character's motivation, Shepard created a biography that included the character's "home life, religious experience, and sense of grief." Doing research, he also "went to a lot of charismatic churches where they lay on hands."

In the end, the work Shepard did paid great dividends. Although *Resurrection* was not a great success at the box office, his performance was praised by a wide variety of critics. In her *New York Times* review, Janet Maslin wrote, "The whole cast is outstanding. The playwright Sam Shepard, who showed so much promise in *Days of Heaven*, realizes that promise here. As Edna's hot-tempered lover, he brings a keen, nervous alertness to the role, and a presumptuousness that turns very appealing."

In *The New Yorker*, Pauline Kael praised Shepard for bringing "some sexy tension" to the film. In *The Village Voice*, Carrie Rickey called him "a cross between Peter Fonda and heaven." In *Newsweek*, David Ansen wrote, "Shepard invests his role with the same sense of lurking psychic violence that permeates his plays. If he wants it, he stands on the brink of an extraordinary new career in the movies."

"Sam?" Ellen Burstyn said. "Sam is Gary Cooper."

However, the single best review Shepard received for his performance came from his wife. In Jones's words, "Sam was so hot in *Resurrection* that I wrote him a filthy fan letter."

ON APRIL 15, 1979, THE day shooting wrapped on *Resurrection*, Shepard loaded his truck and began the long journey back to Mill Valley. On his way home, he stopped in Santa Fe, New Mexico, to visit his father, whom he had not seen in more than fifteen years. Unlikely as this seems even now, their reunion occurred on the day Shepard won the Pulitzer Prize.

After leaving California, Sam Rogers had gone to Texas, where he had been "in and out of jail" for offenses related to his chronic alcoholism. Moving to New Mexico in 1975, he had settled in Santa Fe. Shortly before his son came to see him, Rogers was working as a janitor at the historic hotel now known as La Fonda on the Plaza in the heart of the city's downtown area. While living in a series of cheap apartments and, at one point, a trailer, he had also worked in a warehouse. By the time Shepard visited him, Rogers was no longer working at all. Subsisting on his monthly government Veterans Pension checks and on money his son sent him, he now just drank.

After having no real contact with his son for years, Rogers had begun reaching out to him by writing letters in which he described the dire nature of his current situation and asked for money. In a letter dated January 4, 1976, cited by biographer John J. Winters, Rogers asked for financial help so he could cover his back rent and pay a hospital bill he had incurred while being treated for a wound that became infected. Six weeks later, he wrote to thank his son for the money he had sent. Drowning in the kind of self-pity that is a hallmark of alcoholism, Rogers described how "desolate" he now felt after a young man whom he had let sleep on the floor of his motel room for six months had just taken off one day and disappeared. Although both his daughters had recently come to see him, Rogers wished they had never done so because he was now "miserable" and crying because they were gone. He closed his letter by writing that the only thing he had ever done in his life "worth a shit" was raising "three great kids." He then added that his "selfish" ex-wife would no doubt take "all the credit for that," too.

When Rogers learned that his son had won a Pulitzer Prize, Shepard said, "He wrote me a note saying, 'I don't understand what the hell you're writing, I can't make hide nor hair of this shit, but I have to congratulate you nevertheless.'" In another letter, Rogers wrote to say how proud he was of his son and that his literary genius must have come from him because he had been the sports editor of his high school newspaper.

In *Motel Chronicles,* the collection of Shepard's short prose and poems published in 1982 by City Lights Books, there are two untitled entries about the visits Shepard made to see his father in New Mexico. Dated "4/79 Santa Fe, New Mexico," Shepard's first account begins with a description of the records his father kept in cardboard boxes along his bedroom wall "collecting New Mexican dust." His father's prized possession is an original Al Jolson 78 "with the jacket taped and even the tape is ripped." Convinced that it must be "worth at least a grand," Rogers tries to bribe his son "into taking it back to L.A. and selling it for a bundle."

In the hovel where Rogers lives, all the walls are covered with pictures he's clipped out of magazines. In a Yuban coffee can, he keeps "a collection of cigarette butts." Although Shepard has brought his father a carton of Old Golds, Rogers will not touch them. Instead, he keeps "twisting tobacco out of butts and rolling re-makes over a grocery bag so as not to lose the slightest bit." Having already spent all the money Shepard gave him for food on the bottles of bourbon that now fill his icebox, Rogers also has had "his hair cut short like a World War II fighter pilot." After explaining that they did this back then so their helmets would fit, he shows his son the shrapnel scars on the back of his neck. Shepard concludes the piece by writing, "My Dad lives alone in the desert. He says he doesn't fit with people."

The black-and-white photograph of Shepard and his father accompanying this account was taken by Johnny Dark during a later visit described in an entry dated "4/14/82—Bluewater, New Mexico thru 4/18/82 Barstow, Ca." In a white straw Resistol cowboy hat, Rogers stares at something over his son's left shoulder. A thick beard covers the lower part of his face, which, despite his drinking, is not overly weathered. His dark quilted jacket and striped shirt with a white T-shirt peeping out at the collar make him look like he has just come in from a hard day's work on horseback. By far, the most striking aspect of the photograph is Sam Rogers's eyes. Hollow and empty, they look like portholes into the void.

In a longer entry that begins with Shepard and Dark telling stories as they drive for hours and with Shepard's extended recollection of an experience he had in the desert as a teenager while still living in Duarte, both men, accompanied by Scarlett and O-Lan, stop off to visit Rogers, who was then sixty-five years old. In much worse shape than when Shepard last saw him, his father was "hunched over in a Maple rocker with stained pillows strapped to the seat and back . . . His hands trembled as he made a vain attempt to stand for the visitors but couldn't make it more than halfway before he dropped back into the rocker breathing in short desperate bursts. His eyes were blue and wild with a frightened child-like amazement."

In a brown paper bag on the floor, Rogers keeps a bottle of George Dickel Sour Mash Whisky. Beside it, a white plastic plate filled with cigarette butts lies next to a cardboard box with a newspaper sticking out of the top. Hands shaking violently, Rogers begins reaching into the box and unwrapping the newspaper from a series of objects he hands to Shepard, among them a small black-and-white plastic horse;

a silver belt buckle with a star and the words "State of Texas" on it; a small, green ceramic frog; and a black rock from the high desert. Collecting the objects in his lap, Shepard "wished he'd brought something for the old man." Taking off his straw Resistol hat, he reaches over and places it on his father's head, where "It fit perfect." Dark then snapped the photographs of Shepard and his father that appear in *Motel Chronicles*.

So that they could take more photographs out in the sunshine, Shepard and Dark help Rogers leave the room. "He stumbled just outside the door and fell into a curtain of aluminum flip-tops from empty beer cans that he'd strung together himself." Cursing the gravel beneath his feet, Rogers "staggered toward a little patch of brown grass" he had sown himself. Standing on it, he proudly proclaims, "The only real lawn in town."

After they helped him back inside, "he collapsed into his rocker again." When they said goodbye to him, "he clasped their hands very firmly. They were surprised he had that much strength left." Sam Shepard never saw his father alive again.

AFTER THEY HAD RIDDEN their bicycles through the streets of Mill Valley to the marsh by Highway 101 on Saturday, September 29, 1979, Shepard, Jones, and Dark were sitting on a bench watching a snowy egret poking holes in the mud with its beak when they heard a siren wailing in the distance. On their way back home, an ambulance heading in the opposite direction went screaming past them.

When they reached their house on Evergreen Avenue, they found it empty. After calling 911, Shepard learned that while they were gone, Scarlett, his mother-in-law, had passed out in the house. After regaining consciousness, she had called for an ambulance and was taken to the emergency ward of the nearest hospital.

Suspecting that she had suffered a cerebral hemorrhage the doctors there sent Scarlett in an ambulance to another hospital, where a brain scan verified that she had suffered an aneurysm in the basilar artery of her brain. Because the aneurysm was "like a time bomb," the artery could rupture at any moment. The surgeon who had viewed her brain scan informed Shepard, Jones, and Dark that the chances that she would live long enough for them to perform surgery were very slim.

After making calls to people in New York, Boston, and Los Angeles, Shepard was given the name of a surgeon who had performed this operation sixty times while only ever having lost a single patient. Because he was now practicing at a hospital in San Francisco, Scarlett had to be moved there so he could operate on her.

The surgery took six hours. For a week, Scarlett lay unconscious in the intensive care unit. The day she finally woke up, "one eye looked straight ahead while the other one stared to the side." Her arms were strapped down so she would not pull the breathing tube from her nose. When they asked her if she knew who they were, she smiled but could not speak.

Once Scarlett was able to recognize them, she "started to speak in a little girl voice. The words would come out in short blurts like a code from a mixed-up machine." She was easily distracted by noises or by "dust balls blowing across the floor or paper flapping in a trash can," and when being fed, she would "stare at the spoonful of food and weep. Her whole body would weep. Then she'd fall asleep and we couldn't wake her for hours."

Although the hospital recommended transferring her to a therapy center, Shepard, Jones, and Dark decided to take her home instead. In Shepard's words, "That night was the beginning of the worst. She began to moan in an agonizing animal voice." Keeping this up for hours, she would then start screaming that one of them was going to kill her. Afraid of everything and everyone, she jumped "if someone turned on the water or flushed the toilet."

Convinced that the sleeping pills they had given her were meant to kill her, she would spit them out when no one was looking. After she finally fell asleep late each night, Shepard, Jones, and Dark held meetings at which they soon began arguing about how each of them was dealing with her. They also "began having nightmares that *she* was trying to kill us."

In his account dated one year to the day after Scarlett suffered the aneurysm, Shepard wrote that she was now walking on her own, feeding herself, and taking part in conversations while still speaking with a strange accent. Suddenly falling silent, she would sit and stare off into space for long periods of time. Shepard ended his report by writing, "She refers to her past as the time before she was 'blown away.'"

In his long and detailed account of the incident, Shepard never singles himself out as being the one in charge. Nor does the playwright take any credit for the selfless manner in which he devoted so much of his time and energy to caring for his mother-in-law. What does emerge from this harrowing true-life tale is just how much Sam Shepard wanted to look after his family, as his father had never been able to do after a certain point in time.

TWENTY-ONE

TRUE WEST

I wanted to write a play about double nature,
one that wouldn't be symbolic or metaphorical
or any of that stuff. I just wanted to give a
taste of what it feels like to be two-sided.

—SAM SHEPARD, IN 1980
NEW YORK TIMES MAGAZINE
PROFILE

A FTER SAM SHEPARD WON THE PULITZER PRIZE, HIS AGENT joked the playwright was now in such great demand that she could have sold anything he wrote, including his recipe for chili. While this was an exaggeration on her part, Shepard viewed his new standing in theater in an entirely different manner. In part, his dismissive attitude about having won the prize was motivated by knowing he now had to come up with a play that would be a worthy successor to *Buried Child*. He also understood that from this point on, all his work would be judged far more critically than it had ever been before.

At a crucial turning point in his career, Shepard responded by writing *True West*, a play that, as one critic wrote, soon became "an established contemporary masterpiece, and much beloved of actors wanting to test their acting mettle." Thirty-six years later, the playwright would describe how he conceived of *True West* by saying, "My mother had gone to Alaska, and I was house sitting for her in California and I was completely alone, with crickets, and I started to dream this thing up. It just started to come. I wrote it in its entirety in that house."

Although Shepard may have completed the first draft of the play in his mother's house in Pasadena during the summer of 1979, he continued rewriting it for months in Mill Valley. After working his way through thirteen drafts, he brought *True West* to John Lion at the Magic Theatre for Robert Woodruff to direct. As Shepard told Robert Coe of *The New York Times Magazine* a month before *True West* opened at the Public Theater, "I worked harder on this play than anything I've ever written. The play's down to the bone. It opens up new ground for me. I can see a lot of new directions."

The brilliance of *True West* begins with Shepard's incredibly specific character descriptions and precisely detailed notes on the set, costumes, and sound design. Lee, the older of the two brothers who are the play's central characters, is clad in a "filthy white t-shirt, tattered brown overcoat covered with dust, dark blue baggy suit pants from the Salvation Army, pink suede belt, pointed black forties dress shoes scuffed up, holes in the soles, no socks, no hat, long pronounced sideburns, 'Gene Vincent' hairdo, two days' growth of beard, bad teeth."

Concerning the sound design, Shepard wrote, "The Coyote of Southern California has a distinct yapping, dog-like bark similar to a Hyena. This yapping grows more intense and maniacal as the pack grows in numbers, which is usually the case when they lure and kill pets from suburban yards ... In any case, these Coyotes never make the long, mournful, solitary howl of the Hollywood stereotype." The playwright then added, "The sound of Crickets can speak for itself."

True West opens with Lee's younger brother, Austin, writing madly in his notebook in the kitchen of their mother's house as Lee, mildly drunk, leans against the sink with a beer in his hand. From their first words, Lee's feelings of inferiority to his highly educated brother are obvious. Both brothers have recently seen their father, yet another version of Sam Rogers, who lives on his own in the desert. When Austin asks his brother how long he plans to stay in their mother's house, Lee says it depends on what he will be able to steal from other houses in the neighborhood.

After Saul Zimmer, a fairly stereotypical Hollywood producer, arrives to discuss a project with Austin, Lee enters with a television set he has just stolen. Lying about having lived in Palm Springs, he persuades Zimmer to arrange for the two of them to play golf together. He also pitches him on an idea for a Western the producer suggests

Austin put down on paper for him to read. The two brothers then begin working together on this treatment.

The reversal of roles begins in Act 2 with Lee struggling to peck out words on a typewriter as Austin, who is now drunk, sprawls on the kitchen floor with a bottle of whisky in his hand. In the next scene, Lee smashes the typewriter with a golf club while dropping script pages into a burning bowl on the floor. As drunk as his brother, Austin carefully polishes the numerous toasters he stole the night before while making multiple slices of toast. Having abandoned his marriage and career, he now wants to go live with Lee in the desert. In return for all the expected money from their screenplay, Lee offers to take him there and so Austin agrees to the deal.

The final scene of the play begins with the "ravaged" stage littered with "debris from previous scene," all of it "now starkly visible in intense yellow light." The overall effect is of "a desert junkyard at high noon." Back early from her trip to Alaska, their mother enters. Abandoning work on their screenplay, Lee begins pulling her antique plates and silverware from the cupboards to take with him back to the desert. Infuriated, Austin knocks him backward. Picking up the telephone, he wraps the cord around Lee's neck and begins choking his brother while forcing him face-first into the sink.

Even after Austin has loosened the cord from around his brother's neck, Lee, who seems to be dead, makes no response. But when Austin tries to leave, Lee suddenly leaps to his feet to block his escape. As the two brothers square off, a single coyote is heard off in the distance. Ending the play, the lights slowly go to black as "the figures of the brothers now appear to be caught in a vast desert-like landscape" where they are "very still but watchful for the next move." Warring halves of one personality, they remain frozen in perpetual conflict.

A play in two acts consisting of just nine brief scenes, *True West* is far more concise, focused, and realistic than *Buried Child*. Having decided to embrace the elegance of simplicity for the first time in his work, Shepard had written a play that was basically a classic two-hander replete with the utterly surreal moments that had characterized much of his early work. In every way, *True West* was a major step forward in his career.

As always, Shepard also scattered direct references to his own life throughout the play. When Austin talks about having gone to visit his father in the desert to offer him money he then spent on alcohol, he says that all the old man did "was play Al Jolson records and spit at me." In one of the few extended monologues in the play, Austin describes what actually happened when Shepard's sisters visited their father only to have Rogers get so drunk that he lost his false teeth by leaving them at a bar, in a doggie bag of chop suey.

By far the most personal aspect of *True West* was how Shepard chose to portray his own dual nature through two brothers whom many critics compared to Cain and Abel. As the playwright wrote in a letter to Johnny Dark on November 28, 1983, "I know I've got two sides in me that are very irreconcilable. One's totally undisciplined & just wants to wander into some adventure . . . and the other side has this image of an orderly, disciplined life."

IN PART, PERHAPS, BECAUSE of the explosively violent nature of the conflict between its two central characters, *True West* seemed to engender far more offstage drama than any other play Shepard ever wrote, a pattern that began when it first went into rehearsals before opening at the Magic Theatre on July 10, 1980.

When it came to casting the show, director Robert Woodruff and Shepard decided to tap into the rich legacy of the Magic Theatre company of actors. Jim Haynie, who was cast as Lee, had begun his career in theater as the technical director of the San Francisco Mime Troupe founded in 1959 by R. G. "Ronny" Davis, who had studied corporeal mime with Étienne Decroux in Paris. Peter Coyote, who portrayed Austin, had joined the Mime Troupe as an actor and director because "they had the two most beautiful women I had seen in my life." He had also spent more than one Thanksgiving with Shepard and his family in Mill Valley, where he also lived at the time.

Two years older than Shepard, Peter Coyote was born Robert Peter Cohon in Manhattan. Although his father worked as an investment banker, Coyote described his parents as "Lefty Jewish Intellectuals" and "Commie Jew Reds." After graduating with a B.A. in English literature from Grinnell College in 1964, he was accepted to the Iowa Writers' Workshop but instead began working toward his master's degree in creative writing at San Francisco State University. In the mid-1970s, Coyote began studying Zen Buddhism and in time would become an ordained Zen priest and teacher. In 1976, Governor Jerry Brown appointed him to the California Arts Council, which he chaired for three years. In that role, he distributed funds to the Magic Theatre. After not acting for a decade, he decided to begin performing again and appeared in back-to-back productions at the Magic, *Inacoma* by Shepard and Joe Chaikin being one of them.

In *The Rainman's Third Cure: An Irregular Education*, his second autobiography, Coyote writes that Shepard had "spent an apprenticeship similar to mine in the counterculture but blessed with extraordinary talent and iconic American looks, he was already a star and a Pulitzer Prize winner. It was a big boost to my confidence when he asked me to be one of his leading men in a production that would undeniably attract a great deal of attention."

Despite his expectations, Coyote found himself engaged in constant conflict with Shepard during the production of *True West* at the Magic. Unlike Coyote, Shepard had never been a hippie. In other ways, however, the two men were oddly alike. Blessed with leading-man good looks that made them irresistible to women, both were hipsters who shared a deep and abiding love for rock 'n' roll. For the first time in his theatrical career, Shepard was not reacting to an older male authority figure who evoked memories of his father but rather to someone he perceived as a threat to his standing as the alpha male in the room. Exacerbating the problem, the playwright was also so enthralled by this production that he showed up at virtually every rehearsal.

On June 20, 1980, less than three weeks before *True West* was to open, Shepard was sitting at the back of the Magic Theatre smoking an Old Gold cigarette while watching Woodruff run a scene onstage with Haynie and Coyote. When the scene came to a halt and Woodruff was huddling with both actors, he looked out into the house and said, "What do you think of this, Sam?"

Grinding his cigarette out with the heel of his boot, Shepard said,

The Holy Modal
Rounders, circa 1968—
Sam second from left

Sam and O-Lan joined
in holy matrimony on
the altar of St. Mark's
Church in-the-Bowery,
November 9, 1969

Sam Shepard and
O-Lan Jones,
Fairfax, California,
1970

Sam and Patti Smith
on a balcony of
the Chelsea Hotel,
May 7, 1971

Bob Dylan and Sam
at Jack Kerouac's grave,
November 3, 1975

Sam and
Brooke Adams
on location for
Days of Heaven,
fall 1976

Sam Rogers,
Santa Fe,
New Mexico,
1980

Sam and Jessica Lange while filming *Frances*, October 1981

Johnny Dark
and Sam,
Mill Valley,
California,
1982

Sam as Chuck Yeager in *The Right Stuff*, the role for which he was nominated for a Best Supporting Actor Oscar, 1982

Sam and Jessica Lange, Santa Fe, New Mexico, 1983

Sam's photo from
the cover of
Newsweek,
November 11, 1985

Sam and Jessica Lange in their final scene together
onscreen in *Don't Come Knocking*

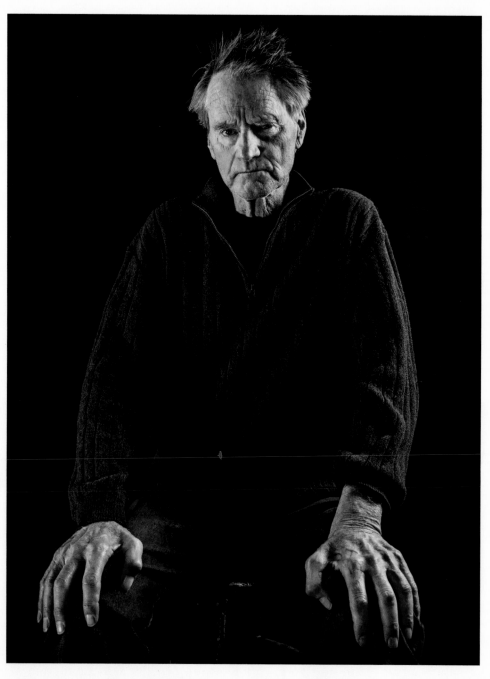

Sam Shepard, already suffering from ALS,
January 28, 2016

"It's hard to keep open in this scene. It can't go right down the track because you'll miss the whole town. Austin has come into the meat and potatoes of the situation. Lee is taking his movie job. He's got to be willing to face that situation. He's not condescending anymore. He has to open to the guy, which also makes Lee have to figure out where he stands. That's the life of the scene. All the rest of it's just clever Ping-Pong."

As Shepard said this, Robert Coe, who was researching the extensive profile of the playwright that would appear five months later in *The New York Times Magazine*, was sitting right beside him. By then, Shepard had already imprinted Coe with the message he wanted to communicate to the world. As Coe wrote, "Friendly, unassuming, Shepard nevertheless has a habit of avoiding a stranger's eyes. He is naturally wary of journalists and gives few interviews. Writing plays, he tells me, 'isn't something you talk about. It's something you do.' He would rather talk about head-roping steers."

After Haynie and Coyote had run the scene again, Shepard praised their work by saying, "That section about the Mojave was really breathing. You didn't have to do nothing but just *be*. It needs to be continually simplified like that." Telling Shepard the scene changed every time the actors performed it, Woodruff noted that "the bottom line" was that as long as Haynie and Coyote remained emotionally connected to each other, they could do whatever they liked, because "the words are there."

That night, Shepard drove with Coe in his pickup truck to the San Francisco Civic Auditorium so they could watch the closed-circuit broadcast of "The Brawl in Montreal," the Roberto Duran–Sugar Ray Leonard welterweight championship boxing match. With the arrival of Woodruff, who had stayed behind to continue rehearsing, Shepard proposed that they "make this interesting" by coming up with a variety of bets on each round and on whether there would be a knockout, with a bonus if there was a knockout in the round that one of them had chosen.

At the end of what Shepard called "the greatest fight" he had ever seen, the referee announced Duran had won by a unanimous decision. As Mexican firecrackers began exploding in the front rows, Shepard quickly ran up the stairs so he could exit the building before the crowd began doing so. It was the instinctive reaction of a playwright accustomed to leaving a theater before the audience could let him know what they thought of his work.

Perhaps because Coe had been allowed to attend only a single rehearsal, he did not witness how Shepard's dismissive attitude toward Coyote influenced those working on the production. And so while the show's stage manager was only too happy to bring Shepard coffee during rehearsals, her response when Coyote asked her to do this for him was "Do I look like a short-order cook to you?" When Coyote complained about halfway through *True West*'s run at the Magic Theatre that, unlike his co-star Jim Haynie, his photograph had not been posted in the lobby, the company responded by putting up a photograph of the actor lying onstage covering his head and face as Haynie kicked him.

When Coyote was asked to continue playing Austin when *True West* moved to the larger Marines' Memorial Theatre in San Francisco, his response was "Are you fucking crazy? You guys have treated me terribly. Why would I do that?"

ON JULY 10, 1980, SHEPARD showed up for the world premiere of *True West* at the Magic Theatre wearing an orange T-shirt, blue jeans held up by a belt with a silver-and-turquoise buckle, cowboy boots, and a pair of aviator glasses. On an opening night, as biographer Don Shewey noted, "drama critics from all over the country outnumbered the paying customers in the audience" and the playwright reacted with pleasure to what he saw onstage. As he had never done before, Shepard then began returning frequently to watch the production. In his words, "This is the first one of my plays I've been able to sit through night after night and not have my stomach ball up in knots of embarrassment."

Excitedly, he called Joe Papp in New York to tell him that *True West* was the best play he had ever written. A month earlier, Shepard had told Coe he had "no plans" to attend the Public Theater production of *True West* in New York City, scheduled to open on December 23, 1980. Had Papp known this before Coe's article appeared less than a month before opening night, much of the conflict between him and Shepard might have been avoided. However, because Papp and Shepard were already at odds about *True West* while the play was still running at the Magic, it also might not have made any difference at all.

Their initial disagreement concerned who would direct the play in New York. Papp suggested JoAnne Akalaitis, an Obie Award–winning director and writer who had studied at the San Francisco Actor's Workshop, with the San Francisco Mime Troupe, and with Jerzy Grotowski in Paris. Along with others, Akalaitis and Philip Glass, who was her husband at the time, had founded the Mabou Mines experimental theater group in 1970. Whether Shepard knew they had done so while living in the house Glass had built on the land he and Rudy Wurlitzer purchased in Nova Scotia and had then named the troupe after the nearby town, no one can say for certain. Based on Shepard's feelings about Akalaitis's ability to direct *True West,* nor would it have mattered one way or the other.

After he spoke with Akalaitis on the phone, Shepard told Papp, "No, no, a woman can't understand this play." In 1991, Shepard also said, "I wouldn't want to see *True West* done by women because it's a scam on the play, it's not the play. I don't have anything against women. I'm just telling you it would distort the play." As immune to the changing tide of gender perception in the culture as he had been to the social and political turbulence that had swirled around him on the Lower East Side during the 1960s, Shepard blithely continued to maintain this attitude throughout his career.

In 2004, Shepard would go to great lengths—through his then agent, Judy Boals—to shut down a production of *True West* that was being performed only on weekends in a seventy-four-seat college theater with two women in the central roles. As Boals told *The New York Times,* the issue was "not that women are playing the brothers. It's that they changed the words." The words in question were the pronouns the characters used to refer to one another onstage.

Several years later, Shepard would put the kibosh on Ethan Hawke's attempt to direct a version of the play starring the Tony Award–winning actress Marin Ireland, who had appeared in the revival of *A*

Lie of the Mind that Hawke directed, and Martha Plimpton, the film and stage actress who had been nominated for three Tony Awards. Although Hawke later described the production as "amazing," Shepard ordered it shut down because, in Hawke's words, "Sam's cut from another cloth. He's from a different tree in the forest—an older part of the forest!"

Although Shepard's steadfast refusal to allow women to play Lee and Austin, both of whose names are gender neutral, might now seem like sexism of the first order, his primary aim in *True West* was to examine the dual nature of personality while also continuing to explore the violence and anger he believed lay at the heart of what now passed for American manhood. And while the mother, the only female character in *True West*, is as much a stereotype and plot device as the Jewish producer from Hollywood, her utter failure to recognize that her two sons are now engaged in a life-and-death struggle speaks volumes about what is obviously yet another supremely dysfunctional Shepard family.

Concerning the way the playwright dealt with gender issues throughout his entire body of work, the critic and director Florence Falk wrote, "In the plays of Sam Shepard, the cowboy is the reigning male; consequently, *any* female is, perforce, marginalized," while also noting that "women in Shepard's world are often victims, but they are also hardier than their oppressors, more skilled in survival strategies." In her essay in the *Journal of Dramatic Theory and Criticism*, Carla J. McDonough offered another perspective on the roles played by women in Shepard's plays. "Given the activities that usually occupy Shepard's center stage, perhaps the wisest choice is that taken by many of his women characters, to exit into a different world."

Nonetheless, it seems eminently fair to say that the world of theater would have been greatly enriched by a production of *True West* directed by Ethan Hawke in which two gifted women played the leading roles, thereby providing an entirely new context for the intense dramatic interaction Shepard had created between a pair of siblings who apparently could not be more different yet who are inextricably linked together in ways even they do not understand.

IN HIS PHONE CONVERSATIONS with Papp in 1980, Shepard insisted
that Robert Woodruff be allowed to direct *True West* at the Public
Theater. Although Papp had not had any problems with Woodruff
when Woodruff directed *Curse of the Starving Class* for him, the producer did not want him to direct this play because he "was so tied" into
Shepard that "he was pale with his subjugation to this man that he
stood in awe of." Although Papp would later claim that his primary
concern was for the "good of the play," he was also trying to exert control over a playwright who had already defied him by allowing another
company to produce the first Off-Off-Broadway play ever to win the
Pulitzer Prize for Drama.

As the two men battled it out from opposite coasts—just as they
had done over where in New York *Curse of the Starving Class* should be
staged—Shepard refused to give ground. Nor did anything Papp said
on the subject make him change his mind. As Papp told Kenneth
Turan, "I could have said, 'Well, fuck you. I don't want to do your play
then. Forget it.'" Because this was never really an option for Papp, the
producer decided to proceed with the play the way Shepard wanted
him to. In Papp's words, "That began the nightmare."

With Woodruff now set to direct, the next problem was deciding
who would play the two central roles. Peter Coyote was no longer involved in the show, but Shepard and Woodruff wanted Jim Haynie to
repeat his performance as Lee and so he was brought to New York to
audition for Papp. Haynie had already performed the role onstage at
the Magic, but he did not do well interacting with a reader during his
audition. Given a second chance, he improved enough for Papp to say
that if Woodruff wanted the actor for the role, he would not stand in
his way.

While all this was going on, the casting director at the Public Theater began looking for "two major actors" to play the parts. If the reviews were good, this would have greatly increased the chances of
moving the play to Broadway. Because this was a purely commercial
decision, it did not add to the existing tension between Shepard and
Papp. In the end, Tommy Lee Jones was cast as Austin and Peter Boyle

was selected to play Lee. Extraordinarily gifted actors, they were also extraordinarily different from each other in virtually every way.

The son of an oil field worker in Midland, Texas, Jones was thirty-four years old. Admitted to Harvard on a financial need scholarship, he had played guard on the school's undefeated football team while rooming with future vice president Al Gore. After beginning his career as a stage actor in New York, Jones won his first Golden Globe for his performance as Loretta Lynn's husband in *Coal Miner's Daughter*, the box-office smash released earlier that year.

Eleven years older than Jones, Peter Boyle was the son of a children's television show host in Philadelphia. After spending three years as a seminarian, Boyle served briefly in the navy before suffering a nervous breakdown. While working as a postal clerk in New York City, he studied acting with Uta Hagen. After making his career in films, Boyle had appeared on Broadway for the first time six months earlier in a comedy that closed after two nights.

While Papp was delighted to have "ended up with two marvelous actors," Woodruff "went along with it" because he "was playing both sides to stay alive." Shepard—who by then was in Texas acting in *Raggedy Man*, a film starring Sissy Spacek and directed by her husband, Jack Fisk, whom Shepard had met when Fisk was the art director on *Days of Heaven*—refused to agree with the decision. Nonetheless, Papp managed to win this argument. In his words, "I also kept saying . . . [']If you're in New York, come here and we can talk about it. But I can't do this thing on the telephone.'"

Although Shepard had attended virtually every rehearsal and multiple performances of *True West* at the Magic Theatre, he wanted as little as possible to do with the Public Theater production. Insofar as his own works were concerned, he had already learned that his most effective weapon in any struggle for theatrical control was to make himself inaccessible. And while Shepard would later claim that Tommy Lee Jones and Peter Boyle were forced upon him to perform in *True West*, Woodruff said of Joe Papp, "He didn't cast the play. I cast the play. Nobody twisted my arm."

Although the stage at the Public Theater had now been set for melodrama of the first order, no one was prepared for a production that then went totally off the rails. Unable to get what he wanted from actors who were more experienced than he but who were also having real problems embodying their characters onstage, Woodruff described the rehearsal process for *True West* as "the most difficult experience I've had in theater."

As Gail Merrifield Papp says, "I don't know if Robert Woodruff was cowed by the situation or what, but we had a public pay phone in the lobby and I would see him there every night talking long distance to Sam. Every night, they would have these long, long conversations and he had to put a lot of money into that pay phone just to be able to stay on the line."

From afar, it seemed that Shepard could not just hop into his truck to drive to New York City because he was playing an integral character in *Raggedy Man* so needed to stay on location until principal photography had been completed. In fact, nothing could have been further from the truth. Playing the title role of the "raggedy man," a mysterious figure who stumbles around the small town where Sissy Spacek, who portrays his wife and the mother of their two children, lives without ever being able to recognize him as her long-lost husband, Shepard had no dialogue and just a few brief scenes in the film. As Vincent Canby wrote in his *New York Times* review, "Sam Shepard, as fine an actor as he is a playwright, has an opportunity to be little more than a passing presence as Nita's wayward husband."

Whatever Shepard's real reasons were for staying as far away from the show as possible, Woodruff already knew the play was going to be a disaster. After three and a half weeks of rehearsal, Papp attended a run-through only to discover that the actors were not yet ready to perform the final fifteen minutes. Virtually everything about the set and the lighting also seemed wrong to him and as he told Fred Ferretti of *The New York Times*, "I've been around long enough to know that when the housekeeping is bad, the play is in trouble."

When none of these elements improved over the next few days, Papp began speaking directly to Shepard on the phone while also conveying messages to him through Woodruff. Convinced that the actors were no longer listening to the director because his primary concern seemed to be what Shepard thought about his decisions, Papp told

Woodruff, "I'd love to be able to fire you." Woodruff relayed this information to Shepard, who told Papp that if he went ahead and did so,
True West would be "the last play of his I'd ever get." Shepard also suggested that Papp replace both actors and start all over again. As the
Public Theater had, in Gail Merrifield Papp's words, "never put on a
play before where the author could not even show up," Shepard's "effort to salvage something" fell on deaf ears.

Much like Austin and Lee in *True West,* Papp and Shepard were
now fully engaged in open combat. Furious "that he didn't have his
own people in the show," Shepard threatened to withdraw the play. No
stranger to such arguments, Papp responded by saying, "You can't
withdraw the play. It's on. Why the hell don't you come to goddamn
New York and see what's going on?" Shepard's answer was he did not
want to fly there.

With Peter Boyle now threatening "to quit every day," and with the
very real fear that he and Tommy Lee Jones might actually start physically fighting with each other, the situation was deteriorating so rap-
idly that Papp called Shepard again and demanded that he come to
New York immediately. When the playwright responded by shouting
that he was not about to do this, Papp said, "I never heard a more hysterical voice in my life. High-pitched, completely out of character with
Sam's image as this close-lipped taciturn Western character." Papp also
called Shepard "a screamer, a hysteric of the first water."

On December 5, 1980, during the third week of previews and a few
days before the press opening, Woodruff, who for weeks had been
"waking up in the proverbial cold sweat and screaming" and whose
own "mental health at this point was not doing well," told Papp he was
leaving the show because Shepard had "already disowned" the production by telling the director "it's not what he wants on stage." Woodruff
later remembered the producer telling him, "You can't go around being
a messenger boy for a playwright all your life." And then Joe Papp
himself took over the show.

Because he was then also directing Meryl Streep in *Alice in Concert,*
a musical by Elizabeth Swados, Papp was unable to do more than
spend a few hours a day discussing the play with Boyle and Jones.
Adding yet more fuel to the fire, Fred Ferretti of *The New York Times*

interviewed both Papp and Shepard, who by now was back home in Mill Valley, for an article entitled "Joe Papp: A 'Divisive' Force or a 'Healing' One?," which ran on December 20, 1980, three days before opening night.

In the article, Shepard made it plain that Papp would "never see another play of mine." He accused him of "acting like a high handed Zanuck" (a reference to the famed Hollywood studio executive and Academy Award–winning producer Darryl Zanuck) while also saying that Papp's judgments were "out to lunch." Without any firsthand knowledge of what had happened in New York, Shepard added that he had also heard that the actors were "paraphrasing my lines" and "not using the language I'd written." Shepard acknowledged that he had accepted five thousand dollars from Papp for the rights to produce his plays—"when I was broke"—but vowed "to refund the money and terminate the whole thing. I just can't have a relationship where I have to beg. He's not the only game in town."

After not leaving the house where he was staying in New York City for days, Woodruff finally emerged on a Saturday morning only to discover Shepard and Papp discussing him in a *New York Times* article that ran across four columns alongside photographs of the two men. As Woodruff said, "The last thing I wanted to see is these guys talking about me. I mean, fuck, you two have some problems here, argue it between yourselves." For the director, the article became "a whole new insight in the way the world works, the way history is written and who writes it. Because I realized that Joe was writing it and Sam was writing it and, if anything, I was going to be a footnote."

ALTHOUGH SHEPARD AND PAPP had now gone public with the messy details of their intense personal and professional feud, this did nothing to lower the temperature of the simmering backstage melodrama at the Public Theater. Instead, the tension reached an even higher level. Because Tommy Lee Jones and Peter Boyle were both powerful men and it seemed that they might soon come to blows before, during, or after a performance, the play's stage manager was, in Gail Merrifield Papp's words, "terrified violence might break out, because she did not know how to handle it. To avoid this possibility, Papp told Jones and Boyle, 'Look, you guys, I'm going to send Gail in and she'll always be there for every performance. So if you have any problems, just talk to Gail.'"

As a result, Gail Merrifield Papp saw "every performance of *True West* that was ever given at the Public Theater. I would check in with both guys, whom I liked, because they were interesting fellows, before the show. I would be visible to them during the play and then I would be around afterward. Tommy Lee Jones was interested in the Civil War and I was a Civil War buff and so we had a lot to talk about."

Graciously, Tommy Lee Jones later said that, despite all the difficulties, he "felt proud to be an actor at the Public, happy to be an actor, privileged to be an actor, and that's not very common in my profession." But, as he also noted, "Of all the versions of that play that were done at that time, around New York and around the country, ours was distinguished by being the worst."

Frank Rich began his review of the play in *The New York Times* on December 24, 1980, by writing, "Some day, when the warring parties get around to writing their memoirs, we may actually discover who killed 'True West.'" He then noted, "'True West' seems to be a very good Shepard play—which means that it's one of American theater's most precious natural resources. But no play can hold the stage all by itself.

"This play hasn't been misdirected: it really looks as if it hasn't been directed at all"; the "evening's climax—the mystical death embrace of two fratricidal brothers—is so vaguely choreographed it looks like a polka." Rich concluded his review by writing, "Who's to blame? Please address your inquiries to Messrs. Shepard, Woodruff and Papp. And while you're writing, demand restitution. These men owe New York a *true* 'True West.'"

TWENTY-TWO

TRUE WEST REDUX

Just got back from N.Y. where they were working
on another production of *True West* with a couple of
funny and interesting new actors. Amazing to see a
twenty year old play have a brand new life.

—SAM SHEPARD,
TWO PROSPECTORS

BY 1981, GARY SINISE HAD ALREADY BECOME A DYED-IN-THE-
wool Sam Shepard devotee. In a tiny theater in Hollywood two years
earlier, Sinise had played Wesley in a production of *Curse of the Starving Class* featuring James Gammon, who had created the role of
Weston at the Public Theater. Now twenty-six years old, Sinise had
also directed and acted in a production of *Action* at the Steppenwolf
Theatre, the company he had co-founded with his friend and fellow
classmate Jeff Perry in 1974 while both were students at Highland Park
High School in Chicago.

By the time John Malkovich joined the troupe two years later,
Sinise had become Steppenwolf's artistic director. Because Wayne
Adams, who had produced a Steppenwolf show in Chicago, wanted to
bring one of the company's productions to New York, Sinise began his
quest to acquire the rights to *True West* by flying east to plead his case
in person to Shepard's agent, Lois Berman. In a futile attempt to look
like a theatrical impresario, Sinise dressed up "in a nerdy corduroy
jacket, slacks, and paisley tie." As unimpressed with his outfit as she
was with him, Berman told Sinise she wanted the far-better-known
Goodman Theatre to produce the play in Chicago. In defeat, Sinise
went back home.

Nonetheless, as he wrote in his autobiography, "The play wouldn't leave me. I *had* to direct this, and I knew it would be great for the company." Refusing to give up, Sinise began calling Berman on a regular basis. Whenever he did so, she would tell him, "We don't know who you are. We have no idea who Steppenwolf is. We want the Goodman to do it."

Unable to interest the Goodman Theatre in the play, Berman finally gave Sinise the rights to produce *True West* at the Steppenwolf. Sinise then cast John Malkovich as Lee and Jeff Perry as Austin. After the play opened on March 31, 1982, *Chicago Sun-Times* critic Glenna Syse wrote, "Simply the best production I've seen in Chicago all season . . . The Steppenwolf production of Sam Shepard's *True West* is a beaut . . . This is a script with perfect pitch, a rare sense of diminuendo and crescendo, meticulously punctuated and paced for maximum theatrics."

The play then moved to the 440-seat Apollo Theater in Chicago, where it ran for five weeks. Convinced that this was the play Steppenwolf was meant to present in New York, Sinise called Wayne Adams, who came to Chicago to see it. He and his partner then raised $120,000, an extraordinary sum of money for a four-character play performed on a single set (and the equivalent of nearly $325,000 today) to put *True West* on in New York.

At some point during the play's run at the Apollo, Tom Irwin replaced Jeff Perry as Austin. Having spent a semester as John Malkovich's roommate at Illinois State University, Irwin had joined the Steppenwolf company in 1979. In his words, "This was a time when Chicago was pretty insular, and so New York? Los Angeles? They were unimaginable." And while the play's New York City producers intended to come back to Chicago to see Irwin and Malkovich in *True West,* they never did. Nonetheless, both actors were told they would continue to perform their roles when the production moved to the 180-seat Cherry Lane Theatre in Greenwich Village. For various reasons, among them their concern that, as artistic director, Sinise was now spending too much time away from Chicago and the ensemble, the company refused to allow him to bill this version of *True West* as a Steppenwolf Theatre production.

After arriving in New York for his first visit to the city, Tom Irwin was taken to the Top of the Sixes by his aunt for his first martini. On the day before rehearsals were to begin, the producers asked him and John Malkovich to run through a scene onstage at the Cherry Lane, as Irwin said, "just to see how it would feel in that space. Which was the way they put it and that was that."

When Irwin arrived at the theater the next day to begin rehearsals, Wayne Adams was sitting on a bicycle waiting for him. Balding, "with a longish fringe of white hair and wearing a cape," he looked "like a Dickens character." Adams told Irwin that the producers had "decided to go in another direction." In Irwin's words, "No notes, no nothing. My thought was like, 'What the fuck?' I was both devastated and confused. For me, it became a sort of a Holden Caulfield moment in that I then walked all the way from the Cherry Lane Theatre to Central Park."

Describing Tom Irwin as "a fantastic actor" in his autobiography, Sinise writes that "after we started rehearsals . . . one of the producers took me aside and said I needed to play Tom's role." Over the next several days, Sinise writes, "both producers kept encouraging" him to make this change. "But no matter how hard I tried to avoid making this decision, I felt I could do a good job in the role and the producers kept urging me to make the change. So I did."

After Irwin returned to Chicago, "the hardest part of the whole thing was trying to explain it to everyone." None too pleased by the way Sinise had gone off to New York City on his own and then allowed his producers to fire a fellow member of the ensemble so that he could assume his role, the company voted to remove him as artistic director. Despite feeling "crushed" by their decision, Sinise wrote, "Thankfully, down the road there were no hard feelings between Tom and me, and he appeared in three out of the next four shows" Sinise directed at Steppenwolf. Irwin himself then went on to a long and successful career in television and movies.

Nonetheless, the offstage drama that seemed to accompany *True West* whenever it was staged had manifested itself yet again.

ON OCTOBER 17, 1982, THE opening night party for *True West* was held at Chumley's, the historic pub and former speakeasy on Bedford

Street just a four-minute walk from the Cherry Lane Theatre. As the evening wore on, someone brought in a copy of the next day's *New York Times*. In a scene right out of a 1930s movie, Wayne Adams stood up on a table to read out the review.

"As performed by John Malkovich and Gary Sinise, two members of Chicago's Steppenwolf Theater [*sic*] Company making their New York debuts, and as directed by Mr. Sinise, this is the true 'True West,'" critic Mel Gussow wrote. "Though the two actors are a symbiotic team, it is Mr. Malkovich who ambles away with the evening's acting trophy . . . his performance is a comic original . . . 'True West,' revivified, should now take its rightful place in the company of the best of Shepard—along with 'The Tooth of Crime,' 'The [*sic*] Curse of the Starving Class,' and 'Buried Child.'"

As it had never been at the Public Theater, *True West* now seemed funny, albeit in the surreal, somewhat terrifying manner Shepard had intended. "With perfect timing and inexhaustible expressiveness," Gussow wrote of Malkovich's performance as Lee, "he is amusing and menacing at the same time."

With the publication of this review, the phones at the Cherry Lane Theatre began ringing off the hook the next morning as theatergoers called to order tickets for what soon became the hottest show in town. Based on the brilliance of his performance, Malkovich became the flavor of the moment in Manhattan, with celebrities like Jacqueline Kennedy Onassis; her son, John F. Kennedy, Jr.; Bernardo Bertolucci; Kurt Vonnegut; Lauren Bacall; Robert Duvall; and Susan Sarandon coming backstage after performances to meet him.

Malkovich, who won the Obie Award for Best Actor, was also given the Clarence Derwent Award by Actors' Equity as Most Promising Male Actor. Sinise received the Obie Award for Best Director. The production was also nominated for the 1983 Pulitzer Prize for Drama, which was won by Marsha Norman for 'Night, Mother. Far more significantly, this production of *True West* elevated Steppenwolf to a level of national prominence that was confirmed when, in 1985, the company won the Tony Award for Regional Theatre Excellence.

Although Malkovich and Sinise left the New York production after their six-month commitment was over, *True West* continued to run at the Cherry Lane until August 4, 1984. Over the course of its 762 performances, Jim Belushi and Gary Cole as well as a pair of real-life brothers, Dennis and Randy Quaid, performed the leading roles, with Sinise returning to direct each new cast.

Shortly before leaving the show in the spring of 1983, Malkovich and Sinise re-created their roles for an hour-and-fifty-minute video-taped episode of *American Playhouse* that was broadcast nationwide on PBS on January 31, 1984. This version laid the foundation for the play's enduring legacy.

In terms of the continuing role that *True West* would come to play in Sam Shepard's career, the final word belongs to John Malkovich. As he said in an article by Don Shewey in *The Village Voice* on November 30, 1982, "The play is a little unfinished, I think, in Sam's mind. People kept saying *True West* is so commercial, but I think it's a more personal play than most of his. Shepard, like Lee, defies all the things we're told we have to do to be successful. He spent years in a loft picking his nose and writing really punk stuff with Patti Smith, and then he wins a Pulitzer. He's like Austin when he shrugs off his writing to go make all these movies, but then he'll turn around and, like, trash Papp in the *New York Times*—that's such a Lee-like thing to do . . . Lee is the side of Shepard that's always being strangled but never quite killed."

—

TWENTY-THREE

WHEN SAM MET JESSICA

I go through such inner dramas over Jessica—
the whole spectrum of emotions from teen-age
jealousies to the most tender love I've ever known.
I just can't believe she gets to me like that.

—SAM SHEPARD,
TWO PROSPECTORS

THE SILENCE WAS AWKWARD. AS THEY SAT TOGETHER IN A director's office on Santa Monica Boulevard in the fall of 1982, Sam Shepard and Jessica Lange had run out of things to say to each other. With Lange already cast in the lead role in *Frances,* the life story of Frances Farmer, the Hollywood actress who battled the studio system only to be declared legally insane and involuntarily committed to a mental institution for six years, the pressure in this meeting was squarely on Shepard.

Because Graeme Clifford, the Australian film editor who was about to direct his first feature, was still considering other actors, Shepard needed to demonstrate that he and Lange had the kind of personal chemistry that would translate to the screen, thereby enabling him to play Harry York, the fictional character who reappears constantly throughout the film as Farmer's friend and lover.

For reasons that may have had little to do with his desire for the part, Shepard had been unusually concerned about his appearance that day. In his motel room, he changed his clothes three times before deciding on, as biographer John J. Winters wrote, "a pair of old black corduroys, a brown-and-white checked shirt, and western boots." Unwilling to appear "too Hollywood," he then deliberated on whether to leave his shirt collar open or snap it shut. Deciding to go with the more casual look, he left the collar open. Determined not to show up early, he also drove around for a while only to find himself sitting in the waiting room leafing through magazines before the meeting began.

For her part, Jessica Lange, who would win the Academy Award for Best Supporting Actress for her role in *Tootsie* that year while also nominated as Best Actress for *Frances*, had chosen an entirely different kind of look. Pushing her six-month-old daughter, Alexandra "Shura" Lange Baryshnikov, in a baby carriage, Lange wore "a loose blue sweater, white skirt, penny loafers with white socks, and horn-rimmed glasses."

By then, Lange had played the role of the classic blond damsel in distress created by Fay Wray in the original version of *King Kong* in Dino De Laurentiis's 1976 remake of that classic movie. She had appeared in Bob Fosse's *All That Jazz* and had played Cora, the role originated by Lana Turner, the archetypal sultry platinum-blond temptress, in Bob Rafelson's 1981 remake of *The Postman Always Rings Twice*.

Having seen Lange in two of those movies, Shepard was well aware of how much she looked like his great teenage crush, Tuesday Weld. The actresses were actually close friends who had once planned to play sisters in a film. Weld had also wanted to portray Frances Farmer before losing the part to Lange, who was so obsessed with the story that she had tried to option a book about Farmer in order to portray her onscreen. At the time, Weld was also dating Mikhail Baryshnikov, the Russian ballet dancer, choreographer, and actor, who was the father of Lange's daughter.

Barely making eye contact with Shepard as they exchanged initial pleasantries, Lange then busied herself by tending to her infant daughter and seemed to come alive only while talking about Frances Farmer. When their conversation eventually fizzled out into extended silence, Shepard got to his feet, shook Lange's hand, and left the room.

In a notebook entry quoted by Winters, entitled "Ruthless" and dated November 10, 1982—about a month after filming on *Frances* began and after Shepard and Lange were already involved—the playwright wondered whether Lange's appearance at their first meeting had been intended to show Shepard that "she was more than just another great piece of ass." Disdainfully, Shepard also wrote that she had seemed to him like "a college girl. One of those dumb sorority chicks."

Although Graeme Clifford remembered Shepard and Lange "getting along like a house on fire," Lange said, "It was one of those horrible meetings in the director's office . . . The director introduced us and then he just up and left. We're both terribly shy and we're just sitting there. I had Shura in her stroller and Sam looked like he was ready to run out . . . We're both very judgmental, so we were judging each other." Having seen Shepard in *Resurrection*, Lange was also already somewhat in thrall to him because "there was something about him that struck such a familiar chord . . . his long legs . . . I immediately felt I knew something about him, that wildness, that typically American wildness, a no-restraints outlaw quality."

On October 12, 1981, filming began on *Frances* in Seattle, where Farmer was born and raised. Six days later, Shepard joined the cast in the waterfront hotel where his third-floor room was adjacent to the one where Lange was staying with her baby daughter and her nanny. At Graeme Clifford's invitation, Shepard joined the director and some cast members for dinner that evening.

When Lange, who was wearing "a green silk dress that was semi-transparent," stood up to leave the table, Shepard watched her walk away. Stunned by her beauty, he felt an immediate attraction to her that was purely physical. And yet, as he would later write in his notebook, he also recognized his "strong feelings" for her. After Lange had "fixed her hair and put on some makeup," she sat back down at the table. As soon as she began stirring the ice in her drink with her finger, Shepard knew she was also interested in him.

The next morning, Shepard and Lange shot their first scene on a beach where they had to walk together for a while before stopping to kiss. Not surprisingly, they were both nervous. When they kissed, Lange opened her mouth. Losing his balance, Shepard fell on top of her. Along with the crew, they both began to laugh.

Recording all this in detail in his notebook a month later, Shepard wrote that he called O-Lan that night only to have her say how much she missed him. Doing his best to fight the urge to visit Lange next door, Shepard went out for a drink. After returning to his room, the playwright lay in bed trying to fall asleep but could not get Lange out of his mind.

As though to prove he was in control of himself, Shepard made a point of walking right by Lange's trailer on the set the next day without even bothering to knock on her door to say hello. But then, as Lange noted, "Movie sets are the most seductive places in the world—there's nothing like them for creating an ambience of romance and passion. I had a feeling Sam and I were going to fall in love." Concerning her relationship with Shepard, she also said, "When it started, it was never with the intention that we were going to run off, live together, have a family, do all these . . . regular things. It was just this unbelievably passionate love affair. But then we just couldn't give it up."

SIX YEARS YOUNGER THAN Shepard, Jessica Phyllis Lange, who could "sing every lyric Dylan ever wrote" because he had been "a transformational artist in her life," was very much a girl from the North Country. Born on April 20, 1949, in Cloquet, Minnesota, which she remembered as "a worn-out little mill town" about half an hour from Duluth, where Dylan had been born and then lived until he was six, Lange moved with her family twelve times and attended eight different schools before finally returning to Cloquet when she was sixteen. "I was always the new girl in town," she said, "the outsider looking in. I've felt that way my whole life, like I never belonged in one particular place."

Changing jobs constantly, her father, Al, whom Lange described as "a drinker" for whom "nothing I did was ever good enough," worked as a traveling salesman, a car dealer, and a teacher. A powerful and charismatic figure who, much like Shepard's father, had also experienced "a certain degree of disappointment" in his life, Al Lange taught his young daughter how to swim by throwing her off a pier. "The first time I rode a horse," Lange said, "he gave it a smack on the ass and the horse ran off and he expected you to hold on, and I did."

After graduating from Cloquet High School in 1967, Lange attended the University of Minnesota on a scholarship. Enrolling in the fine arts program, she intended to "get my BFA, go on to get an MFA," and then "devote my life to painting." When she learned that the drawing class she wanted to attend during the second quarter of her freshman year was full, she decided to sign up instead for a class in photography. At some point during the semester, the instructor introduced her to two young photographers who were, in Lange's words, "leaving for Spain to make a documentary about flamenco Gypsies in Andalusia. And they asked me, did I want to come along? Yes, I said."

The photographers were Francisco "Paco" Grande and Danny Seymour. Twenty-four years old, Grande had been born in Madrid into a family known for "its long line of distinguished doctors and scientists." Seymour's mother was the poet and actress Isabella Gardner. His father was the Russian-born celebrity photographer Maurice Seymour.

Lange and Grande, who by then had become lovers, then set off with Seymour on an international odyssey. After living with the Romany while following flamenco fairs around Seville, Lange was teargassed while taking part in the May 1968 street demonstrations in Paris led by Daniel Cohn-Bendit (aka "Danny the Red"), the organizer of the student strike that had shut down the entire country. After a year in Europe, Lange and Grande took up residence in one of the three lofts on the Bowery in Lower Manhattan that Seymour had purchased with family money. Having just parted company with his first wife, Robert Frank moved into another loft and became Seymour's friend, collaborator, and mentor.

While working on a documentary about drug smugglers, Grande got busted when the pilot of a plane loaded with 920 pounds of marijuana on which he was a passenger crash-landed in the New Mexico desert. Leaving Grande behind to get arrested, the pilot disappeared before the authorities arrived. Because Grande's lawyer told Lange it would help his case, she agreed to marry him. After they returned to New York City in the fall of 1971, Robert Frank and Seymour collaborated on *Home Is Where the Heart Is*, an eighteen-minute color film about loneliness and drug use in which Lange made her first onscreen appearance, as a waitress.

Having already performed mime for free on the streets of New

York, Lange went off on her own to Paris to study with Étienne De-croux just as Ronny Davis of the San Francisco Mime Troupe had done before her. "An adventure," Lange would later say, "that's all I was interested in. That's why I did everything—hooked up with all the men I did, tried all the drugs I tried, lived all the different life-styles. I had no fear."

During the two years she spent in Paris, Lange had several boy-friends, reunited with Grande only to break up with him again, and was taken up by Antonio Lopez, the fashion illustrator who had dis-covered Jerry Hall and Tina Chow. While Lopez was photographing Lange all over Paris in high-fashion couture, Frank and Seymour were filming *Cocksucker Blues,* the documentary of the 1972 Rolling Stones tour of the United States.

When the tour ended, Seymour bought a thirty-eight-foot yacht and set sail for South America only to then vanish at sea. Returning from Paris, Lange flew with Grande to Colombia to look for their friend. Although the yacht was eventually found, Seymour's body never was. Brought back together by the loss, Lange and Grande began living together in a fifth-floor walk-up in Greenwich Village.

While taking acting classes with Herbert Berghof, who had trained Geraldine Page, Anne Bancroft, Liza Minnelli, Al Pacino, and Robert De Niro, Lange worked as a waitress at the Lion's Head tavern on Christopher Street in Greenwich Village. As Claudia Carr Levy says, "I knew Jessica because when I first came to New York, a writer friend got me a job working at the Lion's Head. It really was a very macho place, but Jessica trained me and taught me how to deal with those guys. She was sweet and very determined and focused and at the Lion's Head, they called her 'The Beautiful One.'"

In 1975, Lange was cast to play the heroine in *King Kong.* Al-though she won the Golden Globe for Best Acting Debut in a Motion Picture—Female, she did not appear in another movie for three years until she was cast as Angelique, the angel of death in *All That Jazz,* Bob Fosse's autobiographical musical drama. "There were a couple of men who were crazy about me when they saw *Kong.* Fosse was one," Lange said. The two became "friends and lovers" and had "a wonderful relationship." Initially attracted to Fosse "because he was a renegade and there was such a dark side to him," Lange discovered that "there was, about Fosse, something sad. Profoundly lonely. That's what I connected with more than anything, because I understood that loneliness."

In 1981, Lange co-starred with Jack Nicholson in Bob Rafelson's remake of the classic 1946 John Garfield–Lana Turner movie *The Postman Always Rings Twice*, with a script by David Mamet based on James M. Cain's novel. As it had been during the final stages of the casting process for *King Kong*, the last two actresses considered for the leading female role in the movie were Lange and Meryl Streep.

Paul Pascarella, an abstract artist who would become one of Sam Shepard's closest friends, was hanging out in Hollywood with Rafelson while the director was trying to decide between Lange and Streep. "It was just two of us together," Pascarella says. "Just Bob and I and he said, 'Now, in this situation, you always go with the better actress.' And then he said, 'But who would you *really* want to fuck?'"

In his *New York Times* review of *The Postman Always Rings Twice*, in March 1981, Vincent Canby wrote, "At the heart of the film, though, is Jessica Lange . . . Miss Lange is not a bad actress, but her miscasting is fatal to the picture and exemplifies its tiresomely genteel artfulness . . . In these circumstances, Miss Lange's low-voltage sexuality recalls Marilyn Chambers, the classy, suburban-looking pornographic star." Undeterred by such reviews, Lange was then cast in both *Tootsie* and *Frances*. After they had co-starred in *The Postman Always Rings Twice*, Jack Nicholson famously described Lange as "a cross between a fawn and a Buick." As she herself said, "I never accepted failure at anything. There was no doubt I was going to succeed."

Characterizing what her life was like until seven months before she began filming *Frances*, Lange said, "From about seventeen until I had my first child, I lived like a madwoman. I really burnt out my cylinders. There is nothing that I feel I've missed. I lived everywhere and, believe me, did everything. I have gone down the road full tilt."

RELEASED TWO WEEKS BEFORE *Tootsie*, in December 1982, *Frances* featured Lange in the role for which she was nominated for an Academy Award for Best Actress. Although Vincent Canby described the film in his *New York Times* review as "such a mixed up movie that it still seems to be unfinished," he also wrote, "Yet it also contains a magnificent performance by Jessica Lange in the title role. Here is a performance so unfaltering, so tough, so intelligent and so humane that it seems as if Miss Lange is just now, at long last, making her motion picture debut."

Playing a character whose identity, Canby noted, "was difficult to understand" except as "a figment of the writer's desperation," Shepard first appears in the film wearing a hat that makes him look very much like his father during his stint as a reporter in Chicago before World War II. Although Shepard did the best he could with a seriously underwritten role, the obviously fake moustache he had to wear for the rest of the movie did nothing to enhance his performance.

And while Lange and Shepard played lovers in *Frances,* the heat they generated onscreen paled in comparison to the intensity of an affair that became even more feverish after the movie was released. Nor were Shepard and Lange particularly discreet about their behavior when they were out together in Los Angeles. In her extensive 1991 profile of Lange in *Vanity Fair,* Nancy Collins quoted an unnamed television producer who had seen Lange and Shepard having dinner together during this period in a restaurant near the Chateau Marmont: "I've never seen anything like it in a restaurant . . . They were literally attached to each other over the top of the table. They kept twisting around, holding hands, then a hand would go up the arm, into Jessica's mouth. I don't think a lot of eating was going on, because her mouth was constantly full of his hand. They were just gorgeous and madly, wildly, passionately involved with each other."

In Lange's words, "It was a no-win situation. He was married and I had a little year-old baby. And when we were together we were so wild—drinking, getting into fights, walking down the freeway trying to get away—I mean, just really wild stuff."

On January 27, 1982, Shepard and Lange went out for a quiet dinner at Ports, the hip restaurant hidden behind a nondescript black metal door on Santa Monica Boulevard. On any given night in Ports, celebrities like Francis Ford Coppola, Tom Wolfe, Oliver Stone, Warren Beatty, Julie Christie, and Robert Redford could be found dining in the small front room. After they had finished their dinner, Shepard left the restaurant a step behind Lange. Clad in a light-colored jacket and jeans with a woolen scarf around her neck, a cloth handbag over her shoulder, and her hair pulled back, Lange looked nothing at all as she had in *Frances* or *Tootsie*. Shepard was just as casual in a dark ribbed long-sleeve sweater, tapered Western-style jeans, and cowboy boots. Holding his down vest in both hands, he followed Lange into the street with a lit cigarette dangling from his mouth and his hair cut relatively short.

Unfortunately for them both, Ron Galella, the world-famous paparazzo who by then had already been sued by Jacqueline Kennedy Onassis and punched in the face by Marlon Brando, was lying in wait for them on the sidewalk along with two of his fellow paparazzi. Four black-and-white photographs taken by Galella that night eloquently tell the story of what then happened.

In the first, Lange sees Galella as she comes out of the restaurant. Involuntarily, she looks right into his camera. In the second, she turns her back on him as Shepard follows her onto the street. In the third, which became the image picked up by the wire services who then distributed it to newspapers all over America, Shepard does not turn away as Lange has done. Instead, completely losing his cool, he begins screaming obscenities at the paparazzi. As they go right on clicking away, Shepard hauls off with the only thing he can get his hands on and flings his vest at them. The fourth image is the most telling by far. Standing with one hand on the front door handle of Shepard's pickup truck, Lange covers her eyes and forehead with her other hand as though she cannot believe what has just happened.

Far more media savvy than Shepard, especially where Hollywood celebrity culture was concerned, Lange knew their hitherto relatively secret affair would now become public knowledge. She also knew that the two people most affected by this would be O-Lan Jones and Misha Baryshnikov, with whom Lange was then still living.

SAM SHEPARD WAS STAYING at the Chateau Marmont during one of his regular visits to Los Angeles during this period to spend time with

Lange when he first read the script for *The Right Stuff*, the film based on the bestselling book by Tom Wolfe. That the screenplay had been personally delivered to him by Philip Kaufman, who had written it and was now about to direct the $22 million movie, spoke volumes about just how much he wanted Shepard in his film.

Kaufman had made his major studio debut in 1972 by writing and directing *The Great Northfield Minnesota Raid*. He then directed *The White Dawn* and a remake of the 1956 science-fiction classic *Invasion of the Body Snatchers*. Able to work in a variety of genres, he and his wife, Rose, co-wrote the script for *The Wanderers*, a gritty working-class drama based on the novel by Richard Price, which Kaufman also directed. After creating the story for *Raiders of the Lost Ark*, Kaufman was hired by producers Robert Chartoff and Irwin Winkler to direct *The Right Stuff*.

Having produced the first two *Rocky* movies, which grossed $356 million worldwide (the equivalent of more than $1 billion today), Chartoff and Winkler had bought the film rights to Wolfe's 1979 account of the seven original American astronauts for $350,000. Sparing no expense, they hired William Goldman, then the highest-priced screenwriter in Hollywood, to write the script.

Focusing his story on the astronauts, Goldman made no mention at all of Chuck Yeager, the fabled World War II fighter pilot who had shot down five enemy aircraft in a single day before becoming the first man to break the sound barrier by flying the Bell X-1 experimental jet seven hundred miles an hour, thereby creating the world's first sonic boom. Recognizing that Yeager personified the kind of ineffable cool that was the essence of "the right stuff," Kaufman made him a key supporting character in the new version he wrote in just eight weeks. The first actor he considered for the part was Robert Duvall, whom Kaufman had directed in *The Great Northfield Minnesota Raid*, but he then decided Duvall was too old for the part.

In 1982, Kaufman and his wife attended a reading Shepard gave from *Motel Chronicles* in San Francisco. At one point during the evening, Rose Kaufman poked her husband and said, "That's your guy."

Kaufman, who had no idea what she was talking about, asked, "For what?"

"Yeager," she said.

Even though "Sam was this tall, gangly guy who looked nothing like Yeager," Kaufman realized the actor-playwright "had a cowboy quality to him. He was Gary Cooper." Shepard then became the director's first choice to play a man born and raised in rural West Virginia who had enlisted in the U.S. Army Air Force at the age of eighteen and then became the commander of the Aerospace Research Pilot School at Edwards Air Force Base, where the astronauts trained in 1962.

This did not mean Shepard was all that eager to play the role. "Phil offered the part to me a few times," he said, "and I refused. I felt like it was ridiculous to play a living person. I knew Chuck and I didn't feel like I was him at all." Despite Shepard's reluctance to commit to the part, Kaufman "kept hounding" him about it. Because Shepard "did like Phil a lot" and also "liked a lot of the actors" who had already been cast in the movie—like Ed Harris, who had been in *Cowboy Mouth* and *True West* in Los Angeles, and Fred Ward, who had appeared in *Inacoma* at the Magic Theatre—the playwright thought, "Well, maybe it wouldn't hurt to do it."

Because Shepard had not, in Kaufman's words, "ever been in a successful film" and "wasn't a magic name to the studio," Chartoff and Winkler were not nearly so eager to see him in the part. Refusing to give up, Kaufman rewrote the script, eliminating much of Shepard's dialogue so he could replace it with physical action. When the producers saw Shepard in a leather jacket on horseback in the film's opening scene, they immediately claimed to have been on board with Kaufman's choice all along.

And while the director said Shepard and Yeager "didn't hit it off right away" because Yeager "was a conservative general, and Sam was a freewheeling, progressive-thinking guy," they both came to realize that "there were certain things they didn't really talk about, and that was the quality—called 'the right stuff'—that they each understood the other had."

On his first day on location in Lancaster, a city in the high desert about seventy miles from Los Angeles, Shepard ran into Yeager outside the motel where both were staying. When Shepard said he was about to change the oil in his truck, Yeager, who served as a technical consultant for the film and played a bit part as well and who had driven to the set in his own Ford pickup truck, joined him and they did the job together.

Nor was the great irony of being cast to play Chuck Yeager after not setting foot in an airplane in seventeen years lost on Shepard. Because a part of his process as an actor was to bond with his subject in every possible way, Shepard said, "I went up with Yeager in a Piper Cub. I figured if I died while flying with the greatest pilot in the world, it would be OK." By then, the cast of *The Right Stuff* included several members of Shepard's Bay Area acting circle—like Jim Haynie, Jane Dornacker, John Lion, Kathy Baker, and, in a brief appearance as a girl in Pancho's bar, where the astronauts drink at night, Shepard's wife, O-Lan Jones. In all, more than twenty actors from the Magic Theatre appeared in the movie.

Once filming moved back to the Bay Area, Shepard and Ed Harris could often be found drinking together in the Tosca Cafe on Columbus Avenue in the heart of North Beach, in San Francisco. "Eddie and me were big buddies," Shepard said, "and we liked liquor a little bit more than we should have. And yeah, we got into some fights in that bar."

Filmed by Caleb Deschanel, who was nominated for an Academy Award for his work, Shepard's first scene in *The Right Stuff* features him galloping madly through the desert (on one of his own horses no less) as he chases Barbara Hershey, who portrays Glennis, Yeager's wife. Throughout the film, Shepard is always so relaxed that he never seems to be acting. In a flashback to the day in 1947 when Yeager broke the sound barrier, Shepard boards a vintage B-29 while wearing a leather helmet, goggles, and an oxygen mask and looking very much like his father during World War II.

Making it plain that Chuck Yeager's spirit inspired those who came after him to venture into space, Kaufman began and ended *The Right Stuff* with him. During the film's final sequence, the director cuts back and forth between the astronauts watching Sally Rand perform her famous fan dance at a barbecue celebrating the opening of the NASA Space Center in Houston and Shepard at the controls of a Lockheed

NF-104A as it spirals out of control and begins plummeting toward the desert. Finally managing to eject himself from the cockpit, he struggles to open his parachute as smoke billows from his flight suit. In Houston, the astronauts continue enjoying themselves only to suddenly all look up at once as though they have just heard the thunderous sound of Yeager's jet crashing outside Edwards Air Force Base sixteen hundred miles away.

A huge plume of black smoke wells up from the desert. Kicking up dust, an army ambulance speeds toward the crash site. As stirring music wells up in the background, Shepard, his face blackened with grease and oil, comes walking slowly toward the camera with his parachute neatly folded under his right arm. In cinematic terms, the scene defined Yeager as the greatest American aeronautic hero of all time.

Although *Newsweek* magazine wanted to do a cover story on Shepard, and the producers were more than eager for him to participate, Shepard was the only actor in *The Right Stuff* with a clause in his contract specifying he would not have to do publicity for the film after its October 1983 release. Nonetheless, he was singled out by critics for his breakthrough performance. Despite being part of an outstanding ensemble of actors that included Ed Harris, Scott Glenn, and Dennis Quaid, Shepard was the only one to be nominated for an Academy Award for his performance as Best Supporting Actor. Ironically, Jack Nicholson won an Oscar that year for his leading role as a retired astronaut in *Terms of Endearment*.

Shepard himself chose not to attend the 1984 Academy Awards ceremony at the Dorothy Chandler Pavilion in Los Angeles, which was being televised live internationally to seventy-six countries. Asked why he was not there, he said, "It was too many people. I've never felt great in crowds, and certainly not when they're putting the spotlight on you like that." By then, he was also no longer living with his wife, son, and extended family in Mill Valley.

TWENTY-FOUR

FOOL FOR LOVE

I'm in the third week of rehearsal here at the Magic
for my new play called *Fool for Love,* which is really
the outcome of all this tumultuous feeling I've been
going through for the past year. It's a very emotional
play and, in some ways, it's embarrassing for me to
witness yet somehow necessary at the same time.

—SAM SHEPARD,
LETTERS AND TEXTS,
1972–1984

DURING THE EARLY DAYS OF FILMING *THE RIGHT STUFF* ABOUT
two months after the incident outside Ports restaurant, Shepard came
up with the basic scenario for *Fool for Love,* the fourth work in the
series of family dramas that remains the high-water mark of his career.
By far his most perfectly polished play, *Fool for Love* has the great
economy of a brilliant screenplay. At the same time, the play is so intrinsically theatrical that the 1985 movie based upon it, directed by
Robert Altman with a script by Shepard himself, who also starred in
the film, was both a critical and a commercial disaster of the first order.

Nor was it an accident that the forty-six-page one-act play that
took just an hour and fifteen minutes to perform onstage was so intri-
cately constructed. Mad with desire for a woman he could not live
without, but unwilling to abandon his wife and teenage son as his father had done before him, Shepard was driven by an obsessive need to
make everything work perfectly on the page in this play even as his
own life was spinning madly out of control. "I wrote about sixteen versions of it," he said, "and every time I came back to the first five pages.

I'd write like seventy, eighty pages and then bring it all the way back to the first five pages and start again . . . So, I've got literally at least a dozen different versions of the play, but the first five pages are the same in every one . . . They weren't just drafts—I wrote twelve *plays*."

At one point, Shepard became so thoroughly lost in the writing process that he enlisted Johnny Dark, who had no theatrical experience and was more often stoned than not, to serve as his dramaturge. In a conversation Dark taped that was published in *Two Prospectors*, Shepard asked him to picture three characters onstage, two of whom were in the present, with the third "in the past, like a memory." This character, whom Dark called "a visual memory," talked "directly" to one character but did not exist for the other.

Explaining how this would work onstage, Shepard said, "It's like the old ghost thing in *Our Town*." And while the Stage Manager, presumably the character in Thornton Wilder's Pulitzer Prize–winning play to which Shepard was referring, was not a ghost, the point was not lost on Dark. And so when Dark brought up *Topper*, a 1937 movie featuring Cary Grant and Constance Bennett in which a dead couple talk only to the title character, a film that then became a popular television series during the mid-1950s, Shepard confirmed this was in fact precisely what he meant.

Pursuing his line of questioning further, Shepard asked Dark how he would feel if the visual memory character suddenly began talking to the character who had not yet been able to see or hear him. When Dark said this absolutely should not happen, Shepard asked, "He shouldn't suddenly start talking to him? . . . It would be clearer the other way?"

"Yeah," Dark said.

"You wouldn't buy it?" Shepard asked.

"No," Dark said. "Not at all."

Shepard then ended what may have been a truly significant conversation insofar as the final version of *Fool for Love* was concerned by simply saying, "O.K. I just wanted to know."

Relentlessly continuing to rewrite, Shepard showed up one day at the Magic Theatre, where the opening of *Fool for Love* had already been delayed because of the playwright's involvement as an actor in

The Right Stuff, to show John Lion the eleventh and penultimate version of the play. Although Lion had not yet read the script, he had already "auditioned about a hundred actresses" to portray a character who now did not appear onstage. Nor was the "visual memory character" even in this draft.

Nonetheless, because "the story was essentially there," Lion "was convinced it would play like gangbusters." After saying that the play "somehow seemed 'square'" because it "was pretty linear" which was "unusual for Sam," Lion suggested, "Maybe it needs a three-quarter circle surrounding three points of the square." Three weeks later, Shepard returned with the completed version of the script.

In bold type, the first line of his stage notes, which he wrote after directing the play at the Magic Theatre, reads, **"This play is to be performed relentlessly without a break."** Having established how he wanted *Fool for Love* to be paced, the playwright then specifies exactly how the low-rent motel room on the edge of the Mojave Desert where all the action takes place should look. In granular detail, he describes the "faded blue chenille bedspread" on the four-poster bed, the "well-worn yellow Formica top" of the metal table, and the subdued "grays and blacks" of the horse blanket "laced to the back" of the old maple rocking chair on the small extended platform framed with black curtains located extreme downstage left.

As Merle Haggard's "Wake Up" from *The Way I Am* album plays, the lights rise in tempo to the music until three actors are revealed onstage. Pouring whisky from the bottle by his side into a Styrofoam cup, the Old Man sits in profile to the house on the platform. He sports "a scraggly red beard" and wears "an old stained 'open-road' Stetson hat," a "dark quilted jacket with the stuffing coming out at the elbows," a pair of "black-and-white checkered slacks" that are "too short in the legs," and a pair of "beat up, dark western boots." This is yet another version of Sam Rogers. In this incarnation, however, "He exists only in the minds" of the other two characters, "even though they might talk to him directly and acknowledge his physical presence." For his part, the Old Man "treats them as though they all existed in the same time and place."

Absolutely still, May, who is in her early thirties, sits on the bed facing the audience with her head down, staring at the floor. She is barefoot, with a silver ankle bracelet, and wears a blue denim skirt and a baggy white T-shirt. In "muddy, broken-down cowboy boots with silver gaffer's tape wrapped around them at the toes," Eddie sits in a chair upstage by the table, facing May. His "well-worn, faded, dirty jeans . . . smell like horse sweat. A pair of spurs dangle from his belt." Eddie limps when he walks, and "there is a peculiar broken-down quality about his body in general, as though he's aged long before his time."

While Eddie stares at May, he works resin from a small white bag into the bucking glove on his right hand. Sticking his gloved hand into the handle of the leather bucking strap, he twists it up so the strap and glove make "a weird stretching sound." As the song ends and the lights come up full, he pulls out his hand and takes off the glove.

Before either character has said a word, Shepard has presented the audience with a compelling visual portrait of what *Fool for Love* is all about. As Shepard biographer Don Shewey writes, the play is "basically a continuation of *True West* by other means, an investigation of 'double nature' pitting not man against himself but man against woman, or the male part against the female part of the same person."

In the months since Shepard had begun his relationship with Lange, the playwright had lived in a state of constant turmoil, torn between conflicting emotions he found impossible to resolve. In his words, "The play came out of falling in love. It's such a dumbfounding experience. In one way you wouldn't trade it for the world. In another way it's absolute hell. More than anything, falling in love causes a certain female thing in a man to manifest, oddly enough."

The unceasing combat between Eddie and May, a pair of truly star-crossed lovers, forms the dramatic spine of *Fool for Love*. Like two heavyweight fighters who have met many times before in the ring, they exchange charges, threats, and accusations throughout the play as, despite it all, Eddie just keeps right on proclaiming his undying love for her.

Shepard's great reveal occurs about ten pages before *Fool for Love* ends. Although Eddie and May had different mothers, the Old Man fathered them both. As half sister and half brother, they are literally and figuratively one half of each other. Together, they form one complete human being.

The level of theatrical craft in *Fool for Love* is astonishing. The timing of the many exits and entrances, which Shepard made even more dramatic by wiring the walls and doors of the set and putting speakers in the house so the sound of doors being slammed onstage would reverberate throughout the theater, is exquisite.

No less extraordinary is the way the Old Man appears and then fades back into darkness until Eddie and May begin recounting the story of their father's double life as well as how they first fell in love as teenagers without knowing they were related. The way Shepard uses the Countess, a high-fashion model in love with Eddie who has followed him to this motel, to move the plot forward without ever bringing her onstage is also impressive. In different ways, both May and the Countess embody different aspects of Lange's public persona and personality as well as Shepard's own divided nature.

So much of the dialogue in *Fool for Love* is about Shepard's ongoing affair with Lange that it should come as no surprise that the playwright felt embarrassed to reveal his feelings onstage. Speaking about May's mother, the Old Man says, "She drew me to her . . . She was a force . . . But she kept opening up her heart to me. How could I turn away from her? We were completely whole." The Old Man's double life also mirrors Shepard's domestic situation at the time.

Shepard's other great breakthrough in *Fool for Love* was to ground a story that might have seemed too fantastical to believe in a physical reality that was incontrovertibly real. By doing so, he made it plain the real drama in American lives often occurred in the low-rent motel rooms on the edge of nowhere where he himself had spent so many nights on his own while on the road heading somewhere in his pickup truck.

AFTER *FOOL FOR LOVE* opened at the Magic Theatre on February 3, 1983, the play moved to the Circle Repertory Company Theater at 99 Seventh Avenue South in Greenwich Village. In his *New York Times* review on May 27, 1983, Frank Rich called *Fool for Love* "a western for our time. We watch a pair of figurative gunslingers fight to the finish—not with bullets, but with piercing words that give ballast to the weight of a nation's buried dreams."

Quickly becoming a smash hit, *Fool for Love* moved to Broadway six months later, where it ran for another two years. All told, the play was performed one thousand times in New York City, outstripping the Steppenwolf Theatre production of *True West* by more than two hundred performances. A finalist for the 1984 Pulitzer Prize for Drama, *Fool for Love* won the Obie Award for Best New American Play, for Best Director for Shepard, and for Best Actor for Ed Harris, Kathy Baker, and Will Patton, who followed Harris as Eddie in the New York City production.

Despite all the acclaim, Shepard himself had decidedly mixed feelings about the work. "That play baffles me," he said. "I love the opening, in the sense that I couldn't get enough of this thing between Eddie and May. I just wanted that to go on and on and on. But I knew that was impossible. One way out was to bring the father in. Part of me looks at *Fool for Love* and says, 'This is great,' and part of me says, 'This is really corny' . . . It's still not satisfying. I don't think the play really found itself."

FIVE WEEKS AFTER *Fool for Love* opened at the Magic Theatre, Shepard and Johnny Dark had breakfast together on St. Patrick's Day in the IHOP on Fourth Street in downtown San Rafael. After spending more than a year trying to decide whether to leave his wife, son, and extended family for the woman he could not live without, Shepard had finally reached the breaking point.

In his words, "completely strung out about whether I should stay or go," he appealed to his friend for help. Dark, who, with Scarlett's knowledge and consent, had long since been having affairs with other women, told Shepard he might as well go, because if he stayed, the playwright was going to tear himself to pieces. One way or the other, Dark said Shepard would just have to learn to live with being pulled in two different directions at once.

After driving back to Evergreen Avenue, Shepard rushed around the house trying to pack before anyone else came home. At one point, without really expecting an answer, he began shouting, "Where's my fucking bag?" Throwing his guitar into his truck, he got behind the wheel, put on a Hank Williams tape, and headed south on Highway 5 to Los Angeles. Behind him, he had left his wife, his son, his extended family, and what he would later recall as the happiest time of his life.

In a story entitled "Coalinga ½ Way" published nineteen years later in *great dream of heaven,* Shepard wrote that after reaching the halfway point on his journey, he pulled over to the side of the road to make a phone call. Although Johnny Dark and Sandy Rogers both confirmed he did in fact make this call that day and that much of the dialogue is what he actually said, Shepard chose to set his story in the blazing heat of summer in the San Joaquin Valley rather than on the cool and rainy St. Patrick's Day in 1983 when it all really occurred.

Written in the third person and in present tense, "Coalinga ½ Way" opens with an unnamed driver pulling over to the side of the road. Despite the dread he feels, he knows it is time to make the call and so forces himself to walk to a pay phone with a commanding view of the feed lots outside Coalinga where "pathetic groups of steers stand on tall black mounds of their own shit, waiting for slaughter."

Even before the narrator drops his quarter into the pay phone to call his wife long distance, person-to-person and collect, he can see her face and big eyes and hear her voice. After accepting the call, the first thing she says is, "Where are you?"

"Coalinga," he answers. After she asks him what he is doing all the way down there, he tells her he is on his way south.

"Why?" she asks.

"I'm just—going," he responds.

"Going?" she says. "When are you coming back?"

"I'm not," he tells her.

"You mean, ever? You're not ever coming back?"

"I don't think so," he says.

Gasping as the shock of what he has just said hits her, she says nothing at all for a while. As a truck blasts by and a cow moans, he waits.

"Listen," she suddenly says. "Why don't I drive halfway down and meet you? You drive halfway back, and I'll drive halfway down. Does that sound fair? Just to talk?"

"I don't think so," he says.

When she asks whether he is going to tell their son about this, he says, "Not right now." When she presses him about it, he says, "Tell him I'll call him."

"When?"

"I'm not sure," he says. After a long period of silence that makes him wonder if she is still on the line, he asks, "Are you still there?"

"Where am I supposed to go?" she says. Then she asks, "Is this about her? Is that what this is? You're going down there to be with her?"

"Yeah," he says. "I am."

When she asks him if the woman has told her man about this, he says, "She's going to tell him, I guess."

Unable to believe he is still going down there to be with the woman despite this, she brings up her own family history and then his as well. Just like Sam Rogers, her father walked out on her family. After mentioning their son again, she begins choking up. Pursuing a different line of inquiry, she asks what he thinks this will change. Because whatever is causing this is inside him, swapping women is not going to solve the problem.

Agreeing with her, he says, "No. Probably not."

"It didn't solve it when you changed over to me, did it?"

"No," he says.

"How many times have you done this and what's it come to?" After he says he does not know, she asks, "So why are you doing it again?"

To this, he also has no answer.

As the steers begin bawling, the combination of the awful stink and the heat begins making his eyes water. For a moment, he fools himself into thinking he is crying while knowing he is not. As though he were now looking down at himself from the perspective of a hawk high in the sky, he sees himself as "a tiny man in vast space, clutching a chunk of black plastic."

After she asks when he will call again, he says, "Tomorrow."

She says he has to tell their son about this because she cannot.

After he says he will, she hangs up the phone "with a soft click." Hearing it, he knows a door has shut behind him through which he can never go again.

As the narrator continues driving south with the air-conditioning in his pickup truck turned up high, all he can think about is the imaginary conversation he had with his wife less than a month ago on his way back home from Los Angeles. Talking out loud to himself, he swore he would never leave her, never repeat his father's mistakes, and never abandon his son. Feeling like an honest man filled with conviction, he could hardly wait to tell her all this as she came running from their house to greet him. Only he never did.

With night falling, "a scared boy takes the place of the man" behind the wheel as he "rides the snaking mountain down into the wild lights of L.A." Driving past the intersection of Sunset and Highland in West Hollywood, he sees the "the shiny movie-star faces" leering down at him from huge billboards. "Stretch limos with tinted windows and thumping, subsonic bass lines" haunt "the streets with secret cargo" as "coveys of hysterical, screaming girls, hair teased, tattooed and pierced in every department" run toward "a nightclub framed in pulsing lavender neon."

Without a bag, a toothbrush, or even a change of underwear, he checks into the Tropicana Motel, then still the low-rent residence of choice for rock stars who had not yet lost all contact with ordinary reality. In a room that smells like "bad Chinese food," he picks up the phone. Having "called this number from every conceivable dark corner for the past two years," he has long since memorized it.

When she answers and begins to laugh with delight at the sound of his voice, he feels "a rush of white excitement like falling from a rope swing into icy water."

When she asks what he is doing at the Tropicana, he says, "I've left."

Suddenly, she stops laughing. After learning he has told his wife everything and then driven to Los Angeles today, she laughs again. Only, now it sounds like an expression of worry and concern.

Giving her his room number, he asks if she can come over now. "I need to see you," he says.

Telling him she was just going out the door when he called, she says she is about to fly to the Midwest to join her man.

For a long while, he says nothing.

"Are you still there?" she asks.

Repeating what his wife said when he asked her the same question, he says, "Where am I supposed to go?" With this question, the story ends.

Now roughly the same age as Sam Rogers when he abandoned his wife and children in Duarte, Sam Shepard had long since left that world far behind him only to now find himself repeating the very same pattern of behavior. Nor did his ability to recognize what he was doing stop him from pursuing what he now saw as his only real chance at personal happiness. And while all this might have been viewed by some as a simple case of the sins of the father being visited upon the son, Shepard explained his own behavior in the epigraph he selected for *Fool for Love:* "The proper response to love is to accept it. There is nothing to do."

TWENTY-FIVE

COUNTRY MATTERS

I love this woman in a way I can't describe & a
feeling of belonging to each other that reaches
across all the pain. It's as though we answered
something in each other that was almost forgotten.

—SAM SHEPARD,
TWO PROSPECTORS

NINE DAYS AFTER HE ARRIVED IN LOS ANGELES, SHEPARD WAS
happily ensconced with Lange in what he described as "her remote
cabin hideaway in the deep forests of Northern Minnesota surrounded
by snow. Everything's white & silent as far as the eye can see & the ear
can hear. It's like sitting in the middle of a Christmas postcard & it's
almost the end of March. Very cold outside but warm as toast in here
with the wood fires burning."

After they had spent three blissful days together "absolutely alone,"
Shepard realized Lange's remote hideaway outside Wrenshall, a village
where the city hall was located on Alcohol Road, was just ten miles
from Cloquet, where Lange was born and graduated from high school
and where her parents still lived.

In Shepard's truck, they then went to visit them so Lange could
pick up her two-year-old daughter and four- and six-year-old neph-
ews. Leading Shepard into the kitchen, Lange's father, "a gruff old
country guy with a black plow horse out back & broken down tractors
all sitting around the yard buried in snow," thumbed through his
daughter's fan mail before handing Shepard two letters with his name
on them. Still traumatized by his decision to leave home, Shepard
knew immediately the letters were from Johnny Dark but then as he

would write to Dark on March 29, 1983, "Everything strikes me on the raw nerves these days—even the recognition of your handwriting."

After driving Lange and the three young children down a winding back country road covered so deeply in mud, slush, and snow that he had to put the truck into four-wheel drive so they could reach her cabin, Shepard received an abrupt introduction to what family life in rural Minnesota could be like at this time of year. Promptly falling down a flight of stairs, Lange's nephew cracked his head open so badly that he began "crying like crazy" and "screaming for Mom" as they applied ice packs to his head and wrapped him in blankets. With the nearest doctor thirty miles away, Shepard worried the child might have suffered a concussion and so he and Lange began waking the boy up every fifteen minutes to ensure he had not lost consciousness only to then realize he was fine.

The next day, Shepard and Lange spent time together in Duluth, which he described as "a town right out of Kerouac . . . on the shores of Lake Superior with brick industrial buildings . . . I can't describe the feeling I had walking side by side with her down those streets knowing this was her hometown & she was a child in this place . . . & here I was *with* her & we were really together after all those agonizing months of being separated." Nonetheless, he still missed "the family & Jesse & O-Lan & all of you—sometimes with a terrible sadness that seizes me completely. The thing that hurts me the most is knowing I abandoned everyone. That I ran off & left everyone high and dry." Even though they were all "self-sufficient more or less & resilient & able to continue no matter what—I still get swamped by this feeling of betrayal. Especially for O-Lan."

At the same time, Shepard also knew he could not turn back now, because "there is a rightness in this direction" that had led him to realize that he had spent the last ten years of his life "hunting desperately for something I wasn't finding." Although the Gurdjieff point of view was that life was inside and that "nothing outside can ever finally answer our yearning . . . in some way, finding Jessie has reached something inside me. A part of me feels brand new—re-awakened."

In a letter that may have prompted Shepard to describe his current state of mind in detail, Dark had written him that O-Lan "says she suffers at least once heavily a day" and that Shepard's son "Jesse is quiet and seems mainly concerned about comforting her." In another letter, Dark wrote that O-Lan "was concerned" for Shepard because "you sounded like you didn't know what you were doing and any information she got she had to pull out of you" because "you were only saying yep and nope."

Assuring Shepard that everything back home in Mill Valley was "OK under control," Dark urged the playwright not to worry, as "Everyone's thinking you'll either come back or you'll never come back. It probably won't be as big a shock to them when the time comes as you think." He closed his letter by writing, "Between the two of us we can take care of *everybody*. You and me, we're family—like brothers—so there's never any problem. Jack and Neal."

Leaving Minnesota behind for Santa Fe, New Mexico, Shepard then drove with Lange and her young daughter for three days through freezing cold weather. In a motel room in Pueblo, Colorado, where Lange and the girl were both already fast asleep, Shepard added to his March 29 letter to Dark. Stunned by what he had seen on his way through the Midwest, Shepard noted, "The cities all have the feeling of communist countries. People are super depressed & very poor. All the small farms are being auctioned off. Every cafe you stop in there's notices up for farm auctions."

THIRTEEN DAYS LATER, JESSICA LANGE was sitting in the audience in the Dorothy Chandler Pavilion in Los Angeles as Robert Mitchum and Sigourney Weaver announced the five nominees for that year's Academy Award for Best Supporting Actress.

After she was named the winner, Lange, looking pale in a loose-fitting glittery gray-green dress, got to her feet and made her way to the stage while swinging her arms like a high-fashion model on the runway. Very composed as she made a short and charming acceptance speech, she thanked her fellow actors in *Tootsie* and her director before noting how lucky she had been to have Dustin Hoffman as her "leading lady."

Because Shepard still would not fly, the playwright did not accompany her to the ceremony. As he would prove again a year later after being nominated for the Academy Award for Best Supporting Actor in *The Right Stuff,* Shepard had no interest in being part of Hollywood's most highly prized tribal rite. The same could not be said for Scarlett, Johnny Dark, and Jesse Shepard, who in a month would be fourteen years old. Much like the rest of America, they eagerly watched on television what was then the greatest star-filled evening of the year. "With Jess," Dark wrote Shepard the next day, "it was like someone in the family had won the Oscar. He really lit up."

By the end of April 1983, Shepard, Lange, and her daughter were living in a small rented house in Santa Fe. On a daily basis, Shepard was working with the German director Wim Wenders in his motel room to cut and rewrite the screenplay they had begun collaborating on three months earlier as *Fool for Love* was in rehearsals at the Magic Theatre in San Francisco.

Thirty-eight years old, Wenders had by then already been recognized as one of the leading figures of the New Wave movement in German cinema. In 1977, *The American Friend,* a film Wenders wrote and directed based on the novel *Ripley's Game* by Patricia Highsmith with Dennis Hopper in the starring role, brought him to the attention of the film business in America. Francis Ford Coppola then hired him to direct *Hammett,* a film in which the famed author of hardboiled detective novels like *The Maltese Falcon* finds himself drawn into a mystery in San Francisco that, much like Sam Spade, only he can solve.

Based solely on Shepard's appearance in *Days of Heaven,* Wenders wanted him to play the leading role. But, as Shepard said, "Coppola didn't want me. He thought of me as a writer, not a movie star. He was a dictatorial producer." Coppola, who had final say in the matter, decided instead to cast Frederic Forrest, who would appear in five of Coppola's movies, in the title role. In what then became a minor cause célèbre in the world of independent film in America, Wenders shot *Hammett* entirely on location in San Francisco only to have Orion Pictures, the film company financing the movie, order him to reshoot it all on a sound stage in Hollywood. Orion then junked and destroyed his original version.

"After Wim finished that nightmarish production," Shepard said, "he asked me if I would be interested in writing a script based on some of my short stories." Although there is no apparent story line linking the unnamed prose pieces in *Motel Chronicles,* Wenders characterized it as the kind of book "you can carry with you, open up to any page, and have someone to talk to." Less than a page long, the entry that had inspired Wenders was dated "2/17/80 Santa Rosa, Ca."

In it, Shepard describes a man who has apparently come to the end of his rope. After smashing his suitcase so that everything he owns lies before him on a solitary blacktop road in the desert, he looks through it all, searching for "some memento" to bring back to a woman after having spent months "doing nothing more than drifting." Unable to find anything worth saving, he strips naked, throws his clothes on top of his worldly belongings, and sets it all on fire. Turning his back on the highway, he walks off "straight out into open land." According to Shepard biographer John J. Winters, Wenders was also struck by the image "of someone looking at a roadmap of the United States, ready to leave at any moment for some place he has found on the map. The film really began with that sentence."

Rather than create a screenplay literally based on the book, Wenders used *Motel Chronicles* as the jumping-off point for a film about the basic rootlessness of American life and the obsessive need to always be on the road, a predilection Shepard shared in both his life and work with Jack Kerouac. Coming together after rehearsals for *Fool for Love* ended at the Magic Theatre, Shepard and Wenders would drink and talk and shoot pool together at Tosca, where the playwright had become a regular during the filming of *The Right Stuff.*

From the start, they were both determined to avoid writing a conventional Hollywood screenplay. Instead, they spent their time coming up with scenes for which Shepard would then write the dialogue. Purposely, they also avoided creating an ending for the film. Instead, they focused on the central character, a worn and heavily bearded drifter named Travis who does not speak but who begins the film by walking out of the desert. They named the film *Paris, Texas* after the small city about a hundred miles northeast of Dallas–Fort Worth where the character was born.

Working together in the director's motel room in Santa Fe, Wenders and Shepard cut down "to regulation Hollywood size" a script that had ballooned to 160 pages. As Shepard noted in a letter to Dark, their ideal cast turned out "to be almost identical to *One from the Heart.*" A 1981 musical co-written and directed by Francis Ford Coppola with an original score by Tom Waits, *One from the Heart* was a failure at the box office only to be reassessed as a visually impressive cinematic fantasy. Along with Harry Dean Stanton and Nastassja Kinski, both of whom would appear in *Paris, Texas,* Shepard's wish list for his cast also included Frederic Forrest and Shepard's longtime crush Tuesday Weld, neither of whom joined the cast.

Although Wenders wanted Shepard to play the leading role in the film, the director said, "He adamantly insisted that being the writer precluded him from acting in the film." Having met Harry Dean Stanton on the Rolling Thunder tour, Shepard had run into the actor again as they were both drinking tequila in a crowded barroom during a film festival in Santa Fe. The two men talked at length, but Stanton had no idea Shepard was already thinking about casting him as Travis in *Paris, Texas.*

Acting more like a producer than a screenwriter, Shepard then called Stanton in Los Angeles to offer him the part. Despite having worked constantly in episodic television during the past four decades while appearing in forty films, Stanton had never played a leading role. In his widely praised breakthrough performance, he was finally given the opportunity for the first time to demonstrate his great range as an actor.

Although *Paris, Texas* had originally been scheduled to start filming in late spring, principal photography did not begin until October 1983. While on location with a full crew on a state highway in a remote section of Brewster County in Southwest Texas, Wenders was then forced to shut down production as he waited for more funding to arrive from Europe. After he had watched the dailies, the director decided to rewrite the film's ending. Along with a request for Shepard to convert the material into screenplay form, Wenders sent him a seventeen-page typed outline for the film.

By then, Shepard was on location in Iowa co-starring with Lange in *Country.* Informing Wenders that he could not possibly find the time to revise the entire thing, Shepard did promise to write the final scene of *Paris, Texas* if the director got that far without him. Wenders then enlisted screenwriter, director, and producer L. M. Kit Carson—who was on the set of *Paris, Texas* because his eight-year-old son, Hunter, had been cast as Harry Dean Stanton's grandson—to convert his new outline into scenes he could film.

At one point during filming, Stanton, who was unsure about how he should approach a monologue Shepard had written, called the playwright for advice only to have him say, "It's all there. Just don't act it. Don't act it." Carson then recalled watching Stanton as he sat in a chair on the set reading the monologue out loud over and over again. Suddenly, Carson began to "hear something under the flow of speech—a heart-breaking pulse-like rhythm." The words made the hairs "stand up on the back of my neck. Shepard was right—*don't act this.* He'd put all the terrible, necessary power of the scenes into just the bare, unhidden sequence of the words."

As filming on *Paris, Texas* neared an end, Shepard fulfilled the promise he had made to Wenders by writing the final scene while on location in Iowa. In a marathon phone call that began at midnight and did not end until six o'clock in the morning, he relayed the material to Wenders, who then filmed it. For his work on the script, L. M. Kit Carson received an "Adapted by" credit. Nonetheless, the headline of Vincent Canby's review of the film in *The New York Times* read, "'Paris, Texas,' Written by Sam Shepard."

Winning all three jury awards at the 1984 Cannes Film Festival, the highly coveted Palme d'Or foremost among them, *Paris, Texas* went on to become both a critical and commercial success. Insofar as Shepard was concerned, he had now joined the company of a select few in the film business. Although his name was not above the title in Canby's *New York Times* review of *Paris, Texas,* it was right there beside it.

ON LOCATION IN WATERLOO, IOWA, where *Country* was being filmed, Shepard again found himself trapped inside a trailer "in the mouth of the mad movie machine." On a film set with Lange for the first time since they had begun their affair while filming *Frances,* Shepard was acutely aware of how much more comfortable she was in this world than he would ever be.

Pouring his heart out to Dark in a series of letters and in a conversation Dark taped when he visited the set with his current girlfriend, Shepard repeatedly acknowledged how much he was in love with Lange and so could not conceive of ever living without her. Nonetheless, he had walked out on her more than once while on location, driving off in his truck only to find himself sitting alone at some hamburger stand entertaining fantasies of escaping by going to live with his sister Sandy in California. Inevitably, the playwright then returned to apologize to Lange for what he had done, while saying, "I just want to sleep with you, okay? I want to hold you and fuck you and I'm sure sorry. It won't ever happen again." Further complicating matters between them, Lange now wanted to get pregnant and go to Europe to give birth so they could live somewhere other than Santa Fe when they returned. About to turn forty and with his traveling days behind him, Shepard was stunned when Lange suggested they board the Orient Express in the summer so they could then journey on to the Himalayas.

Despite their problems—or, perhaps, because of them—Shepard and Lange became engaged on December 9, 1983. After buying her an antique sapphire-and-gold ring, he stuffed it into his pocket and waited until Lange had walked into the room where they watched the dailies each day. He then led her back outside into the freezing wind and snow and asked her to marry him. Like children, they both began jumping up and down while giggling in the snow. Although O-Lan Jones had Shepard served with papers on the set for a divorce that became final in July 1984, he and Lange then spent the next three decades together without ever getting married.

FILMED AT A TIME in America when small farmers throughout the Midwest were confusing their self-worth with their net worth and committing suicide after being forced to sell land that had been in their families for generations, *Country* was a sincere effort to bring widespread attention to this state of affairs a year before Willie Nelson and Neil Young mounted the initial Farm Aid benefit concert.

With her own family background in mind, Lange had commissioned William D. Wittliff, who had written *Raggedy Man* and would later write *Lonesome Dove*, *Legends of the Fall*, and *The Perfect Storm*, to write *Country*. Although Wittliff had never directed before, she also hired him to fill that role.

Two weeks into production, Lange, who along with Wittliff was also producing *Country*, decided to fire the cinematographer, thereby shutting down production on the set. As Shepard told biographer Don Shewey, "Jessica just didn't like what she was seeing in the dailies, and that was flat *it*, you know? She should be a director. She's got a great eye." Wittliff himself then decided to step down as director.

For reasons known only to him, Shepard also "quit until they get a replacement. They've threatened to sue me if I don't go back to work but threats always make me more stubborn." Richard Pearce, a skilled documentary filmmaker and cinematographer who had already directed two feature films, *Heartland* among them, replaced Wittliff. In addition to playing the male lead in *Country*, Shepard also now began doing rewrites on the script.

Shot on location in rural Iowa in brutally cold weather, *Country* is the story of Gil (Shepard) and Jewell (Lange) Ivy, who struggle to hold on to their family farm after a tornado ravages their corn harvest and the local bank calls in their Farmers Home Administration loans, thereby forcing them into bankruptcy. Shepard's character reacts to this situation by getting drunk and taking his anger out on his teenage son, whom he throws into the sheep pen and then beats senseless. When Lange's character comes out to stop him, Shepard half-punches, half-slaps her in the face. Grabbing a fence post, she wallops him with it. When he keeps coming at her, she finishes the job by hitting him with it in the head. After he drops onto the snow-covered ground, she orders him to leave the farm because no one needs him there anymore.

In his *Chicago Sun-Times* review, Roger Ebert gave *Country* three and a half stars (out of a possible four) and wrote, "The most touching scenes, though, are the ones showing how abstract economic policies cause specific human suffering, cause lives to be interrupted and families to be torn apart, all in the name of the balance sheet. 'Country' is as political, as unforgiving, as 'The Grapes of Wrath.'"

For Shepard, acting in *Country* only served to confirm that even when he was co-starring with the woman he loved in a film with a real purpose, the experience was "like being sentenced to a trailer for twelve weeks. With people walking around with walkie-talkies, banging on your door . . . I don't know if I'll do it much longer."

TWENTY-SIX

SEE YOU IN MY DREAMS

You may think this great calamity that happened,
way back when—this so-called disaster between
me and your mother—you might actually think that
it had something to do with you, but you're dead
wrong. Whatever took place between me and her
was strictly personal. See you in my dreams.

—SAM ROGERS,
IN *CRUISING PARADISE*

THE WAY SAM SHEPARD RECONSTRUCTED THE STORY AFTER IT
was too late for him to do anything but write about it was by talking
to Esteban, the "little Mexican man" who had been looking after Sam
Rogers for the last ten years while the two had lived across a concrete
courtyard from each other in Santa Fe. According to Esteban, it had
all started when Shepard's father unexpectedly received a big check
from the Veterans Administration in the mail. After cashing it, Rogers
went to a nearby shopping mall to get the kind of crew cut he had
sported as a bomber pilot in World War II. At a gun store, he bought
himself a fishing license and traveled sixty-five miles by cab to Pecos,
a small village on the Pecos River where the fishing was good.

Concerned about that much money "in the hands of a professional
drunk," Esteban had tracked Rogers there but was too afraid to approach him because Rogers was already drunk and dangerous as well.
By then, he had "hooked up with a very large Indian woman ... and
they'd both gone upriver to trout-fish with a bottle of gin." Knowing
how violent Rogers could sometimes be when he was this drunk, Esteban decided not to follow them into the mountains.

After they had spent three days fishing and drinking in the Pecos Wilderness area of the Sangre de Cristo Mountains, Shepard's father and his female companion returned to Pecos, where Rogers hired another cab to take them sixty-five miles to Bernalillo, a small city about twenty minutes north of Albuquerque. By now, they were no longer getting along and there were "reports of out-and-out fistfights between them in the local bars."

As Shepard wrote in a short story in *Cruising Paradise* entitled "See you in my Dreams," "They were easy to remember: a very fat Apache woman with bare feet, and a tall, stringy white man with a red beard and a crew cut, both raging drunk. They careened their way from one end of town to the other, getting rousted from every bar until the money ran out. At that point, my dad staggered into the middle of the road and met his death."

According to biographer John J. Winters, Sam Rogers stumbled out of a bar at 7:45 in the evening on Saturday, March 24, 1984. Until the moment of impact, the driver of the car that hit Rogers never saw him. At the time, his blood alcohol level was three times the legal limit, an amount sufficient to cause alcohol poisoning and loss of consciousness and nearly enough to bring on a coma, respiratory arrest, and death.

In a short prose piece entitled "Bernalillo," published sixteen years later in *Day out of Days,* Shepard writes, "When they loaded my father's mangled body on the gurney they asked him if he knew his name. 'Just Sam,' he said and then died right away. Ever since then I've had a stark terror of being blindsided by cars."

Rogers was actually taken to a hospital in Albuquerque where he died from his injuries the next day at the age of sixty-seven. In a notebook entry dated a few weeks later, Shepard expressed the overwhelming anger he felt about his father's passing. As quoted by Winters, he called it a "miserable, contemptible death ... as if he had purposely gone out of his way to lay a curse on me and all those left in his wake."

On March 25, Shepard appeared at the funeral home to sign an official certificate stating that he wanted his father to be cremated. He describes his actions in detail in "See you in my Dreams." "Since the

body was so badly mangled, that seemed to be the appropriate procedure." All the items Sam Rogers had been carrying with him when he
died—"his jackknife; his coins; his fishing license; and a strange iron-
colored stone with a hole through the middle of it"—were lined up
neatly on a glass-topped desk for Shepard to identify.

After Shepard had signed a form verifying that he was "the responsible party," the funeral director "began reciting all the options for
burial containers, cemetery sites, and headstones." Because Rogers had
served in the U.S. Army Air Force during World War II, Shepard
chose to have his father's ashes buried in "a plain pine box, about eight
inches square" in the National Cemetery in Santa Fe.

Shepard spent the rest of the day in Esteban's little front room,
listening to him describe how Sam Rogers would never pay attention
when he talked to him about his drinking. But then, as his son well
knew, Sam Rogers never listened to anyone. When he was off on another one of his epic drunks and had not come out of his house or
eaten for a week or more, Esteban would bring black bean soup to his
door only to hear Rogers "yell that he needed no food. Food was for
the living!"

After Esteban left the soup, Rogers would come out and kick it
into the yard. Sometimes, he would try to chase Esteban. He would
always fall down without getting very far. If Esteban tried to help him
up, Rogers would curse him "in the worst Spanish, calling me *cabron*
and things like that." Knowing it was "the booze causing the devil in
him," Esteban never took any of this personally, even though "it hurt
my feelings sometimes."

After their conversation, Esteban walked Shepard over to his father's one-room apartment. Touching Shepard's shoulder very softly,
he then walked away. For a while, the playwright just stood there,
afraid to go inside. It was "the same fear that invaded me at his door
when he was alive. The very same fear."

The sign his father had nailed to the door read MAD DOG in red letters with "a cartoon face of a snarling bulldog, foaming at the mouth."
Hanging from the green fiberglass awning above the door were "long
chains made from aluminum pop-off tabs of beer cans, all linked to-

gether and tinkling in the desert breeze." Threading his way through the curtain his father had assembled, Shepard opened the door and walked into the dark room.

As though his father were still sitting "hunkered over" in the "broken-down rocker" Shepard had bought him years ago, the playwright felt his entire body begin "throbbing" with "pounding fear." Parting the plastic curtains on the windows, he let sunlight come flooding into the room, illuminating walls "collaged with pictures" his father had "torn from magazines and Scotch-taped to the plaster."

The "opened cans of half-eaten tuna fish and a crusty bowl of Esteban's black bean soup" on the little table in front of the rocking chair, the stacks of magazines "with a narrow alleyway leading out toward the sink," the peanut butter jar on the floor "half-filled with brown water and soggy cigarette butts," and the piles of letters his father had written but never sent, among them one that ended with the words "See you in my dreams"—all reflected how his father had lived within these four walls.

Shepard's aunt and uncle soon arrived along with Shepard's sisters, Sandy and Roxanne. The next morning, they all drove out to the National Cemetery, about six miles from downtown Santa Fe. Although Shepard had asked for "one of those upright marble crosses" for his father's headstone, none was available and so he "settled for a little white slab, set flat in the ground, engraved with his name, rank, and the dates of his life."

Up on a hill, a green canvas awning had been set up over rows of benches and folding chairs for the service. "There was a larger gathering than I'd expected," Shepard writes. "Mostly alcoholics or exalcoholics. You could see it in their ravaged faces." Others who had known his father from the housing complex where he once lived were also there. The only one Shepard recognized was Esteban, who smiled at him and then lowered his head.

Beginning the service, Shepard and Roxanne took turns reading poems by Federico García Lorca, who had always been one of Rogers's great favorites. Shepard then tried to read a passage from the Bible, only to choke "on the words 'All is vanity,' because I suddenly saw my own in reading this as though I understood its true meaning." For a while, he could not speak. "Nothing came out," and his "whole face quivered."

Although Shepard "could sense the embarrassment from the gathering," he "felt no embarrassment at all, only a terrible knotted grief that couldn't find expression," and so he just stood there in silence, waiting for this to pass. When "finally it dissolved enough" to allow him to finish, he read the rest of the passage "without emotion and with no connection to any of the words" while just feeling grateful to get through it.

Looking more like "a CIA agent than a mediator for the dead," in his gray suit and dark glasses, the funeral director stood up and read the standard military funeral sermon that had been provided to him by the government. He then presented Shepard with an American flag folded into the traditional triangle appropriate for a military funeral and shook his hand. As everyone was leaving, Shepard turned back toward the green canvas awning and saw the little pine box with his father's ashes on a folding table with no one else around. "I felt pulled back to him as if by gravity; as though there were still something unfinished in this ceremony."

Off to one side by a yellow backhoe were "two Chicano men," a term his father had always refused to use. They were waiting for everyone to leave so they could put the box in the ground and cover it with dirt. When Shepard approached and picked up the pine box, he was "surprised by how much it weighed. Just ashes from a dead man." Out of respect for his loss, "the gravediggers turned their backs toward me and lowered their heads. I was grateful to them for that." Written in Los Angeles five years after his father died, "See you in my Dreams" ends there.

AS GOOD AS *Fool for Love* had been as a play, it was just that bad as a movie. Without question, the blame for this calamity rested squarely on the shoulders of Robert Altman, the filmmaker who during his forty-five-year career would be nominated five times for the Academy Award for Best Director. Like Charles Marowitz and Joe Papp before him, but with the added fillip of having also served at the controls of a

B-24 Liberator bomber as a co-pilot in World War II, Altman took his place in the long line of powerful male authority figures with whom Sam Shepard came into conflict during his career.

Unlike Sam Rogers, Altman had not liked or responded positively in any way whatsoever to military life. As soon as he was discharged, he went to Los Angeles where his parents owned a home in the Malibu hills. In 1948, he received his first shared story credit from RKO Pictures. After directing sixty-five industrial films, Altman spent more than fifteen years directing episodic television drama series.

A supremely talented craftsman who was often fired for refusing to conform to network standards, Altman saw his great breakthrough come when he directed *M*A*S*H,* a wildly original black comedy about two anti-establishment surgeons stationed at a Mobile Army Surgical Hospital as the Korean War raged around them. Released in 1970, just two months before National Guardsmen killed four students at Kent State University during a protest against the war in Vietnam, the film was widely perceived as a political statement about that conflict. A huge box-office smash, *M*A*S*H* won the Palme d'Or at the Cannes Film Festival and was nominated for five Academy Awards, with Ring Lardner, Jr., winning the Oscar for Best Adapted Screenplay.

Altman's subsequent films, including *McCabe and Mrs. Miller, The Long Goodbye,* and *Nashville,* firmly established his reputation as an American director of the first order. However, after his fairly disastrous attempt to transform *Popeye* into a big-screen musical in 1980, Altman could no longer persuade major studios to finance his projects. To continue working, the director began optioning plays he could film fairly quickly with budgets that were a fraction of the twenty million dollars *Popeye* had cost.

Bankrolled for two million dollars by Cannon Films, a company run by Menahem Golan and Yoram Globus, two Israeli cousins who specialized in negotiating foreign distribution deals before production even began so as to cover a film's budget, *Fool for Love* was the fourth play Altman had filmed in the past three years.

Because of a heart condition, the director, at sixty years old, was no longer drinking as heavily as he had been while filming *Popeye,* but he had begun smoking marijuana in the mid-1960s and so was still a dedicated stoner. Despite how high he might get at night, though, he was usually the first person on the set the next morning. In terms of his anti-establishment attitude, lifestyle, and filmography, he seemed like the perfect director to bring one of Shepard's plays to the big screen for the first time.

Although Shepard had seen some of Altman's films, the two had never met until the director approached him with the idea of making *Fool for Love* into a movie. At the time, Shepard "wasn't that turned on" by the notion. After Altman had sold him on it, Shepard wanted his good friend Ed Harris to play Eddie "because he was so great in the play." For reasons that may have had to do more with his limited budget than with casting, Altman "kept insisting" that the playwright accept the role.

Altman also wanted Jessica Lange to portray May. Locked in combat onscreen, Lange and Shepard would have made a brilliant pair. Sensing this, Altman may also have realized his only chance to cast an Academy Award–winning actress in what was essentially a low-budget movie was by having Shepard as her co-star. But Lange discovered she was pregnant with their first child shortly before filming began in New Mexico in May 1985 and so withdrew from the project.

Altman then cast Kim Basinger as May. Decidedly beautiful, she had just appeared with Robert Redford, Glenn Close, and Robert Duvall in Barry Levinson's film of Bernard Malamud's novel *The Natural.* Basinger would go on to become an Academy Award–winning actress, but in *Fool for Love,* she was badly miscast. So was Harry Dean Stanton, who as the Old Man had little to do but walk around the rundown motel where the film takes place, peering into windows as Eddie and May talk. Only Randy Quaid, as Martin, delivers a credible performance.

The single most astonishing aspect of *Fool for Love* is watching Shepard speaking dialogue he wrote that worked brilliantly onstage but falls so flat in front of the camera that it seems false and hollow. "I felt very uncomfortable," Shepard said. "I was *not* having a good time . . . This was a situation I tried to avoid for a long, long time—acting in my own stuff—because I always felt it was silly and pretentious— And I don't think I'll ever do it again if I can help it."

Tempering his remarks when he was interviewed by Mitchell Zuckoff for *Robert Altman: The Oral Biography*, Shepard said of *Fool for Love*, "Onstage, it was huge. It had a frightening physical reality to it, because of the intensity and presence of the actors. On film it comes across as kind of a quaint little Western tale of two people lost in a motel room. It doesn't have the power. In the theater it was right in front of your face, it was so intense it was kind of scary." Summing up the experience without mentioning Altman's name, he added, "There's never been any of my plays that was turned into a movie that was worth a shit. A lot of people have tried it and one after another they don't work."

Nonetheless, Shepard did say he had found it "weird" that Altman agreed to have the playwright "involved in the editing process" only to then take the film with him to Paris where "he cut the whole thing there and that was it." Shepard then said, "And I love Bob." In an article in *Interview* magazine in 1988, he was much less diplomatic. "I liked Altman's stuff up to a certain point," he said. "And I was fooled into believing that he was going to have integrity in this thing. Later on, I just felt he kind of shined me on."

According to Sandy Rogers, who wrote and performed eight songs on the film's soundtrack, "Sam was not real happy with what Robert Altman did, because they had an agreement that Sam would have a say in the final cut and then Altman took the film to Europe because he knew Sam wouldn't go there. It was one of those things where Sam got tricked and he really didn't like the guy after that."

DURING THE FIRST WEEK in December 1985, *Fool for Love* was released at the same time as *A Lie of the Mind*, the last of Shepard's great family plays, was opening at the Promenade Theatre in New York City. The synchronicity of these two events served to create a blitzkrieg of publicity that suddenly elevated Shepard to a brand-new level as an authentic American celebrity.

Although he still viewed the press "as hostile and intrusive," Shepard had agreed to promote *A Lie of the Mind* by doing interviews with *The New York Times*, *The Village Voice*, and *Newsweek*. At the time, *Newsweek* relied heavily on the celebrity value of its front cover to boost its newsstand sales in order to compete with *Time*, its weekly news magazine rival. Well aware of this, the playwright had consented to speak with Jack Kroll, *Newsweek*'s film and drama critic, on the condition his article not appear as a cover story, an offer he had also turned down after *The Right Stuff*.

Both *Time* and *Newsweek* were published on Mondays. On Friday, November 8, 1985, Shepard learned the extensive piece Kroll had written about him would appear three days later on the cover of the magazine. Going "ballistic," Shepard called Kroll and told him he was on his way to "bust him up" and "break all the furniture" in his house. In tears, Kroll called a friend and said he was going to pull the story. As no magazine back then could possibly do this seventy-two hours before issues were mailed to subscribers and shipped to newsstands, Kroll's friend simply laughed at the idea.

On Monday night, Shepard called producer Albert Poland at home. "Guess what I'm doing?" Poland said. "I'm looking at you on the cover of *Newsweek* and talking to you at the same time." Sounding far more relaxed about it all than when he had called Kroll on Friday, Shepard said, "Yeah, I'm doing the same thing." Whatever the source of the playwright's apparent newfound nonchalance over the cover might have been, the seven-page *Newsweek* story, entitled "Who's That Tall, Dark Stranger" was a paean of embarrassing proportions to his overwhelming success as both a brilliant playwright and a newly christened major Hollywood star.

Beneath a big black headline reading, "TRUE WEST," with the words "SAM SHEPARD Leading Man, Playwright, Maverick" stacked in smaller print by the side of his face, Shepard gazed out at the world from the cover of *Newsweek* on November 11, 1986. In the cover photo, the playwright-actor wore the white Stetson hat he had sported in *Fool for Love* and a dark-blue Western shirt. With his eyes hidden behind dark aviator shades, his utterly impassive look harkened back to an earlier and far more heroic era in America. The hyperbolic level of praise heaped upon him in the article only served to compound the intended effect of the image, which was to announce that a brand-new star had just been born.

Characterizing Shepard as "the most challenging American playwright of his time," whose appearance in *Fool for Love* would only "add to his rocketlike emergence as a movie star of potent popular appeal," Kroll wrote as if Ernest Hemingway had appeared in the movie version of *For Whom the Bell Tolls*, F. Scott Fitzgerald had chosen "an additional career as Hollywood's golden leading man," or Clark Gable and Humphrey Bogart had "dashed off plays in their spare time to rival Tennessee Williams or Arthur Miller." In what Kroll called "an almost embarrassing excess of good fortune," he noted that with his "young-Lincoln looks and brainy carnality," Shepard had "jumped the gap from screen to audience with the spark power of a Redford or Newman . . . At 42, Sam Shepard has become an American fantasy."

—

TWENTY-SEVEN

A LIE OF
THE MIND

It's a big-assed play. That's twenty-one
years of work there.

—SAM SHEPARD,
ON *A LIE OF THE MIND*

NINE MONTHS BEFORE *A LIE OF THE MIND* WAS SCHEDULED
to open at the Promenade Theatre in New York City on December 5,
1985, Shepard was still trying to complete the play in a way that satisfied him. There was nothing new about the difficulty he was experiencing. In a letter to Joe Chaikin fifteen months earlier, Shepard had
written, "Mostly, I've been working on my new play. Rewriting and
continuing it. It looks like it wants to be a long one this time. About
twelve characters—three acts and about thirty scenes. I hope I can find
the right actors for it. Maybe you can help me, once I get it started."

Much as he had done with *Fool for Love,* Shepard eventually wrote
"eleven or twelve drafts" of *A Lie of the Mind.* Because the play kept
"changing and shifting directions" on him, he would return to "where
it had gone wrong" and "throw everything away up to that point" and
then "start over again at that moment." And while this sometimes resulted in his discarding as many as twenty-five or thirty pages each
time he did so, Shepard remained committed to the process. As he
told Jonathan Cott in a *Rolling Stone* interview published shortly after
A Lie of the Mind opened, "It was a tough play to write, because I had
the first act very clearly in mind, then went off on a tangent and had to
throw away two acts and start again. And then it began to tell itself."

Deciding that he would direct this play, Shepard also began look-ing for actors to cast in it. At around the same time he wrote to Joe Chaikin in the fall of 1984, Shepard happened to run into John Malkovich outside the Circle Repertory Company Theater in Green-wich Village. Although the two had never met, Shepard invited the actor to take part in a reading of scenes from *A Lie of the Mind* at the Minetta Lane Theatre.

To his surprise, Malkovich found himself onstage alongside Harry Dean Stanton and Geraldine Page. And while Shepard was "shooting for a dream cast that included Malkovich, Page, Amanda Plummer, Jessica Tandy, Jason Robards, Ed Harris, and Amy Madigan," only Page and Plummer would appear in the final production. Shepard also had bigger plans for *A Lie of the Mind* than to present it at the Magic Theatre in San Francisco. Intent on opening the play in New York, he allied himself with Lewis M. Allen, a noted film and theater producer, and Stephen Graham, whose mother, Katharine, was the publisher of *The Washington Post*.

In late September, Shepard drove nearly two thousand miles from Santa Fe to Manhattan with Lange, who was now six months preg-nant, and her daughter, Shura, so he could begin rehearsals for *A Lie of the Mind*. "Blown away" when he learned Shepard had specifically asked the producers to hire him as the play's general manager, Albert Poland had arranged for Shepard, Lange, and Shura to stay in director Jack Garfein's "luxury apartment" on Broadway and Sixty-second Street. Instructed to do so by Poland, the garage attendant in the building called him at three in the morning to report Shepard, Lange, and Shura had arrived safely in the city. Because they were all going to be in New York for a while, Lange enrolled her daughter in kindergar-ten on the Upper East Side, where Shepard would often drop her off before heading to rehearsals.

During the first production meeting for *A Lie of the Mind*, Shepard made it plain he would be running the show by pointedly ignoring both producers. Instead, he directed his attention to Poland, with whom he had worked before and who was "still in awe of" the play-wright and "intimidated" by him because he was "hip" and "seemed to be in on something I wasn't and never would be. It was unsettling."

Two weeks into rehearsals, Shepard told Poland he wanted the Red Clay Ramblers, a North Carolina string band that played old-time mountain music and bluegrass, at rehearsals the next day. Canceling all their existing bookings, the band flew to New York and appeared at the Promenade Theatre at two in the afternoon as Shepard had requested. By attending rehearsals on a daily basis, the band was able to develop the songs they performed to open and close each act while also supplying the background music for scene changes and underscoring.

As he never had done before, Shepard also went to great pains to assemble a cast of actors who were not just talented but would also bring people into the theater. After John Malkovich decided to pass on playing Jake in *A Lie of the Mind*—he felt the role was too similar not only to Lee in *True West* but also to Wesley in *Curse of the Starving Class*, a role he had played in a Steppenwolf production—Shepard chose Harvey Keitel, an actor best known for his work in *Mean Streets* and *Taxi Driver*, for the part. The rest of the cast included Amanda Plummer, who had won a Tony Award for her work with Geraldine Page in *Agnes of God;* Ann Wedgeworth, whom Shepard had met while she was playing Jessica Lange's mother in the Patsy Cline biopic *Sweet Dreams;* James Gammon, who by now had become a regular member of Shepard's acting company; Will Patton and Aidan Quinn, both of whom had played Eddie in *Fool for Love* during its long run at the Circle Repertory Company Theater; and Page, an Academy Award–winning actress who had been nominated for her first Tony Award twenty-five years earlier for her performance in Tennessee Williams's *Sweet Bird of Youth*. At some point, Judith Ivey, who had appeared with Keitel in the Broadway production of David Rabe's *Hurlyburly*, left the production. She was replaced by Rebecca De Mornay, who had recently co-starred with Tom Cruise in the box-office smash *Risky Business*. Six weeks into rehearsal, Shepard instructed Poland to fire De Mornay. The playwright then replaced her with Karen Young.

All told, Shepard spent two months in rehearsals on *A Lie of the Mind*. By any standard, this was a long time to work on a show, much less a production with eight actors, all of whom were being paid on a weekly basis. Often, the cast was struggling to understand what Shepard wanted from them onstage. "This is a very competitive bunch of actors, to put it mildly," Geraldine Page said. "Sometimes I'd get weary fighting for my share of space. I'd feel like saying, 'Sam, you've got to block this.'"

As always where Shepard was concerned, there was a method to his madness. The vital lesson he had learned after having first become a director was that he could really experience the full impact of what he had written only when an actor was performing his work before him. As Amanda Plummer said of Shepard, "He's quiet—he doesn't talk much. Then, when he gets excited, his eyes come out. They look out in wonder as if he's never seen this before."

As opposed to working from an established text so he could concentrate on blocking and movement during rehearsals, Shepard used that time to reshape the play. By doing so, he ended up jettisoning entire sections from what had begun as an epic dramatic marathon that could take anywhere from five to seven hours to perform. Throughout it all, he was in control of every aspect of the production.

To help him, he brought in his younger sister Roxanne as his assistant director. She described her role to *People* magazine by saying, "I took care of the rehearsal process. I made sure Sam had everything he needed. I made suggestions. I thought most people were very open to me. Because Sam trusted me, they would ask, 'What do you think? What's Sam planning here?'"

Continuing to tinker with the script even after previews began, Shepard brought Robert Woodruff in to "help him figure out how to cut it" and to give the playwright "some notes on what was happening." When Woodruff directed the Los Angeles debut of the play at the Mark Taper Forum in 1988, he restored some of the scenes Shepard had removed from the play. This led to a "parting of the ways" between the two men, who then did not see each other again for twenty years.

Belying the appearance Shepard presented during rehearsals for *A Lie of the Mind,* the playwright was also still struggling with his decision to debut another new play in New York City as well as his role as a playwright. Each day, he found himself wanting only "to be with Jessica & Shura & the new baby & some life in the country—far away."

Without being privy to the self-doubt Shepard never shared with anyone but Dark and Lange, Albert Poland gathered his staff together on the morning of December 5, 1985. With *A Lie of the Mind* scheduled to open that evening, he told them, "Tonight there will be fisticuffs thrown at the opening night party. If the reviews are bad, it will happen inside the party. If the reviews are good, it will happen outside. And the thrower of the fisticuffs will be Sam Shepard."

THROUGH THE USE OF a four-foot-wide ramp suspended twelve feet in the air, a pair of one-foot-high platforms located extreme downstage right and left, and a bare, wide-open central area designed to give the impression "of infinite space, going off to nowhere," Shepard created a set for *A Lie of the Mind* that enabled his characters to transcend both space and time.

As a playwright, he had now also significantly raised the degree of difficulty in terms of what he was trying to accomplish on that stage by presenting two separate, but equally dysfunctional families who are inextricably linked together as a result of the violent beating that Jake, the son of one family, has administered to his wife, Beth, the daughter of the other. While each family is engaged in their own drama on one side of the stage, they also become involved in what is occurring on the other.

Yet again in the world according to Sam Shepard, the characters in *A Lie of the Mind* are all out of tune not just with themselves but also with the world in which they live. Talking at cross-purposes to one another, they continually revisit the past without ever coming to a clear understanding of it. They also engage in random acts of casual madness that verge on psychosis but make eminent sense within the alternate reality Shepard had created for them.

By far the most sympathetic character in the play, Beth, is the North Star around which *A Lie of the Mind* revolves. Much like Shepard's mother-in-law Scarlett and Joe Chaikin after he suffered a stroke, Beth has great difficulty speaking because of the serious brain damage she suffered when Jake beat her. Nonetheless, she is still able to communicate through the sometimes barely comprehensible but brilliantly rendered childlike language Shepard created for her.

Responding in part to the criticism that had been leveled at him for writing about dysfunctional men trying to find their way in the modern world, Shepard made a conscious effort to explore the other side of the equation in *A Lie of the Mind*. Despite how odd and distracted they seem, the female characters in the play are all more powerful and interesting than their male counterparts.

As he had done in the four plays preceding *A Lie of the Mind*, Shepard had strewn references to his own life throughout the work. Just as they had in the playwright's bedroom in Duarte, plastic models of "World War II fighters and bombers" hang from the ceiling above the bed in which Jake slept as a boy. Beneath the bed, his mother stores the dusty American flag folded into a military-style triangle from his father's funeral and the small leather box containing his ashes. Describing how he died, she tells her son, "He was no hero. Got hit by a truck. Drunk as a snake in the middle of the highway."

Shepard ended the first act by blacking out the entire stage except for a spotlight on the box containing the ashes. Picking up the box, Jake opens the lid and stares inside it for a moment. Blowing "lightly into the box," he sends "a soft puff of ashes into the beam of spotlight," which then fades softly to black. Later in the play, echoing how Jane Rogers must have felt after her husband walked out on her and their three children, Jake's mother tells her daughter, "You know a man your whole life. You grow up with him. You're almost raised with him . . . And then one day he just up and disappears into thin air."

In his *New York Times* review of *A Lie of the Mind*, Frank Rich called it Shepard's "most romantic play . . . By turns aching and hilarious—and always as lyrical as its accompanying country music— 'A Lie of the Mind' is the unmistakable expression of a major writer nearing the height of his powers." In the *New York Post*, Clive Barnes described *A Lie of the Mind* as "the event of the season." The reviews in *Time, Newsweek, The Village Voice,* and *The New Republic* were no less laudatory. Albert Poland described them as filled with "wall to wall superlatives."

As was then customary in New York whenever a play was deemed a hit by the all-powerful daily newspaper theater critics, the line to buy tickets the next morning wound around the block. The Promenade

Theatre box office take that day was a record-shattering $37,000. The next day, the theater took in nearly $8,000 more.

TWENTY-FIVE YEARS LATER, WHILE promoting *Ages of the Moon*, his new two-character play, Shepard told Patrick Healy of *The New York Times*, "I have to admit . . . with 'Lie of the Mind,' I've come to see it as a bit of an awkward play . . . If you were to talk about it in terms of cars, it's like an old, broken-down Buick that you kind of hold together to just get down the road. All of the characters are in a fractured place, broken into pieces, and the pieces don't really fit together. So it feels kind of rickety to me now."

Whether any of these thoughts was running through the playwright's mind as he sat at a corner table in Sardi's at the opening night party with a small group of friends and associates that included the actor Danny DeVito, no one can say for sure. After the issue of *The New York Times* containing Frank Rich's rave review had been brought into the room and everyone there had been apprised of its contents, Poland went over to Shepard's table to congratulate him.

By then, Shepard was already, in Poland's words, "well oiled." Recalling their last opening night together, when Clive Barnes had used his *New York Times* review of *The Unseen Hand* and *Forensic and the Navigators* to call Shepard "perhaps the first person to write good disposable plays," Poland asked the playwright, "Well, how do you feel?" When Shepard mockingly replied, "I'm ecstatic, Al," Poland immediately knew "we were on our way to the dark side."

Going into great detail about an incident that does not seem to have ever been independently corroborated, Poland describes how in a strange yet also somehow entirely predictable replay of the incident at Ports in Los Angeles, Shepard then violently assaulted a photographer who had been lying in wait for him outside Sardi's on West Forty-fourth Street.

When the playwright called Poland some months later to say he would be returning to the city in May 1986 to be inducted into the American Academy of Arts and Letters, Poland advised him to "dress up like Sam Beckett" so he could avoid being arrested for what he had done that night. Puzzled by this advice, Shepard asked Poland what he was talking about. After Poland described the incident to him, Shepard said, "To tell you the truth, I don't even remember it."

Despite how much the playwright's intake of alcohol that night might have influenced his behavior, Shepard's initial reaction to the critical praise being heaped on *A Lie of the Mind* speaks volumes about his state of mind at the time. For Shepard, professional success and personal happiness were no longer one and the same. Whether they ever had been was a question only he could have answered.

—

TWENTY-EIGHT

HORSE COUNTRY

The only really intimidating thing
in life is a bad horse.

—SAM SHEPARD, IN 1988
WASHINGTON POST
PROFILE

AS THOUGH THE WAY SHE WAS RAISED STILL MADE IT IMPOS-
sible for her to live in one place for very long, Jessica Lange suddenly
decided the time had come for her and Shepard and her daughter,
Shura, to leave Santa Fe. During the months Lange had spent in New
York as Shepard was readying *A Lie of the Mind* for the stage, she had
gained fifty pounds before giving birth to their daughter, Hannah, on
January 13, 1986. "It was great," Lange said, "except I get real dark
sometimes when I'm pregnant. My mood swings are extreme anyhow,
but when I'm pregnant I could be like Medea at any moment." Moody
and restless one day while also "feeling crazy," Lange "looked in *The
New York Times* and I saw this picture of a farm down in Virginia and
I thought, 'Well, we're going to look at this place.' And that was it."

After Shepard and Lange had returned to their $450,000 (the
equivalent of more than $1 million now) "log cabin on five acres with a
barn and a state-of-the-art security system" in Santa Fe, continuing to
live there "just didn't feel right" to her. "You know you can feel when
you're meant to be in some place and then you know your time there
is past," Lange said. "And it's time to move on. And I really felt that
strongly." Shepard explained their decision by saying, "It just got inun-
dated with Texas oil people. And the face of it changed into this

shopping-mall thing with adobe siding. It was getting weird. You couldn't even get across the downtown plaza, it was so full of tourists."

Along with their two daughters, Shepard and Lange took up residence in a two-story Federal-style white clapboard farmhouse with three brick chimneys, wraparound porches, and extensive brick patios on Totier Creek Farm, about twenty miles south of Charlottesville, Virginia. Located on a road outside the tiny town of Scottsville, the house, which had been built in 1799, sat on 107 acres of verdant pastureland studded with linden, beech, maple, and elm trees, some as old as the house itself.

The interior of the house resembled an English country manor. The ceilings were eleven feet high. The highly polished floors had been fashioned from wide-plank heart pine. All six working fireplaces had period mantels. The estate also included a horse barn, two cottages, a three-car garage, and additional farm buildings. Despite never having lived in such a grand manner before, Shepard seemed very much at home there.

At Totier Creek Farm, the playwright's obsessive interest in acquiring, riding, and breeding horses became his central focus. Shortly after he had sold his first yearling at a prestigious thoroughbred auction in Kentucky, Shepard's stables housed two brood mares, ten polo ponies, and three hunter jumpers he and Lange both rode. They also took up fox hunting, a pursuit that resulted in Lange's suffering a concussion after she was thrown from her horse.

"Sam was a good rider," his close friend Paul Pascarella says. "And he was a good horseman. He had horses in Santa Fe and first started playing cowboy polo there with a volleyball. Then he got into real polo, which was pretty serious because of all these guys from South America who could really play, and they had a decent little polo group going. When Sam and Jessica lived in Charlottesville, he always had really good polo horses. The minimum that would have cost him back then would have been about seventy thousand dollars a year. But money always went right through Sam."

To afford his new lifestyle, Shepard began accepting roles in mainstream Hollywood movies. Although he appeared onscreen during this period opposite Lange, Diane Keaton, Sissy Spacek, Sally Field,

Dolly Parton, Julia Roberts, and Daryl Hannah in *Crimes of the Heart, Baby Boom,* and *Steel Magnolias,* the playwright continued going to extraordinary lengths to safeguard his privacy.

And so when a member of Woody Allen's staff called to inform Shepard the director had decided to replace Christopher Walken in his new film and wanted to send a driver from New York to bring Shepard the screenplay, the playwright did not feel comfortable letting someone he did not know come to his house. Instead, he had the script for *September* delivered to the nearby hardware store where he sometimes picked up his mail. Although Shepard accepted the role, Allen eventually scrapped all the footage he had already shot and rewrote the script and so the playwright did not appear in the film.

After cracking two vertebrae in his back playing polo, Shepard completed the screenplay for *Far North,* the first movie he directed. Based on an accident Lange's father had suffered while riding a horse, the film, which had a five-million-dollar budget and was shot in and around Duluth, Minnesota, starred Lange, Charles Durning, and Tess Harper.

The total U.S. gross for *Far North* was less than $150,000. The reviews were no better. In *The New York Times,* Janet Maslin wrote, "It doesn't help that the above-mentioned horse, Mel, happens to have the film's best role." Taking an even harsher tack, Roger Ebert noted, "'Far North' is a disorganized, undisciplined, pointless exercise in undigested material, and you can't blame the actors, the technicians, or the middle men. This movie fails at the level of writing and direction."

To help promote the film two months after it was released, Shepard granted an interview to David Richards, the theater critic for *The Washington Post.* In it, the playwright exhibited a brand-new level of paranoia. "Sam Shepard doesn't just guard his privacy," Richards wrote, "he patrols it. Not only does the 45-year-old playwright, actor and now first-time movie director not want it known where he is granting one of his rare interviews, he doesn't want it known why he doesn't want it known."

When Richards began the interview by asking Shepard if his desire for privacy was motivated by the need to avoid paparazzi or "the loonies out there," the playwright replied, "I'd rather not answer that question, because that in itself becomes a provocation. It doesn't matter what the reason is. It's my private life and it's not up for grabs." He then added, "Can't you just say we're meeting in a Holiday Inn in Atlanta, Georgia?" In fact, Shepard and Richards were meeting in the faux-English pub of the Holiday Inn in Charlottesville, Virginia, where Shepard came so often that when the hostess ushered Richards to the corner table where the playwright always sat, she said, "Mr. Shepard prefers to have his back to the room."

Making it plain he did not want to talk about his life, because "I've had it up to my ears with the personal mythology," and it was "now getting kind of personally sickening," Shepard was willing to talk about *Far North*, a film about which Richards noted "critical reaction has been glum." Having made precisely the kind of film he had wanted to make, Shepard said, "The fact that it has had across-the-board bad reviews doesn't bother me." Later in the interview, he added, "Hell, there were only two good reviews out of the whole batch."

While the reviews *Far North* had just received may have done little to improve his attitude toward the media, Shepard was hardly a recluse in Charlottesville. He was a regular at many of the university town's restaurants and bars and local residents later saw him as "a colorful, flirtatious and gregarious character." Occasionally, he also sat in on drums with the Kokomotions, then the hottest band in what was essentially a college town.

The most significant event in Shepard's life during this period took place on June 14, 1987, when Jessica Lange gave birth to a son. Following in the Rogers family tradition, the boy was named Samuel Walker Shepard, the understanding being that he would be called by his middle name.

BY THE FALL OF 1989, with four incomplete plays and seven stories on his desk, none of which he had been able to finish, Shepard had "been having one hell of a time with my writing lately." Compounding his problems, he and Lange had now reached an impasse in their relationship that neither seemed willing or able to solve. Much like Shepard's obsessive need to write, Lange was not about to give up her career.

Nor was she content to remain at home for extended periods of time. As she said, "It's a regular existence but after a couple of months of it, I'm ready to go mad. I can't wait to go on location, start a movie, study a character—anything that gives me a release."

Acknowledging that her career was the overriding issue in her relationship with Shepard, Lange said, "The worst part is the separations." Nonetheless, during the nine years she and Shepard lived together on Totier Creek Farm, Lange appeared in eleven feature films and two made-for-television movies, among them *A Streetcar Named Desire*, in which she played Blanche with Alec Baldwin as Stanley Kowalski and Diane Lane as Stella. Because the actress always took her children with her wherever she was filming, Shepard would "come see us, but he's not going to pack his bags, sit on my location for three months, and twiddle with the kids ... Sam would've been happy if I never made another movie, if we could've lived together in the wild, idyllic manner we had in the beginning. But I kept wanting to act."

Responding to a question from *Vanity Fair* writer Nancy Collins, Lange also said, "It would never occur to me that Sam would be unfaithful, although he has a long history of it." When Collins asked Lange what she would do if he were, her laughing reply was "I'd kill him." Lange also confessed she was still hoping her relationship with Shepard would settle "into a certain dynamic where there'll be no question Sam and I are best friends, which is hard to come by ... You get inextricable connections with people ... Sam actually buried my dad—he dug the grave. I was the one who told him his dad died. He was with me when I gave birth to two children. I never discard the possibility of anything happening in life, but his leaving would surprise me."

IN MARCH 1990, SHEPARD LEFT Totier Creek Farm to portray Walter Faber, the central character in *Voyager*, a film directed by Volker Schlöndorff with a script written by him and Shepard's old friend Rudy Wurlitzer based on *Homo Faber* (Latin for *Man the Maker*), a novel by the Swiss playwright and author Max Frisch.

Much as he had done on the Rolling Thunder tour fifteen years earlier, Shepard transformed the experience into his own personal drama and wrote three stories about it that were then published in *The New Yorker*, thereby beginning his association with the magazine as a contributor.

Unlike the fluffy, lighter-than-air Hollywood movies in which Shepard had appeared during the past five years, *Voyager* offered the playwright the opportunity to take a giant step forward as an actor. Set in the summer of 1957, *Voyager* is the story of Walter Faber, an engineer who after having survived a plane crash meets and falls in love with Sabeth, a younger woman played by Julie Delpy who reminds him of his former girlfriend Hannah. Together, they travel to Greece, where Faber learns that Hannah is in fact Sabeth's mother and he is her father. After Sabeth suddenly dies from a poisonous snakebite, the film ends with Faber sitting alone and dejected in the airport after the flight taking him back home has been announced.

Knowing principal photography was scheduled to take place in Greece, California, Germany, Mexico, New York City, and Italy, Shepard was willing to forsake his usual practice of driving to locations to appear in this film. As the days of transatlantic ocean liners were over and crossing the Atlantic by freighter took two weeks, he agreed to spend three and a half hours on the Concorde from New York to Paris, a one-way fare that cost the equivalent of $12,000 today.

Before doing so, Shepard had to join the rest of the company on location in a remote village in Mexico. As he wrote in a story entitled "Spencer Tracy Is Not Dead" in *Cruising Paradise*, "This morning I'm leaving for Mexico to shoot a film directed by a German, written by a Swiss, photographed by a Greek, with a crew of Frenchmen. It should be interesting." After traveling by train from Charlottesville to Los Angeles, where filming on *Voyager* had already begun, the playwright planned to pick up a rental car so he could drive fourteen hundred miles through Arizona and Texas and then south another six hundred miles to Poza Rica in the Veracruz region of Mexico. As no American automobile rental agency would allow any of its cars to be taken across the border, Shepard first had to be driven to Laredo, Texas, in a blue Lincoln stretch limousine by an Austrian chauffeur clad in "a shiny tuxedo, complete with cummerbund" and a ruffled shirt. From there, he continued on a long and difficult journey through Mexico to where *Voyager* was being filmed.

Once he finally arrived, Shepard began what soon became a complicated relationship with Schlöndorff. Much like Wim Wenders, Schlöndorff was an internationally known member of the German New Wave movement. A decade earlier, he had won the Palme d'Or at the Cannes Film Festival and the Academy Award for Best Foreign Language Film for his cinematic adaptation of Günter Grass's 1959 novel, *The Tin Drum*. As Shepard said of the director, "I never met anyone I liked so much off the set that I felt so much hostility to *on* the set."

In "Winging It," one of the stories about the film in *Cruising Paradise,* Shepard's character is asked to do six takes of a scene by an unnamed director who screams at him for improvising. The process continues until Shepard decides to "smash a radio to the floor with my fist," an action the director joyously proclaims to be "Absolutely perfect!" Shepard's ironic postscript to the story, which he attributes to Marlon Brando, reads, *"Just because they say* 'Action!' *doesn't mean you have to do anything."*

At one point during another scene Schlöndorff was shooting from long distance, Shepard was sitting beside a German actor who had to drive their truck across a shallow river. When the vehicle got stuck in the mud, everyone who was clustered around the camera began shouting at them to keep going. Taking charge of the situation, Shepard yelled *"Cut the camera!"* When the German actor told Shepard, "In Europe, only the director can say 'Cut,'" Shepard replied, "This ain't Europe, it's Mexico, and any fool can tell the shot's over."

For his part, Schlöndorff would later remember shooting a scene in Paris where Shepard was saying goodbye to Julie Delpy, whose character he would most likely never see again. "He walked out of the café," Schlöndorff said, "and I yelled 'cut,' and we waited for him to come back and do another take." When Shepard did not return, Schlöndorff went looking for his star, only to find him standing outside the café with his face against a wall. When the director asked if he was all right, there was a long pause, and then Shepard said, "I just realized I couldn't tolerate another loss in my life."

Nor was Shepard's state of mind lost on his twenty-year-old co-star. As Julie Delpy said of him, "Sometimes the writer would take over the actor, and he would get a little moody and insecure . . . so you never knew what day it was going to be in the morning, when you went on the set, whether it was going to be the moody guy or the, you know, very sweet, sensitive person in front of you. So it was unsettling, but after a while I got used to it."

What Delpy never mentioned and Shepard did not write about was an incident that occurred while they were filming *Voyager* in a rugged mountainous region in Greece. In a sequence that begins when Shepard's character goes for a swim as Delpy's naps in a red polka-dot two-piece bathing suit, Delpy's character falls backward after being bitten by a snake and strikes her head on a rock. When Shepard returns, he lifts her into his arms and carries her down the stony slope to a highway.

"I once spent an evening talking about Sam with Volker Schlöndorff," Jacob Brackman says. "The backstory was that there was this young girl in the film who must have rebuffed Sam and there was a scene where she had injured her leg and he was carrying her down the mountain. And whenever Volker would yell 'Cut!,' Sam would whip his arms away and let her fall into the gravel and she was getting scraped up. Volker was saying all this in a sympathetic way, because if you'd had the kind of childhood Sam did, you never get over it. Knowing Sam had some really bad holes in his bucket he was never going to fill, Volker was always very sympathetic to him."

Although it earned less than half a million dollars at the box office, *Voyager* fared somewhat better with the critics, most of whom appreciated the film without finding it entirely successful. Giving it three stars in his *Chicago Sun-Times* review, Roger Ebert wrote, "The end of *Voyager* does not leave us with very much . . . Thinking back, we realize we've met some interesting people and heard some good talk, and that it's a shame all those contrived plot points about incest got in the way of what was otherwise a perfectly stimulating relationship. This is a movie that is good in spite of what it thinks it's about." The review in *Variety* noted, "Sam Shepard is ideal as Faber, the quintessentially cool cowboy-loner-businessman."

Having returned to Totier Creek Farm in September 1990 to re-
sume his domestic life, Shepard wrote Johnny Dark he had been going
through "heart-wrenching stuff" with Lange. Eight months later, he
wrote Dark again. Although the playwright was "in deep shit again
with money," because he could not "seem to earn enough of it these
days," he also noted, "Me & Jessie are in love again & everything is
hunky-dorey [*sic*]."

IN THE SUMMER OF 1993, Jane Schook Rogers came to Baileys Harbor, Wisconsin, to visit her sister Dorothy, who was still living in "the
Schook Shack" where they had both spent their summers as children.
Rogers, now seventy-six years old, had experienced heart problems in
her sixties only to be diagnosed with cancer. Moving north to be near
her daughter Sandy, who was then living on the ranch in Santa Rosa,
California, that her brother now owned, Rogers took up residence in a
nearby trailer park. Aware that his mother's disease was nearing its
final stages, Shepard and his son Jesse, who was now twenty-three
years old, accompanied Jane Rogers on what became her final visit to
Baileys Harbor.

Beset by his usual concerns about privacy even in a town of a thousand people on the edge of Lake Michigan, Shepard was talking to
someone when Margaret Poole, the great-granddaughter of the co-
founder of the Frogtown Art Colony, walked up behind him with her
sister. Politely, they waited for his conversation to end. When it did,
Shepard slowly turned around with a look of exasperation on his face,
"as if he was expecting fans or photographers." It was only after Margaret Poole asked him, "Is Jane home?" that he "smiled with surprise
and led them into the house."

In a story entitled "Place," published in *Cruising Paradise* three
years later, Shepard describes how he and his son had dragged "a huge
slab of limestone off the shore of Lake Michigan up to the little cemetery overlooking the hayfields of Door County." Working together,
they dug a trench for the slab between two red cedar trees and "dropped
it in edgewise, so the flat white side of the rock would face the morning sun."

For more than seventy years, Shepard's grandparents on his mother's side of the family had been buried in this cemetery in unmarked graves, as per their request. Because this had always disturbed his mother, Shepard was trying to rectify the problem by marking the site with "a native stone from the same beach where her father had built his cabin, back at the turn of the century."

Later in the day, when Jane Rogers came to look at what they had done, she walked around the slab with "her arms crossed softly on her chest and a worried look in her eyes." She smiled and thanked them for their efforts and then "stared hard at the two cedar trees, her eyes running up the shaggy bark to the thick fernlike canopy." Turning around, she stared across "the little gravel path that divided" Saint Mary's of the Lake Catholic Cemetery on the south from Baileys Harbor Cemetery on the north. Apologetically, she said, "I think it's the wrong place."

Trying to remember her father's funeral of fifty-one years before, she could recall only that her parents had wanted to be buried side by side without a stone, so they would "dissolve back into the earth and disappear." When Shepard and his son offered to move the slab for her, she also could not remember the exact site of their graves and thought her son and grandson might actually have put up the slab on the plot belonging to the Poole family. "It's terrible when you get your funerals mixed up," she said, looking out across "the shimmering vast surface of Lake Michigan. The wind caught a wisp of her white hair and blew it across her mouth, but she didn't move." When Shepard offered to consult the caretaker, she said, "I suppose so . . . We'd better just leave it like it is for now."

During the last week in February 1994, Shepard was staying in a hotel overlooking Central Park in New York City while filming *Safe Passage,* a movie in which he was starring with Susan Sarandon. Learning his mother did not have long to live, he boarded a train and arrived at the hospital in time to be with Jane Schook Rogers before she died on March 10, 1994, at the age of seventy-six. Noting that she had not suffered all that much before the end, Shepard wrote Joe Chaikin that "her living and her dying were precious gifts to me."

The following summer, almost a year to the day after Shepard and his son visited Baileys Harbor, and with her daughters, Sandy and Roxanne, in attendance, Jane Rogers's ashes were buried "slightly to the left of the two red cedars." After checking with those who ran the cemetery, Shepard had learned that the limestone slab was in fact "in the wrong spot, so we dug it up and moved it again. It lined up right behind my mother's grave. Everything was in its place now, and we left it just like that."

SHEPARD WAS DRIVING HIS pickup truck west on Route 40 to Los Angeles when he began writing *Simpatico,* the three-act play that would open two years later at the recently renamed Joseph Papp Public Theater in New York City. Having pinned a sheaf of papers to the steering wheel, he was using his free hand to scrawl the first draft of a work he then called *One Last Favor.*

"You have to do it on an open highway," he told Ben Brantley of *The New York Times* during a break in rehearsals before the show opened on November 11, 1994. "You wouldn't want to do it in New York City. But on Highway 40 West or some of those big open highways, you can hold the wheel with one hand and write with the other. It's a good discipline because sometimes you can only write two or three words at a time before you have to look back at the road, so those three words have to count. The problem is whether you can read the damn thing by the time you reach your destination." By the end of his five-hundred-mile journey, Shepard had written the first twenty-five pages of what he thought was a one-act play. Because new characters just kept popping up, the playwright then spent the next year adding a second act and then a third.

When it became known Sam Shepard had a new three-act play he was also going to direct, Lewis Allen, who had co-produced *A Lie of the Mind,* immediately began trying to raise $800,000 (the equivalent of $1.5 million now) to bring the show to Broadway. The star-studded cast Shepard had in mind, which included Ed Harris, Jennifer Jason Leigh, Frederic Forrest, and Beverly D'Angelo (only Harris and

D'Angelo appeared in the final production), also made the play a hot property that seemed destined for success.

Despite all he had accomplished during the past twenty years, the truth of the situation was that as a playwright, Shepard needed a hit. Five years after *A Lie of the Mind* closed at the Promenade Theatre in the spring of 1986, he had returned to the stage in New York City with *States of Shock,* a one-act play inspired by the Persian Gulf War, which opened at the American Place Theatre on May 16, 1991. Notwithstanding the efforts of "the indispensable" John Malkovich, Frank Rich of *The New York Times* wondered if Shepard had "been hibernating since his East Village emergence in the Vietnam era," while noting that the play "does not really go anywhere once it has established its basic thematic attack."

Realizing a Broadway production for *Simpatico* was not going to be feasible, Lewis Allen then set his sights on presenting the play Off-Broadway and so cut his fundraising goal in half to $400,000, a sum Shepard dismissively characterized as "gas money on a movie." When this goal also proved impossible to achieve, Shepard contacted George C. Wolfe, who had taken over the Public Theater after Joe Papp died of prostate cancer three years earlier at the age of seventy. Once Wolfe had agreed to put on the play, Lewis Allen "contributed" $325,000 to the Public Theater's nonprofit Shakespeare Festival. In return, if *Simpatico* was a success, Allen would have the right to transfer it to a Broadway or Off-Broadway venue.

Having "started and abandoned eight or nine plays" about the two male characters in *Simpatico,* Shepard said, "It's an old, old situation that I've been struggling with for years." He had also dabbled with similar ideas in a story entitled "Thin Skin" written in 1989 and published in *Cruising Paradise* that featured a character named "J.D.," based on Johnny Dark. Calling *Simpatico* "elegiac" in his *New York Times* review, Stephen Holden wrote, "Mr. Shepard's ear for the American vernacular and his foreboding view of life at the end of the 20th century fuse into a terse, bitterly scornful poetry of regret." In his annual *New York Times* year-end assessment of theater, Vincent Canby named *Simpatico* "one of the year's best in New York plays."

ON THE NIGHT BEFORE *Simpatico* opened in New York, a truly innovative production of *True West* directed by Matthew Warchus premiered at the Donmar Warehouse, in London's Covent Garden.

The son of an actor who had become a vicar, Warchus had grown up in "a village in the middle of nowhere with an extraordinary name—Drax. Which is also the name of a James Bond villain. The only thing in Drax was Europe's largest coal-fired power station and a small cluster of houses. There was one bus in and one bus out a day and it was twenty-five miles to the nearest cinema." After seeing John Malkovich and Gary Sinise in the *American Playhouse* production of *True West* on "regular television" in England, Warchus remembers "not really talking for about two days. It really stunned me and made me very, very quiet." Although he had never before seen or even heard of John Malkovich, he was astonished by the "unassailable" way the actor "played the part completely on his own terms. He constructed a version of Lee no one could get to because he had no obvious Achilles' heel. His appetite for cruelty and meanness was massive and constant and so everything Gary Sinise said as Austin was just an opportunity for more punishment by Lee. And there was a sly glee in the way he did it that was beautiful."

After graduating from Bristol University, Warchus became the resident director of the West Yorkshire Playhouse in Leeds. In October 1994, he staged the first revival of *True West* in England since John Schlesinger had directed Bob Hoskins as Lee at the National Theatre in London thirteen years earlier. Warchus had just directed Mark Rylance in *Much Ado About Nothing* in the West End and so he enlisted the actor to co-star in the production alongside Michael Rudko, with whom Rylance had worked at Theatre for a New Audience, where *Buried Child* was first presented in New York City.

"It was my idea for them to switch roles on a nightly basis," Warchus says, "and they both played it as Americans. Mark had grown up in Minnesota and so had no trouble with the accent and the play became a sensation in Leeds. Sam Mendes, who was then the director of the Donmar Warehouse in London, asked if he could co-produce the show and take it there for a run and it became a great success there as well."

Despite how brilliant the concept of having the actors portraying Lee and Austin switch roles on a nightly basis initially seemed, putting it into practice during rehearsals proved to be "a grueling experience" for all concerned. As each actor was "trying to find his own way through the play, he's watching another actor go through the process and find things that he may have been missing. It's a great opportunity for paranoia."

Although Warchus had written Shepard to ask for his approval for the actor switch, which the playwright granted, the two men did not meet until 1998. However, four months after *True West* closed at the Donmar, Warchus, who was heading off to go hiking by himself in the Lake District the next day, went to see the London production of *Simpatico* directed by James Macdonald at the Royal Court. Along with the program that night, everyone in the theater received a copy of the script. On sabbatical with nothing else to read, Warchus decided to try to convert the play into a film script as a writing exercise. After he had enlisted his friend David Nicholls to join him in the project, the two men began working on the screenplay of *Simpatico* together. As Warchus recounts, he then told Albert Finney—who owned horses and whom he had directed in *Art,* by Yasmina Reza, in the West End— that "I was now working on a screenplay about horse racing, but as I didn't know anything at all about the subject, I wanted to send him the script so he could tell me what was right and what was wrong."

After Finney gave Warchus some pointers, the actor said he wanted to "show it to a producer and some other people. Before I knew it, the script had gone to Sam Shepard and Nick Nolte and he had given it to someone else and I was in Jeff Bridges's house in Los Angeles and Sharon Stone's trailer on the lot at Paramount. *Simpatico* had a ten-million-dollar budget and as I had never made a movie before, that was my film school." Although Shepard was not a producer, he did have "to sign off on every draft of the screenplay and so the script would come back to me with his signature on it. Occasionally, I would talk to him about characters and casting and at one point, he was also going to act in it, but then could not do so."

In an only-in-Hollywood moment, Warchus, who had never been to a horse race, found himself shooting the movie's final scenes at the 1998 Kentucky Derby before the project had even been greenlit. Much as Shepard's upstairs neighbor in London had done when the playwright took him to watch the greyhound races for the first time, Warchus asked Shepard on which horse he should place the first bet of his life.

"Yeah," Shepard told him. "You want to put your money on Real Quiet."

"So I went to the window and put two hundred dollars on that horse," Warchus says, "and then I watched Real Quiet come all the way around and win." Because the horse had gone off at nine to one, Warchus earned what would now be the equivalent of three thousand dollars.

—

TWENTY-NINE

STILLWATER

Seems like playwrights hit a certain place
where they're either repeating past work or trying
to invent new stuff that has nowhere near
the impact of the earlier work.

—SAM SHEPARD, IN 1996
NEW YORKER PROFILE

O
N MARCH 27, 1995, JESSICA LANGE WON THE ACADEMY AWARD
for Best Actress for her performance in *Blue Sky* as the mentally un-
stable wife of an army major who unwittingly finds himself involved in
the cover-up of a secret nuclear bomb test. Shot in 1990 and completed a year later, the film had lain in a bank vault for three years after
Orion Pictures went bankrupt.

Giggling repeatedly as she thanked her co-star Tommy Lee Jones
by name and her late director, Tony Richardson, who had died of complications from AIDS at the age of sixty-three in 1991, Lange ended
her Academy Award acceptance speech by thanking her three children
for making it all possible through their love and patience. As she never
once mentioned Shepard's name during her speech, some people
began speculating their relationship was on the rocks.

About four months later, Shepard and Lange and their three children left Totier Creek Farm and moved to Stillwater, Minnesota, a
small city about twenty-five miles east of Minneapolis on the banks of
the St. Croix River that forms the border with Wisconsin. For $415,000
(about $720,000 now), they purchased what was then a four-bedroom,
four-bath white farmhouse built in 1892 on two and a half acres of land
on Fourth Street North. Located atop a knoll on one of the largest lots

in Stillwater, the house featured "sweeping views of the town, the St. Croix River, and the historic lift bridge."

Although the house needed work and the grounds were nothing but scrubland dotted with trees and bushes, Lange had wanted to move to Stillwater because she had "this kind of romantic image of the children growing up not dissimilarly to the way I grew up, in a small town where they could walk to school. And I wanted to raise them close to their extended family." She also wanted to be closer to her mother, Dorothy. Widowed six years earlier, Dorothy lived right next door to Shepard and Lange's new home. Lange's two older sisters, her brother, and their children were also nearby and so there was always family around to interact with her three children.

About a month after they had moved to Stillwater, Lange told Shepard that "she was profoundly depressed about returning to the land of her childhood & that everything she'd imagined about being here in Minnesota was a total fantasy & the actual reality of 'being' here was something she couldn't foresee." Determined nonetheless to make the best of their new living situation, Lange threw herself into renovating and reconstructing the house into a fifty-five-hundred-square-foot, five-bedroom mansion. Having never gardened before, she also spent the next decade transforming the grounds into an elaborate floral fantasia.

After having the two acres surrounding the house cleared, Lange terraced the sloping grounds. With the zeal she had demonstrated while pursuing her acting career, she created an elaborate garden for each of her children. In 2003, Shura would be married in the garden her mother had planted for her. Inspired by Monet, Lange had a pond dug "surrounded by yellow- and blue-flowering plants." Where a large oak tree had come down in a storm, she built "a Buddha garden based on the wheel of dharma." At the bottom of the hill, she installed a large lily pond flanked by a stone terrace covered with wild daisies. She also created her own version of Sissinghurst, the garden Vita Sackville-West and Harold Nicolson had worked on in Kent, England, for thirty years, by planting "every white flower" she could grow.

After she and Shepard acquired the lot adjacent to their property, Lange oversaw construction of their second guesthouse and had the pool and pool house remodeled. In part because of all the work she had done on the property over the years, Shepard and Lange would sell their house at 903 Fourth Street North in 2008 for $1.85 million, more than four times what they had paid for it.

As Lange was doing all this, she continued going off to make movies on location, although not as frequently as when the family had lived in Scottsville. In Stillwater, Shepard created a daily domestic routine of his own. Rising on weekdays at six A.M., he would make breakfast for the children, take them to school, and then either return home to write or continue on to the three-hundred-acre ranch he had purchased twenty miles away in River Falls, Wisconsin, where he had horses and fifty head of cattle.

"The first thing Sam ever did," Johnny Dark said, "wherever he lived, was to always get another place. When they lived in Minnesota, he bought a place in Wisconsin. When they lived in New York, he bought a place in Kentucky. He was a pretty complex guy." Asked if Shepard had done this for solitude or to pursue sexual conquests, Dark replied, "Both."

Despite Shepard's ongoing need to have his own space, the move to Minnesota had led him and Lange to realize that "we both come from almost identical transient backgrounds, children of alcoholic fathers & neither one of us know where we want to live & call 'home.'" Nonetheless, Shepard had urged Lange to make a go of it in Stillwater by saying they "should at least stick it out during the winter before we picked up sticks again. I mean seeing as how we've both invested close to 2 million in land & houses." He then added, "In any case, so long as we stick together I told her we can't stray far from what's right. Where we ought to be is together & so far, that's holding. The beat goes on."

FOURTEEN YEARS AFTER GARY SINISE had rescued *True West* from the mountain of criticism beneath which it had been buried when the play first opened at the Public Theater in December 1980, he turned his attention to *Buried Child,* the play for which Shepard had won the Pulitzer Prize but that had not been seen since it closed in New York after a four-and-a-half-month run in the spring of 1978.

With a cast that included James Gammon as Dodge, Lois Smith as Halie, and Ethan Hawke as Vince, Sinise began rehearsals for the Steppenwolf Theatre revival of *Buried Child* in Chicago shortly after Shepard and Lange had moved to Stillwater. As the playwright was now just a six-hour drive away, Sinise invited him to come watch the company work on the play. To their great surprise, Shepard not only made several trips from his new home to the theater but also began rewriting the script and showing up with brand-new pages for Sinise to share with his cast.

"I was never real happy with the play," Shepard said. "It was somewhat raggedy, areas of it were sloppy. When the Steppenwolf production started, a whole territory of the play became clear to me. I started tailor-making it for this production. What triggered a lot of the rewriting was that I saw these weird actors and a director who intuitively understood the humor that couches the tragedy, and I wanted to reinforce that." Fairly quickly, he cut "the length of some of the dialogue, including Dodge's last will, and added to the tension of the mystery of the buried child." He also clarified Vince's character and removed "some of the ambiguity over who had fathered the buried child out back."

Despite how impressive Shepard's revisions seemed to the company, as Richard Christiansen wrote in the *Chicago Tribune*, "The script was transformed and revivified by the electric-shock treatment of director Gary Sinise into a roaring, stomping, wheezing, unfailingly fascinating gallery of American grotesques . . . Thunder crashes, villains cackle, a jazz saxophone wails, an endless staircase leads to the farmhouse's second floor. It's all so eerie." While praising Sinise for assembling such "a bravura cast of weirdos," Christiansen also noted, "Shepard's script does not achieve a satisfying resolution," but then concluded his review by writing, "But, oh, with this cast blasting away at full force, what a fireworks display it makes."

Buoyed by such reviews and the enthusiastic audience response on a nightly basis during its six-week run in Chicago, the Steppenwolf company joined forces with New York producer Fred Zollo to move *Buried Child* to Broadway. The show opened in the 1,069-seat Brooks Atkinson Theatre on April 30, 1996. As he had never done before,

Shepard accompanied the play to New York, where he continued tinkering with the text during rehearsals.

In his *New York Times* review of the show, Ben Brantley refuted the notion that Shepard had now become "a relic of a chapter in experimental theater, saturated in symbolism, willfully obscure and given to bashing the American Dream with two heavy hands." As Brantley wrote, "In this exuberant staging by Gary Sinise, 'Buried Child' emerges as a play for the ages . . . 'Buried Child' operates successfully on so many levels that you get dizzy watching it. It has the intangible spookiness of nightmares about home and dispossession, yet it involves you in its tawdry, mystery-driven plot with the old-fashioned verve of an Erskine Caldwell novel."

In suitably raucous fashion, Shepard celebrated at the opening night party with John Malkovich, Tom Waits, and T Bone Burnett. The party was held in the Harley-Davidson Cafe, a garish Midtown joint dedicated to the iconic motorcycle of the same name with a thirty-eight-foot-long illuminated fiber-optic American flag running across the ceiling. Twenty years earlier, Shepard would never have been caught dead in such a place. But for him, the night was just another stop along the way in what, as Stephen Schiff wrote in *The New Yorker,* "is beginning to look like a Shepard jubilee year."

In May, *Buried Child* was nominated for five Tony Awards. Hoping it would help lure people to the box office, Sinise had persuaded the awards committee that the show should be included in the Best Play category rather than Best Revival. In the end, the strategy was not successful and the show wound up not winning any awards. Despite unanimously positive reviews, *Buried Child* closed three weeks later on June 30, 1996, after fourteen previews and seventy-two performances. Having returned to watch the production several times during its run, Shepard "was dragged on stage to take a reluctant bow at the last performance."

As though he was now committed to recycling his previous work, Shepard had already begun rewriting *The Tooth of Crime* with a brand-new score by T Bone Burnett. Agreeing to allow artistic director James Houghton to present a full season of his plays—ranging from *The Rock Garden* and *Chicago* to *Action* and *Killer's Head*—at his downtown Signature Theatre and at the Public Theater, Shepard made his newly re-titled *Tooth of Crime (Second Dance)* part of the program.

With Bill Hart set to direct, Shepard changed the names of some of the supporting characters while also eliminating references to rock stars like Bob Dylan, Mick Jagger, and Pete Townshend, all of whom were about the same age as Shepard, who was now fifty-three. Burnett's score, which he later released as an album, was "a vast improvement over Shepard's original music," but "its grunge-rock flavor unavoidably linked Hoss to Eddie Vedder and Kurt Cobain, charismatic icons of 90's rock."

Noting that when the original version of the play was presented at Princeton's McCarter Theatre in 1972, "angry audience members fled in disgust," Ben Brantley wrote in his *New York Times* review of Shepard's reboot that even "in the enlightened year of 1996, audience members are fleeing in disgust at intermission." Despite calling the new version "a fascinating, even brilliant work," the critic added, "More than two decades after its inception, 'Tooth of Crime' is still waiting for the production that can do it justice."

WITH HIS "JUBILEE YEAR" having not turned out as he might have expected, Shepard's emotional situation was now also complicated by his sudden inability to earn a living by acting in movies. Before filming *Voyager* seven years earlier, he had written an entry in his journal that read, "I'm an actor now; I confess."

Now, in 1997, after having listed all the factors that made the profession more difficult for him than for those who pursued it on a full-time basis—among them, his refusal to live in Los Angeles or "own a fax machine or an answering service or a cellular car phone or a word processor"—Shepard got to the crux of the matter: "On top of this, I'm not getting any younger and my face is falling apart. Most of my lower teeth were knocked out by a yearling in the spring of '75. Half my upper teeth are badly discolored, and one of them's been dead for as long as I can remember. When you get right down to it, I'm lucky to even have an agent at this point in time."

Nonetheless, Shepard had somehow managed to continue being

cast as either the leading male character or in a primary supporting role in at least one high-paying project a year. Now sounding very much like an aggrieved out-of-work actor, he wrote Johnny Dark on October 6, 1997, to complain that he had no job, had not worked in a year, and "there is *nothing* on the horizon." After acting in films for twenty-two years without ever "imagining that one day the well would run dry," he wrote, "now it's come." To bail himself out, he had begun thinking about liquidating his assets by selling his truck and his horses in what would have been a vain attempt to keep himself afloat financially.

Regaining some degree of perspective while continuing to agonize over his predicament, Shepard had realized that "this was bound to happen—things go in cycles—you've had your day in the sun & now the rug's going to get pulled out." Feeling "slightly liberated" by his current situation, the playwright confessed he had "absolutely no idea what's up ahead," but that was all right because "something will happen . . . I'm completely in the grip of forces I can't control."

A month later, Shepard wrote Dark to thank him for the letter and photographs he had sent the playwright on his fifty-fourth birthday, which Shepard had celebrated with a family dinner at a restaurant in a nearby small town. Despite enjoying a great meal "surrounded by the ones I love," he "kept having little glimmers of the truth" about "how incredibly selfish I've lived my whole life—everything geared to what I might gain out of it—even in my relationships with family & those I think I'm closest to." He signed the letter "Your aging friend, Sam."

Notwithstanding how harshly Shepard had judged himself on his fifty-fourth birthday, the playwright had, as his father had never done, devoted himself wholeheartedly to his children during their time in Minnesota. To celebrate his son Walker's twelfth birthday in 1999, Shepard took him and four of his friends camping along the Saint Croix River and cooked them all cheeseburgers, beans, and hot dogs, with marshmallows and Hershey bars for dessert. Finding it amazing to hang out with adolescent boys because they were all "totally insane & hysterical," Shepard was delighted when his son was asked whom he would eat first if he had to kill someone to survive and calmly replied, "My dad."

Over the course of one Sunday eight months later, Shepard had sat on the floor of a gym shouting encouragement to his son as he played basketball, taken him to McDonald's for cheeseburgers ("one of his mother's specific taboos"), played nine holes of indoor pitch-and-putt golf with him, gone shopping at a "monster shopping goods store," and then eaten dinner with him in a Mexican restaurant before they returned home together to watch action movies like *Alcatraz* and *Armageddon.*

In "Berlin Wall Piece," a story published in his 2002 collection *great dream of heaven,* Shepard portrays himself as the hapless father of a teenage girl and boy, both of whom are now far sharper than he. As the narrator, a seventh-grade boy who has to interview his father to write an essay about the 1980s, observes, "My dad's fucking crazy . . . my sister knows more about the eighties than my dad does and she's only a year or so older than me." As his sister continues doing her own homework, she keeps coming up with more tidbits of pop culture information about the era. It's "as though her mind is able to split right down the middle and do two things at once. She's totally brilliant, I think." All the while, their father is busily wiping black ants off a kitchen counter with a wet sponge while making certain not to step on any of them, because, as he says, they remind him "of summer and hot places" and "We always had ants when I was growing up." And then, when his daughter asks him her one and only question about the eighties, he is unable to answer it.

Shepard paints a far different picture of domestic life in Minnesota in a story entitled "An Unfair Question." Also published in *great dream of heaven,* the piece is a first-person narrative reminiscent of the way John Cheever portrayed the everyday madness of upper-class white suburban life in America in the 1950s and '60s. With a party in full swing in the house in Stillwater, a strange and distracted version of Shepard is sent by his wife to bring back some basil from a supermarket in town. In the deserted parking lot of what was once a busy shopping mall but is now lined with abandoned storefronts, he begins a pattern of truly odd behavior by pushing the security button on his car key over and over again so he can watch the headlights blink and listen to the honking of the horn. By the end of the story, he stands in the cellar of his house pointing a loaded shotgun at a terrified female party guest, who screams so loudly that she immediately brings the noisy party going on above them to a screeching halt.

What lies right beneath the surface of "An Unfair Question" is the overwhelming sense of utter dislocation Shepard was now experiencing in a place he had never been able to call home. Confirming this in a letter to Johnny Dark dated March 18, 2002, he wrote, "I don't know what to do with myself. I'm beyond 'Eeyore' in the self-pity department. I have no friends. I feel alienated from my own family and all of Jessica's relatives. I can't stand Minnesota—the climate, the people, the whole stupid place—and yet I don't have any idea what to do or where to go or what the answer is. This really is the pits."

THIRTY

THE LATE
HENRY MOSS

My story? Oh, I don't know. Again, percentage wise,
I couldn't tell you. Seventy-five, eighty
percent, eighty-five percent? I don't know . . .
My intention is not to make a Xerox of my life.

—SAM SHEPARD,
IN *THIS SO-CALLED DISASTER*

IN A VERY REAL SENSE, *THE LATE HENRY MOSS,* A PLAY ORIGINALLY entitled *Sierra Madre* on which Shepard had worked for ten years before finally allowing it to be produced in 2000, was his last great theatrical hurrah. As befitting his usual style, he went out in a blaze of glory. Although the play itself left much to be desired, the bells and whistles accompanying the production, many of which Shepard himself had attached and/or engineered, made *The Late Henry Moss* the subject of intense media attention on both coasts before it was ever performed.

Although John Lion had died a year earlier and Robert Woodruff was now teaching at Columbia University's School of the Arts, Shepard chose to stage the world premiere of *The Late Henry Moss,* which he was also directing, at the Magic Theatre in San Francisco. Because it had been seventeen years since *Fool for Love* opened there, his decision to do this made for a Bay Area story that wrote itself.

And so, when the *San Francisco Chronicle* decided to run "a package of stories" about *The Late Henry Moss* a week before the play opened, the editor in charge of the project wrote, "Normally we don't talk to all the principals in a new play, but this one is special. Opening night on Nov. 14 [2000] has attracted the attention of the national press, and the entire run is already sold out." But then, as the reporter who had conducted the interviews noted. "Among Sam Shepard aficionados, this is a major event." And while the play was going to be performed in the 729-seat Theatre on the Square in downtown San Francisco, rehearsals were being held at the Magic Theatre, which, as the reporter added, "is where [Shepard] started. It's like seeing Bob Dylan at Gerde's Folk City."

And then there was the cast. More than a year earlier when Shepard was still months away from finishing *The Late Henry Moss*, Sean Penn and Nick Nolte had already agreed to play Ray and Earl Moss, two brothers who return home after many years to try to determine the events that led to their father's death. The two actors had worked sparingly in theater before and they had never appeared onstage together. However, with both of them having already been nominated twice for the Academy Award for Best Actor, Penn and Nolte were at the height of their careers. Both had also earned well-deserved reputations as hard-drinking men with independent spirits.

As though the onstage chemistry between them was not enough to ensure *The Late Henry Moss* would be a box-office bonanza in San Francisco, the cast also featured Woody Harrelson, who had spent eight seasons as the bartender on the multiple Emmy Award–winning NBC television series *Cheers* before being nominated for an Academy Award for Best Actor for his performance in the 1996 film *The People vs. Larry Flint*.

Formerly one half of the super-stoned hippie comedy duo Cheech and Chong, Cheech Marin had never appeared onstage but was cast to play Esteban, the character Shepard had named after his father's friend, neighbor, and caretaker. The cast was anchored by longtime Shepard stalwart James Gammon as Henry Moss and Sheila Tousey, a Native American actress who had worked with Shepard in the two movies he had written and directed, as Conchalla, Henry Moss's lover.

Wearing "black slacks, a black mock-turtleneck sweater and a glossy black leather jacket" at a star-studded benefit in San Francisco to raise funds for the Magic Theatre, Shepard told *Salon*'s Kevin

Berger, "I didn't set out to cast movie stars. It just happens that every single one of them is a dynamite actor. The fact that they're movie stars is something else." After dining with Philip Kaufman and T Bone Burnett, Shepard joined the musicians who had been hired to play at the party by taking over behind the drums as Burnett sang and played "Long Tall Texan." As the last guests straggled out the door, Shepard thrashed his way through Chuck Berry's "Too Much Monkey Business."

The extensive media coverage generated by *The Late Henry Moss* was not restricted to San Francisco. After journeying there so he could review the play for *The New Yorker* nearly a year before it would open in New York, John Lahr wrote, "And for this outing, one of his first since the creative glitch of 'Simpatico' in 1994, Shepard has brought insurance: a troupe of actors one could call the Sam Shepard All Stars . . . The amperage of their combined star power, and the novelty of a new Shepard tale, has quickly turned a tryout into a sell out, with tickets being hawked on eBay at two hundred and fifty dollars each."

As understandable as this excitement over a production with this much star power may have been, all the media coverage was restricted to events occurring outside rehearsals. In a complete reversal of the way Shepard had always zealously guarded his privacy and personal space, the playwright invited Michael Almereyda, who had directed Shepard in an ultra-hip version of *Hamlet*, to film the process of bringing *The Late Henry Moss* to the stage for the first time. "The documentary began very casually," Almereyda said, "with Sam calling up after 'Hamlet' and asking if I'd be interested in making a record of his play. He had assembled a phenomenal cast—I assumed he didn't want to just have the experience vanish without a trace. I didn't even ask why he wanted me to show up with a camera. I just said 'Sure.'"

Working with a small crew as Shepard put the cast through their paces, Almereyda ended up shooting 140 hours of film he then edited into a 1 hour, 29-minute documentary entitled *This So-Called Disaster*, which was theatrically released in 2003. When an interviewer asked Almereyda if Shepard had placed any limits on what could be filmed, the director said, "The restriction was that we were only shooting in the theater. Outside of that, I interviewed Sam on his ranch, much later, and Nick [Nolte] at home in Malibu. But the task before us was to make a record of the play. And then it became more layered, because it became apparent to me that you couldn't make a true record of the play without understanding the parallel story, the semi-camouflaged story of Sam and his father." Without being specific, the director also conceded, "Sifting through the 140 hours of footage, you could come up with an alternate movie, and there's an alternate tale I could tell that had to do with after-hours activity. But that still doesn't refute or contradict the impression the movie gives of people revealing themselves through their work."

Undeniably the star of the film, Shepard himself supplies the most combative element in *This So-Called Disaster*. Right at the start of the documentary, the playwright is being interviewed by Kim Curtis, an entertainment reporter from the Associated Press. Looking worn, he does his best to answer her question about the different challenges presented by writing a play and directing it. In response to how closely *The Late Henry Moss* has been drawn from his own life, he says, "My story? Oh, I don't know. Again, percentage wise, I couldn't tell you. Seventy-five, eighty percent, eighty-five percent? I don't know. Sure, it's partly personal and it's partly not. It has to come out of a personal vein, but I'm not interested in . . . the intention of the play is not to—" Suddenly grinding to a halt, Shepard waves his hand at the photographer, who has begun leaning in too closely as he continues taking pictures of the playwright. "Back off!" he snaps. And then, in a gesture any director would have loved to film, he rubs both hands over his face and through his hair. Picking up right where he left off, he completes his answer and ends the scene by saying, "My intention is not to make a Xerox of my life."

Asked about this moment while he was publicizing the film three years later, Almereyda said, "There was always this implicit contradiction in Sam's invitation to make this movie. He didn't want it to be a profile about him, but the play is deeply personal . . . Somebody said a writer is someone who hides his secrets in print. And that's true of Sam, I think. Because he's intensely private, but anyone who's read his work knows him very well."

The most revealing moment in *This So-Called Disaster*, which takes its title from a letter written to Shepard by his father in which he used that phrase, was filmed after the play had closed. As Shepard sits in a wooden rocking chair on the porch of a rustic cabin with chinked walls behind him, he supplies the on-camera narration as well as the voiceover for photographs of his father. In a dispassionate manner that at times becomes hauntingly strange, Shepard recounts the details of his father's life. He describes the last time they ever saw each other by saying:

> It was one of those meetings you never forget and it was horrible because he was absolutely smashed and I should have known better over the years [than] to try to sit down with him when he was in that state, because he was a madman. He was crazy. He was totally crazy. This Dr. Jekyll Mr. Hyde personality thing that happens with true alcoholics . . . just POW!
>
> So I made the mistake of sitting down with him and trying to have just a normal conversation, but he was ranting and raving and carrying on and I remember his main thing was that he wanted me to take him with me back to this little ranch I had in Northern California so he could work there as a hand. He was in no condition to do that. He'd burn the fucking place down.
>
> And I was trying to find sort of a diplomatic way of refusing him this. Anyway, once he got wind of the fact that I wasn't going to do that, he just had a fit and he started screaming and yelling and telling me to get out of the place. So as I was backing out of the door, I remember the last thought I had was, "Don't retaliate. Whatever you do in this moment, don't retaliate because you'll regret it for the rest of your life."
>
> I don't know why I had that thought in my head, but he was just gone. Frothing at the mouth. Screaming. Throwing shit at me. And I was in this little screen door. Yelling. I was between the screen door and those flip-top beer curtains and I thought, "If I retaliate in any way, verbally or in any kind of way, it would be a bad deal." And so I just kind of walked away and that was the last I ever saw of him. About three weeks later, they picked him up in an ambulance and he died in the ambulance.

———

WITH A RUNNING TIME of three hours, *The Late Henry Moss* was, in terms of form at least, a return to *A Lie of the Mind.* The title of the play was inspired by "The Late Henry Conran," a 1931 short story by Frank O'Connor in which an alcoholic man discovers his wife has declared him dead in a notice published in the newspaper announcing their son's wedding. As a play, *The Late Henry Moss* also recycled many of the details about Sam Rogers's death in 1984 that had appeared in "See you in my Dreams," published in *Cruising Paradise* in 1989.

Talking about the story, Shepard told Kevin Berger, "It took me five years to even consider writing about it. Finally, I came to the point where I thought that if I don't write about it, some aspect of it may be lost." As John Lahr pointed out in *The New Yorker,* a character with the same last name had appeared in Shepard's *The Holy Ghostly,* "a 1969 one-act exercise in Oedipal mayhem." Called "Stanley Moss" then, "he is gunned down by his son, a cool renegade customer called Ice, who like Shepard, has shed his family name." In truth, the sixteen years that had passed between Rogers's death and the completion of· *The Late Henry Moss* had done nothing to enhance or transform the material or the way in which Shepard had now chosen to present it onstage.

And so as the two brothers at the center of *The Late Henry Moss,* who seem no more than pale shadows of those in *True West,* examine the shared trauma of their childhoods while arguing about who deserves possession of their father's few belongings, not much else really happens. What does stand out is how the nature of the violence wreaked upon the family by their alcoholic father has escalated to yet another level.

During the big blowout between the older brother, Earl, and Henry Moss, all the windows in the house explode as Earl breaks them one by one. Leaving his mother trapped under the sink as his father keeps on kicking her while she waits for someone to help her, Earl gets into his 1951 Chevy and drives away and Ray does not see him again for seven years. Near the end of the play, Henry says to his sons, "Your mother threw me out. She locked me out of the house ... I saw the blood and thought I killed her, but it was me that I killed." Addressing

Earl directly, he adds, "You were there the whole time and you could've stopped me," only to have Earl reply, "I couldn't. I was scared, I was just too scared."

On November 14, 2000, when *The Late Henry Moss* opened in San Francisco, two tickets for the opening night performance were sold for nine hundred dollars on the street. Although the entire seven-week run had already sold out, one reviewer noted, "During the past week it seems either Nick Nolte or Sean Penn has been out due to 'sickness.' It is a lucky person who gets to see both of these men on stage at the same time." In *The New Yorker,* John Lahr observed, "Whatever the audience paid to get in, it was more than the producers seem to have shelled out for the set." Concluding his review, Lahr wrote, "'The Late Henry Moss' will no doubt make it to New York. I hope the play stops along the way for repairs; it has its narrative problems, which must by now be obvious to its subtle creator, but there is nothing that a new first act, a new set, and a new director couldn't fix."

A little more than ten months later, on September 24, 2001, *The Late Henry Moss* opened at the Signature Theatre Company's 176-seat performance space on West Forty-second Street in Manhattan. With Joe Chaikin directing a two-and-a-half-hour version of the play, Sheila Tousey was the only member of the San Francisco cast who was still with the show. As Charles Isherwood, *Variety*'s chief theater critic, wrote, "The play had its world preem last fall at San Francisco's Magic Theater, in a production starring Sean Penn, Nick Nolte and Woody Harrelson, among others, and their high-voltage personalities may have helped to mask some of the watery patches in the writing. The New York premiere features Arliss Howard and an egregiously miscast Ethan Hawke, in a staging from Joseph Chaikin that reveals this long-time Shepard collaborator to be in rusty form."

In his *New York Times* review of the play, entitled "No-Good Dad Whose Tale Is Told Repeatedly," Ben Brantley wrote, "The play itself is long, plodding and diminishingly crowded with echoes from stronger Shepard works . . . The title character here is dear old destructive Dad, a seedy, hard-drinking figure who has shown up in many of Mr. Shepard's plays . . . 'Henry Moss' is Mr. Shepard's most earnest and direct attempt to pin down this festering paternal ghost and to find the attendant filial guilt and responsibility. The results suggest that Mr. Shepard, of all people, may be ripe for a guest spot on 'Oprah.'"

EVEN AS SAM SHEPARD was being roundly pilloried for returning to material in *The Late Henry Moss* he had already dealt with onstage in a far more effective dramatic manner, Matthew Warchus, who had originated the idea of having the lead actors in *True West* switch roles for every performance, was mounting a Broadway revival of that play. As Shepard himself had been unable to do in his recent work, the revival would serve to enhance his standing as a seminal American playwright of the first order.

With the production scheduled to open at the Circle in the Square Theatre on March 9, 2000, Warchus began the difficult process of trying to cast two actors who could not only alternate playing Austin and Lee at each show, but also bring the kind of star power that would draw people into the theater, thereby helping make this version of the play a critical and commercial success. "Among what you might call many of the usual suspects at the time," Warchus would later say, "Jim Carnahan, the casting director, brought in Ethan Hawke, who was a bit on the young side but not that far off. And then John C. Reilly came in and read for me." Reilly, who had appeared on Broadway two years earlier as Tom Joad's older brother, Noah, in the Steppenwolf Theatre production of John Steinbeck's *Grapes of Wrath,* had just played a policeman in Paul Thomas Anderson's *Magnolia,* in which the actor Philip Seymour Hoffman played a hospice nurse.

"I was really struck by how unlike the sort of heroic chiseled cowboy John was in that film," Warchus says. "There was something hapless about him and so all the anger and passion and desperation seemed to come from that place as well. There were quite a lot of younger swarthy and sexy actors interested in *True West* and although John did not obviously fit in that world, I suddenly saw it all in a new light. As in, 'Okay, what about these brothers as hapless losers, without the heroism?'"

Having decided that Reilly could play Austin and Lee in successive shows, Warchus asked the actor if he had any thoughts about whom he might want to do this with. By then, Warchus had already checked on Philip Seymour Hoffman's availability, only to be told he could not even come in for a meeting about the play. Nor had Hoffman's agent exhibited any interest in the project. When Reilly brought up Hoffman's name, Warchus said, "'Would you try him yourself, actor to actor?' And so that was how we approached Phil and he said yes."

Thirty-three years old, Hoffman had by then already established himself as the actor of choice for an astonishing variety of character parts in both independent films and big-budget Hollywood movies. In 1992, he was one of the founders of the LAByrinth Theater Company, a nonprofit Off-Broadway ensemble of actors. In Warchus's words, "The way Phil played Lee wasn't like a shark or a hawk or a predator. He was just repellent and nasty with a bit of a gut hanging out of his shirt and drool coming out of his mouth. He was like a disgusting, vile, cruel, nasty creature. Both Phil and John were terrifying as Lee, making you think you were dealing with the most unfortunate version of a human being."

After theatergoers had seen one version of the play, Warchus remembered them saying, "'I'm so glad I saw it this way, because there is no way the other version would have worked.' And so they would go away satisfied but occasionally they would come back and see it the other way and then be completely confused, because it was different but just as good."

As Ben Brantley wrote in his *New York Times* review of *True West*, "Rest assured that no matter which performance of the production you attend, there's no way you're going to lose . . . If you've followed Mr. Hoffman's and Mr. Reilly's work on film, you probably have your own ideas of who was meant for which part. Forget it. Whichever way you've sliced it, you're right . . . Twist my arm, and I still wouldn't be able to tell you which version of 'True West' I prefer." Calling Warchus's direction "pitch perfect," Brantley added, "To see both versions of the current 'True West'—and if you have the time and the money, you must—is to enrich deeply your experience of what good actors can do with the limited instruments known as the human body and voice."

Noting the "production makes a persuasive case for 'True West' as a great American play, arguably Mr. Shepard's finest," Brantley accurately foresaw that *True West* would continue being presented regularly for the next two decades by writing that the play "also shows the incredible variety that can be harvested from a work this fertile without betraying its essential nature."

Unlike the way he had reacted to the Public Theater production of *True West*, Shepard himself seemed as pleased by this version of the play as he had been during its initial run at the Magic. Finding himself in New York at the time, the playwright asked Warchus "if it would be okay if he came to rehearsals. Of course I said yes and he made it all just as casual and informal as possible. Sam also came to a couple of previews because he got such a kick out of watching those two actors and because they made him laugh a lot, which he liked. When Sam used to talk to me about them, he would compare them to two great racehorses."

—

THIRTY-ONE

DON'T COME KNOCKING

I'm going through an enormously painful time
right now with Jessica & finally beginning to realize
all the pain I've caused her over the years. I don't
know what's wrong with me. That's the hard part.

—SAM SHEPARD,
TWO PROSPECTORS

O N JULY 5, 2003, SHURA BARYSHNIKOV, WHO WAS TWENTY-TWO
years old and had recently graduated from Marlboro College in Vermont, married her college boyfriend, Bruce Bryan, in the garden her
mother had designed for her below the family house in Stillwater. Although Shepard had once been forced to go shopping at the last moment for a white shirt and tie in New York City so he could attend an
event—he did not then own either of those items—the playwright
decided to mark the occasion by purchasing the kind of white suit he
had seen in old movies and had always thought would look good on a
man once he reached the age of sixty.

On the day before the ceremony, Lange welcomed the wedding
guests while also celebrating the Fourth of July on the Saint Croix
River by hosting a party on a rented white yacht staffed by crew wearing white shirts and black shorts and serving drinks and appetizers
from silver trays. Because the groom's family was from New England,
Shepard noted that Lange's relatives, all of whom were "big, raw-
boned Minnesotans," made them look "like little Hobbits."

In hot, steamy weather, the wedding took place the following day.

As Lange and Shepard's seventeen-year-old daughter, Hannah, played "a fantastic Bach piece on her cello" and the bride and groom passed their three-month-old daughter back and forth, the couple were married by a friend. With a band playing, everyone then began eating, drinking, dancing, and carrying on. Although his white suit was now "getting sweaty," Shepard was "getting along splendidly" with the father of the bride, telling Mikhail Baryshnikov what it had been like to bring up Shura only to have him say "how he's grateful to me for having helped raise her."

As the night wore on, Shepard began getting "pretty drunk" and then saw Hannah's boyfriend openly flirting with one of her best friends. Acting on "some weird impulse (this is how I always get into trouble)," Shepard promptly marched over to "the doofus" and asked him to leave the party. Understandably intimidated, the boyfriend slid off into the night. Once word got out about what Shepard had done, "Hannah's crying—Jessica's livid, blaming it all on my alcoholic ways & I've jumped into the pool in my Armani white suit, splashing around with all the other drunken revelers & having a great old time— oblivious to the ruckus I've caused."

The next day, Lange and Hannah had "teamed up against me in some female covenant" only to have Shepard "tell them I'm not feeling the least bit guilty—the ass-hole kid had it coming—his behavior was entirely inappropriate (of course mine was atrocious but who cares)." Continuing to make his case, Shepard informed them that, in "a different culture—say Mexican," if both the stepfather and father of the bride had witnessed "the shameful behavior of the boyfriend—the Mexican man might have shot the kid. Justifiably."

As Lange and Hannah stood there "stupefied, unable to follow any of my reasoning," Shepard left them to meet his son Jesse and his girlfriend at a breakfast thrown by Shura's father-in-law at the historic Water Street Inn on the river in downtown Stillwater. When Jesse and his girlfriend wondered why Shepard was there without Lange or Hannah, the playwright went off into "fantasies of me going off to live by myself in Montana somewhere with only my horses." A few days later, however, it had "all blown over" because his daughter "didn't really like the guy" and "Jessica seems to have seen my side of the issue."

Over the course of the following year, the problems that had plagued Shepard and Lange's never-tranquil relationship continued to multiply while also becoming deeper and far more protracted than they had ever been before. When the two of them stopped speaking to each other shortly before setting off with their children on a family vacation in Mexico, Shepard wrote that it was like "the bottom fell out on us. I don't know what happened."

In a letter to Johnny Dark written on April 28, 2004, he described how this situation had come about. "I don't know why I keep returning to these horrible bouts of drinking & bad behavior," he wrote. "I've ruined an amazing relationship just out of a callous disregard for anyone else's feelings & the worst part of it is that I don't really know how it all happened. Anyhow, she has finally come to the end of the rope with me." Nonetheless, Shepard also noted, "We've decided to soldier on for a while because of the kids."

After twenty-three years together, Sam Shepard and Jessica Lange had finally agreed to continue their relationship by entering into what was known in many marriages as "the arrangement," the decision by partners unable or unwilling to reconcile their differences to remain together solely for the sake of the children. Compounding the drama of their current situation, Lange and Shepard then co-starred in the movie that would become their final onscreen appearance together.

IN THE SUMMER OF 2004, Sam Shepard and Jessica Lange went off on location to make *Don't Come Knocking,* the first movie they appeared in together in eighteen years. Working from a story they had written together, Shepard and director Wim Wenders had first begun the project three years earlier when Wenders presented Shepard with a treatment he felt "wasn't down his alley." After discussing it at length, Wenders junked what he had written and the two men began, as Wenders said, "to shape a new story."

Although the director had "asked Sam on my knees" to play the leading character in *Paris, Texas,* he had steadfastly refused to do so. Insofar as *Don't Come Knocking* was concerned, though, Shepard informed Wenders "very early on" that he wanted to portray Howard

Spence, the aging cowboy movie star who begins the film by riding off the set of a movie entitled *Phantom of the West* with no intention of ever going back. To play Doreen, the waitress in Butte, Montana, with whom Spence had been involved in an affair while filming on location there twenty years before, Wenders "immediately knew" he also wanted Lange, whom he described as "any director's dream."

With production scheduled for 2002 and 2003 only to have been postponed twice at the last minute due to financing problems, filming on *Don't Come Knocking* began on July 18, 2004, in Montana, Utah, Nevada, and Los Angeles. With a budget of $11 million, the film was ten times more expensive to make than *Paris, Texas* had been.

Beautifully shot but burdened by a plot that constantly wanders off in one direction after another, *Don't Come Knocking* follows Howard Spence as he goes on a journey that begins with a visit to his mother, played by Eva Marie Saint, who was then eighty years old. Returning to Butte, Spence discovers his former flame Doreen, who is now managing the bar and restaurant where she once worked as a waitress. As they sit at the bar watching a young man perform onstage, she informs Spence he is now looking at the son he has never seen before. Spence then also meets the daughter he fathered with another woman there.

The single best moment Lange and Shepard have together in the film occurs as they walk down the main street of town and Shepard's character suddenly realizes the real reason he came back there was to see Doreen. When he tells her they should have gotten married, she loses all patience with him. Showing anger for the first time, she begins beating him about the head and chest with her handbag.

After telling him he is an idiot and gutless for not reconciling with his son, she adds, "You're a coward, Howard! *Hah!* That rhymes, doesn't it?" Stalking off, Lange suddenly wheels around and comes up close to Shepard. Putting her hand around his throat, she kisses him. Fiercely, they begin making out. Breaking it off just as suddenly as she began it, Lange hits him three times in the chest with her fist and walks off again, this time for good. Brilliantly, Jessica Lange had just encapsulated her long-running relationship with Sam Shepard into a single scene.

In her words, "The night before we were doing that scene I was thinking about it and I thought, at the end of this scene I'm going to go over to him and I'm going to kiss him, I'm going to kiss him really hard, and then I'm going to slug him. And that's just for all the years you wasted." Asked by an interviewer if it had helped being in a relationship with her co-star, Lange said, "Sure, I know some couples don't like to work together, but I've always found it easy working with Sam. And in this case, it's a little different than just working with your partner because he also wrote it; so I'm speaking his words. But, as soon as you start saying those trigger words, just because you're in a heightened emotional state anyhow, it brings up a whole well of emotion that you're not even aware of that you're going to touch on."

ON SEPTEMBER 30, 2004, JACQUES Levy, the man who had brought Sam Shepard to Bob Dylan, died of cancer at the age of sixty-nine. Fifteen days later, Shepard wrote a letter to Johnny Dark in which he described going to the "uptown, very Jewish" funeral of an old friend where something had happened Shepard thought "could probably be some kind of story or movie or something."

At the funeral, Shepard had run into an old girlfriend of the deceased whom he had also been "balling on the side back then" when the woman had, in the words of T Bone Burnett, "a body that could jump start a car." As he was "trying to plow through the crowd of Jewish mourners in black caps & black suits to get to the man's wife" to offer his condolences, the woman began tugging on his elbow. Only, now she looked "like Cruella De Vil from 101 Dalmatians." Her face was wrinkled and her body had "deflated in all the places" he remembered lusting after wildly. When she offered to share a cab with him downtown, Shepard said he had an appointment and could not do so. As she would not give up, he had "to ditch her in the crowd after a hasty, 'I'm sorry' to the widowed wife." Without ever mentioning the name of the deceased, this was Shepard's complete account of having attended the funeral of Jacques Levy, whom he not seen or spoken to in twenty-seven years.

"I had just buried my husband, whom I had adored," Claudia Carr Levy said, "and I was stunned to see Sam there. He said something like, 'I don't know what to say,' and I said, 'Sam, I have to tell you something. Jacques always loved you.' And he just broke down and began crying. The way I always saw Sam was that he had never come to terms with his own family background and the pain he had grown up with and so I always felt he was a rather tortured man. But Jacques always adored him and never blamed him. Never."

Some months later, Jacques Levy's sixteen-year-old son, Julien, happened to cross paths with Shepard on Prince Street in Lower Manhattan. By way of introducing himself, Julien said, "I'm Jacques Levy's son."

"Do you still live in the same place on West Broadway with your mother?" Shepard asked.

When Julien Levy told him he did, Shepard said, "That's nice." And then he turned and walked away.

—

THIRTY-TWO

THE FEELING
OF NUMBNESS

Little did I know that aging & alcohol are
sympathetic. I must admit that I like getting drunk.
I like the feeling that comes over me. The numb-
ness. The moving into a different state. All that stuff.

—SAM SHEPARD,
TWO PROSPECTORS

SAM SHEPARD HAD NOW REACHED THE STAGE IN HIS LIFE WHERE
even though he knew that many of the things he was doing were not
good for him, he kept right on doing them all the same. While the
physical toll he had wreaked upon his body was a legitimate source of
concern to him, he also used his medical issues as the subject matter
for his short fiction and would continue doing so until his death.

In the story "Indio, California," published in *Day out of Days*, Shepard writes about "diving down deep into the slimy green water" of the
bass pond on his Wisconsin ranch while "trying to retrieve an old
sunken raft" with his son in the summer of 2000. "I came up gasping,"
he writes. "That was the very first indication I had something seriously
wrong with my heart: Desperate breath. Ache in the armpit. Ropes in
the neck. The panic, although I kept it hidden from my son."

Having accurately described the symptoms associated with angina,
Shepard ends the story by listing two drugs designed to lower blood
cholesterol and an enzyme inhibitor prescribed to prevent heart at-
tacks and strokes in high-risk patients over the age of fifty-five: "Lipi-
tor. Zetia. Ramipril. If this were 1876, I'd be dead in a heartbeat."

Three months later, while he was in San Francisco about to begin rehearsals for *The Late Henry Moss,* Shepard had what he later describes as a "little 'almost' heart-attack experience." One minute, the playwright was eating sushi on Sutter Street while, the next, he suddenly found himself "collapsed at the bottom of the glass steps of the hotel, tourists brushing past him with their black luggage." Rather than summon an ambulance, Shepard got behind the wheel of his white Suburban and drove from downtown San Francisco to a clinic in Oakland. After he failed a stress test, an angiogram revealed he had a blockage in the left anterior artery of his heart. Due to the high death rate it caused, a coronary occlusion in this artery was commonly referred to as "the widow maker." Shepard was then wheeled into an operating room to undergo angioplasty and have a stent inserted into the blocked artery.

Four months later, he "was intentionally going out of his way to exercise and raise his heart rate like some aerobic moron" by snowshoeing as hard he could through snow and ice in subzero temperature in the Wisconsin wilderness. Gasping for breath as his heart pounded madly and "the back of his skull felt like it might blow off," he kept going "as though he had become possessed by a maniac intent and he was just along for the ride."

Fifteen months later, Shepard took another stress test only to be informed that the results had "turned up a glitch of some sort in the area where they did the procedure a year & a half ago." To his great relief, he then learned that the problem was not serious.

The most powerful message the surgeon who inserted the stent into Shepard's left anterior coronary artery had tried to impress upon him was the urgent need for him to stop smoking cigarettes. In an attempt to explain his deep, lifelong attachment to smoking, Shepard wrote of himself, using the third person, "How could he suddenly forsake his most sacred obsessions, abandoning entire aspects of character he had taken to be immutable?" He had started down this road by "pilfering Chesterfield butts from his old man's ashtray" and had been "a solid, deep-inhaling smoker" since he was twelve years old. "By the age of sixteen," he wrote, "he was totally addicted and indoctrinated into the strong belief that manhood and smoking were synonymous."

And so there "was nothing he did without a cigarette clenched between his teeth or his fingers: mowing lawns, working under cars, saddling horses, even necking with girls, the ubiquitous cigarette became a prop of necessity."

Nonetheless, Shepard made a serious effort to quit the habit that had defined him for more than half a century. On the day he had pushed himself to the edge of exhaustion on snowshoes in Wisconsin, he had "actually managed to go cold-turkey for two and a half months" but "could still feel his tongue yearning for the bright sting of smoke."

In a letter to Dark written eighteen months after that incident, Shepard wrote that the screened-in porch of his house in Stillwater was his "favorite place to be in the summer," surrounded by "all my books & writing piled up in stacks" and by "a silver ash tray & macanudo [sic] cigars (which I don't inhale)."

HEADING NORTHWEST ON U.S. Route 62 to his horse farm in Kentucky, Sam Shepard would have driven past endless vistas of rolling green pastureland before proceeding down the main street of Midway, the small town named for its location about halfway between Lexington and Frankfort, the state capital. Turning left onto Leestown Road and then right onto Fishers Mill Road would have brought him to the extensive acreage and weathered two-story brick house on Sharp Lane he had purchased two years after *Simpatico* was filmed in and around the area during the fall of 1998.

Having sold his first thoroughbred at an auction in Kentucky while he and Lange were living outside Charlottesville, Virginia, Shepard chose to continue using the name "Totier Creek Farm" for his new venture so buyers would know the breeding history of his stock. Now living in the heart of bluegrass country, where the distilling of fine bourbon whisky and the breeding of championship thoroughbred horses had long since been staples of the local economy, Shepard returned regularly to his farm from the acting jobs that enabled him to pay his bills.

From 2004 to 2008, he appeared as a trainer in a television movie about the acclaimed thoroughbred filly Ruffian and in eight feature films, most notably *The Assassination of Jesse James by the Coward Robert Ford*, in which he played the outlaw's older brother, Frank. The playwright could also be heard as the narrator of the animated version of E. B. White's classic children's book *Charlotte's Web*. As the manager of a neighboring horse farm said of Shepard, "He used to always say, 'I just stay in the movie business to feed my horses.'"

By the fall of 2006, Shepard, who was still working on the stories that would be published in *Day out of Days*, began writing a new one-act, one-character play entitled *Kicking a Dead Horse*. Sparked by a request from his old friend Stephen Rea to come up with something the actor could perform at the Abbey Theatre in Dublin, Ireland, Shepard created an eighty-minute monologue he then directed in Dublin and New York. Throughout the show, Rea, who portrayed a Manhattan art dealer named Hobart Struther, shared the stage with a very large and realistic-looking dead horse, a prop on which he leaned and leisurely reclined and also turned over on its back so all four legs stuck straight up in the air.

In his *New York Times* review of the 2008 production at the Public Theater, Charles Isherwood called the play "a conscious homage to Beckett" while noting Shepard had "covered much of this territory before, far more subtly." The critic John Simon wrote, "Though the Irish designer Brien Vahey has created a terrific equine carcass—Shepard would have preferred a real horse—the author is kicking a dead horse in more ways than one."

By March 2008, Shepard had nearly completed a one-act play entitled *Ages of the Moon*. Starring Stephen Rea and Sean McGinley, the show opened a year later at Dublin's Abbey Theatre and was then presented in New York by the Atlantic Theater Company at the 199-seat Linda Gross Theater in the Gothic Revival St. Peter's Parish House on West Twentieth Street between Eighth and Ninth avenues in Manhattan.

On a hot summer night in August 2007, Ames and Byron, two old friends now in their sixties, sit together on a porch talking about their shared past while drinking bourbon as they wait for the lunar eclipse. "Even as they face their twilight years," Ben Brantley wrote in his *New York Times* review of the play, "those Shepard boys are still tearing down the house . . . Ames and Byron confirm that in Mr. Shepard's universe it is hard to be close to someone without wanting to kill that person and occasionally acting on the instinct." Nonetheless, Brantley also felt *Ages of the Moon* "exudes a contagious weariness" and "is essentially static."

Despite how much Shepard prized the solitary nature of his life on his horse farm in Kentucky, he expressed an entirely different feeling about it in a letter to Dark in September 2008. "I've decided," Shepard wrote, "it's not so great living so much of the time alone & I've told Jessica that I think we should find a way to spend most of our time together."

Ten months after they left Stillwater, Shepard and Lange had purchased a two-unit apartment at One Fifth Avenue for $3.4 million (the equivalent of about $5 million today). Built as a hotel in 1927, the iconic twenty-seven-story building overlooking Washington Square Park in the heart of Greenwich Village had long been one of the most coveted residences in Lower Manhattan. Located on the ninth floor, their unit consisted of two separate apartments, one with a single bedroom and the other with two bedrooms, thereby allowing Shepard and Lange to live entirely separate lives while remaining together.

Four years later, Shepard no longer had any desire whatsoever to live with Lange in Manhattan, but he did think a reasonable compromise might be for them to settle in Upstate New York, "in order to be close to Shura's little girls . . . When you know you have a destiny with someone, why put it off? We were meant to live together for the rest of our lives & that's now become more important than horses & farms & fishing & New Mexico & Kentucky & running up & down the American road like a chicken with a head cut off."

AT AROUND TWO IN the morning on Thursday, January 3, 2008, Shepard was driving north in his white Chevy Tahoe on Main Street in Normal, Illinois, when police officers observed him going forty-six miles an hour in a thirty-mile-an-hour zone. "The way he pulled up on the curb," one of them told a reporter from the local newspaper, "it appeared he was driving under the influence." After the officers arrested

Shepard on charges of drunk driving, speeding fifteen to twenty miles above the posted limit, and improper lane usage, a test revealed his blood alcohol level to be 0.175, more than twice the legal limit of 0.08 in Illinois. This was about half the alcohol level in Sam Rogers's bloodstream when he was struck by a car and killed in New Mexico nearly twenty-five years earlier.

In Normal, where the founding members of the Steppenwolf Theatre Company had met while attending what by then had become Illinois State University, Shepard had been drinking in Fat Jack's, a bar he had visited "at least four or five times before" after "hitting it off with a bartender who recognized him." The playwright liked the place so much that he had even autographed a bottle of Woodford Reserve, "reportedly his favorite drink," which had been distilled and bottled about twenty-five minutes from his horse farm in Kentucky.

"I wasn't speeding," Shepard told a writer from *Time Out Chicago*. "I was just drunk. In fact, I was under the speed limit. It was the day after New Year's, and the cops were staked out, and they saw me come out of a bar and get into my car. They stopped me, like, a block later." In a letter to Dark written five weeks later, he was more specific, describing what he had done that night as "driving blind drunk (which I've been doing for 50 years & just now got caught)."

Unable to name anyone who could wire him the one hundred fifty dollars he needed to complete his three-hundred-dollar bail, Shepard spent the rest of the night in jail. In a poem he included in a story entitled "Normal (Highway 39 South)," published in *Day out of Days*, he wrote, "they must have thought I was lying / so they threw me in here / slammed the door . . . / I'm not in here for lying / I know that much / I'm in here for blowing / twice the state limit."

Lying on a cot so short he had to bend his knees to fit on it, with a "weird light green plastic burlap-sack style mattress propped under his head," Shepard wrote he had "nothing much else to do" but study the cinder-block walls of his cell "under the blaring neon of the drunk-tank lockup." Having never been in jail before, he found the "remarkable absence of graffiti" most astonishing. Instead, "Someone had attempted some desperate scrapings on the steel frame of the window but there were no letters; no words of any kind. Not even a lover's name or a racial slur . . . Just random gashes in the steel." As the night wore on, those "raw wall scrapings" began "to move all by themselves. Flicker and dance."

Back in Kentucky thirteen days later, the playwright seemed far more concerned about having forgotten to call his daughter, Hannah, on her twenty-third birthday on January 13 than about his drunk-driving arrest in Normal. In a letter to Dark four days later, he wrote that he had called his daughter frantically from a "twisting Kentucky country road" to apologize, "but she just laughs hysterically & I realize I've become the crazy old coot of a father who always forgets her birthday plus now also gets arrested for drunk driving with his loopy mug-shot all over CNN & *People* Magazine. Great! A laughingstock—at my age when I should be revered and honored."

About a month after he was arrested there and a day before his trial, Shepard returned to Normal to confer with Hal Jennings, "a great old guy with a gray beard" who had been practicing law there for five decades and so knew "everyone in town, which is the reason I hired him." Sitting with Shepard in a booth in the restaurant of the Mark Twain Hotel in Peoria, Illinois, where the playwright had decided to stay so he would not be bothered by reporters, Jennings instructed him on "how I should respond—what not to say—how to behave as though I'm the nicest, most polite citizen on earth & how I've learned my lesson & never ever again will I even think about stepping into a vehicle of any kind having even had a swallow of beer."

In a letter to Dark on February 11, 2009, Shepard wrote that a "woman with a huge nose & tiny nostrils" who worked for the court had then asked him an extensive series of questions about his drinking, all of which he answered by saying, "No." Alongside his lawyer, he then walked through the pouring rain to the courthouse. When "a couple of pathetic photographers" from the local newspapers tried to take his picture, he had his "raincoat hood pulled tight around my head & my shades on (Hell man, I've dodged Italian paparazzi with Brad Pitt! This is nothing—This is Normal fucking Illinois!)."

In a courtroom that "reek[ed] of boredom and bureaucracy," he was "suddenly glad to be a drunken playwright/actor ass hole with no connection to the world of law & order. It all looks like living death . . . I suddenly think of Lenny Bruce. Poor Lenny! How he must have suffered." After his name was called, Shepard approached the bench. When the judge asked what he had been doing getting so drunk in a city where he did not live and was only passing through, Shepard told a story about having met two guys in the bar who had been "helicopter pilots in the original 'Blackhawk Down' incident in Somalia (true) & how I started drinking with them & swapping stories—since I was in the movie & they were in the actual real-life catastrophe." (In 2001, Shepard had portrayed General William F. Garrison in *Black Hawk Down*, Ridley Scott's film about the incident.)

Although Shepard had indeed met these men in Normal, he had done so a year before his arrest, "but I figured the military aspect of it would appeal to their gung-ho enthusiasm for sobriety & it worked. No conviction on the DUI—which means it won't show up on my future license record." In truth, Shepard pleaded guilty to the charge of driving under the influence and paid a six-hundred-dollar fine. As would most likely have happened even if he had not elected to commit perjury on the stand, he was also placed on two years of court supervision with the provision that if he completed twenty-two and half hours of alcohol treatment and performed one hundred hours of community service, his Kentucky driver's license would be suspended for a month but the conviction would then be expunged from his record.

Explaining to Dark that he would wait out that month "in New York or Dublin where I won't need a car," he added, "Long story short—I won't be caught dead drinking & driving again. Which is a good thing, I think. God knows how dangerous it could have been—if I ran someone down in the street." Even as he was writing the letter, Sam Shepard was drinking a Negra Modelo beer.

A YEAR LATER, SHEPARD was staying with Lange in their apartment at One Fifth Avenue as *Ages of the Moon* and a highly praised revival of *A Lie of the Mind* directed by Ethan Hawke opened within weeks of each other Off-Broadway. Twice a week, Shepard was also signing in at an alcohol counseling office on Forty-sixth Street just off Broadway, giving a urine sample to prove he had not been drinking and then sitting down on a swivel chair in "a blank room" alongside "6 to 14 raving addicts—some on heroin, Methadone, crack, pills, pot, alcohol—you name it."

In a letter to Johnny Dark a year after he had completed the program, Shepard created a well-written quasi-short play about it with multiple characters, all of whom he described in meticulous detail without exhibiting any compassion whatsoever for how they had managed to destroy their lives with a variety of drugs. He also never mentioned whether he had shared his own story in these sessions.

AS OPPOSED TO THE WAY he had felt about his court-ordered alcohol treatment program, Shepard found himself in far more comfortable surroundings when he began the one hundred hours of community service the judge had ordered him to perform before his DUI conviction could be expunged from his driving record.

Having collaborated with Joe Chaikin and appeared in several of Jean-Claude van Itallie's plays, Rosemary Quinn, the director of the Experimental Theatre Wing of the Tisch School of the Arts at New York University, arranged for Shepard to work there with twenty-seven students on their independent projects. According to Jeff Ward, an actor who in the spring of 2010 was completing his senior year in the studio, "ETW was very much built on the work of Sam Shepard, Elizabeth Swados, and everyone at Café La MaMa during the late sixties and early seventies. That was the scene the people who ran ETW had come up worshipping and all of it had gone on literally about a quarter of a mile from NYU. I was twenty years old when Sam walked into ETW for the first time and I felt like I was seeing someone who basically was a god. Anybody who looked at him then would have thought, 'Wow! This is the coolest guy I have ever seen in my life.'"

When Ward, who would go on to appear in a wide variety of television shows and series, including a Lifetime movie in which he played Charles Manson, worked on his independent project with Shepard, the young actor ran through the first twenty minutes of his one-man show and then stopped so the playwright could give him notes on what he had seen so far. "What I will never forget as long as I live," Ward says, "is that Sam took my script, stood up, and started going through my play like he was me. As he was acting, Sam was also doing the blocking and saying, 'See, now you should be here and then you run over here and do this.' Because there was no ego at all on his part, he made me feel like I was working with a peer."

Four months later, on July 1, 2010, Shepard woke up with no idea where he was. As the playwright wrote to Dark later that day, "I waited for the usual panic to set in but it didn't come." Staring at the "patterns of white & dark on the ceiling," he tried "to figure out what motel" he might be in as well as "—what country I was in." Although it seemed like Mexico, the sound of the birds and the wind conveyed a different message. After he had stared at the walls for a while, it finally came to him. He was in Kentucky and although he loved being there, it had "never felt exactly like home" to him. But then, as he conceded, "I don't exactly know what 'home' would feel like."

Sixty-seven years old, Sam Shepard had now begun regularly experiencing the very same kind of self-pity his father had expressed in letters he had written to his son asking for money. And while the fact that Sam Rogers had died at the age of sixty-seven might have been a coincidence, the trait both men shared that helped generate this state of mind was their persistent abuse of alcohol.

—

THIRTY-THREE

SHEPARD & DARK

My life is falling apart. Falling apart at the seams.
I can see it. It's just that I continually make the same
mistakes over and over again. It's pretty obvious.
But still not enough to prevent me from making
them. And I don't quite understand it.

—SAM SHEPARD,
IN *SHEPARD & DARK*

ALTHOUGH SAM SHEPARD HAD BEEN IN DIRE FINANCIAL straits many times before because of the extravagant manner in which he had always spent his money, his current situation seemed far worse to him because of his age. After his accountant called in May 2009 to inform him he now had "no money" and so could not pay his bills, Shepard replied by saying he had no idea what to do about it because there were "no movies out there" and "the ones they do end up making aren't anything like the movies I used to make."

Taking his complaint to yet another level, he wrote, "My days are over. I'm an old fart sitting in my 200 year old brick cabin on a farm in Kentucky, by the fire, reading obscure literature & making up stories & plays. Movies have passed me by. Come and gone. Now I just want to be left alone in peace & poverty."

Facetiously, he considered going out to find a job. "I could go back to washing dishes in restaurants, busing tables, washing UPS trucks in Times Square, working as a guard for the Burns Detective Agency." Conceding he really had no idea how to solve his financial problems, he added, "Throw me in Debtor's Prison, just like the Dickens characters. Let me live out my days in stone walls sipping soup."

Two months later, he was working alongside Dermot Mulroney, Diane Kruger, and Rosanna Arquette shooting a movie entitled *Inhale*. Although the film earned a little more than four thousand dollars in the United States and only eighty thousand dollars worldwide, it had a ten-million-dollar budget and so Shepard would have been well compensated for a supporting role for which he was billed fourth in the credits. A year later, he was cast in the starring role in *Blackthorn*, a movie with a fifteen-million-dollar budget in which he portrayed an aging Butch Cassidy who after having lived in a secluded village in Bolivia for twenty years decides to return to America.

During the next seven years, Shepard continued earning a regular income by appearing in twelve movies and in multiple episodes of two cable television miniseries, *Klondike*, on the Discovery Channel, and *Bloodline*, on Netflix.

HAD IT NOT BEEN for Howard Gotlieb, writers like Sam Shepard who suddenly found themselves in financial need, if only on a temporary basis, might never have been able to bail themselves out by selling their archives to the highest bidder. Leaving Yale in 1963, where he had worked as a teaching associate and an archivist of historical manuscripts, Gotlieb was hired by Boston University to head their newly formed Special Collections division. After learning he had no budget for making acquisitions, Gotlieb decided he "would choose living writers and public figures, some almost unknown when he identified them, and persuade them to donate papers and possessions before they were discarded or dispersed." Although no one before him had ever done so, he began personally importuning authors like Isaac Asimov, Martha Gellhorn, and Elie Wiesel; movie stars like Bette Davis and Fred Astaire; journalists like Dan Rather; playwrights like Shepard; and political leaders like Dr. Martin Luther King, Jr., to donate their private papers and artifacts. Gotlieb eventually amassed a collection that now occupies forty thousand linear feet of space: about seven miles long.

Shepard responded to Gotlieb's requests for material by donating several original manuscripts, notebooks, and journals from the 1970s as well as personal and professional correspondence; black-and-white photographs dating back to his days with the Bishop's Company; a short journal kept by Patti Smith; and the Obie Award he won for *Action* in 1975. Without receiving any compensation, he had also begun contributing archival material in 1992 to the Southwestern Writers Collection at Texas State University in San Marcos, Texas. Because the collection had been founded six years earlier by Bill Wittliff, who wrote *Raggedy Man* and *Country*, Shepard often drove there to visit his old friend after having loaded boxes of his papers into the bed of his pickup truck.

Inspired by Gotlieb's archival work, major universities then began bidding against one another to acquire the work of living writers. For an undisclosed sum of money in 2006, the University of Texas in Austin made "a large acquisition" of Sam Shepard's papers from the playwright. The collection included the original script for *The Tooth of Crime*, the manuscript for *great dream of heaven*, eight Obie awards, and his personal copy of the published version of *Buried Child*, which became the nine-millionth volume held by the university's library. Four years later, this collection was transferred to the Harry Ransom Center at the university, which then purchased another collection of Shepard's papers from the University of Virginia library along with yet more material supplied by Shepard.

By the third week in July 2010, Shepard had agreed for Wittliff (for whom the archives at Texas State University had been renamed) to purchase what came to be known as the Sam Shepard and Johnny Dark Collection. In a letter to Dark written on July 26, 2010, Shepard promised to bring all the letters they had written to each other over the past four decades to Deming, New Mexico, where Dark was now living alone after Scarlett's death five months earlier from what seems to have been kidney failure.

Two days later, Shepard wrote Dark again to report that he had tried to assemble the letters in chronological order only to realize he "wasn't ready for the deep sorrow in re-visiting our past lives." On the back of a postcard with Allen Ginsberg's black-and-white photograph of Jack Kerouac smoking a cigarette on the balcony of a tenement building in Lower Manhattan, Shepard wrote Dark again a day later to say his continuing search for letters had now "turned into some crazy-ass treasure hunt—letters turning up everywhere old luggage, mildewed envelopes—folded up in books, closets, laundry rooms . . . Water-stained pictures—old crumbling, cardboard boxes, rusty paper clips. Ancient artifacts . . . Here's to the book of letters. It may be our last HURRAH!"

Devoting himself wholeheartedly to the task, Shepard spent the next several weeks finding, reading, and sorting through letters he had received from Dark. While doing so, the playwright realized what he had always loved about the letter as a form was that it was "conversation . . . It's not just a solo act. You're writing in response to or in relationship to someone else . . ." Doing so over time, he noted, was the key element in a true correspondence and he counted himself lucky that the two of them had "continued the desire to talk to one another by mail for forty years . . . It is probably the strongest through-line I've maintained in this life. Everything else seems broken—."

Shepard also wrote that he had not seen Lange for six months but did expect her to be in Galway at Thanksgiving when their daughter, Hannah, graduated from the National University of Ireland. Although the news would not become public knowledge until *People* magazine reported it in December 2011, the couple had now finally parted with no intention of getting back together again.

Although neither of them ever spoke publicly about their breakup, Lange did provide Shepard with cash in 2013 by buying his share of their condominium at One Fifth Avenue for $1.64 million. Continuing to act in television miniseries and series, *American Horror Story* among them, she then acquired the two-bedroom, two-bath unit directly above their unit for $3.3 million in 2018.

In mid-September 2010, Shepard set off by himself on the 1,350-mile drive from Midway to Santa Fe, New Mexico. With him, the playwright brought all the letters he had spent the summer collecting so he could work on them with Dark before presenting the collection to Wittliff at Texas State University in San Marcos, about thirty miles south of Austin.

Shortly after giving a reading from *Day out of Days* at the Inn and Spa at Loretto in downtown Santa Fe on Thursday, September 23,

Shepard drove to Deming, where he checked in at the Vagabond Inn. Sitting beneath an umbrella by the motel pool, he transferred material from a notebook onto the page with his white portable typewriter. Along with beautifully framed shots of downtown Deming that then give way to a white-haired Johnny Dark sitting in his house typing away madly on an ancient computer keyboard while smoking marijuana from a bong, this is how *Shepard & Dark,* Treva Wurmfeld's feature-length documentary about the two men, begins.

Wurmfeld, who was thirty-two years old, first met Shepard in 2009, while working as the set videographer on Doug Liman's *Fair Game,* a movie in which Shepard played the father of CIA agent Valerie Plame. After she had interviewed Shepard for the film's electronic press kit, she sent the playwright a handwritten letter asking if he would be interested in letting her make a documentary film about him. Shepard had then called her and invited her to Santa Fe where she filmed his reading, beginning a process that continued for the next eighteen months.

Early in *Shepard & Dark,* the playwright talks on a cell phone, explaining to someone that he is now in Deming, New Mexico, to make a book deal for all the letters he and Dark exchanged over the years, along with Dark's photographs. "So, that is what I'm doing just to make some bread," Shepard says. "Since the TV gig fell through, I got no money coming in, etcetera, okay? So that's where I'm going, just to pay the rent." When Shepard delivers the letters, Bill Wittliff says it would be good if Dark joined them, so he and Shepard could specify the ones they wanted to be published. After telling Wittliff that Dark, who was now working behind the delicatessen counter in Peppers Supermarket in Deming, could not afford to travel to Santa Fe, Shepard says, "So, I am not negotiating just for myself on this. I'm kind of looking out for him."

After we have seen a series of Dark's photographs as well as some of his Super 8 footage of him and Shepard in Mill Valley, Dark reveals how much Texas State University is paying them for their letters by saying, "We signed a contract, and I think we are getting two hundred and fifty thousand dollars apiece . . . for selling all these artifacts to the Sam Shepard archives. Which included all my movies and all my tapes and all my photographs and all our letters."

Dark then comes to work on the project with Shepard in the play-wright's office at the Santa Fe Institute, where, as the recipient of a prestigious Miller Scholarship, Shepard had spent the past year work-ing on what would be his final play. After Shepard leads Dark to an-other desk, Dark unpacks a large Ziploc bag filled with marijuana buds and another containing rolling papers in brown vials while eating a hash cookie. Already looking loaded, he then smokes a joint on the patio outside the office.

When they begin working together, Shepard notes there are no dates on some of Johnny's letters, thereby making this task "suddenly daunting." He then points out how helpful it would have been if Dark had ever also thought about numbering pages or dating his letters. However, when Dark reads a letter from 1998 in which he listed the seven things he had learned from Shepard—among them, "Try to get someone else to wash your underwear," "Keep driving even if you for-get where you're going," and "Spend all your money & then get some more"—the playwright laughs out loud.

At another point while they are working together, Shepard makes a joke of hitting Dark in the head with a sheaf of papers for driving him crazy by constantly clearing his throat. Masking his very real an-noyance, the playwright laughs at what he has just done only to then imitate the coughing for Dark, who explains this is what happens when you live alone like him.

Inside his well-appointed house behind a high red adobe wall in Santa Fe, Shepard sits on a bed singing and playing guitar as Dark avidly watches *The Real Housewives of Beverly Hills,* apparently for the first time. When Dark again begins coughing, Shepard says he is prob-ably dying and will soon have to carry oxygen with him. Accustomed to eating dinner at five P.M., Dark begins complaining about how hun-gry he feels. Suddenly, Shepard snaps, "Will you stop bitching and whining? Jesus Christ!"

Putting a sudden and unexpected end to their collaborative effort in Santa Fe, Dark then gets up at three in the morning and drives back home to Deming. Once he is there, he notes there was always a kind of tension when he and Shepard were together because the playwright was such a moody person. Even though "all the little jabs of criticism" he had been getting from Shepard in Santa Fe had gone in "like arrows," Dark could not tell if Shepard was just getting old or if it had always been this way between them. Dark then wrote the playwright a letter in which he said, "You're starting to sound just like your old man. And like my old man."

In March 2011, Dark came home to find several FedEx boxes outside his front door filled with all the letters and photos that were to be published in their book. There was also a relatively brief note from Shepard. Addressed to "John," it read, "Here are all the letters of yours back. I've just realized that I have come to the end of this obsession & long to be free of it. I'm no longer interested in poring over the past—re-making the past—goofing on the past—reminiscing about the past or re-writing the past. I need to move on to my own stuff & leave this behind . . . As far as I'm concerned you can continue in any way you want. You can arrange them in any order—with or without dates—I don't care—be my guest. Take it away, Johnny & good luck." The note was signed, "Sam."

With this note, *Two Prospectors: The Letters of Sam Shepard and Johnny Dark,* edited by Chad Hammett and published by the University of Texas Press in 2013, ends. However, as the documentary *Shepard & Dark* makes clear, this was not the end of their relationship. As Shepard sits being interviewed in Kentucky after having sent Dark back all the letters and his photos along with that brief note, he explains, "I didn't mean it to be pejorative. I just like said, 'Take it. Run with it. I don't care.'" Turning to the camera, he clarifies his position by saying, "I stopped caring about it. I just stopped caring about it as an artistic adventure."

Although Dark was convinced he would never hear from or see Shepard again, the playwright says, "It will heal up, and it will blow away in the wind and the dust, but I realize that what exists between us is stronger than that, you know. But for a while, it just left me with a bad taste, y'know? And I'm glad I got out of it . . . I wanted to get on with my own work and that was the only way I saw how to do it."

A year later, Shepard wrote Dark to say he had recently spoken to Wittliff only to learn that the book was still a long way from being published. Although the playwright did not know "why there is so much red tape in Texas," he also noted that he would try to come visit Dark in Deming. Completing the final exchange between them in the documentary, Dark reads a letter he wrote to Shepard about his hope that one day they would be able to go back to the way it was between them so they could amble around digging things in each other, "because my feelings for you, my admiration, love, remains intact in spite of limitations of time and situation, and so regardless of how long, I'll never let us lose touch. Your pal, Johnny."

According to Chad Hammett, the senior lecturer in English at Texas State who put Shepard and Dark's letters into book form, "Sam was absolutely telling Johnny things in those letters he did not tell anyone else. But Sam was also sometimes writing to himself and knew he was making a myth. I also think Sam's letters were completely stream of consciousness because there was not a lot of crossing out in them and I make that argument in the foreword to the book."

By allowing *Two Prospectors* to be published, Shepard provided researchers with material they could never have found in any collection of his papers and artifacts—an authentic first-person narrative in which he wrote about his deepest feelings in an entirely unfiltered voice that was all his own.

THIRTY-FOUR

A PARTICLE OF DREAD

We're in this trance. We don't see ourselves.
We don't know who we are. And that's the way I feel
about my life. That I've gone through all these
things having hurt people and it's not something
you go to somebody and you lay on the couch and
you talk about . . . I find destiny and fate far more
plausible than all this psychological stuff, you know.

—SAM SHEPARD,
IN *SHEPARD & DARK*

ASIDE FROM BEING THE LAST PLAY SHEPARD WROTE, *A Particle of Dread (Oedipus Variations)* remains of interest because of his decision to explore familiar themes in a form that harkened back to the avant-garde work he did with Joe Chaikin in Lower Manhattan in the 1960s. With Stephen Rea in the lead role and Nancy Meckler directing, both of whom Shepard had known for five decades, *A Particle of Dread* became the playwright's bittersweet farewell to one of the most extraordinary careers in modern American theater.

Commissioned by the Field Day Theatre Company in Ireland, which was founded in 1980 by the playwright Brian Friel and Rea, *A Particle of Dread* was presented for the first time on November 30, 2013, at the Playhouse in Londonderry (called Derry by Irish nationalists) as part of its City of Culture celebration. Shepard had written the play three years earlier while in residence as a Miller Scholar at the Santa Fe Institute. In *Shepard & Dark*, copies of Sophocles's *Oedipus the King* and *The Great Myth* by Robert Graves can be seen lying on the desk in Shepard's office.

The subject itself had intrigued him for more than thirty-five years. As Shepard told Jonathan Cott in their 1986 *Rolling Stone* interview, he had never "read any plays except for a couple of Brecht things when I was living in New York City. But when I went to England in the early Seventies, I suddenly found myself having a kind of dry spell. It was difficult for me to write, so I started to read. And I read most of the Greek guys—Aeschylus, Sophocles . . . I studied up on those guys, and I'm glad I did."

What amazed him about these plays was how simple they were, with "nothing complex or tricky" about them. "They're all about destiny! That's the most powerful thing. Everything is foreseen, and we just play it out." In response to Cott's question as to when the playwright first recognized his own destiny, Shepard said, "I'm not so sure I do. I'm not saying I know my destiny; I'm saying that it exists. It exists, and it can become a duty to discover it. Or it can be shirked . . . But it's more interesting to try to find it and know it."

A Particle of Dread takes its title from a line spoken by the leader of the chorus in Sophocles's play, who tells Oedipus, "If the killer can feel a particle of dread / Your curse will bring him out of hiding." In Shepard's version of *Oedipus Rex*, there is no chorus nor is the line ever spoken but the basic plotline remains the same. To rid his people of the plague, a king begins searching for the man who killed his predecessor only to learn he unknowingly fulfilled a prophecy by murdering his own father and then marrying his own mother. At the end of the play, his mother hangs herself and Oedipus puts out his eyes before going off into exile for his sins.

In *A Particle of Dread*, Shepard jumps back and forth from Sophocles's characters to a modern time in which an unsolved triple murder involving a Las Vegas casino owner has taken place on Highway 15 near Barstow, California. Structurally, the play comprises thirty-three short scenes, many of which consist of a soliloquy delivered by one of the play's seven actors, five of whom portray multiple roles. Making it all yet more complex, Shepard interpolates a police procedural of the kind in which he so often acted in television series and movies.

Setting the tone for all that follows, *A Particle of Dread* opens with Stephen Rea as Oedipus in a pair of large, blood-soaked eyeglasses with blood running down his face as he mops up yet more blood from the stage while wondering if this is where his mother left him to die as an infant so he would never fulfill the prophecy.

Although the reviews of the production in Ireland were for the most part respectable, the same could not be said for the critical reaction the play generated when it opened a year later at the 191-seat Alice Griffin Jewel Box Theatre at the Pershing Square Signature Center on Forty-second Street in New York City. In *The Village Voice,* Tom Sellar wrote, "Approach *A Particle of Dread* with a particle of dread." In his *New York Times* review, titled "Call Out the Patricide Squad," Ben Brantley quoted a character who questions the value of tragedy during the play by asking, "Why waste my time? Why waste yours? What's it for? Catharsis? Purging? Metaphor?" Brantley then wrote, "That's a fair summing up of the form and substance of this endlessly circular play."

While Shepard had long since learned how to inoculate himself from all such thoroughly negative reviews, the playwright seems to have finally realized he really had nothing more to say on the stage. Seventy-one years old, Sam Shepard instead turned his attention to the short fiction and prose that had always sustained him as a writer during the periods of his life when he simply was unable to come up with an idea for yet another brand-new play.

NEVER SOMEONE WHO WILLINGLY went to see a doctor if he could possibly avoid doing so, Shepard had now begun experiencing a wide range of symptoms, including extreme fatigue and an inability to catch his breath, without attributing them to anything other than just getting old. "I do think the sickness that came over Sam had been already there for a long while," Sandy Rogers says, "because I remember talking to him about how much trouble I had been having getting on my horse because she wouldn't hold still and he said, 'Shit, I can't even get a saddle on a horse anymore.' I remember laughing with him about that because he didn't know what he had. He just had a sense of being diminished. Not just growing old but also getting weak."

Referring to a movie that began shooting on July 29, 2013, Rogers adds, "If you take a look at *Cold in July* with him and Don Johnson, Sam takes his shirt off and you can see how skinny his arms are and he never had skinny arms. And so I could tell by looking at his body that he was not just growing older."

At some point during this period, Shepard sought medical help and went to a series of doctors, one of whom diagnosed him with Lyme disease. As a result of a lifetime of heavy smoking, the playwright had also begun suffering from chronic obstructive pulmonary disease (COPD), which in his case included emphysema. During a visit to the Mayo Clinic in Scottsdale, Arizona, in early September 2014, he finally learned the cause of his symptoms.

As he wrote in *Spy of the First Person,* "They gave me all these tests ... blood tests, of course. All kinds of blood tests, testing my white corpuscles, testing my red corpuscles, testing one against the other." He also underwent a spinal tap and a series of MRIs "to see if there was any paralysis in any bones or muscles ... And they looked at decay and they looked at all kinds of things and they couldn't come up with an answer until finally one guy, I think some kind of neurosurgeon" administered a needle electromyography (EMG), a procedure that measured the electrical activity in Shepard's muscles, by inserting a "steel rod" into "each arm and an electric current pulsed through and I could feel the shocks in my arms."

The playwright was then told he was suffering from progressive muscular atrophy (PMA), a motor neuron disease that was then still considered a precursor to rather than a subtype of amyotrophic lateral sclerosis, or ALS. As there was no known treatment for PMA, Shepard was instructed to perform physical exercises to mitigate the weakness in his arms and hands. Willing to try anything to improve his health, he also went to a doctor of Chinese medicine who prescribed a variety of herbs, a course of action that may not have helped the playwright but that at least made him feel he was doing something to combat his condition.

A month or so later, Shepard was cast to play Robert Rayburn, the aging patriarch of a spectacularly dysfunctional family involved in a web of nefarious schemes in *Bloodline,* a thirteen-episode series set in the Florida Keys and produced by Netflix in partnership with Sony

Pictures. Concerning her brother's appearance in the second and fourth episodes of the first season of the series, which began screening on Netflix in March 2015, Sandy Rogers, who then still had no idea her brother was ill, says, "There was this scene where Sam had to paddle a kayak, and he was very uncoordinated, and I thought, 'Wow, he's acting like an old man really well.' In retrospect, he was actually having trouble paddling. Then they had him playing the ukulele and he was playing like shit and he could play the ukulele really well. Although Sam had finally gone to the Mayo Clinic in Arizona by then, no one knew how long he'd already had it."

ON MEMORIAL DAY, MONDAY, May 25, 2015, Sam Shepard went out for dinner at La Choza, a popular Mexican restaurant in Santa Fe. The playwright was such a regular that whenever he and his friend Paul Pascarella went there together, the bartender would motion them both to their regular spot at the far end of the bar where they could sit and drink in peace, and Shepard would invariably pick up the check. "What happened that night," Pascarella says, "was that Sam walked out of the restaurant into the parking lot but because it was always so crazy there, he had parked his truck on the street. The parking lot attendant saw Sam staggering around and trying to open the door of his truck and said, 'Oh, this guy is really drunk. I'm calling the cops.' Of course, this was the beginning of his ALS period."

In the police dashcam video of the arrest, Shepard sits behind the wheel of his blue Toyota Tacoma truck. Leaving their patrol car, two uniformed Santa Fe County police officers approach him on either side of the truck's cab. Under his own power, Shepard responds to their request to exit the vehicle by walking away from it, albeit a bit unsteadily. Taking up a position directly in front of Shepard, one officer begins administering a series of field sobriety tests by moving the index finger of his right hand from left to right and back again and then up and down. Standing stock still while flexing and extending his fingers, Shepard follows the motion with his eyes. After the officer has repeatedly demonstrated how he wants Shepard to walk, in a straight line with one foot behind the other, the playwright follows the command but in a halting manner, with his legs and body as stiff as a board. Testing Shepard's balance, the officer asks him to lift one foot at a time while standing in place. Having barely said a word during the entire procedure, Shepard is unable to stand like that for very long. In light of how physically compromised he already was by that point, his silent compliance with each direction he is being given is truly heart-breaking in retrospect.

Turning Shepard around, the officer who administered the tests cuffs the playwright's hands behind his back. A third policeman then heads to Shepard's truck so he can drive it to an impound lot. Be-cause Shepard refused to take a Breathalyzer test, he was automatically charged with aggravated DWI in accordance with New Mexico state law and then taken to the Santa Fe County Adult Detention Center. During the night, Shepard had so much trouble breathing that he had to be given oxygen. After getting no sleep at all, he was released on bail the next morning.

By then, the media was already having a field day with the news that the seventy-two-year-old Pulitzer Prize–winning playwright and Academy Award–nominated actor had been arrested again for driving while intoxicated. Stories based on the account furnished by wire ser-vices ran in newspapers throughout the United States and in *The Guardian* in Britain. The most terrifying aspect of the coverage was Shepard's mug shot. Unshaven and unkempt, with his long hair wildly askew, the playwright looked like a homeless person who was not at all well—which was in fact the case.

As though Shepard had now somehow come to represent the left-wing, progressive Hollywood elite, Breitbart, the archconservative website founded as "the *Huffington Post* of the right," ran his mug shot in full color atop an article that concluded, "According to his official biography, Sam's father, also named Sam Shepard, was an alcoholic, and his dysfunctional ways heavily influenced his son's work, which includes his writing." Nor was the furor generated by Shepard's sec-ond arrest for drunk driving restricted to print, electronic, and social media. In Santa Fe, people whom the playwright did not know but who had already judged him as guilty made loud comments as he walked down the street or sat trying to have dinner with friends in a restaurant.

Throughout it all, Shepard just kept getting sicker. Because Santa Fe is located at an altitude of 7,200 feet, his COPD symptoms had become so severe that he now had to rely constantly on supplemental oxygen to help him breathe. The effects of the muscular atrophy from which he was suffering were also progressing.

In a brief passage that his longtime editor in New York City had "read right past" in fall 2015 when Shepard submitted the manuscript of *The One Inside*, a novel published in February 2017, the playwright wrote, "Something in his body refuses to get up . . . The appendages don't seem connected to the motor—whatever that is—driving this thing. They won't take direction—won't be dictated to—the arms, legs, feet, hands. Nothing moves. Nothing even wants to. The brain isn't sending signals."

Shepard went into even more detail about his condition in another chapter in *The One Inside*, entitled "Back across the Desert Floor." At two thirty in the morning in early June 2015, he suddenly began bleeding from his left nostril. "I thought I could stop it easily by stuffing my nose full of toilet paper and laying my head back on the bed," he writes. "When I pulled the toilet paper out of my left nostril, it went right on bleeding. More blood now came out of my right."

Two and a half hours later, Shepard, who was staying in the guesthouse of a woman who had "already been kind enough to go my bail and find me a crackerjack DUI lawyer and drive me around town on shortcuts when they'd taken away my driver's license," slowly made his way to the main house to ask for her help. After she drove him to the emergency room of a hospital in Santa Fe, Shepard was taken inside in a wheelchair. A doctor then packed his "left nostril with a cotton material she said was impregnated with cocaine. (It's hard to believe how much stuff will fit up inside your nose.)" As soon as he had returned to his host's house, Shepard's nose began to bleed again. "She called my doctor in Phoenix and he thought I should come down and get checked into the hospital just to make sure." After she volunteered to make the seven-and-a-half-hour drive with him, as Shepard writes,

"Off we went to Phoenix, across the desert floor ... with my nose packed and oxygen tanks clanking around in the back seat."

At the hospital, Shepard saw many people who "seemed much worse off than me," and so he "wondered what would happen if you were very much alive but looked dead, seemed dead, and were surrounded by the living who also believed you were dead but you had no way to communicate you weren't dead. Very much like life itself." Alluding to the condition that had caused his nosebleed without naming it, Shepard writes that he described the events that had brought him to the hospital to people who "said they understood. They realized there was something wrong with me even if they didn't know how to describe it."

A nurse who Shepard thought was "very cute" told him that as soon as he came into the building, she had known "there was something about me that was catastrophic. That's the word she used— 'catastrophic' ... She just knew my condition was 'catastrophic' and that I'd always remain that way."

USING HIS KENTUCKY DRIVER'S license about a week after his hospital visit, Shepard drove four and a half hours south to Deming, New Mexico, to visit Johnny Dark, whom he had not seen since their breakup four years earlier while filming *Shepard & Dark*. In Deming, where the altitude was 4,334 feet, he was able to breathe much easier than he had in Santa Fe.

In an obituary for Shepard that would appear in *The Guardian* in 2017, Dark wrote, "I was a writer and he was a writer and we both loved movies. He was an alcoholic and I was a drug addict. And we had an inflated sense of how wonderful we were." Noting they had been "friends in our 20s, 30s, part of our 40s," Dark added, "I was never particularly interested in his plays: they were filled with humour, but also with violence and chaos, so it always amazed me that people were attracted to him based on his plays."

Describing Shepard's final visit to Deming, Dark noted, "He knew he was dying ... From what I could see he was getting more depressed, more angry, going through all the stages people go through when they're dying. He had been busted for the second time driving drunk. All of these things were happening at once for him. His life was literally falling apart. The last time he came through here he was having a lot of trouble driving. He shouldn't have been driving at all. He was losing control of his whole upper body, having trouble controlling the truck. He was driving to his farm in Kentucky, travelling with a large oxygen machine because of his difficulty breathing."

In fact, Shepard was returning to Santa Fe. After his annoyance at Dark's persistent coughing in *Shepard & Dark*, the playwright had jokingly suggested his friend would soon need an oxygen machine. The irony that Shepard was now traveling with one himself was apparently lost on Dark, who ended his 1,200-word obituary by writing, "So it goes from the light in the 60s, and youth, to the dark at the end. He had a great need to be adored, and applauded. I have some of that too. We were very similar in a lot of ways, but we had very different styles in the way we dealt with each other and other people. He was a big influence on me, in a good way and a bad way. He was a big part of my life."

AT SOME POINT DURING the early fall of 2014, Shepard was finally diagnosed with ALS. As Dr. Mel Wichter, a professor of clinical neurology at the University of Illinois Chicago, who lost his own mother to the disease, explains, "Because the disease had first presented itself in his limbs and he did not yet have difficulty swallowing, eating, or breathing, you would never jump into saying definitively it was ALS because that is a terminal diagnosis. Spinal cord compression, lead poisoning, West Nile virus, and polio-like viruses can all look exactly like ALS."

Defining Shepard's illness in clinical terms, Wichter adds, "There are two presentations of ALS, or amyotrophic lateral sclerosis. One presentation is the effect on the brain stem, which controls vital functions like swallowing, speaking, and breathing. You can't hide that form of the disease for very long. It's the one that leads to aspiration pneumonia and the inability to eat. The form from which he was suffering had presented itself in his limbs, resulting in a shrinkage and twitching of his muscles called fasciculation, as well as weakness and brisk reflexes, all of which indicate spinal cord dysfunction. As such, he would have had a much longer prognosis. The proof being Stephen Hawking, who survived for tens of years with that form of ALS."

Although Shepard's immediate family and small circle of friends, including his editor in New York City, learned about his condition in the fall of 2015, the information never became public. In part, this was because of how Shepard's drunk-driving charge was handled. Although the district attorney in Santa Fe was determined to make an example of the playwright by prosecuting him to the full extent of the law, Shepard's attorney used the playwright's credit card and eyewitness accounts to prove that he had drunk only "one and a half margaritas and had a sip of mescal" before leaving La Choza on Memorial Day weekend, not nearly enough alcohol "to raise his blood alcohol level to New Mexico's presumed level of intoxication." In addition, the arresting officer had failed to ask Shepard if he had any physical conditions that might cause him to be unsteady or lose his balance. The officer had also administered the incorrect field sobriety test for someone of the playwright's age. And so, without Shepard's attorney having to submit evidence of his client's disease in court, thereby making it public record, the charge against the playwright, who by then had already left Santa Fe for good, was dismissed by prosecutors on December 18, 2015.

Two days later, filming on the second season of *Bloodline* began in the Florida Keys. Although Shepard's character, Robert Rayburn, had been killed off before the midpoint of the first season, he reappears in a flashback in the second season's tenth and final episode. In what critic Brian Tallerico called "one of the second season's best scenes," Shepard sits across a table from actor Ben Mendelsohn. Looking wrinkled and somewhat hollow-eyed but much better than in his mug shot, he is filmed from the waist up and so his hands and arms are never seen. Focused on the scene, he delivers his dialogue in a gravelly voice that seems appropriate for his character. Although his hair is gray and his face is worn, he does not look appreciably diminished or obviously ill. Only in comparison to how animated he was a year earlier while filming the series does the radical decline in his physical condition become apparent. Shepard's ability to perform despite his condition was enhanced by the warm weather and moist air at sea level, which made it possible for him to breathe as he could no longer do at altitude.

By the time all ten episodes of the second season of *Bloodline*, including the one in which Shepard makes his final appearance as an actor, were released on May 27, 2016, the playwright was on his horse farm in Midway, where, as Paul Pascarella says, "Sam didn't need a wheelchair yet and he taught me how to drive a tractor by telling me how to do it. One day, we were like two old guys sitting on a bench by the side log wall of the barn, looking out over the ranch. We looked at each other and said, 'Well, at least we don't smoke anymore.' A message that should be passed on to all young kids everywhere.

"We didn't talk much about the ALS thing but he had this girl who looked after him and helped him with his driving and I think [she] also cooked for him but he would still have a glass or two of wine and I remember going out with him to this really good restaurant where there was this incredibly beautiful and really sweet female bartender.

"Sam always had his own corner in a bar and we were sitting there and she was bringing him something to drink and he had to use two hands to lift the glass. He had, like, these crab hands. But even when he got worse, Sam never complained about any of it. Not once. Not, 'Ah, this is so bad. I can't even pick up a fucking cup of coffee.' None of that. And he also never stopped going out so people wouldn't see him like that. In that sense, he really was heroic."

THIRTY-FIVE

SPY OF THE FIRST PERSON

Nothing seems to be working now. Hands.
Arms. Legs. I just lie here. Waiting for someone
to find me. I just look up at the sky.

—SAM SHEPARD,
SPY OF THE FIRST PERSON

I N MARCH 2005, THIRTY-FOUR YEARS AFTER HE HAD LEFT HER
waiting for him in the American Place Theatre in New York City so
they could appear together onstage in *Cowboy Mouth*, Patti Smith
called Shepard from "out of the blue" to ask if they could see each
other again. In a letter to Dark, Shepard says that they then met "at
Cafe Dante down in the West Village where Dylan used to play & I
was a busboy right around the corner about a hundred years ago."

Describing Smith as still being "as sweet as ever," Shepard also
noted she was "somewhat haggard around the edges like all of us. She
has 2 teen-age kids from a guitar player husband who drank himself to
death & she's had a lot of death in her immediate family but nonetheless still maintains a great bravado about life. One of the things I always liked about her." In another letter to Johnny Dark, he wrote, "As
Patti said to me once, 'Aw hell let's just all go kill ourselves'—I like that
one too. What else are you going to do?"

With Jessica Lange about to open on Broadway in a revival of Tennessee Williams's *The Glass Menagerie,* Shepard invited Smith and her
daughter to join him, Hannah, and Walker in the audience on opening
night. At the party after the performance, Shepard found himself

standing with Smith "around a plate of cookies kind of giggling like kids." Completely confused, he confessed it felt "exactly the same being around her now as it did then except now we've got these grown kids." Making everything even more astonishing, he wrote, "Now, my son Walker might be going out on a date with Patti's daughter whose name just happens to be—Jesse! Unbelievable."

Three years later, in January 2008, *Patti Smith: Dream of Life,* a documentary Steven Sebring had begun filming in 1995, premiered at the Sundance Film Festival, where it won the Excellence in Cinematography Award. It was then shown by PBS on *POV,* the network's long-running independent documentary series.

In the film—as though he had been passing by and just decided on the spur of the moment to drop in on Patti Smith in her New York City apartment only to discover a film crew was already there—Shepard sits in her living room strumming chords on a guitar while singing nonsense syllables to help lead Smith through a ragged version of "You Are My Sunshine." On the black 1931 Gibson guitar he bought her in a pawnshop on the Lower East Side in 1971 for two hundred dollars, she then launches into "Sittin' on Top of the World" with Shepard singing lead.

Looking directly into the camera, Smith starts talking about the first time she ever saw Shepard, as he was singing "Blind Rage" from behind his drum kit onstage with the Holy Modal Rounders at the Village Gate. Cracking Shepard up, Smith says, "I thought, 'That is one hillbilly son of a bitch.'" Completely at ease with one another, they seem to vibrate at an even higher frequency together than either of them could attain on their own.

Continuing their newfound relationship, Shepard brought Smith to a rehearsal of *Heartless,* a new play he had written about women with Lois Smith in the leading role, before it opened on August 27, 2012, at the Pershing Square Signature Theatre in New York City. "When Sam talked to me about her," says Daniel Aukin—who directed the play and whose mother, Nancy Meckler, had taken him to see *Buried Child* at the Hampstead Theatre in London in 1980 when he was just ten—"he explained who she was to him by saying, 'Like, she taught me everything. I didn't know anything before I met Patti.' And the way Sam always behaved around her was like she was his mentor as well as the artistic colossus and senior partner in their relationship."

Shepard also brought Smith to a rehearsal before one of the show's final previews. "They were both at the back of the house," Aukin says, "and I was midway down the aisle with the sound designer and after we had tried some new idea, Sam would come forward and suggest an adjustment and we would try that out. And once this had happened two or three more times, it became apparent to me these were not Sam's suggestions. They were coming from Patti. And so I looked at her and said, 'Patti, come on down here and tell me what you're seeing.' And what she was seeing involved a change in some blocking and I tried it and it worked and that was what we went with. It was a lovely moment because I don't think I would have been alone in being willing to listen to a note from Patti Smith or be really happy to hear whatever she had to say."

After Shepard had returned to his horse farm in Kentucky for good, he continued calling Smith as he had always done before "from somewhere on the road, a ghost town in Texas, a rest stop near Pittsburgh, or from Santa Fe, where he was parked in the desert, listening to the coyotes howling." As Smith writes in "My Buddy," her remembrance of Shepard that appeared in *The New Yorker* four days after his death, "Just a late-night phone call out of a blue, as startling as a canvas by Yves Klein; a blue to get lost in, a blue that might lead anywhere. I'd happily awake, stir up some Nescafé and we'd talk about anything. About the emeralds of Cortez, or the white crosses in Flanders Fields, about our kids, or the history of the Kentucky Derby. But mostly we talked about writers and their books. Latin writers. Rudy Wurlitzer. Nabokov. Bruno Schulz."

In November 2016, more than a year after Shepard had submitted the manuscript for *The One Inside* to his publisher, he was still editing the book and asked Smith to come work on it with him in Midway at Thanksgiving. "With some effort," he met her at the airport in his pickup truck, driving, as she wrote, by "using his elbows to guide the steering wheel. He did the things he could, and when he couldn't he adjusted."

Waking up early each day, they would work on the book together for several hours and then take a break. Falling right back into the way they had collaborated while creating *Cowboy Mouth* on a single typewriter in their room at the Chelsea Hotel forty-five years earlier, Smith realized Shepard was in "the homestretch" of the book. Because writing was physically tiresome for him, she would read the manuscript to him so he could make edits that "required more thinking than writing, searching for the desired combination of words."

"As the book unfolded," Smith writes in *Year of the Monkey*, a memoir published in 2019, "I was dazzled by the bravado of his language, a narrative mix of cinematic poetry, pictures of the Southwest, surreal dreams and his singular dark humor. Inklings of his present challenges emerged here and there, vague yet undeniable." And while Shepard never spoke to her about his horses, which they could both see from his kitchen window but he could no longer ride, the playwright did look "down at the hands that were slowly losing their strength and say, 'Everybody dies . . . though I never saw this coming. But I'm alright with it. I've lived my life the way I wanted.'"

Published on February 7, 2017, *The One Inside* features a foreword by Smith that begins with her describing the "golden Kentucky afternoon" when she sat reading the completed manuscript at Shepard's kitchen table as he stood looking out the window at his horses. She then identifies "the shifting core of the narrator" as "a loner who doesn't want to be alone" and "is just going to keep on living until he dies."

Unlike Smith, no one who did not know about Shepard's condition could have fully understood her meaning. After she finally "set down the manuscript," she writes, "It's him, sort of him, not him at all. It's an entity trying to break out, make sense of things . . . *The One Inside* is a coalescing atlas, marked by the boot heels of one who instinctively tramps, with open eyes, the stretches of its unearthly roads."

In her *New York Times* review of *The One Inside*, Michiko Kakutani compared the overall effect of the book to Fellini's *8½* and Bob Fosse's *All That Jazz*. Despite what he described as Patti Smith's "fawning introduction," *Washington Post* critic Ron Charles wrote, "The best parts of 'The One Inside' are those least hobbled by its fractured structure and mannered dialogue." Had any reviewer known how hard Shepard labored just to get the book into print, their assessment of *The One Inside* might have been radically different.

On the occasion of her seventieth birthday, on December 30, 2016, Smith wrote, "One year to the day when Sam was still able to make a cup of coffee, and write with his own hand." Having known about her brother's condition since the fall of 2015, Sandy Rogers had repeatedly told him, "'Well, if you need help, let me know.' But Sam just kept right on saying, 'No, no, no, not yet, not yet' and so I didn't get there until March. By then, he had been driving his truck with his legs and his elbows and going up to a window at a coffee place so the girl there would come outside to give him his coffee. He was tough."

AT SOME POINT EARLY in 2016, Hannah Shepard bought her father a tape recorder she would set up by his side in the garden so he could dictate the thirty-seven separate sections that eventually comprised *Spy of the First Person*. Relying on the ability that had enabled him to write all those first-draft stream-of-consciousness letters to Johnny Dark over the years with almost no crossing out, Shepard would sit there reciting text into the machine.

Whenever the playwright was ready for a break or had decided he was done for the day, he would signal to his daughter, who would come to turn the tape recorder off. Shepard's sisters, Sandy and Roxanne, both of whom were now living with him in Midway, would then transcribe the tapes so he could read what he had written.

"At the beginning," Sandy Rogers says, "Sam would always say, 'This isn't writing. This isn't really writing,' but we just kept encouraging him to do it and so he adapted to it. We'd turn on this little tape recorder for him and then he'd just sit there and rattle this shit off for an hour and a half or two hours and then hardly change a single word. I think he had thought about it all day long and then just went through it all, because he couldn't turn off the machine or erase anything and then go back over what he had said. It was amazing. Sam then came to believe the first thing that came out of his brain was in fact the real thing."

In an email quoted by Alexandra Alter in an article about the book that appeared in *The New York Times* after Shepard's death, his son Walker said of his father, "He was always a very private writer, and the fact that he was now having to involve his family in his process was not easy for him. I think it was a relief for him to work with Patti because she is not family." In late August, Smith returned to Midway to work with Shepard again. Because he was "now writing out loud in real time," the deeper task had become "to rescue" the aloneness he had always required in order to write. Fully comprehending the existential absurdity of their current situation, Shepard good-naturedly told Smith, "We've become a Beckett play . . . Yep, a Beckett play."

One day after they had been working together for most of the afternoon, Smith left the house to take a short break at twilight and saw the stone ledge surrounding the garden was covered with black butterflies. When she went back inside, she noticed Shepard's old Gibson in a corner of the room, "a guitar he can no longer play. And the reality of the present hits hard, no banging on the typewriter keys, no roping cattle, no more struggling with his cowboy boots. Still I say nothing of these things and neither does Sam. He fills in the silences with the written word, seeing a perfection he alone can dictate."

Unable to sleep that night, Smith got up from "her makeshift bed" to go outside to breathe the air and look at the stars. The black butterflies were still there, "motionless, covering a portion of the garden wall, but I can't really tell if they are dead or just sleeping." The last time she ever saw Shepard, the manuscript of *Spy of the First Person* "was all but done. It was there on the kitchen table like a small monolith, containing the uncontainable, a bright flicker that could not be extinguished."

As she writes in the final paragraph of *Year of the Monkey*, "And I saw myself with Sam in his kitchen in Kentucky and we were talking about writing. In the end, he was saying, everything is fodder for a story, which means, I guess, that we're all fodder. I was sitting on a straight-back wooden chair. He was standing looking down at me just as always. *Papa Was a Rolling Stone* was playing on the radio, which was brown tweed, sort of forties-looking. And I thought, as he reached down to brush the hair from my eyes, the trouble with dreaming is that we eventually wake up."

———

AS HE BEGAN HIS second autumn on the farm in Midway, Shepard wrote of himself in the third person in *Spy of the First Person*, "One year ago exactly he could drive across the great divide ... One year ago exactly more or less, he could walk with his head up. He could see through the air. He could wipe his own ass."

"Actually," Sandy Rogers says, "Sam was walking right up until the day he died but couldn't stand up on his own, because his balance was off and so he had to get into a wheelchair to keep from falling. He couldn't use his arms and hands to push himself out of a chair. And his head would fall forward because the muscles in his neck were also gone."

In *Spy of the First Person*, the unnamed person who observes the Shepard character from across the road notes, "He eats cheese and crackers all day long ... But he has particular trouble with his hands and arms, I've noticed ... He uses his legs, his knees, his thighs, to bring his arms and hands to his face in order to be able to eat his cheese and crackers. It seems that periodically he has to go to the bathroom or something. He stands ... He looks like he's going to fall over. Topple. ... He wavers from side to side."

After calling for "one of his people—one of his sons or daughters or someone else closely related to him like his sisters," they come out on the porch to "tend to him. They take him inside the house ... When he comes back out, often with the same person, arm in arm, they either zip him up or zip him down ... In other words he's done something very private. He's either urinated or gone number two and they help him with this." Then they "stick him back in his rocking chair" by gently lowering him "down although at a certain point he kind of falls into the chair backwards panting and gasping. He says, the more helpless I become, the more remote I become."

Unwilling to spend the winter in Kentucky, Shepard flew on a private plane to Northern California where he took up residence in Healdsburg, the small city on the Russian River in Sonoma County where Johnny Dark and Scarlett had lived for a while in the late 1990s. His son Jesse, who was forty-six years old, had lived and worked as a ranch manager in Healdsburg for more than twenty years. Jesse and his wife, Maura, rented a house for Shepard, where he was cared for by both his sisters and his son and daughter-in-law.

In the thirty-seventh and final section of *Spy of the First Person*, Shepard vividly portrays his relationship with his children and immediate family by describing an evening when he went out to dinner with them in Healdsburg. "I was in a wheelchair with a shaggy sheepskin covering the seat and a Navajo blanket over my knees," he writes, "and my two sons . . . Jesse and Walker, were on either side pushing me . . . I'll never forget the strength I felt from my two boys behind me. Following us were my daughter Hannah, her two friends, both of my sisters, and my daughter-in-law, nine of us altogether."

Having reached El Farolito, a Mexican restaurant in the center of town, Shepard's sons pushed him "boldly in the wheelchair from the quiet street through two swinging doors into the reverberations of an enormous room." After everyone ordered margaritas and Shepard asked for "a beef enchilada and a Cabo Wabo," there was "a lot of conversation, a lot of people talking at once, the whole table bustling with conversation."

Once the meal had ended, "Our whole troupe, our little band, hit the street. The thing I remember most is being more or less helpless and the strength of my sons. A man pushed by his sons in a wheelchair from a crowded restaurant to a street with nobody on it. A man sitting on shaggy wool with a Navajo blanket across his knees."

WITH HIS SISTER SANDY having already flown back to Kentucky to prepare the house for his return, Shepard left Healdsburg for home at the end of March 2017 in an RV with Roxanne, Jesse, and Maura Shepard. In Midway, the playwright continued growing weaker. Still able to walk, although usually with assistance, he was now locked inside the prison his body had become. Nonetheless, his cognitive abilities and perception remained unaffected. As Sandy Rogers says, "His mind was like a steel trap."

Describing his condition in *Spy of the First Person*, Shepard writes, "Sometimes he does this thing where he shakes his head violently from side to side as though a bug of some kind is bugging him as though the bug is trying to get into his nostrils but it's not a bug at all it's the hair on his face or the imagined hair on his face or him trying to prevent the imagined hair getting on his face." To keep this from happening, "one of his sisters stands and combs his hair with a brush, a brush with tiny plastic teeth. She also uses hairspray, women's hairspray, to keep the hair back. The imagined hair. He always closes his nose or tries to close his nose because evidently the spray is perfumed and he's trying not to smell it. He also has this one gesture that is very curious where he rocks back and forth. He rocks and he'll clasp both hands together like he's praying and ... He'll brace both elbows against his stomach and then he'll raise both hands to his face using the left knee in this jerky sort of fashion where the leg is propelling the arms toward his face" so he can scratch the itch on his upper lip.

Noting he now had to ask other people for help and could not manage without them, Shepard ends this section of *Spy of the First Person* by writing, "Can you imagine for instance something crawling up your ear? It's easy to imagine something like that. Crawling up your ear ... and then you go on to imagine the itch and pretty soon you have one. You have an itch. And pretty soon you ask for help."

Unlike Stephen Hawking, Shepard had made it plain he did not want a tracheotomy so he could breathe with the help of a ventilator. He also did not want a feeding tube inserted into his stomach. "I mean," Sandy Rogers says, "he could have just been like a drunk asshole. He could have been one of those guys who wreaked havoc from his wheelchair. He could have been like that, because he had that kind of stuff inside him. But he never was. He was quiet. He was calm. And he didn't complain. He never complained. And he had to sit and be still. He couldn't move. He was good on talking and he could still eat but towards the end, it was just pudding and stuff like that."

On Wednesday, July 26, 2017, Sandy Rogers received a call from Roxanne in which "she said, 'You know, I think you better get back here.' And so I got a plane ticket and flew out that night and arrived the next morning and when I first walked into the house, I thought, 'Oh man, he's not going to die.' Sam was skinnier than when I had last seen him but just as chippy as ever and he was giving me shit and telling people where to put things, which was amazing to me. I got about four hours with him, and then he was eating lunch and we said, 'Do you want to take a nap?' And he took a nap, and that was it. And if there was ever anyone who was ready to go, it was Sam. He was conscious right up until the very last second and it was a very beautiful experience and just so peaceful and we were all there with him when it happened."

At 2:20 in the afternoon on Thursday, July 27, 2017, Sam Shepard, whose occupation on the death certificate issued by the Commonwealth of Kentucky was listed as "playwright," died of respiratory failure caused by ALS, pneumonia, and COPD. After reviewing *Spy of the First Person* with his family, he had "dictated his final edits a few days before he passed away." He was seventy-three years old.

ENDGAME

Finished, it's finished, nearly finished,
it must be nearly finished.

—CLOV, IN SAMUEL BECKETT'S
ENDGAME

FIVE WEEKS AFTER SHEPARD'S BODY HAD BEEN CREMATED, about a hundred people gathered together on Labor Day weekend on the horse farm in Midway to honor him. Along with his sisters and his children, O-Lan Jones and Jessica Lange, both of whom spoke that day along with many others, were there. Patti Smith, who had performed in Mexico City on Saturday afternoon, flew in to join the assemblage shortly before the ceremony ended.

In October, with Lange and her children in attendance, the playwright Jean-Claude van Itallie hosted a tribute to Shepard at La MaMa in Lower Manhattan. The panel included Joyce Aaron, Charles Mingus III, and Sandy Rogers, who also performed one of her songs from the film version of *Fool for Love*.

A month later, Nancy Meckler, Stephen Rea, and Lloyd Hutchinson, who had appeared with Rea in *A Particle of Dread*, presented "Sam Shepard: A Celebration" at the Royal Court Theatre in London. According to Nicholas Wright, who had worked there with Shepard in the early 1970s, "O-Lan Jones spoke most beautifully and revealingly" about her relationship with the playwright and about "their eventual breakup."

In December, Patti Smith performed her own tribute to Shepard at the St. Ann and the Holy Trinity Church in Brooklyn by reading from his work. Accompanied by Lenny Kaye and Tony Shanahan, Smith sang "Freight Train," "Streets of Bakersfield," "Bury Me Not on the Lone Prairie," and her own composition "Dancing Barefoot," as Shepard's children watched from the second row.

The two actors with whom Shepard had maintained his longest working relationship both expressed their sorrow at his passing in *The Guardian*. In an interview, Ed Harris characterized Shepard as "a man who did not relinquish power, but in his work he allowed himself to be vulnerable and uncertain . . . As a really private guy, Sam didn't talk a lot about his feelings . . . When he found out he was seriously ill, he became more open and accessible. A kindness crept into him. It allowed me to feel the nature of our friendship, and I'd like to think it was the same for him."

In his essay about Shepard, Stephen Rea noted, "I wrote an introduction to one of his plays in which I said that the three great writers of the English-speaking theatre at the end of the 20th century were Beckett, Pinter and Sam. He said to me at the time: 'You shouldn't include me in that company,' but he more than belonged there. His writing is heroic, he himself was heroic and he was heroic in the stoical way he faced his death."

Having worked both onstage and in film with Shepard, Matthew Warchus says, "When I was in my twenties, I spent some time with Arthur Miller and I felt the same way about Sam as I did about him, because in many ways Sam was also a titan and the same kind of king as Arthur Miller. For me, it was a privilege and an honor just to be close to somebody like Sam, who could have such profound feelings about human nature and then be able to turn them into drama that chronicled the human psyche in that way."

Perhaps the most eloquent recognition of the unique role Shepard played in American popular culture for seven decades was the photograph the editors of *The New York Times Magazine* chose for the front cover of their annual "The Lives They Lived" issue, published in December of the year Shepard died. Before a rough green plaster wall in Walker Shepard's home in Louisville, Kentucky, without any accompanying text, a cowboy hat very much like the one Shepard wore in *Don't Come Knocking* sits atop a light-brown tablecloth speckled with painted white flowers.

Inside an issue that memorialized the lives of Mary Tyler Moore, Glen Campbell, Dick Gregory, Harry Dean Stanton, John Ashbery, and Derek Walcott (as well as others who had passed away that year), there was a single paragraph about Shepard. Written by his son Jesse, it read in part, "He was always a pinch-front kind of guy, the style is kind of a triangular crease in the front. It's a strong reminder of the man—of him being outside and on location and involved in the day. There is a practicality and a confidence to it. It's a well-worn hat. His work was key to his day and it was always about process and project."

Unlike his hats, Sam Shepard himself was never easy to describe or understand. Complicated and complex as both an artist and a man, he created work of the first order but always remained a puzzle, not just to others, but himself as well.

TRUE WEST, AGAIN

A S IF TO CONFIRM BEYOND ANY DOUBT THAT THE PLAY WHICH had come to define Sam Shepard's career would continue being performed even when he was no longer able to see it, yet another revival of *True West,* presented by the Roundabout Theatre Company, opened on Broadway on January 24, 2019, seventeen months after the playwright passed away.

Much like Matthew Warchus in England, Ethan Hawke, who had first seen the PBS production of *True West* when he was fourteen and was inspired by it to seek his own career in the performing arts, had been cast as Lee. Despite spending years acting in and directing Sam Shepard's plays and appearing with him in films, Hawke accepted the part only after learning Shepard wanted it restored to its original form, with a distinct age gap between the two brothers—and so Paul Dano was cast as Austin.

Before going onstage for each performance, Hawke would carefully apply an inked crescent between the thumb and forefinger of his left hand. By doing so, he was re-creating the hawk moon tattoo Shepard had received while living with Patti Smith at the Chelsea Hotel. As Hawke said, "There's something about this play that feels directly distilled from his heart, his brain, and so I wear the tattoo for the run in kind of homage to the playwright."

In *The New York Times*, Ben Brantley concluded his review by describing *True West* as "a play that seems to grow in disturbing depth every time it comes back to haunt us." In suitably dramatic fashion, *True West* also illustrates the indelible power of a true work of art to inspire others to create something of equal magnitude, thereby continuing the unbroken chain of artistic achievement that links us all to the past in a timeless manner.

ACKNOWLEDGMENTS

ONE DAY, MY AGENT AND LONGTIME FRIEND PAUL BRESNICK called me to ask, "Are you the right guy to write the Sam Shepard biography?" While the answer to that remains to be seen, this book is the result and I thank Paul for asking the question that began it all.

I am also beyond truly fortunate to have had an editor like Kevin Doughten, a veritable font of musical knowledge who stayed with me as I blew right through one deadline after another. For his keeping faith in this book as well as the extraordinary way in which he edited it, I will be eternally grateful.

For favors both great and small—and in alphabetical order—I would like to thank Richard Adams, Andrew Bailey, Harriet Brand, Carlton Carl, Chris Cochran, David Coleman, Johnny Dark, Steve Davis, Emily Ekstrand-Brunner, the late Tony Elliott, James Fox, Chad Hammett, Teri Keating, Alicia Kershaw and Peter Rose, Brian Lipson, Joshua Maurer, Nancy Meckler, Tom Morse, the late Johnnie Planco, Tyler Pulkkinen, Jane Rose, Ben Schafer, Peter Stampfel, Patrick Tourville, and Dr. Mel Wichter.

For helping me make it through these mad and troubled times—also in alphabetical order—thanks to John de Menil, Dr. Trevor Fogg, Robin Goldschmidt and Emiliya Suezaki, Jeff and Debbie Greenberg, John and Jean Gulliver, Brian Higgins and Janice Pober Higgins, Don Hubbard and Darrah Blanton Hubbard, Raimie Kriste, Anne-Louise Marquis and Mike Capoferri, Seth and Naomi Pollock, Jerry Pompili and Nancy Taylor Pompili, Richard and Kate Rosenthal, Stephen and Cathy Seagrave, Johnny Simmons and Katie Benz Olsen, Jill Warner, Shelley Weinberg, and Jeff White and Allie Maffei. Special thanks to Martha Thomas, for all the time on the telephone from Santa Fe.

As they have always been, Sandy and Anna continue to be the great joys of my life, as is the loving being who brought them into this world and now still looks after us all.

AUTHOR'S NOTE

WHEN IT CAME TO MAKING PUBLIC STATEMENTS ABOUT HIS life in many of the interviews he did over the course of his long and illustrious career, Sam Shepard could often be the very definition of an unreliable narrator. And so it was only in his letters to Johnny Dark and his short fiction that Shepard ever seemed able to truly express his deepest feelings about his past and whatever highly emotional situation in which he currently found himself involved.

In compiling this biography, I have relied on those two sources as the framework for a life in which Shepard also spent a good deal of time developing a persona so brilliantly crafted that few were ever able to see the man behind it. Knowing full well Shepard also fictionalized some details of the real-life experiences that formed the basis of much of his short fiction, I have nonetheless tried to let him tell the story of his life in his own words as much as possible. I have done so in the belief that an artist can sometimes be best understood by how they choose to portray themselves in their work.

Having lived at the same time as Shepard in many of the places where he made his home during various periods of his life—New York City, London, and Northern California among them, as well as in Los Angeles, where he spent time becoming a movie star and courting Jessica Lange—I have done my best to convey the tenor of those times without supplying a laundry list of the most salient historical events of each era except, as with the Vietnam draft, when Shepard himself was personally affected by them.

A case study in contradictions about whom completely conflicting statements were often equally true, Sam Shepard was an artist of the first order who never truly understood the enormity of his gift and so was always blinded by his own light. Utterly subsumed by his work whether he was writing, acting, or directing, he could also seem entirely removed from a project once it was done. A pure product of an America that no longer exists, he spent six decades producing an astonishing volume of work and then, despite seemingly impossible hardships, continued to go on writing until just before his death.

And while it may be true that no man is a hero to his biographer, I remain convinced, as I hope this book makes plain, that Sam Shepard deserves to be honored for his life as well as all the work he did in the times in which he lived.

—ROBERT GREENFIELD

SOURCES

To date, three other biographies of sam shepard (four, if you count the revised edition of the first to appear in print, which was reissued twelve years later) have already been published. I am indebted to Don Shewey, Ellen Oumano, and John J. Winters for the work they did before me.

While, to varying degrees, I have drawn on all these biographies for information, I have used them primarily as a guide for my own research into Shepard's life, work, and times. All direct quotes from the biographies and other published sources are cited in the following notes. Quotes that are not sourced—which can also be identified by dialogue tags in the present tense (e.g., he says, she says)—come from interviews I conducted.

As I have done in all my previous work, I reached out to all those who figured prominently in Shepard's life and career with interview requests. Those whose names do not appear in the list of interviewees did not respond, thereby making it plain they did not wish to participate in this project. Respecting their desires, I have quoted their published statements and cited the sources where they appeared.

INTERVIEWS

Joyce Aaron	— 6/5/18	Chad Hammett	— 11/14/19
Richard Adams	— 9/24/18	Thelma Holt	— 9/25/18
Gretchen Amussen	— 11/4/19	Tom Irwin	— 5/22/19
John Ashford	— 9/20/18	Teri Keating	— 10/1/19
Daniel Aukin	— 5/22/19	Lee Kissman	— 6/21/18, 6/25/18
Jacob Brackman	— 1/24/19	Claudia Carr Levy	— 11/16/18, 11/2/20
Roger Croucher	— 10/2/18	Michael March	— 9/8/18
Johnny Dark	— 6/2/18	Jane Windsor Marowitz	— 9/26/18
Marianne de Pury	— 7/24/18	Lee Mason	— 7/2/18
Spencer Earnshaw	— 12/19/19	Nancy Meckler	— 9/17/18
Ramblin' Jack Elliott	— 3/14/18	Charles Mingus III	— 6/5/18

Chip Monck	— 9/24/18	Michael Smith	— 7/23/18
Chris O'Dell	— 11/12/18	Peter Stampfel	— 6/12/18
Gail Merrifield Papp	— 1/10/19	Kenneth Turan	— 11/29/18
Paul Pascarella	— 11/5/19	Matthew Warchus	— 4/12/19
Sandy Rogers	— 6/14/18,	Jeff Ward	— 6/10/19
	11/25/19,	Michael Weller	— 9/24/18
	11/26/19	Mel Wichter	— 11/18/19
Ben Schafer	— 11/15/18	Nicholas Wright	— 10/9/18
Larry Sloman	— 11/10/18	Rudy Wurlitzer	— 1/18/19

BOOKS

Allen, Michael, ed. *This Time, This Place.* New York: Bobbs-Merrill, 1971.

Beckett, Samuel. *"Endgame" and "Act without Words."* New York: Grove Press, 2009.

Campbell, Joseph, with Bill Moyers. *The Power of Myth.* New York: Doubleday, 1988.

Chaikin, Joseph, and Sam Shepard. *Letters and Texts, 1972–1984.* Ed. Barry Daniels. New York: Theatre Communications Group, 1989.

Coyote, Peter. *The Rainman's Third Cure: An Irregular Education.* Berkeley, Calif.: Counterpoint Press, 2015.

Daltrey, Roger. *Thanks a Lot Mr Kibblewhite.* New York: Henry Holt and Company, 2018.

DeRose, David. *Sam Shepard.* New York: Twayne/Macmillan, 1992.

Dorr, Robert F. *B-24 Liberator Units of the Fifteenth Air Force.* Botley, UK: Osprey Publishing, 2000.

Flores, Angel. *The Anchor Anthology of French Poetry.* New York: Anchor Books, 2000.

Gerard, Jeremy. *Wynn Place Show: A Biased History of the Rollicking Life and Extreme Times of Wynn Handman and the American Place Theatre.* Hanover, N.H.: Smith and Kraus, 2015.

Graham, Bill, and Robert Greenfield. *Bill Graham Presents: My Life Inside Rock and Out.* New York: Doubleday, 1992.

Gussow, Mel. *Conversations with and about Beckett.* New York: Grove Press, 1996.

Hermes, Will. *Love Goes to Buildings on Fire.* New York: Faber and Faber, 2011.

Junker, Patricia, and Charles C. Eldredge. *John Steuart Curry: Inventing the Middle West.* New York: Hudson Hills, 1998.

Leech, Jeanette. *Seasons They Change: The Story of Acid and Psychedelic Rock.* London: Jawbone Press, 2010.

Little, Ruth, and Emily McLaughlin. *The Royal Court Theatre Inside Out.* London: Oberon Books, 2007.

Marranca, Bonnie, ed. *American Dreams: The Imagination of Sam Shepard.* New York: Performing Arts Journal Publications, 1981.

Mayer, John. *Steppenwolf Theatre Company of Chicago: In Their Own Words.* London: Bloomsbury, 2016.

Middleton, William. *Double Vision.* New York: Alfred A. Knopf, 2018.

Miles, Barry. *In the Sixties.* London: Jonathan Cape, 2002.

Mingus, Charles. *Beneath the Underdog.* New York: Vintage Books, 1991.

Morrisroe, Patricia. *Mapplethorpe: A Biography.* New York: Random House, 1995.

O'Dell, Chris, with Katherine Ketcham. *Miss O'Dell.* New York: Touchstone/Simon and Schuster, 2009.

Oumano, Ellen. *Sam Shepard: The Life and Work of an American.* New York: St. Martin's Press, 1986.

Poland, Albert. *Stages: A Theater Memoir.* Wappinger Falls, N.Y.: Albert Poland, 2019.

Rosen, Carol. *Sam Shepard: A Poetic Rodeo.* Basingstoke, UK: Palgrave Macmillan, 2004.

Roudané, Matthew, ed. *The Cambridge Companion to Sam Shepard.* Cambridge, UK: Cambridge University Press, 2002.

Santoro, Gene. *Myself When I Am Real: The Life and Music of Charles Mingus.* New York: Oxford University Press, 2000.

Shepard, Jesse. *Jubilee King.* New York: Bloomsbury, 2004.

Shepard, Sam. *Ages of the Moon.* New York: Dramatists Play Service, 2015.

———. *Cruising Paradise.* New York: Vintage Books, 1997.

———. *Day out of Days.* New York: Alfred A. Knopf, 2010.

———. *Fifteen One-Act Plays.* New York: Vintage Books, 2012.

———. *Five Plays.* New York: Bobbs-Merrill, 1967.

———. *"Fool for Love" and Other Plays.* New York: Bantam Books, 1988.

———. *Great dream of heaven.* New York: Alfred A. Knopf, 2002.

———. *Hawk Moon: Short Stories, Poems, and Monologues.* New York: PAJ Books, 1981.

———. *Heartless: A Play.* New York: Vintage Books, 2013.

———. *"The Late Henry Moss," "Eyes for Consuela," "When the World Was Green."* New York: Vintage Books, 2003.

———. *A Lie of the Mind.* New York: Dramatists Play Service, 1986.

———. *"Mad Dog Blues" & Other Plays.* (The Winter Repertory 4). New York: Winter House, 1972.

———. *"Maxagasm."* Unpublished screenplay, n.d. Sam Shepard, Bancroft Library Special Collections, University of California at Berkeley.

———. *Motel Chronicles.* San Francisco, Calif.: City Lights Books, 1982.

———. *The One Inside.* New York: Vintage Books, 2018.

———. *A Particle of Dread (Oedipus Variations).* New York: Vintage Books, 2017.

———. *The Rolling Thunder Logbook.* Cambridge, Mass.: Da Capo Press, 2004. First published in 1978 by Penguin Books (New York).

———. *Seven Plays.* New York: Bantam Books, 1981.

———. *Spy of the First Person.* New York: Vintage Books, 2018.

———. *"The Tooth of Crime" and "Geography of a Horse Dreamer."* New York: Grove Press, 1974.

———. *The Tooth of Crime (Second Dance): A Play with Music in Two Acts.* New York: Vintage Books, 2006. Originally published 1974.

———. *"The Unseen Hand" and Other Plays.* New York: Applause Books, 2000.

Shepard, Sam, and Johnny Dark. *Two Prospectors: The Letters of Sam Shepard and Johnny Dark.* Ed. Chad Hammett. Austin: University of Texas Press, 2013.

Shewey, Don. *Sam Shepard.* New York: Da Capo Press, 1997. First published in 1984 by Dell.

Sinise, Gary, with Marcus Brotherton. *Grateful American: A Journey from Self to Service.* Nashville, Tenn.: Nelson Books, 2019.

Sloman, Larry "Ratso." *On the Road with Bob Dylan.* New York: Three Rivers Press, 2002.

Smith, Patti. *Just Kids.* New York: Ecco, 2010.

———. *Year of the Monkey.* New York: Alfred A. Knopf, 2019.

Townshend, Pete. *Who I Am.* New York: HarperCollins, 2012.

Turan, Kenneth, and Joseph Papp. *Free for All: Joe Papp, the Public, and the Greatest Theater Story Ever Told.* New York: Doubleday, 2009.

Williams, Heathcote. *AC/DC and the Local Stigmatic.* New York: Viking Press, 1973.

Winters, John J. *Sam Shepard: A Life.* Berkeley, Calif.: Counterpoint, 2017.

Yaffe, David. *Reckless Daughter: A Portrait of Joni Mitchell.* New York: Sarah Crichton Books/Farrar, Straus and Giroux, 2017.

Zuckoff, Mitchell. *Robert Altman: The Oral Biography.* New York: Alfred A. Knopf, 2009.

ARTICLES

Albee, Edward. "Edward Albee Reviews Sam Shepard's 'Icarus's Mother.'" *The Village Voice,* November 25, 1965.

Almereyda, Michael. "Sam Shepard." *Interview,* September 24, 2011.

Als, Hilton. "Hungry Hearts." *The New Yorker,* May 27, 2019.

———. "Sam Shepard's Soul." *The New Yorker,* August 2, 2017.

Alter, Alexandra. "A Final Work by Sam Shepard Reveals His Struggle with Lou Gehrig's Disease." *The New York Times,* December 4, 2017.

"Amy Victoria Schook." Obituary. *The Chicago Daily Tribune,* December 8, 1940.

Ansen, David. "The 'True West' Interviews." *Newsweek,* November 11, 1985.

Associated Press. "Sam Shepard's Drunk-Driving Charge Dismissed in Court." *Toronto Star,* December 18, 2015.

Barnes, Clive. "Stage Lizard vs. Snake." *The New York Times,* March 13, 1970.

———. "The Theater: Sam Shepard's 'The Tooth of Crime.'" *The New York Times,* November 12, 1972.

———. "Theater: Shepard's 'Tooth of Crime.'" *The New York Times,* March 8, 1973.

————. "Theater: 2 by Shepard." *The New York Times,* April 16, 1975.

————. "Theater: 'The Unseen Hand' and 'Forensic and the Navigators.'" *The New York Times,* April 2, 1970.

Bartels, Brian. "Sam Shepard's Master Class in Playwriting." Interview, Cherry Lane Theatre, November 5, 2006. *Missouri Review,* Spring 2007.

Berger, Kevin. "Sam Shepard." *Salon,* January 3, 2001. www.salon.com/2001/01/02/shepard_6/.

Brantley, Ben. "Ages of the Moon: It's Old Timers' Day at Shepard's Arena." *The New York Times,* January 27, 2010.

————. "Call Out the Patricide Squad." *The New York Times,* November 23, 2014.

————. "A Clash of Rock Stars in an Existential Mode." *The New York Times,* December 24, 1996.

————. "Nothing Is Ever Finished." *The New York Times,* September 22, 2019.

————. "Sam Shepard, Storyteller." *The New York Times,* November 13, 1994.

————. "Theater Review: Finding Out What It's Like to Really Be Your Brother." *The New York Times,* March 10, 2000.

————. "Theater Review: No-Good Dad Whose Tale Is Told Repeatedly." *The New York Times,* September 25, 2001.

————. "Theater Review: A Sam Shepard Revival Gets Him to Broadway." *The New York Times,* May 1, 1996.

————. "Two Satanic Majesties Request All Devouring Fame." *The New York Times,* October 22, 2006.

Browne, David. "The Last Folksinger." *Rolling Stone,* October 10, 2019.

Campion, Chris. "Saturation 70: The Gram Parsons UFO Movie That Never Flew." *The Guardian,* September 5, 2014.

Canby, Vincent. "Film: 'Paris Texas,' Written by Sam Shepard." *The New York Times,* November 9, 1984.

————. "Film: 'Right Stuff'; On Astronauts." *The New York Times,* October 21, 1983.

————. "Frances Farmer Played by Jessica Lange." *The New York Times,* December 3, 1982.

————. "A New 'Postman Always Rings Twice.'" *The New York Times,* March 20, 1981.

————. "Review/Film: A Variation on the Oedipus Theme." *The New York Times,* January 31, 1992.

————. "Sissy Spacek in 'Raggedy Man,' a Violent Melodrama." *The New York Times,* September 18, 1981.

————. "The Year in the Arts: Theater 1994; Strike Zones (and Erogenous Ones, Too)." *The New York Times,* December 25, 1994.

Carpenter, Ellen. "Ethan Hawke Talks Tackling Sam Shepard's 'True West.'" *Hemispheres,* January 1, 2019.

Carroll, Christopher. "Mingus: The Chaos and the Magic." *The New York Review of Books,* February 12, 2013.

Charles, Ron. "'It's Him, It's Sort of Him': Sam Shepard's 'The One Inside' Toys with Fact and Fiction." *The Washington Post,* January 24, 2017.

Christiansen, Richard. "Revived 'Buried Child' Haunting When Not Slow . . ." *Chicago Tribune,* January 23, 1985.

————. "Sinise Breathes Fire into 'Buried Child.'" *Chicago Tribune,* October 2, 1995.

Chubb, Kenneth, and the editors of *Theatre Quarterly.* "Metaphors, Mad Dogs and Old Time Cowboys: Interview with Sam Shepard." *Theatre Quarterly* 4 (August/October 1974), 3–16.

"Clue to the New Album? Patti Smith Hits the Studio with Actor Sam Shepard." *Blackbook,* October 1, 2011.

Coe, Robert. "The Saga of Sam Shepard." *The New York Times Magazine,* November 23, 1980.

Collins, Nancy. "Full-Tilt Jessica." *Vanity Fair,* October 1991.

Connema, Richard. "Regional Reviews: San Francisco The World Premiere of Sam Shepard's 'The Late Henry Moss.'" Talkin' Broadway, n.d. www.talkinbroadway.com/page/regional/sanfran/s82.html.

Cott, Jonathan. "Sam Shepard on Working with Dylan, Why Jim Morrison Has No Sense of Humor." *Rolling Stone,* December 18, 1986.

Coveney, Michael. "Heathcote Williams Obituary." *The Guardian,* July 2, 2017.

Crawley, Peter. "A Particle of Dread (Oedipus Variations)." Review. *The Irish Times,* December 2, 2013.

Da Fonseca-Wollheim, Corinna. "A Mystic's Work Is Cast in a Brilliant Light." *The New York Times,* September 20, 2019.

Dark, Johnny. "Sam Shepard Remembered by Johnny Dark." *The Guardian,* December 17, 2017.

David, Mark. "Sam and Jessica Still Selling Stillwater Estate." *Variety,* July 28, 2008.

Denham, Ryan. "Actor, Playwright Sam Shepard Arrested in Normal for Suspected DUI." *The Pantagraph,* January 3, 2009.

Dieckmann, Katherine. "Wim Wenders: An Interview." *Film Quarterly* 38, no. 2 (1984): 2–7.

Divine, Mary. "Lange Disses Stillwater in NY Daily News." (St. Paul) *Pioneer Press,* March 8, 2008.

———. "Sam Shepard—Pulitzer-Winning Playwright, Actor, and Former Stillwater Resident—Dead at 73." (St. Paul) *Pioneer Press,* July 31, 2017.

Dowd, Maureen. "Rock Star Patti Smith Making Paris Swoon." *The New York Times,* September 19, 2019.

Downey, Roger. "Inside the Words." *Time Out,* April 22–28, 1977.

Ebert, Roger. "Country." *Chicago Sun-Times,* January 1, 1984.

———. "Days of Heaven." *Chicago Sun-Times,* December 7, 1997.

———. "Far North." *Chicago Sun-Times,* November 25, 1988.

———. "Review of 'The River.'" *Chicago Sun-Times,* January 1, 1984.

———. "Voyager." *Chicago Sun-Times,* May 29, 1992.

———. "Zabriskie Point." *Chicago Sun-Times,* January 1, 1970.

Eder, Richard. "Stage: Sam Shepard Offers 'Buried Child.'" *The New York Times,* November 7, 1978.

———. "Theater: 'The Starving.'" *The New York Times,* March 3, 1978.

Ensign, Amy. "Playwright Shepard Has Door County Connection." *Green Bay Press-Gazette,* April 4, 2017.

Evans, Greg. "Ethan Hawke's Blazing Year: The Actor Talks Broadway's 'True West,' His Ambitious New Showtime Series, and the Night Paul Dano Kicked Him." Deadline, April 10, 2019. www.deadline.com/2019/04/ethan-hawke-tony-watch-interview-true-west-good-lord-bird-1202592003/.

"F. de Forrest Schook." Obituary. *The Chicago Daily Tribune,* October 15, 1942.

Faires, Robert. "In Memoriam: Sam Shepard." *The Austin Chronicle,* August 3, 2017.

Farber, Stephen. "East Meets West, Take 2." *The New York Times,* March 12, 2006.

Ferretti, Fred. "Joseph Papp: A 'Divisive Force' or a 'Healing' One?" *The New York Times,* December 20, 1980.

Flatley, Guy. "Antonioni Defends 'Zabriskie Point.'" *The New York Times Magazine,* February 22, 1970.

Ford, Alyssa. "La Vie Boheme: Jessica Lange's Artistic Odyssey." *Artful Living,* March 25, 2015.

French, Alex, and David Kahn. "Punch a Hole in the Sky: An Oral History of 'The Right Stuff.'" *Wired,* November 18, 2014.

Gere, Richard. "Richard Gere Recalls Working with Sam Shepard on 'Days of Heaven.'" Guest Column. *The Hollywood Reporter,* August 1, 2017.

Gindoff, Bryan. "Thalberg Didn't Look Happy: Or, with Antonioni at Zabriskie Point." *Film Quarterly* 24, no. 1 (1970): 3–6, JSTOR, doi.org/10.2307/1211137.

Glicksman, Marlaine. "Highway 61 Revisited: Robert Frank." *Film Comment,* July–August 1987.

Gold, Sylviane. "FILM; Harried Child." *The New York Times,* April 18, 2004.

Goldberg, Robert. "Sam Shepard: American Original." *Playboy,* March 1984.

Gorman, Sophie. "A Particle of Dread." Review. *Irish Independent,* 2014.

Greenfield, Robert. "The Rolling Stones on Tour: Goodbye Great Britain." *Rolling Stone,* April 15, 1971.

Gussow, Mel. "Finally Famous in Films, Back to Theater." *The New York Times,* October 5, 1995.

———. "From Plays to Fiction: Thanks, Dad; Sam Shepard's Rascals Are Inspired by Memories of a Mysterious Father." *The New York Times,* October 15, 2002.

———. "Sam Shepard: Writer on the Way Up." *The New York Times,* November 12, 1969.

———. "Stage: 'Mad Dog Blues.'" *The New York Times,* March 9, 1971.

———. "Stage: Shepard's 'West' Revived and Restored." *The New York Times,* October 18, 1982.

Haldeman, Peter. "Tour Jessica Lange's House in Minnesota." *Architectural Digest,* March 2006.

Hamill, Pete. "The American Hero." *New York,* December 5, 1983.

Harris, Hunter. "How Ethan Hawke Transforms into a 'Cowboy' Drifter for 'True West.'"

Vulture, March 5, 2019. www.vulture.com/2019/03/true-west-broadway-ethan-hawke -backstage-photos.html.

Healy, Patrick. "Getting Faster with Age: Sam Shepard's New Velocity." *The New York Times,* February 12, 2010.

Holden, Stephen. "Film Review: Another True West Tale of Phantom Family Ties." *The New York Times,* March 17, 2006.

Holdren, Sara. "Director Robert Woodruff Remembers Sam Shepard." *Vulture,* August 1, 2017. www.vulture.com/2017/08/director-robert-woodruff-remembers-sam-shepard.html.

Howe, Benjamin Ryder, Jeanne McCulloch, and Mona Simpson. "Sam Shepard: The Art of Theater No. 12." *Paris Review* 142 (Spring 1997).

Ihara, Nathan. "The Drop Edge of Yonder: Rudy Wurlitzer Rides Nowhere Again." *LA Weekly,* June 12, 2008.

Isherwood, Charles. "The Late Henry Moss." *Variety,* September 24, 2001.

———. "Theater Review, 'Kicking a Dead Horse.'" *The New York Times,* July 15, 2008.

Jacobs, Leonard. "NYC 'True West' Defies Agent, Refuses to Close." *Backstage,* March 16, 2004.

"Jessica Lange Interview." *Sunday Observer and Belfast Telegraph,* January 2007. www.sam -shepard.com/pressjessica0107.html/.

Jones, Kipp. "Actor Sam Shepard Arrested for Aggravated D.U.I." Breitbart, May 26, 2015. www.breitbart.com/entertainment/2015/05/26/actor-sam-shepard-arrested-for-aggra vated-d-u-i/.

Jones, O-Lan. "Running Off with Sam." *American Theatre,* August 4, 2017.

Kakutani, Michiko. "Review: 'The One Inside' Presents Sam Shepard in a Minor Key." *The New York Times,* February 20, 2017.

Kaufman, Philip, as told to Gregg Kilday. "'The Right Stuff' Filmmaker Remembers Sam Shepard: He Was 'Born with the Gift of a Golden Ear.'" *The Hollywood Reporter,* August 1, 2017.

Kaur, Anumita. "Japanese Stragglers Remained Hidden in Guam's Jungles for Years after World War II." *Pacific Daily News,* July 1, 2019.

Kihss, Peter. "Shepard Takes Pulitzer for Drama, Baker of Times Wins for Comment." *The New York Times,* April 17, 1979.

Kissman, Lee. "50 Years On: Theater Genesis and Sam Shepard." *Contemporary Theater Review* 25, no. 4 (2015): 573–81.

Kocher, Greg. "Sam Shepard Enjoyed Quiet Life in Midway." *Lexington Herald Leader,* July 31, 2017.

Kroll, Jack, Constance Guthrie, and Janet Huck. "Who's That Tall Dark Stranger." *Newsweek,* November 11, 1985.

Lahr, John. "Giving Up the Ghost." *The New Yorker,* December 4, 2000.

———. "The Pathfinder: Sam Shepard and the Struggles of American Manhood." *The New Yorker,* February 8, 2010.

———. "Postscript: Sam Shepard, Who Brought Rage and Rebellion Onstage." *The New Yorker,* July 31, 2017.

Larson, Sarah. "The Chaos of American Manhood in *True West.*" *The New Yorker,* January 28, 2019.

———. "Home on the Range." *The New Yorker,* February 4, 2019.

Leigh, Spencer. "Jacques Levy: Theatre Director and Songwriter." *The Independent,* October 6, 2004.

Leland, John. "How Sam Shepard Hit Downtown New York and Reinvented Himself." *The New York Times,* August 4, 2017.

Lester, Elenore. "The Pass-the-Hat Theater Circuit." *The New York Times Magazine,* December 5, 1965.

Levy, Emanuel. "Don't Come Knocking: Interview with Wim Wenders." Emanuel Levy Cin ema 24/7, February 14, 2006. www.emanuellevy.com/interviews/wim-wenders-dont-come -knocking-9/.

"Like Father." *Time Out Chicago,* November 11, 2010.

Lion, John. "Rock 'n' Roll Jesus with a Cowboy Mouth." *American Theatre,* April 1, 1984.

Lippman, Amy. "Rhythm & Truths: An Interview with Sam Shepard." *American Theatre,* April 1, 1984.

"The Lives They Lived." *The New York Times Magazine,* December 31, 2017.

"A Look Back at Door County's Art Appeal: Frogtown Art Colony." Door County Pulse, July 7, 2011. doorcountypulse.com/a-look-back-at-door-countys-art-appeal/.

Lufkin, Liz. "'The Late Henry Moss' Very Much Alive in S.F." San Francisco Chronicle, November 5, 2000.

Marowitz, Charles. "Is This Shepard or Saroyan?" The New York Times, May 15, 1977.

Martin, Douglas. "Howard Gotlieb, an Archivist with Persistence, Dies at 79." The New York Times, December 5, 2005.

Maslin, Janet. "Film: 'Resurrection' Has the Manner of a Fairy Tale; Question of Faith." The New York Times, November 7, 1980.

———. "'Renaldo and Clara,' Film by Bob Dylan: Rolling Thunder." The New York Times, January 26, 1978.

———. "Review/Film; 'Far North': Sam Shepard Ventures into Directing." The New York Times, November 9, 1988.

McBride, Stewart. "Sam Shepard." The Christian Science Monitor, December 26, 1980.

McDaniel, John. "Sam Shepard in Midway: He Liked the Town That Honored His Privacy, and He Chose to Spend His Last Days Nearby." The Midway Messenger, August 2, 2017.

McDonough, Carla J. "The Politics of Stage Space: Women and Male Identity in Sam Shepard's Family Plays." Journal of Dramatic Theory and Criticism IX, no. 2 (Spring 1995): 65–83.

McKenzie, Bryan. "Actor, Writer, Former Local Resident Shepard Dies." Daily Progress, July 31, 2017.

Miller, Kenneth. "Jessica Lange Can Finally Relax." AARP: The Magazine, July 18, 2017.

Mingus, Sue Graham. "My Mingus." The New York Times Magazine, March 17, 2002.

Oliver, Myrna. "Howard Gotlieb, 79; Archivist Collected Personal Papers of Notables of the 20th Century." Los Angeles Times, December 8, 2005.

O'Mahony, John. "The Write Stuff." The Guardian, October 11, 2003.

Oppenheim, Irene, and Victor Fascio. "The Most Promising Playwright in America Today Is Sam Shepard." The Village Voice, October 27, 1975.

Penhall, Joe. "The Outsider." The Guardian, June 14, 2006.

Prose, Francine. "The Greatest Year: 1963." New York, January 7, 2011.

"Q&A with Sam Shepard." Details, July 2008.

Rauch, Berna. "Zen Experience at the Theatre: A Non-Symbolic Sam Shepard." Berkeley Barb 21, no. 20 (May 1975).

Rea, Stephen. "Sam Shepard 1943–2017: 'He Was the Kindest Man, Truthful, Witty and Generous.'" The Guardian, August 6, 2017.

Rees, Jasper. "Theatre: American Playwright in London." The Independent, June 25, 1996.

Rich, Frank. "Review/Theater; Sam Shepard Returns, on War and Machismo." The New York Times, May 17, 1991.

———. "Stage: 'Fool for Love.'" The New York Times, May 27, 1983.

———. "Stage: Shepard's 'True West'; Myths vs. Reality." The New York Times, December 24, 1980.

———. "Theater: 'A Lie of the Mind,' by Sam Shepard." The New York Times, December 6, 1985.

Richards, David. "SSSHHHH! IT'S SAM SHEPARD." The Washington Post, December 12, 1988.

Riku, Yuichi, et al. "Differential Motor Neuron Involvement in Progressive Muscular Atrophy: A Comparative Study with Amyotrophic Lateral Sclerosis." BMJ Open 4, no. 5 (May 2014).

Roman, Julian. "Jessica Lange Says Don't Come Knocking." MovieWeb, March 20, 2006. www.movieweb.com/jessica-lange-says-dont-come-knocking/.

Rosen, Carol. "Sam Shepard Speaks: A Rare Interview with the Cowboy Playwright." The Village Voice, September 29, 1992.

Schiff, Stephen. "Showcase: Shepard on Broadway." The New Yorker, April 22, 1996.

Schonberg, Harold C. "At the Movies—'Days of Heaven.'" The New York Times, September 14, 1978.

Sessums, Kevin. "Geography of a Horse Dreamer." Interview, September 1988.

———. "Lange on Life." Vanity Fair, March 1995.

Shapiro, Harriet. "Sam Shepard Has Enough Horse Sense to Corral His Talented Sisters into His Dramatic Stable." People, January 6, 1986.

Shepard, Sam. "My First Year in New York: 1963." The New York Times Magazine, September 17, 2000.

———. "Operation Sidewinder." *Esquire,* May 1960.

———. "True Dylan." *Esquire,* July 1987.

Shewey, Don. "Rock-and-Roll Jesus with a Cowboy Mouth (Revisited)." *American Theatre,* April 2004.

———. "The 'True Story' of 'True West.'" *The Village Voice,* November 30, 1982.

Shirley, Don. "Searching for Sam Shepard." *The Washington Post,* January 14, 1979.

Simon, John. "Stephen Rea Seeks 'True' West in Sam Shepard Fable." Bloomberg News.

Skaggs, Joey. "Lucky Loser: My Abortive Attempt to Kidnap Sam Shepard." *HuffPost,* April 22, 2013. www.huffpost.com/entry/joey-skaggs-sam-shepard_b_3132059.

Smith, Michael. "Cowboys and the Rock Garden." From "A Brief History of Off-Broadway, 1955–1985." Smith's full article originally appeared in *The Village Voice,* October 22, 1964.

Smith, Patti. "My Buddy." *The New Yorker,* August 1, 2017.

Soloski, Alexis. "A Holy Space in More Ways Than One." *The New York Times,* June 19, 2014.

———. "True East: Sam Shepard Returns to New York." *The Village Voice,* June 24, 2008.

Stampfel, Peter. "Sam Shepard: Tribute by Peter Stampfel," Parts 1, 2, and 3. Perfect Sound Forever, October 2017–February 2018.

Steinberg, Claudia. "Volker Schlöndorff." Interview. *BOMB,* Summer 1990.

Sullivan, James. "The Scene: Sam Shepard Joins Jesse Shepard for a Reading at City Lights—Father and Son Share a Moment, but Without the Literary Drama." *San Francisco Chronicle,* April 26, 2003.

Tallerico, Brian. "'Bloodline' Season Finale Recap: Now Leaving the Keys." *Vulture,* June 7, 2016, www.vulture.com/2016/06/bloodline-recap-season-2-episode-10.html.

Tinney, Jason. "The One Inside." *Washington Independent Review of Books,* March 17, 2017.

"Tony Shanahan: Making Music with Patti Smith, Sam Shepard, and the Pope." www.sstrentals.com/tonyshanahan.

Trueman, Matt. "The All-American Realness of the Steppenwolf Theatre Company." *Financial Times,* March 8, 2019.

"Urbane Cowboy." *Vanity Fair,* December 1984.

"Voyager." *Variety,* December 31, 1990.

Wardle, Irving. "Charles Marowitz Obituary." *The Guardian,* May 9, 2014.

Washburn, Martin. "Theatre: Two by Sam Shepard." *The Village Voice,* April 9, 1970.

Weale, Sally. "Dark Victory." *The Guardian,* November 4, 2000.

Weinert-Kendt, Rob. "Rehearsal Note: That Bad Choice Could Be Useful." *The New York Times,* August 10, 2012.

Westbrook, Ray. "Navigator's Job in a B-24 Was Fraught with Danger." *Lubbock Avalanche-Journal,* January 27, 2013.

Wiegand, Chris. "'It Was Like Meeting a Cowboy': Ed Harris, Kathy Burke, and Others Remember Sam Shepard." *The Guardian,* August 2, 2017.

Winn, Steven. "John Lion: Magic Onstage—Theater Rebel Found New Writers, Audiences." *San Francisco Chronicle,* August 4, 1999.

Zakem, Patrick, ed. "The Steppenwolf Ensemble on 'True West.'" Steppenwolf. www.steppenwolf.org/articles/the-steppenwolf-ensemble-on-true-west/.

Zolotow, Sam. "Black Students Block Yale Play: 'Operation Sidewinder' Off Drama School's Schedule." *The New York Times,* December 27, 1969.

FILM AND VIDEO

Almereyda, Michael, dir. *This So-Called Disaster: Sam Shepard Directs "The Late Henry Moss."* 2003.

Brown, Jeffrey. "'True West' Stars Ethan Hawke and Paul Dano on Sam Shepard's Profound Sensibility." Interview footage. *PBS NewsHour,* March 1, 2019. www.pbs.org/newshour/amp/show/true-west-stars-ethan-hawke-and-paul-dano-on-sam-shepards-profound-sensibility/.

Douglas, Sam Wainwright, and Paul Lovelace. *The Holy Modal Rounders: Bound to Lose.* Cav Entertainment, 2008.

Jacoby, Oren, dir. "Sam Shepard: Stalking Himself." *Great Performances.* KQED Productions, July 8, 1998, on Thirteen/WNET and BBC Worldwide.

"Jacques Levy," Parts 1, 2, and 3. YouTube, March 4, 2013. www.youtube.com/watch?v=Hs _NRbODKtM.

"Jessica Lange Wins Supporting Actress: 1983 Oscars." YouTube, October 3, 2008. www .youtube.com/watch?v=9mKLxWrRVMg/.

Lange, Jessica. "Commencement Address." Sarah Lawrence College, May 23, 2008. C-SPAN. www.c-span.org/video/?205589-1/sarah-lawrence-college-commencement-address.

"Patti Smith's First Performance, St Marks [*sic*] Church 2/10/71." YouTube. www.youtube.com /watch?v=klpUlOZyGIs/.

Scorsese, Martin, dir. *Rolling Thunder: A Bob Dylan Story by Martin Scorsese.* Netflix, 2019.

Wadleigh, Michael, dir. *Woodstock.* Warner Bros., 1970.

Wurmfeld, Treva, dir. *Shepard & Dark.* Prime Video, 2012.

NOTES

PROLOGUE: NEW YORK, NEW YORK

3 **In the opening scene** The entire prologue draws on Sam Shepard, "My First Year in New York: 1963," *The New York Times Magazine,* September 17, 2000.

ONE: LIFE DURING WARTIME

9 **"was thick enough to walk on"** Shepard, "My First Year in New York: 1963."
12 **"My name came" . . . "Chicago Mafia"** Sam Shepard, *Motel Chronicles* (San Francisco, Calif.: City Lights Books, 1982).
14 **"had been forced" . . . "projected on a bedsheet"** Don Shewey, *Sam Shepard* (1984; repr. New York: Da Capo Press, 1997).
16 **"was Welsh"** Sam Shepard, *Spy of the First Person* (New York: Vintage Books, 2018).

TWO: THE ROSE PARADE

22 **"I mean, here"** Sam Shepard, www.samshepard.com.
22 **"to bow to"** Matt Hormann, "When South Pasadena Was for Whites Only," September 15, 2014, Hometown Pasadena. (This website is no longer active; the article has been archived at: web.archive.org/web/20200123171338/http://hometown-pasadena.com /history/when-south-pasadena-was-for-whites-only/88641.)
24 **"blue hair" . . . "Arab pride"** Shepard, *Spy of the First Person.*
25 **"been in and out of Juvenile" . . . "never said a word"** Shepard, *Motel Chronicles.*
26 **"a dead bucking horse" . . . "matching silver concho saddles"** Sam Shepard, *Day out of Days* (New York: Alfred A. Knopf, 2010).

THREE: A STRANGE KIND OF MELTING POT

30 **"dry, flat, cracked" . . . "Duarte most of the time"** Sam Shepard, *Hawk Moon: Short Stories, Poems, and Monologues* (New York: PAJ Books, 1981).
32 **"If a formation of P-51's went over"** Shepard, *Motel Chronicles.*
33 **"In that area, fighting was kind of a badge"** Robert Goldberg, "Sam Shepard: American Original," *Playboy,* March 1984.
34 **"a blond crew-cut" . . . "take that away from me"** Sam Shepard, *"The Unseen Hand" and Other Plays* (New York: Applause Books, 2000).
36 **"He was very strict, my father"** Shewey, *Sam Shepard.*
36 **"There was always a kind of"** Ibid.
37 **"Later, I found out"** Sam Shepard, *Cruising Paradise* (New York: Vintage Books, 1997).

FOUR: THE REAL GABBY HAYES

39 **"a veterinarian with a flashy"** Sam Shepard and Johnny Dark, *Two Prospectors: The Letters of Sam Shepard and Johnny Dark,* ed. Chad Hammett (Austin: University of Texas Press, 2013).

39   **"My history with booze"** Benjamin Ryder Howe, Jeanne McCulloch, and Mona Simpson, "Sam Shepard: The Art of Theater No. 12," *Paris Review* 142 (Spring 1997).

41   **"probably shatter my dreams immediately"** John J. Winters, *Sam Shepard: A Life* (Berkeley, Calif.: Counterpoint, 2017).

41   **"There are some who say Sam Rogers left"** Ibid.

42   **"a holocaust"** . . . **"tore the doors off, stuff like that"** Dave Davies, "Fresh Air Remembers Pulitzer Prize–Winning Playwright and Actor Sam Shepard," 1998 Transcript, *Fresh Air,* August 4, 2017, NPR, www.npr.org/2017/08/04/541602156/fresh-air-remembers-pulitzer-prize-winning-playwright-and-actor-sam-shepard.

42   **"a maniac, but"** Howe, McCulloch, and Simpson, "Sam Shepard: The Art of Theater No. 12."

43   **"I thought I had"** Shepard, *Day out of Days.*

44   **"for a community college freshman"** . . . **"lacks a traditional ending"** Winters, *Sam Shepard: A Life.*

46   **"glistening swimming pools"** . . . **"How 'bout that?"** Shepard, *Cruising Paradise.*

47   **"That is my old man talking"** Mel Gussow, "From Plays to Fiction: Thanks, Dad; Sam Shepard's Rascals Are Inspired by Memories of a Mysterious Father," *The New York Times,* October 15, 2002.

FIVE: THE VILLAGE GATE

48   **"three roller chairs"** Thornton Wilder, *The Skin of Our Teeth* (New York: Harper Perennial, 2003).

49   **"When I saw him the second time"** . . . **"he took me home"** Ellen Oumano, *Sam Shepard: The Life and Work of an American* (New York: St. Martin's Press, 1986).

50   **"It was actually a great"** . . . **"'I'm getting off the bus'"** Howe, McCulloch, and Simpson, "Sam Shepard: The Art of Theater No. 12."

51   **"hot tip"** . . . **"vandalize a coal barge"** Shepard, "My First Year in New York: 1963."

52   **"mixing the bitter"** . . . **"which I threw in the East River"** Shepard, *Cruising Paradise.*

53   **"I never shot up"** Jack Kroll, Constance Guthrie, and Janet Huck, "Who's That Tall Dark Stranger," *Newsweek,* November 11, 1985.

53   **"I rode everything with hair"** Ibid.

55   **"very not into selling out"** Bonnie Marranca, ed., *American Dreams: The Imagination of Sam Shepard* (New York: Performing Arts Journal Publications, 1981).

56   **"a particular accomplice"** . . . **"the heroes of that era"** Michael Almereyda, "Sam Shepard," *Interview,* September 24, 2011.

57   **"the brown acid that is circulating"** *Woodstock,* directed by Michael Wadleigh (Warner Bros., 1970).

58   **"After Amiri Baraka"** Hilton Als, "Hungry Hearts," *The New Yorker,* May 27, 2019.

59   **"Dolphy's Egyptian pharaoh"** . . . **"cruel smile"** Shepard, *Day out of Days.*

59   **"unleashing torrential angry riffs"** . . . **"up to the rafters"** Shepard, "My First Year in New York: 1963."

59   **"a whole big gray"** . . . **"was always nice to me"** Shepard, *Motel Chronicles.*

60   **"Underneath,"** Shepard wrote, **"her real"** . . . **"your neck stood up"** Ibid.

60   **"recognized"** . . . **"only thing that makes any sense"** Shepard, "My First Year in New York: 1963."

SIX: THEATRE GENESIS

62   **"is supposedly based on [his] flunking"** Winters, *Sam Shepard: A Life.*

62   **"I was 4F"** David Richards, "SSSHHHH! IT'S SAM SHEPARD," *The Washington Post,* December 12, 1988.

62   **"The sixties, to me"** . . . **"nobody has a *clue*"** Matthew Roudané, ed., *The Cambridge Companion to Sam Shepard* (Cambridge, UK: Cambridge University Press, 2002).

64   **"I was on a different drug—crystal Methedrine"** Goldberg, "Sam Shepard: American Original."

65   **"Sam Shepard never called himself Sam Shepard"** Oumano, *Sam Shepard.*

65 **"Because it's shorter"** Robert Coe, "The Saga of Sam Shepard," *The New York Times Magazine,* November 23, 1980.

66 **"I always thought Rogers was a corny name"** Pete Hamill, "The American Hero," *New York,* December 5, 1983.

66 **"the only guy"** Brian Bartels, "Sam Shepard's Master Class in Playwriting," Interview, Cherry Lane Theatre, November 5, 2006, *Missouri Review* (Spring 2007).

66 **"There was something wrong"** . . . **"to write a play"** Almereyda, "Sam Shepard."

67 **"more depressing sermons"** Michael Allen, ed., *This Time, This Place* (New York: Bobbs-Merrill, 1971).

67 **"a parish-based arts program"** Lee Kissman, "50 Years On: Theater Genesis and Sam Shepard," *Contemporary Theater Review* 25, no. 4 (2015).

68 **"the beginning, the Genesis"** Nick Orzel and Michael Smith, eds., *Eight Plays from Off-Off Broadway* (New York: Bobbs-Merrill, 1966); see also "Theatre Genesis," Wikipedia, en.wikipedia.org/wiki/Theatre_Genesis.

68 **"For me, that wasn't a problem"** Howe, McCulloch, and Simpson, "Sam Shepard: The Art of Theater No. 12."

68 **"a pain in the ass"** . . . **"what *Cowboys* was about"** Allen, ed., *This Time, This Place.*

69 **"about leaving my mom and dad"** Coe, "The Saga of Sam Shepard."

69 **"When I come"** Sam Shepard, *Fifteen One-Act Plays* (New York: Vintage Books, 2012).

69 **"I believe this whole generation of young people"** Shewey, *Sam Shepard.*

70 **"more than a little distressed"** . . . **"move back to California"** Kissman, "50 Years On: Theater Genesis and Sam Shepard."

70 **"It was shocking"** Alexis Soloski, "A Holy Space in More Ways Than One," *The New York Times,* June 19, 2014.

70 **"They have actually found"** Michael Smith, "'Cowboys' and 'The Rock Garden,'" *The Village Voice,* October 22, 1964.

71 **"neither of them could stop"** . . . **"they didn't flinch"** Kissman, "50 Years On: Theater Genesis and Sam Shepard."

SEVEN: LA TURISTA

75 **"Sam didn't care about the outcome"** Oumano, *Sam Shepard.*

75 **"a little family money"** Winters, *Sam Shepard: A Life.*

75 **"one of the great piano players"** . . . **"kind of awesome"** Almereyda, "Sam Shepard."

76 **"one of the youngest and most gifted"** Edward Albee, "Edward Albee Reviews Sam Shepard's 'Icarus's Mother,'" *The Village Voice,* November 25, 1965.

77 **"OOB TALENT"** Elenore Lester, "The Pass-the-Hat Theater Circuit," *The New York Times Magazine,* December 5, 1965.

77 **"in a voice I'd only heard in animals giving birth"** Shepard, *Motel Chronicles.*

78 **"Tuesday Weld–type"** . . . **"carry the bones of my Grandpa's face"** Ibid.

81 **"was just cool"** Joyce Aaron, email to author, June 2, 2020.

81 **"superb"** . . . **"north of Fourteenth Street"** Jeremy Gerard, *Wynn Place Show: A Biased History of the Rollicking Life and Extreme Times of Wynn Handman and the American Place Theatre* (Hanover, N.H.: Smith and Kraus, 2015).

82 **"We struggled"** Ibid.

82 ***La Turista* by Sam Shepard"** Elizabeth Hardwick, "Word of Mouth: 'La Turista,' by Sam Shepard, American Place Theatre," *New York Review of Books,* April 6, 1967.

82 **"We lost a lot of subscribers"** Gerard, *Wynn Place Show.*

82 **"So that was an eye opener"** . . . **"rude and belligerent"** Ibid.

83 **"Whose loving companionship"** Sam Shepard, *Five Plays* (New York: Bobbs-Merrill, 1967).

EIGHT: FORENSIC AND THE NAVIGATORS

85 **"a huge black-and-white"** Sam Shepard, *Fool for Love and Other Plays* (New York: Bantam Books, 1988).

86 **"Being 1967"** Peter Stampfel, "Sam Shepard: Tribute by Peter Stampfel, Part 1," December 2017, Perfect Sound Forever, www.furious.com/perfect/samshepard1.html.

87 **"raised by a free-spirited Philosopher Queen"** O-Lan Jones, Bio, www.o-lanjones.com/.

88 **"He was a quiet guy"** Winters, *Sam Shepard: A Life.*

88 **"quite mystified to audition for a play"** Shewey, *Sam Shepard.*

89 **"appear on one level to be two sides"** . . . **"during the later 1960s"** Stephen J. Bottoms, in Roudané, ed., *The Cambridge Companion to Sam Shepard.*

89 **"this noise that was so bad"** David DeRose, *Sam Shepard* (New York: Twayne/Macmillan, 1992).

89 **"had a red plaid shirt on"** Shepard and Dark, *Two Prospectors.*

89 **"I saw your play last night"** *Shepard & Dark,* directed by Treva Wurmfeld (Prime Video, 2012).

90 **"bought (adopted) in"** . . . **"to call the maid"** Shepard and Dark, *Two Prospectors.*

90 **"I like this guy because he's not a hippy"** Ibid.

90 **"to see America from"** . . . **"riding shotgun"** Ibid.

90 **"Sam said his father"** Wurmfeld, *Shepard & Dark.*

91 **"the playwright's confidant"** Shepard and Dark, *Two Prospectors.*

91 **"a smoke-dream"** Winters, *Sam Shepard: A Life.*

NINE: ZABRISKIE POINT

93 **"about a semi-committed student activist"** Shewey, *Sam Shepard.*

93 **"He got in touch with me"** Irene Oppenheim and Victor Fascio, "The Most Promising Playwright in America Today Is Sam Shepard," *The Village Voice,* October 27, 1975.

94 **"I like Michelangelo a lot"** *Village Voice* interview quoted in Winters, *Sam Shepard: A Life.*

96 **"We were on *Laugh-In*?"** . . . **"verge of success"** Sam Wainwright Douglas and Paul Lovelace. *The Holy Modal Rounders: Bound to Lose* (Cav Entertainment, 2008).

97 **"I wrote the very first version"** Oppenheim and Fascio, "The Most Promising Playwright in America Today Is Sam Shepard."

97 **"emaciated and worn down"** Winters, *Sam Shepard: A Life.*

98 **"to testify about the movie's alleged"** Guy Flatley, "Antonioni Defends 'Zabriskie Point,'" *The New York Times Magazine,* February 22, 1970.

99 **"I think people got screwed on the desert"** Winters, *Sam Shepard: A Life.*

99 **"an ignoramus"** Flatley, "Antonioni Defends 'Zabriskie Point.'"

99 **"a silly and stupid movie"** Roger Ebert, "Zabriskie Point," *Chicago Sun-Times,* January 1, 1970.

99 **"unintentionally funny"** Vincent Canby, "Screen: Antonioni's 'Zabriskie Point,'" *The New York Times,* February 10, 1970.

TEN: MAXAGASM

101 **"feature the group as a band"** Chris Campion, "Saturation 70: The Gram Parsons UFO Movie That Never Flew," *The Guardian,* September 5, 2014.

102 **"With a couple of elderly locals"** . . . **"'groovy,' he recalled"** Winters, *Sam Shepard: A Life.*

102 **"a really great movie"** Ibid.

102 **"A cascading wealth"** . . . **"Negro member"** Sam Shepard, "Maxagasm," Unpublished screenplay, n.d., Sam Shepard, Bancroft Library Special Collections, University of California at Berkeley.

104 **"the cat that gets him"** Heathcote Williams, *AC/DC and the Local Stigmatic* (New York: Viking Press, 1973).

104 **"You can't talk that way about Mick Jagger!"** Shewey, *Sam Shepard.*

104 **"The thing about Keith"** . . . **"crow feather hair"** Shepard, *Hawk Moon.*

105 **"dated"** Winters, *Sam Shepard: A Life.*

ELEVEN: O-LAN

108 **"Well," he said, "Sam Shepard wrote just one"** Marlaine Glicksman, "Highway 61 Revisited: Robert Frank," *Film Comment,* July–August 1987.

109 "off writing a movie with Antonioni" . . . "double-parked in front" O-Lan Jones's account of the beginning of her relationship with Shepard is from "Running Off with Sam," *American Theatre,* August 4, 2017.

112 "He was a tricky guy" Winters, *Sam Shepard: A Life.*

112 "In a broken world" Shewey, *Sam Shepard.*

112 "was wearing a long Empire-waisted" . . . "really kind of cool" Oumano, *Sam Shepard.*

113 "The Rounders played at the wedding" Peter Stampfel, "Sam Shepard: Tribute by Peter Stampfel, Part 2," December 2017, Perfect Sound Forever, www.furious.com/perfect/sam shepard2.html.

113 "We do!" Shewey, *Sam Shepard.*

114 "that before he could proclaim them" Winters, *Sam Shepard: A Life.*

114 In a black-and-white photograph Pinterest, www.pinterest.com/pin/325385141819720773.

TWELVE: OPERATION SIDEWINDER

116 "A lot of the songs we were practicing" Oumano, *Sam Shepard.*

117 "as stereotypes reminiscent of Stepin Fetchit" . . . "free theater in a university setting" Sam Zolotow, "Black Students Block Yale Play: 'Operation Sidewinder' Off Drama School's Schedule," *The New York Times,* December 27, 1969.

118 "not because he agreed with their assessment" Shewey, *Sam Shepard.*

118 "The New Theatre presents" . . . "dressed like Blood" Sam Shepard, "Operation Sidewinder," *Esquire,* May 1969.

119 "No, we're with the Rams" Ibid.

120 "It's impossible to stage in a poverty situation" Mel Gussow, "Sam Shepard: Writer on the Way Up," *The New York Times,* November 12, 1969.

121 "an apocalyptic comic strip" Shewey, *Sam Shepard.*

121 "I couldn't bring myself to go up there" Gussow, "Sam Shepard: Writer on the Way Up."

121 "In the fractious early seventies" John Lahr, "Postscript: Sam Shepard, Who Brought Rage and Rebellion Onstage," *The New Yorker,* July 31, 2017.

121 "a move that in Off-Off-Broadway" John Lahr, "The Pathfinder: Sam Shepard and the Struggles of American Manhood," *The New Yorker,* February 8, 2010.

121 "the bartender tried to shoo us out" Ibid.

121 "The first time he came to rehearsal" Shewey, *Sam Shepard.*

121 "Gee, it's not like" . . . "should be fired" Ibid.

122 "We lost about 10,000 subscribers" Jasper Rees, "Theatre: American Playwright in London," *The Independent,* June 25, 1996.

122 "The difficulty of the play is in the writing" Clive Barnes, "Stage Lizard vs. Snake," *The New York Times,* March 13, 1970.

122 "There is only one thing wrong with Sam Shepard's" Kerr's review quoted in Shewey, *Sam Shepard.*

122 "He told me he'd had awards" Ibid.

123 "funny and charming" performance Martin Washburn, "Theatre: Two by Sam Shepard," *The Village Voice,* April 9, 1970.

123 "Despite my worst instincts" Clive Barnes, "Theater: 'The Unseen Hand' and 'Forensic and the Navigators,'" *The New York Times,* April 2, 1970.

123 "I felt terrible for causing the playwright" Shewey, *Sam Shepard.*

123 "Seeing Sam in the lobby" Lahr, "Postscript."

124 "fine arts painter" . . . "cause him harm" Joey Skaggs, "Lucky Loser: My Abortive Attempt to Kidnap Sam Shepard," *HuffPost,* April 22, 2013.

124 "They recognized me" Oumano, *Sam Shepard.*

124 "started throwing fists" Skaggs, "Lucky Loser."

124 "was freaking out" Oumano, *Sam Shepard.*

124 "made a hasty retreat" Skaggs, "Lucky Loser."

125 "The next morning the *Daily News*" Albert Poland, *Stages: A Theater Memoir* (Wappinger Falls, N.Y.: Albert Poland, 2019).

125 "Sam doesn't want anything moved" Oumano, *Sam Shepard.*

125 "He had a triple whammy" Winters, *Sam Shepard: A Life.*

THIRTEEN: COWBOY MOUTH

126 **"I'm gonna get my gun"** . . . **"the heart and soul"** Patti Smith, *Just Kids* (New York: Ecco, 2010).

127 **"even taller than mine"** Ibid.

127 **"After the set"** Peter Stampfel, "Sam Shepard: Tribute by Peter Stampfel, Part 3," February 2018, Perfect Sound Forever, www.furious.com/perfect/samshepard3.html.

127 **"Okay, sugar, let's eat"** . . . **"trapped in one's skin"** Smith, *Just Kids.*

129 **"Me and his wife still even liked each other"** Patricia Morrisroe, *Mapplethorpe: A Biography* (New York: Random House, 1995).

129 **"the weirdest fight I ever saw"** Oumano, *Sam Shepard.*

129 **"Everything you heard about us in those days"** Morrisroe, *Mapplethorpe.*

129 **"Like any snake, you've rattled your way"** Winters, *Sam Shepard: A Life.*

129 **"beatnik-witch" artist from Australia** Penny Green, "Patti Smith," *Interview,* October 1973, as quoted in www.oceanstar.com/patti/bio/vali.htm.

130 **"Hawk Moon month November month"** Shepard, *Hawk Moon.*

130 **"a battered black Gibson"** . . . **"beautiful gesture"** Smith, *Just Kids.*

131 **"Her writing blew me away"** Joe Penhall, "The Outsider," *The Guardian,* June 14, 2006.

131 **"terrific poet and great songwriter"** "Patti Smith's First Performance, St Marks [*sic*] Church 2/10/71," YouTube, www.youtube.com/watch?v=klpUIOZyGIs.

131 **Smith took to the stage** . . . **"Ballad of a Bad Boy"** Ibid.

132 **"I didn't capitalize on that performance"** Jack Whatley, "Patti Smith Remembers Her First-Ever Gig in New York, 1971," *Far Out,* August 22, 2020.

133 **"Let's write a play"** Smith, *Just Kids.*

133 **"a cat who looks like a coyote"** Sam Shepard, *"Fool for Love" and Other Plays* (New York: Bantam Books, 1988).

133 **"You're on, Patti Lee"** Smith, *Just Kids.*

133 **"a chick who looks"** . . . **"I want her too"** Shepard, *"Fool for Love" and Other Plays.*

134 **"The characters were ourselves"** Smith, *Just Kids.*

135 **"She's great"** . . . **"I said, 'Fine.'"** Gerard, *Wynn Place Show.*

135 **"On the surface"** Ibid.

135 **"because the play was good"** . . . **"egged us on"** Smith, *Just Kids.*

135 **"out of control"** . . . **"a great performance"** Oumano, *Sam Shepard.*

136 **"It didn't work out"** Shewey, *Sam Shepard.*

136 **"You know, the dreams you had for me"** Smith, *Just Kids.*

136 **"O-Lan didn't know where Sam was"** Shewey, *Sam Shepard.*

136 **"would recall an inebriated Smith"** Winters, *Sam Shepard: A Life.*

136 **"stories about me being carried out"** Maureen Dowd, "Rock Star Patti Smith Making Paris Swoon," *The New York Times,* September 19, 2019.

136 **"We were only trying to talk about two people"** Patti Smith, "My Buddy," *The New Yorker,* August 1, 2017.

137 **"informed O-Lan that they were getting back together"** Stampfel, "Sam Shepard: Tribute by Peter Stampfel, Part 3."

137 **"do something drastic"** . . . **"No, I guess I hadn't"** Shepard and Dark, *Two Prospectors.*

FOURTEEN: THE TOOTH OF CRIME

138 **"When I first got to New York"** . . . **"into a rock 'n' roll band"** Kenneth Chubb and the editors of *Theatre Quarterly,* "Metaphors, Mad Dogs and Old Time Cowboys: Interview with Sam Shepard," *Theatre Quarterly* 4 (August/October 1974).

139 **"sat in for Charlie Watts"** Goldberg, "Sam Shepard: American Original."

140 **"At the end," he said** Winters, *Sam Shepard: A Life.*

140 **"a series of lined notebooks"** Shewey, *Sam Shepard.*

140 **"an unrecognizable space and time"** Coe, "The Saga of Sam Shepard."

140 **"using an invented language"** Shewey, *Sam Shepard.*

140 **"Back in the sixties"** Sam Shepard, *"The Tooth of Crime" (Second Dance): A Play with Music in Two Acts* (1974; repr. New York: Vintage Books, 2006).

141 "the first play of the twenty-first century" Marowitz's review quoted in Michael Coveney, "Heathcote Williams Obituary," *The Guardian*, July 2, 2017.

141 "the finest American play" Shewey, *Sam Shepard*.

144 "with a Mephistophelian beard" Irving Wardle, "Charles Marowitz Obituary," *The Guardian*, May 9, 2014.

144 "I guess Marowitz's theater" Hamill, "The American Hero."

145 "on a proscenium stage with amplified rock" Oumano, *Sam Shepard*.

146 "apparently in anger at what they felt" Clive Barnes, "The Theater: Sam Shepard's 'The Tooth of Crime,'" *The New York Times*, November 12, 1972.

146 "in a conventional theater" . . . "between wood and bodies" Clive Barnes, "Theater: Shepard's 'Tooth of Crime,'" *The New York Times*, March 8, 1973.

146 "actively hated" what the Performance Group had done Shewey, *Sam Shepard*.

146 "And in the enlightened year of 1996" Ben Brantley, "A Clash of Rock Stars in an Existential Mode," *The New York Times*, December 24, 1996.

147 "It is both gratifying and a little frightening" Ben Brantley, "Two Satanic Majesties Request All Devouring Fame," *The New York Times*, October 22, 2006.

147 "The idea was like a gang-warfare" . . . "interested in in the play" *Time Out* interview quoted in Shewey, *Sam Shepard*.

148 "But while there exists in your breast of stone" Stéphane Mallarmé, in Angel Flores, ed., *The Anchor Anthology of French Poetry* (New York; Anchor Books, 2000).

148 "white and dressed like a 42nd Street pimp" Sam Shepard, *"The Tooth of Crime" and "Geography of a Horse Dreamer"* (New York: Grove Press, 1974).

149 "dark, heavy, lurking Rock and Roll" . . . "just like Keith Richards" Ibid.

149 "Its central battle to the death" Irving Wardle, review of *The Tooth of Crime*, *The Times of London*, July 18, 1972.

149 "My first reaction was to beg off" Charles Marowitz, "A Sophisticate Abroad," *The Village Voice*, September 7, 1972.

FIFTEEN: THE ROYAL COURT

151 "in one of those transit" . . . "bought for 200 pounds" Naseem Khan, "Free Form Playwright," *Time Out*, July 13–17, 1969.

152 "I really used to like the horse-track" Ibid.

152 "So those few seconds are what it's all about" Shepard's *Time Out* article quoted in Winters, *Sam Shepard: A Life*.

153 "only a few brief meetings" Coe, "The Saga of Sam Shepard."

153 "Character has become much more important" Stewart McBride, "Sam Shepard," *The Christian Science Monitor*, December 26, 1980.

153 "once said that everything" Winters, *Sam Shepard: A Life*.

153 "first re-introduction" . . . "different than we brought with us" Shepard and Dark, *Two Prospectors*.

155 "low and oppressive" ceiling Ruth Little and Emily McLaughlin, *The Royal Court Theatre Inside Out* (London: Oberon Books, 2007).

156 "half an hour of boredom and agony" Heathcote Williams, *AC/DC and the Local Stigmatic* (New York: Viking Press, 1973).

156 "a quarter million bucks in a day" Shepard, *"The Tooth of Crime" and "Geography of a Horse Dreamer."*

157 "work of art that ostensibly deals" Marranca, ed., *American Dreams*.

157 "They were so superb that it was bearing witness" Michael Almereyda, dir., *This So-Called Disaster: Sam Shepard Directs "The Late Henry Moss,"* 2003.

157 "he was sort of resting up" . . . "their favorite author" Little and McLaughlin, *The Royal Court Theatre Inside Out*.

158 "There was no messing about" Rees, "Theatre: American Playwright in London."

158 "a way of sort of getting" . . . "hair falling around his collar" Little and McLaughlin, *The Royal Court Theatre Inside Out*.

160 "vigorous of all companies" David Cleall, "The Freehold," Unfinished Histories: Recording the History of Alternative Theatre, www.unfinishedhistories.com/history/companies/the-freehold/.

160 **"He wrote it about three women"** Rees, "Theatre: American Playwright in London."

160 **"O-Lan's hymn to the masculinity"** Shewey, *Sam Shepard.*

160 **"The play was about being pregnant"** Stephen Rea, "Sam Shepard 1943–2017: 'He Was the Kindest Man, Truthful, Witty and Generous,'" *The Guardian,* August 6, 2017.

161 **"write these fucking letters"** . . . **"Yessir, we're on our way, boy!"** Shepard, in Shepard and Dark, *Two Prospectors.*

SIXTEEN: MAGIC THEATRE

162 **"I came out here because of my family"** Quoted in Shewey, *Sam Shepard.*

163 **"the kind of place with paisley felt wallpaper"** Oumano, *Sam Shepard.*

163 **"an area that looks like the outcome of a recent battle"** Sam Shepard, *The Rolling Thunder Logbook* (1978; repr. Cambridge, Mass.: Da Capo Press, 2004).

163 **"They told me I could maybe do them"** Shewey, *Sam Shepard.*

163 **"The plays are virile and crack like a whip"** Michael McClure, introduction to Sam Shepard, *"Mad Dog Blues" and Other Plays* (The Winter Repertory 4), (New York: Winter House, 1972).

163 **Dubbed "the prince of the San Francisco scene"** Barry Miles, *In the Sixties* (London: Jonathan Cape, 2002).

164 **"Lion's easygoing attitude"** Shewey, *Sam Shepard.*

165 **"no sound, no time, just a cold space"** Clive Barnes, "Theater: 2 by Shepard," *The New York Times,* April 16, 1975.

165 **"the days of mass entertainment"** . . . **"no references for this"** Shepard, *"Fool for Love" and Other Plays.*

165 **"I remember Sam offering"** Nancy Meckler, email to author, March 22, 2019.

165 **"The play is about time and action"** Barnes, "Theater: 2 by Shepard."

166 **"couldn't imagine doing a play"** . . . **"something to go with it"** Gerard, *Wynn Place Show.*

166 **"Hence, *Killer's Head*"** Meckler, email to author.

167 **"a clipped, southwestern rodeo accent"** . . . **"then back to black"** Sam Shepard, *Fifteen One-Act Plays.*

167 **"a sketch" and "a one-joke tragedy"** Barnes, "Theater: 2 by Shepard."

167 **"Wynn was also an acting teacher"** . . . **"feel connected to him"** Meckler, email to author.

168 **"great virtuosity"** Barnes, "Theater: 2 by Shepard."

168 **"I had nothing to use"** Richard Gere, "Richard Gere Recalls Working with Sam Shepard on 'Days of Heaven,'" Guest Column, *The Hollywood Reporter,* August 1, 2017.

168 **"the communication is in the writing"** Berna Rauch, "Zen Experience at the Theatre: A Non-Symbolic Sam Shepard," *Berkeley Barb,* May 9–15, 1975.

168 **"The play was an experiment"** . . . **"I get tired of that"** Ibid.

169 **"At present, he is 'making ends meet'"** . . . **"tickets for productions"** www.rockefeller foundation.org/blog/ctl-stories/decade1960/.

169 **"a pleasure to recite"** Shewey, *Sam Shepard.*

170 **"I feel like I've gone"** . . . **"means to produce my own work"** Shepard's grant application essay quoted in Carol Rosen, *Sam Shepard: A Poetic Rodeo* (Basingstoke, UK: Palgrave Macmillan, 2004).

171 **"The break with Shepard was painful for Lion"** Steven Winn, "John Lion: Magic Onstage—Theater Rebel Found New Writers, Audiences," *San Francisco Chronicle,* August 4, 1999.

172 **"Oh, while we're reminiscing"** Shepard and Dark, *Two Prospectors.*

SEVENTEEN: ROLLING THUNDER

174 **"I couldn't believe you could play"** Unless otherwise cited here, all Sam Shepard quotes in this chapter are from Shepard, *The Rolling Thunder Logbook.*

176 **"Dylan and I wanted to do this tour"** . . . **"I knew Sam would come"** Oumano, *Sam Shepard.*

180 **"good-looking fresh-faced guy"** . . . **"so damn cute"** Chris O'Dell, with Katherine Ketcham, *Miss O'Dell* (New York: Touchstone/Simon and Schuster, 2009).

182 **"two scenes for some movie"** Levy quoted in Oumano, *Sam Shepard.*

182   **"this rock-and-roll lifestyle"** . . . **"didn't want to do *this*"** O'Dell with Ketcham, *Miss O'Dell.*

183   **"He was just sweet"** . . . **"kind of a mess"** Ibid.

184   **"when it snows in your nose"** Allen Ginsberg, *Collected Poems* (New York: HarperCollins, 2007).

184   **"a sweet little smile"** . . . **"It hurt like hell"** O'Dell with Ketcham, *Miss O'Dell.*

185   **"all they wanted to know"** . . . **"the Western greenhorn"** Larry "Ratso" Sloman, *On the Road with Bob Dylan* (New York: Three Rivers Press, 2002).

187   **"I couldn't get past Sam"** Oumano, *Sam Shepard.*

189   **"You know, I really admire"** O'Dell with Ketcham, *Miss O'Dell.*

189   **"a flirtation"** . . . **"I found him very attractive"** David Yaffe, *Reckless Daughter: A Portrait of Joni Mitchell* (New York: Sarah Crichton Books/Farrar, Straus and Giroux, 2017).

192   **"rowdy"** . . . **"in the audience were doing that"** Oumano, *Sam Shepard.*

193   **"responsible for Sam's film career as an actor"** Ibid.

194   **"one of the greatest and most ridiculous"** Robert Christgau, www.robertchristgau.com/get_artist.php?id=169.

194   **"a lot of fun to work with"** Jonathan Cott, "Sam Shepard on Working with Dylan, Why Jim Morrison Has No Sense of Humor," *Rolling Stone,* December 18, 1986.

194   **"A one-act play, as it really happened"** Sam Shepard, "True Dylan," *Esquire,* July 1987.

194   **"a petulant Dylan"** . . . **"attention of an older brother"** Winters, *Sam Shepard: A Life.*

195   **"started thinkin' about the short life of trouble"** Shepard, "True Dylan."

EIGHTEEN: DAYS OF HEAVEN

196   **"to get stoned and talk"** . . . **"Vega club"** Wurmfeld, *Shepard & Dark.*

197   **"a matter of life & death"** . . . **"forty some head of boarding horses"** Shepard and Dark, *Two Prospectors.*

199   **"totally devoted to writing"** . . . **"you got to love him"** Ibid.

199   **"Terry told me very early on"** Rodrigo Perez, "Terrence Malick Wanted John Travolta & 15 Things You Didn't Know about 'Days of Heaven,'" The Playlist, June 9, 2011, theplaylist.net/terrence-malick-wanted-john-travolta-15-things-you-didnt-know-about-days-of-heaven-20110609/3/.

201   **"apparently unruffled by Sam's affair"** Shewey, *Sam Shepard.*

202   **"a thick blanket of snow"** . . . **"yelling things at each other"** Shepard and Dark, *Two Prospectors.*

203   **"The dramatist Sam Shepard demonstrates"** Harold C. Schonberg, "At the Movies—'Days of Heaven,'" *The New York Times,* September 14, 1978.

203   **"'Days of Heaven' is above all"** Roger Ebert, "Days of Heaven," *Chicago Sun-Times,* December 7, 1997.

203   **"I was about to enter a whole new world"** . . . **"until you die"** Shepard and Dark, *Two Prospectors.*

NINETEEN: CURSE OF THE STARVING CLASS

205   **"I was as warm"** . . . **"how many plays he might write"** Kenneth Turan and Joseph Papp, *Free for All: Joe Papp, the Public, and the Greatest Theater Story Ever Told* (New York: Doubleday, 2009).

207   **"How much money will you give me?"** Roger Downey, "Inside the Words," *Time Out,* April 22–28, 1977.

208   **"'Curse' is the first time I've ever tried"** Ibid.

208   **"unshaven and slightly drunk"** . . . **"lizards blowing across it"** Sam Shepard, *Seven Plays* (New York: Bantam Books, 1981).

210   **"sitting in his drawer"** . . . **"So you go to New York"** Sara Holdren, "Director Robert Woodruff Remembers Sam Shepard," *Vulture,* August 1, 2017, www.vulture.com/2017/08/director-robert-woodruff-remembers-sam-shepard.html.

210   **"I loved the material"** . . . **"not concerned about the work"** Turan and Papp, *Free for All.*

210   **"the central notion"** . . . **"self-indulgence"** Richard Eder, "Theater: 'The Starving,'" *The New York Times,* March 3, 1978.

TWENTY: BURIED CHILD

212   **"one of his lowest"** . . . **"talking in phony brogues"** Shewey, *Sam Shepard.*

213   **"allow that thing to grow up"** Shepard, *Seven Plays.*

214   **"had already promised"** . . . **"in a tiny theater"** Shewey, *Sam Shepard.*

214   **"a piece of writing"** . . . **"withered by rootlessness"** Richard Eder, "Stage: Sam Shepard Offers 'Buried Child,'" *The New York Times,* November 7, 1978.

214   **"voted unanimously to recommend"** "In Memoriam: Sam Shepard (1943-2017)," www .pulitzer.org/article/memoriam-sam-shepard-1943-2017.

215   **"the visionary playwright"** . . . **"pleases him no end"** Don Shirley, "Searching for Sam Shepard," *The Washington Post,* January 14, 1979.

216   **"Dealing with the media"** Amy Lippman, "Rhythm & Truths: An Interview with Sam Shepard," *American Theatre,* April 1, 1984.

217   **"a genius"** Shewey, *Sam Shepard.*

217   **"home life, religious experience"** Winters, *Sam Shepard: A Life.*

218   **"The whole cast is outstanding"** Janet Maslin, "Film: 'Resurrection' Has the Manner of a Fairy Tale; Question of Faith," *The New York Times,* November 7, 1980.

218   **"some sexy tension"** Pauline Kael, "Pauline Kael on 'Days of Heaven,'" Castle of Illusion, September 16, 2008, castle.tumblr.com/post/50391722/pauline-kael-on-days-of-heaven -terrence-malick.

218   **"a cross between Peter Fonda and heaven"** Shewey, *Sam Shepard.*

218   **"Shepard invests his role"** David Ansen, "The 'True West' Interviews," *Newsweek,* November 11, 1985.

218   **"Sam is Gary Cooper"** Shewey, *Sam Shepard.*

218   **"Sam was so hot in *Resurrection*"** Ibid.

218   **"in and out of jail"** Winters, *Sam Shepard: A Life.*

219   **"desolate"** . . . **"all the credit for that"** Ibid.

219   **"He wrote me a note saying 'I don't understand'"** Penhall, "The Outsider."

219   **"collecting New Mexican dust"** . . . **"that much strength left"** Shepard, *Motel Chronicles.*

221   **"like a time bomb"** . . . **"she was 'blown away'"** Ibid.

TWENTY-ONE: TRUE WEST

224   **"an established contemporary masterpiece"** Mark Shenton, "True West," London Theatre, June 8, 2016, www.londontheatre.co.uk/reviews/true-west.

224   **"My mother had gone to Alaska"** Bartels, "Sam Shepard's Master Class in Playwriting."

225   **"I worked harder on this play"** Coe, "The Saga of Sam Shepard."

225   **"filthy white t-shirt"** . . . **"Al Jolson records and spit at me"** From *True West,* in Shepard, *Seven Plays.*

227   **"I know I've got two sides in me"** Shepard and Dark, *Two Prospectors.*

227   **"they had the two most beautiful women"** Bill Graham and Robert Greenfield, *Bill Graham Presents: My Life Inside Rock and Out* (New York: Doubleday, 1992).

227   **"Lefty Jewish"** . . . **"attract a great deal of attention"** Peter Coyote, *The Rainman's Third Cure: An Irregular Education* (Berkeley, Calif.: Counterpoint Press, 2015).

228   **"What do you think of this"** . . . **"the greatest fight"** Coe, "The Saga of Sam Shepard."

230   **"Are you fucking crazy?"** Shewey, *Sam Shepard.*

230   **"drama critics from all over the country"** . . . **"knots of embarrassment"** Ibid.

231   **"No, no, a woman can't understand this play"** Turan and Papp, *Free for All.*

231   **"I wouldn't want to see *True West* done"** Carol Rosen, "Sam Shepard Speaks: A Rare Interview with the Cowboy Playwright," *The Village Voice,* September 29, 1992.

231   **"not that women are playing the brothers"** Leonard Jacobs, "NYC 'True West' Defies Agent, Refuses to Close," *Backstage,* March 16, 2004.

232   **"amazing"** Ellen Carpenter, "Ethan Hawke Talks Tackling Sam Shepard's 'True West,'" *Hemispheres,* January 1, 2019.

232   **"Sam's cut from another cloth"** Sarah Larson, "The Chaos of American Manhood in *True West,*" *The New Yorker,* January 28, 2019.

232   **"In the plays of Sam Shepard"** Florence Falk, "Men Without Women: The Shepard Landscape," in Marranca, ed., *American Dreams.*

232   **"Given the activities that usually occupy"** Carla J. McDonough, "The Politics of Stage

Space: Women and Male Identity in Sam Shepard's Family Plays," *Journal of Dramatic Theory and Criticism* IX, no. 2 (Spring 1995).

233 **"was so tied"** . . . **"experience I've had in theater"** Turan and Papp, *Free for All.*

235 **"Sam Shepard, as fine an actor as he is"** Vincent Canby, "Sissy Spacek in 'Raggedy Man,' a Violent Melodrama," *The New York Times,* September 18, 1981.

235 **"I've been around long enough"** Fred Ferretti, "Joseph Papp: A 'Divisive Force' or a 'Healing' One?" *The New York Times,* December 20, 1980.

236 **"I'd love to be able to fire you"** . . . **"for a playwright all your life"** Turan and Papp, *Free for All.*

237 **"never see another play"** . . . **"only game in town"** Ferretti, "Joseph Papp: A 'Divisive Force' or a 'Healing' One?"

237 **"last thing I wanted"** Turan and Papp, *Free for All.*

238 **"felt proud to be an actor"** Ibid.

238 **"Some day, when the warring"** Frank Rich, "Stage: Shepard's 'True West'; Myth vs. Reality," *The New York Times,* December 24, 1980.

TWENTY-TWO: TRUE WEST REDUX

239 **"in a nerdy corduroy jacket"** . . . **"great for the company"** Gary Sinise with Marcus Brotherton, *Grateful American: A Journey from Self to Service* (Nashville, Tenn.: Nelson Books, 2019).

240 **"We don't know who you are"** Patrick Zakem, ed., "The Steppenwolf Ensemble on 'True West,'" Steppenwolf, www.steppenwolf.org/articles/the-steppenwolf-ensemble-on-true-west/.

240 **"Simply the best production"** John Mayer, *Steppenwolf Theatre Company of Chicago: In Their Own Words* (London: Bloomsbury, 2016).

241 **"a fantastic actor"** . . . **"three out of the next four shows"** Sinise with Brotherton, *Grateful American.*

242 **"As performed by John Malkovich"** . . . **"menacing at the same time"** Mel Gussow, "Stage: Shepard's 'West' Revived and Restored," *The New York Times,* October 18, 1982.

243 **"The play is a little unfinished"** Don Shewey, "The 'True Story' of 'True West,'" *The Village Voice,* November 30, 1982.

TWENTY-THREE: WHEN SAM MET JESSICA

244 **"a pair of old black corduroys"** . . . **"like a house on fire"** Winters, *Sam Shepard: A Life.*

246 **"It was one of those horrible meetings"** . . . **"outlaw quality"** Lange quoted in Nancy Collins, "Full-Tilt Jessica," *Vanity Fair,* October 1991.

246 **"a green silk dress"** . . . **"put on some makeup"** Winters, *Sam Shepard: A Life.*

247 **"Movie sets are the most seductive places"** Collins, "Full-Tilt Jessica."

247 **"sing every lyric Dylan ever wrote"** Kenneth Miller, "Jessica Lange Can Finally Relax," *AARP: The Magazine,* July 18, 2017.

247 **"a worn-out little mill town"** Jessica Lange, "Commencement Address," Sarah Lawrence College, May 23, 2008, C-SPAN, www.c-span.org/video/?205589-1/sarah-lawrence-college-commencement-address.

247 **"I was always the new girl in town"** Miller, "Jessica Lange Can Finally Relax."

247 **"a drinker"** . . . **"degree of disappointment"** Collins, "Full-Tilt Jessica."

247 **"The first time I rode"** "Jessica Lange Interview," *Sunday Observer and Belfast Telegraph,* January 2007, www.sam-shepard.com/pressjessica0107.html/.

248 **"get my BFA"** . . . **"Yes, I said"** Lange, "Commencement Address."

248 **"long line of distinguished"** Alyssa Ford, "La Vie Boheme: Jessica Lange's Artistic Odyssey," *Artful Living,* March 25, 2015.

249 **"An adventure"** Collins, "Full-Tilt Jessica."

249 **"There were a couple"** . . . **"understood that loneliness"** Ibid.

250 **"At the heart of the film"** Vincent Canby, "A New 'Postman Always Rings Twice,'" *The New York Times,* March 20, 1981.

250 **"a cross between a fawn and a Buick"** "Jessica Lange Interview," *Sunday Observer and Belfast Telegraph.*

250   "I never accepted failure" . . . "down the road full tilt" Collins, "Full-Tilt Jessica."

251   "such a mixed up movie" . . . "writer's desperation" Vincent Canby, "Frances Farmer Played by Jessica Lange," *The New York Times*, December 3, 1982.

251   "I've never seen" . . . "just really wild stuff" Collins, "Full-Tilt Jessica."

253   "That's your guy" . . . "looked nothing like Yeager" Philip Kaufman, as told to Gregg Kilday, " 'The Right Stuff' Filmmaker Remembers Sam Shepard: He Was 'Born with the Gift of a Golden Ear,' " *The Hollywood Reporter*, August 1, 2017.

254   "had a cowboy quality to him" Winters, *Sam Shepard: A Life*.

254   "Phil offered the part to me" . . . "wouldn't hurt to do it" Alex French and David Kahn, "Punch a Hole in the Sky: An Oral History of 'The Right Stuff,' " *Wired*, November 18, 2014.

254   "ever been in a successful film" Kroll, Guthrie, and Huck, "Who's That Tall Dark Stranger."

254   "didn't hit it off right away" Kaufman with Kilday, " 'The Right Stuff' Filmmaker Remembers Sam Shepard."

255   "I went up with Yeager in a Piper Cub" . . . "some fights in that bar" French and Kahn, "Punch a Hole in the Sky."

256   "It was too many people" "Q&A with Sam Shepard," *Details*, July 2008.

TWENTY-FOUR: FOOL FOR LOVE

257   "I wrote about sixteen versions" Lippman, "Rhythm & Truths."

258   "in the past, like a memory" . . . "I just wanted to know" Shepard and Dark, *Two Prospectors*.

259   "auditioned about a hundred actresses" . . . "three points of the square" John Lion, "Rock 'n' Roll Jesus with a Cowboy Mouth," *American Theatre*, April 1, 1984.

259   "This play is to be performed relentlessly" . . . "a weird stretching sound" Sam Shepard, *"Fool for Love" and Other Plays*.

260   "basically a continuation of *True West*" Shewey, *Sam Shepard*.

260   "The play came out of falling in love" Howe, McCulloch, and Simpson, "Sam Shepard: The Art of Theater No. 12."

261   "She drew me to her" Shepard, *Fool for Love*.

261   "a western for our time" Frank Rich, "Stage: 'Fool for Love,' " *The New York Times*, May 27, 1983.

262   "That play baffles me" Howe, McCulloch, and Simpson, "Sam Shepard: The Art of Theater No. 12."

262   "completely strung out" Shepard and Dark, *Two Prospectors*.

263   "pathetic groups of steers" . . . "supposed to go?" Sam Shepard, *great dream of heaven* (New York: Alfred A. Knopf, 2002).

266   "The proper response to love is to accept it" Shepard, *Fool for Love*.

TWENTY-FIVE: COUNTRY MATTERS

267   "her remote cabin hideaway" . . . "farm auctions" Shepard and Dark, *Two Prospectors*.

269   Dustin Hoffman as her "leading lady" "Jessica Lange Wins Supporting Actress: 1983 Oscars," YouTube, October 3, 2008. www.youtube.com/watch?v=9mKLxWrRVMg/.

270   "With Jess" Shepard and Dark, *Two Prospectors*.

270   "Coppola didn't want me" . . . "some of my short stories" Stephen Farber, "East Meets West, Take 2," *The New York Times*, March 12, 2006.

271   book "you can carry with you" Katherine Dieckmann, "Wim Wenders: An Interview," *Film Quarterly* 38, no. 2 (1984).

271   "some memento" . . . "straight out into open land" Shepard, *Motel Chronicles*.

271   "of someone looking at a roadmap" Winters, *Sam Shepard: A Life*.

272   "to regulation Hollywood size" . . . "*One from the Heart*" Shepard and Dark, *Two Prospectors*.

272   "He adamantly insisted that being the writer" Farber, "East Meets West, Take 2."

273   "It's all there. Just don't act it" . . . "sequence of the words" Shewey, *Sam Shepard*.

273   "in the mouth of the mad movie machine" . . . "won't ever happen again" Shepard and Dark, *Two Prospectors*.

275   "Jessica just didn't like what she was seeing" . . . "make me more stubborn" Shewey, *Sam Shepard.*

275   "The most touching scenes, though" Roger Ebert, "Country," *Chicago Sun-Times,* January 1, 1984.

276   "like being sentenced to a trailer for twelve weeks" Shepard and Dark, *Two Prospectors.*

TWENTY-SIX: SEE YOU IN MY DREAMS

277   "little Mexican man" . . . "met his death" Shepard, *Cruising Paradise.*

278   "When they loaded my father's mangled body" Shepard, *Day out of Days.*

278   "miserable, contemptible death" Winters, *Sam Shepard: A Life.*

278   "Since the body" . . . "I was grateful to them for that" Shepard, *Cruising Paradise.*

283   "wasn't that turned on" . . . "kept insisting" Mitchell Zuckoff, *Robert Altman: The Oral Biography* (New York: Alfred A. Knopf, 2009).

283   "I felt very uncomfortable" Kevin Sessums, "Geography of a Horse Dreamer," *Interview,* September 1988.

284   "Onstage, it was huge" . . . "And I love Bob" Zuckoff, *Robert Altman: The Oral Biography.*

284   "I liked Altman's stuff" Sessums, "Geography of a Horse Dreamer."

285   "as hostile and intrusive" . . . "doing the same thing" Poland, *Stages: A Theater Memoir.*

286   "the most challenging American playwright" . . . "an American fantasy" Kroll, Guthrie, and Huck, "Who's That Tall Dark Stranger."

TWENTY-SEVEN: A LIE OF THE MIND

287   "Mostly, I've been working on" Joseph Chaikin and Sam Shepard, *Letters and Texts, 1972–1984,* ed. Barry Daniels (New York: Theatre Communications Group, 1989).

287   "eleven or twelve drafts" . . . "at that moment" Rosen, *Sam Shepard: A Poetic Rodeo.*

287   "It was a tough play to write" Cott, "Sam Shepard on Working with Dylan, Why Jim Morrison Has No Sense of Humor."

288   "shooting for a dream cast" Shewey, *Sam Shepard.*

288   "Blown away" . . . "It was unsettling" Poland, *Stages: A Theater Memoir.*

290   "This is a very competitive bunch" . . . "never seen this before" Shewey, *Sam Shepard.*

290   "I took care of the rehearsal process" Harriet Shapiro, "Sam Shepard Has Enough Horse Sense to Corral His Talented Sisters into His Dramatic Stable," *People,* January 6, 1986.

290   "help him figure out how to cut it" . . . "parting of the ways" Holdren, "Director Robert Woodruff Remembers Sam Shepard."

290   "to be with Jessica & Shura" Shepard and Dark, *Two Prospectors.*

291   "Tonight there will be fisticuffs" Poland, *Stages: A Theater Memoir.*

291   "of infinite space, going off to nowhere" . . . "disappears into thin air" Sam Shepard, *A Lie of the Mind* (New York: Dramatists Play Service, 1986).

292   Shepard's "most romantic play" Frank Rich, "Theater: 'A Lie of the Mind,' by Sam Shepard," *The New York Times,* December 6, 1985.

292   "the event of the season" Clive Barnes review quoted in Shewey, *Sam Shepard.*

292   "wall to wall superlatives" Poland, *Stages: A Theater Memoir.*

293   "I have to admit" Patrick Healy, "Getting Faster with Age: Sam Shepard's New Velocity," *The New York Times,* February 12, 2010.

293   "well oiled" Poland, *Stages: A Theater Memoir.*

293   "perhaps the first person to write" Barnes, "Theater: 'The Unseen Hand' and 'Forensic and the Navigators.'"

293   "Well, how do you feel?" . . . "don't even remember it" Poland, *Stages: A Theater Memoir.*

TWENTY-EIGHT: HORSE COUNTRY

295   "It was great" . . . "so full of tourists" Shewey, *Sam Shepard.*

297   "It doesn't help that the above-mentioned horse" Janet Maslin, "Review/Film; 'Far North': Sam Shepard Ventures into Directing," *The New York Times,* November 9, 1988.

297   "'Far North' is a disorganized, undisciplined" Roger Ebert, "Far North," *Chicago Sun-Times,* November 25, 1988.

297 **"Sam Shepard doesn't just guard"** . . . **"out of the whole batch"** Richards, "SSSHHHH! IT'S SAM SHEPARD."

298 **"a colorful, flirtatious and gregarious"** Bryan McKenzie, "Actor, Writer, Former Local Resident Shepard Dies," *Daily Progress,* July 31, 2017.

298 **"been having one hell of a time"** Shepard and Dark, *Two Prospectors.*

299 **"It's a regular existence"** . . . **"his leaving would surprise me"** Collins, "Full-Tilt Jessica."

300 **"This morning I'm leaving for Mexico"** . . . **"cummerbund"** Shepard, *Cruising Paradise.*

301 **"I never met anyone I liked so much"** Shewey, *Sam Shepard.*

301 **"smash a radio to the floor"** . . . **"the shot's over"** Shepard, *Cruising Paradise.*

301 **"He walked out of the café"** . . . **"I got used to it"** Winters, *Sam Shepard: A Life.*

302 **"The end of *Voyager*"** Roger Ebert, "Voyager," *Chicago Sun-Times,* May 29, 1992.

302 **"Sam Shepard is ideal as Faber"** "Voyager," *Variety,* December 31, 1990.

303 **"heart-wrenching stuff"** . . . **"hunky-dorey"** Shepard and Dark, *Two Prospectors.*

303 **"as if he was expecting fans or photographers"** Amy Ensign, "Playwright Shepard Has Door County Connection," *Green Bay Press-Gazette,* April 4, 2017.

303 **"a huge slab of limestone"** . . . **"leave it like it is for now"** Shepard, *Cruising Paradise.*

304 **"her living and her dying were precious gifts"** Winters, *Sam Shepard: A Life.*

305 **"slightly to the left of the two red cedars"** . . . **"left it just like that"** Shepard, *Cruising Paradise.*

305 **"You have to do it on an open highway"** Ben Brantley, "Sam Shepard, Storyteller," *The New York Times,* November 13, 1994.

306 **"the indispensable" John Malkovich** Frank Rich, "Review/Theater; Sam Shepard Returns, on War and Machismo," *The New York Times,* May 17, 1991.

306 **"gas money on a movie"** . . . **"struggling with for years"** Shewey, *Sam Shepard.*

306 **"elegiac . . . bitterly scornful poetry of regret"** Stephen Holden, "Film Review: Another True West Tale of Phantom Family Ties," *The New York Times,* March 17, 2006.

306 **"one of the year's best"** Vincent Canby, "The Year in the Arts: Theater 1994; Strike Zones (and Erogenous Ones, Too)," *The New York Times,* December 25, 1994.

308 **"a grueling experience" for all concerned** Matt Wolf, *Sam Mendes at the Donmar: Stepping into Freedom* (Lanham, Md.: Limelight Editons, 2003).

TWENTY-NINE: STILLWATER

311 **"sweeping views of the town"** Winters, *Sam Shepard: A Life.*

311 **"this kind of romantic image"** Peter Haldeman, "Tour Jessica Lange's House in Minnesota," *Architectural Digest,* March 2006.

311 **"she was profoundly depressed"** Shepard and Dark, *Two Prospectors.*

311 **"surrounded by yellow- and blue-flowering plants"** . . . **"every white flower"** Haldeman, "Tour Jessica Lange's House in Minnesota."

312 **"The first thing Sam ever did"** . . . **"The beat goes on"** Shepard and Dark, *Two Prospectors.*

313 **"I was never real happy with the play"** Shewey, *Sam Shepard.*

313 **"the length of some of the dialogue"** Gussow, "From Plays to Fiction."

313 **"The script was transformed and revivified"** Richard Christiansen, "Revived 'Buried Child' Haunting When Not Slow . . . ," *Chicago Tribune,* January 23, 1985.

314 **"a relic of a chapter in experimental theater"** Ben Brantley, "Theater Review: A Sam Shepard Revival Gets Him to Broadway," *The New York Times,* May 1, 1996.

314 **"is beginning to look like a Shepard jubilee year"** Stephen Schiff, "Showcase: Shepard on Broadway," *The New Yorker,* April 22, 1996.

314 **"was dragged on stage to take a reluctant bow"** . . . **"icons of 90's rock"** Shewey, *Sam Shepard.*

315 **"angry audience members fled in disgust"** Ben Brantley, "A Clash of Rock Stars in an Existential Mode."

315 **"I'm an actor now; I confess"** Shepard journal quoted in Shewey, *Sam Shepard.*

315 **"own a fax machine"** . . . **"at this point in time"** Shewey, *Sam Shepard.*

316 **"there is *nothing* on the horizon"** . . . **"totally insane & hysterical"** Shepard and Dark, *Two Prospectors.*

317 **"one of his mother's specific taboos"** . . . **"when I was growing up"** Shepard, *great dream of heaven.*

318 **"I don't know what to do with myself"** Shepard and Dark, *Two Prospectors.*

THIRTY: THE LATE HENRY MOSS

319   **"Normally we don't talk"** Liz Lufkin, "'The Late Henry Moss' Very Much Alive in S.F.," *San Francisco Chronicle,* November 5, 2000.

320   **"black slacks, a black mock-turtleneck sweater"** . . . **"movie stars is something else"** Kevin Berger, "Sam Shepard," *Salon,* January 3, 2001, www.salon.com/2001/01/02/shepard_6/.

321   **"And for this outing"** John Lahr, "Giving Up the Ghost," *The New Yorker,* December 4, 2000.

321   **"The documentary began very casually"** . . . **"through their work"** Almeyreda quoted in Sylviane Gold, "FILM; Harried Child," *The New York Times,* April 18, 2004.

322   **"My story? Oh, I don't know"** . . . **"Xerox of my life"** Almereyda, *This So-Called Disaster.*

322   **"There was always this implicit contradiction"** Gold, "FILM; Harried Child."

323   **"It was one of those meetings"** Almereyda, *This So-Called Disaster.*

324   **"It took me five years"** Berger, "Sam Shepard."

324   **"a 1969 one-act exercise in Oedipal mayhem"** Lahr, "Giving Up the Ghost."

324   **"Your mother threw me out"** Sam Shepard, *"The Late Henry Moss," "Eyes for Consuela," "When the World Was Green"* (New York: Vintage Books, 2003).

325   **"During the past week it seems"** Richard Connema, "Regional Reviews: San Francisco: The World Premiere of Sam Shepard's 'The Late Henry Moss,'" Talkin' Broadway, n.d., www.talkinbroadway.com/page/regional/sanfran/s82.html.

325   **"Whatever the audience paid to get in"** Lahr, "Giving Up the Ghost."

325   **"The play had its world preem last fall"** Charles Isherwood, "'The Late Henry Moss,'" *Variety,* September 24, 2001.

325   **"The play itself is long, plodding"** Ben Brantley, "Theater Review: No-Good Dad Whose Tale Is Told Repeatedly," *The New York Times,* September 25, 2001.

327   **"Rest assured that"** . . . **"betraying its essential nature"** Ben Brantley, "Theater Review: Finding Out What It's Like to Really Be Your Brother," *The New York Times,* March 10, 2000.

THIRTY-ONE: DON'T COME KNOCKING

329   **"big, raw-boned Minnesotans"** . . . **"because of the kids"** Shepard and Dark, *Two Prospectors.*

331   **"wasn't down his alley"** . . . **"any director's dream"** Emanuel Levy, "Don't Come Knocking: Interview with Wim Wenders," Emanuel Levy Cinema 24/7, February 14, 2006, www.emanuellevy.com/interviews/wim-wenders-dont-come-knocking-9/.

332   **"The night before we were doing that scene"** Julian Roman, "Jessica Lange Says Don't Come Knocking," MovieWeb, March 20, 2006, www.movieweb.com/jessica-lange -says-dont-come-knocking/.

333   **"uptown, very Jewish"** . . . **"'I'm sorry' to the widowed wife"** Shepard and Dark, *Two Prospectors.*

THIRTY-TWO: THE FEELING OF NUMBNESS

335   **"diving down deep"** . . **"along for the ride"** Sam Shepard, *Day out of Days.*

336   **"turned up a glitch of some sort"** Shepard and Dark, *Two Prospectors.*

336   **"How could he suddenly forsake"** . . . **"bright sting of smoke"** Shepard, *Day out of Days.*

337   **"favorite place to be in the summer"** Shepard and Dark, *Two Prospectors.*

338   **"He used to always say"** Greg Kocher, "Sam Shepard Enjoyed Quiet Life in Midway," *Lexington Herald Leader,* July 31, 2017.

338   **"a conscious homage to Beckett"** Charles Isherwood, "Theater Review, 'Kicking a Dead Horse.'" *The New York Times,* July 15, 2008.

338   **"Though the Irish designer Brien Vahey"** John Simon, "Stephen Rea Seeks 'True' West in Sam Shepard Fable," Bloomberg News.

338   **"Even as they face their twilight years"** . . . **"essentially static"** Ben Brantley, "Ages of the Moon: It's Old Timers' Day at Shepard's Arena," *The New York Times,* January 27, 2010.

339   **"I've decided"** . . . **"chicken with a head cut off"** Shepard and Dark, *Two Prospectors.*

339   **"The way he pulled up on the curb"** . . . **"reportedly his favorite drink:** Ryan Denham,

"Actor, Playwright Sam Shepard Arrested in Normal for Suspected DUI," *The Pantagraph*, January 3, 2009.

340   **"I wasn't speeding"** "Like Father," *Time Out Chicago*, November 11, 2010.

340   **"driving blind drunk"** Shepard, in Shepard and Dark, *Two Prospectors*.

340   **"they must have thought I was lying"** . . . **"Flicker and dance"** Shepard, *Day out of Days*.

341   **"twisting Kentucky country road"** Shepard and Dark, *Two Prospectors*.

341   **"a great old guy with a gray beard"** . . . **"a swallow of beer"** Shepard, *Day out of Days*.

341   **"woman with a huge nose"** . . . **"you name it"** Shepard and Dark, *Two Prospectors*.

344   **"I waited for the usual panic to set in"** . . . **"would feel like"** Ibid.

THIRTY-THREE: SHEPARD AND DARK

345   **"no money"** . . . **"stone walls sipping soup"** Shepard and Dark, *Two Prospectors*.

346   **"would choose living writers"** Douglas Martin, "Howard Gotlieb, an Archivist with Persistence, Dies at 79," *The New York Times*, December 5, 2005.

347   **"a large acquisition" of Sam Shepard's papers** Robert Faires, "In Memoriam: Sam Shepard," *The Austin Chronicle*, August 3, 2017.

347   **"wasn't ready for the deep sorrow in re-visiting"** . . . **"Everything else seems broken"** Shepard and Dark, *Two Prospectors*.

349   **"So, that is what I'm doing"** . . . **"And like my old man"** Wurmfeld, *Shepard & Dark*.

351   **"Here are all the letters of yours back"** Shepard and Dark, *Two Prospectors*.

THIRTY-FOUR: A PARTICLE OF DREAD

354   **"read any plays except for a couple of Brecht things"** . . . **"find it and know it"** Cott, "Sam Shepard on Working with Dylan, Why Jim Morrison Has No Sense of Humor."

355   **"Why waste my time? Why waste yours?"** Ben Brantley, "Call Out the Patricide Squad," *The New York Times*, November 23, 2014.

356   **"They gave me all these tests"** . . . **"shocks in my arms"** Shepard, *Spy of the First Person*.

358   **"the *Huffington Post* of the right"** "Breitbart News," Ballotpedia, n.d., ballotpedia.org /Breitbart_News.

358   **"According to his official biography"** Kipp Jones, "Actor Sam Shepard Arrested for Aggravated D.U.I.," Breitbart, May 26, 2015, www.breitbart.com/entertainment/2015/05/26 /actor-sam-shepard-arrested-for-aggravated-d-u-i/.

359   **"Something in his body refuses to get up"** . . . **"remain that way"** Sam Shepard, *The One Inside* (New York: Vintage Books, 2018).

360   **"I was a writer"** . . . **"big part of my life"** Johnny Dark, "Sam Shepard Remembered by Johnny Dark," *The Guardian*, December, 17, 2017.

362   **had drunk only "one and a half margaritas and had a sip of mescal"** Associated Press, "Sam Shepard's Drunk-Driving Charge Dismissed in Court," *Toronto Star*, December 18, 2015.

362   **"one of the second season's best scenes"** Brian Tallerico, "'Bloodline' Season Finale Recap: Now Leaving the Keys," *Vulture*, June 7, 2016, www.vulture.com/2016/06 /bloodline-recap-season-2-episode-10.html.

THIRTY-FIVE: SPY OF THE FIRST PERSON

364   **"out of the blue"** . . . **"Unbelievable"** Shepard and Dark, *Two Prospectors*.

365   **In the film** . . . **"'That is one hillbilly son of a bitch'"** *Patti Smith: Dream of Life*, dir. Steven Sebring, *POV*, PBS, aired on December 30, 2009.

366   **"from somewhere on the road"** . . . **"Bruno Schulz"** Smith, "My Buddy."

366   **"With some effort"** . . . **"the way I wanted"** Patti Smith, *Year of the Monkey* (New York: Alfred A. Knopf, 2019).

367   **"golden Kentucky afternoon"** . . . **"unearthly roads"** Shepard, *The One Inside*.

367   **"fawning introduction"** Ron Charles, "'It's Him, It's Sort of Him': Sam Shepard's 'The One Inside' Toys with Fact and Fiction," *The Washington Post*, January 24, 2017.

368   **"One year to the day when Sam was still able"** Smith, *Year of the Monkey*.

369 **"He was always a very private"** Alexandra Alter, "A Final Work by Sam Shepard Reveals His Struggle with Lou Gehrig's Disease," *The New York Times,* December 4, 2017.

369 **"now writing out loud in real time"** . . . **"could not be extinguished"** Shepard, *The One Inside.*

369 **"And I saw myself with Sam"** Smith, *Year of the Monkey.*

370 **"One year ago exactly"** Shepard, *Spy of the First Person.*

370 **"He eats cheese and crackers"** . . . **"across his knees"** Ibid.

371 **"Sometimes he does this thing"** . . . **"ask for help"** Ibid.

373 **"dictated his final edits"** Ibid.

EPILOGUE: ENDGAME

375 **"a man who did not relinquish power"** Hunter Harris, "How Ethan Hawke Transforms into a 'Cowboy' Drifter for 'True West,'" *Vulture,* March 5, 2019, www.vulture.com /2019/03/true-west-broadway-ethan-hawke-backstage-photos.html/.

375 **"I wrote an introduction to one of his plays"** Rea, "Sam Shepard 1943–2017."

376 **"He was always a pinch-front kind of guy"** Jesse Shepard, "Behind the Cover: 12.31.17," *The New York Times Magazine,* December 31, 2017.

CODA: TRUE WEST, AGAIN

377 **"There's something about this play"** Harris, "How Ethan Hawke Transforms into a 'Cowboy' Drifter for 'True West.'"

378 **"a play that seems to grow in disturbing depth"** Ben Brantley, "Ethan Hawke and Paul Dano Go Mano a Mano in the Riveting 'True West,'" *The New York Times,* January 24, 2019.

PHOTO CREDITS

INDEX

ABOUT THE AUTHOR

A former associate editor of the London bureau of *Rolling Stone*, ROBERT GREENFIELD is the author of several classic rock books, among them *S.T.P.: A Journey through America with the Rolling Stones* and the definitive biographies of Bill Graham, Jerry Garcia, Timothy Leary, Ahmet Ertegun, Augustus Owsley Stanley III, and John Perry Barlow. An award-winning novelist, playwright, and screenwriter, he has published short fiction in *GQ, Esquire,* and *Playboy*. He lives in California.